QUEENS PARK RANGERS

PLAYER BY PLAYER

A compendium of every player to have played for QPR

WRITTEN BY IAN WELCH AND JOHN MARKS

This edition first published in the UK in 2009
By Green Umbrella Publishing

www.gupublishing.co.uk

Publishers Jules Gammond and Vanessa Gardner

Printed and bound by J F Print Ltd., Sparkford, Somerset

ISBN: 978-1-906635-96-1

QUEENS PARK RANGERS
PLAYER BY PLAYER

CONTENTS

KEY

The following facts and details relating to a player are given where known:

- Player's full name (popular, abbreviated or nicknames are referred to where relevant).
- Playing positions recorded relate to the terminology of that era, i.e. a midfield player of today would be a wing-half, or an inside-forward of the 1950s. Modern terminology has been shown under the player's name, while the earlier equivalent is in brackets. Height and weight (in feet and inches, and stones [one stone = 14 pounds = c.6.4 kilos] and pounds) follow.
- Date and place of birth are included, likewise that of the player's death if known.
- QPR appearances for all matches (as detailed below) are included, and split as shown. These include substitutions, which have been considered a full appearance and added to the total. Under 'Other' these consist of other first team cup competitions plus Charity matches and acknowledged first team Friendly games.

SURNAME Christian names
(Old) & New positions, height & weight
b: = born, place & date
d: = death, place & date
QPR details, type of transfer and fee
Joining date
(Appearances - Goals), League, FA Cup, Football League Cup, Other, Total
Honours:
(Short biography relating to the player)
Debut: (For QPR) Date… opponents… result… competition/division

GENERAL NOTES:
June 2009 has been taken as a 'cut-off' point for statistical and other details.

Transfer fees and dates: accurate fees are not always made available, and are estimated (normally by the press). Inevitably, different sources will vary and therefore the figures given should often be assumed to be approximate. Where a transfer month is known this information is given, however, different sources again may quote different months, or is often during the close season, therefore some dates may be only approximate.

Clive Allen

A

ABBOTT Harry
ABBOTT Ronald W
ABBOTT Shirley Wray
ABEL Samuel Charles
ADAMS Ernest W
ADDINALL Albert William
ADLAM Leslie William
AGOGO Manuel (Junior)
AGYEMANG Patrick
AINSWORTH Charles
AINSWORTH Gareth
ALBERTI Matteo
ALLEN Bradley James
ALLEN Clive Darren
ALLEN James
ALLEN John C (Ian)
ALLEN Joseph
ALLEN Leslie
ALLEN Martin James
ALLEN Reginald Arthur
ALLUM Albert
ANDERSON Edward T
ANDERSON George Edward
ANDERSON Thomas Cowan
ANDERTON Sylvan James
ANDREWS Cecil J
ANDREWS James Patrick
ANGELL Brett
ANGELL Peter F
ARCHER Arthur
ARDILES Osvaldo Cesar
ARMITAGE Stanley
ARMSTRONG James Harris
ASHFORD Herbert E
ASHMAN Donald
ASTON Charles Lane

ABBOTT Harry

(IL) Mid 5' 9" 11st 4lbs
b: Blackburn, Lancashire, 1883
QPR: 1904
Southern League: 27-4. **FAC:** 1-0. **FLC:** 0-0.
Other: 0-0. **Total:** 28-4.

Harry came to the notice of Blackburn Rovers after some sterling performances for Padiham in the Lancashire Combination League. However he never turned out for the first 11 and drifted south to QPR. He was somewhat impressive as a playmaker, until the arrival of Milward in the side when he was relegated to the reserves. According to the 1905 edition of the *Men Famous in Football* he drifted back north again and was taken on the books of Burnley. However he never turned out for them but he did play for Bolton Wanderers in their promotion campaign of 1905. In 1906 he returned to the Southern League to play for Swindon Town.

Debut: 3 Sep 1904 v Wellingborough (H) 2-0 SL Div 1.

Ronald Abbott

ABBOTT Ronald W

Mid
b: Lambeth, London, 2 Aug 1953
QPR: 1971
Football League: 46-4. **FAC:** 5-0. **FLC:** 3-0.
Other: 0-0. **Total:** 54-4.

Ron made a dream start to his career at the club by scoring the winning goal on his first team debut. West Ham United were beaten in exciting fashion on their own ground by three goals to two in a First Division clash in September 1973. Used as a substitute for most of his time at the club, he proved to be a good stand-in. The arrival of Steve Burtenshaw as manager in 1978 saw the end of his time at QPR and he left for Drogheda.

Debut: 10 Sep 1973 v West Ham United (A) 3-2 Div 1.

ABBOTT Shirley Wray

(LH) Def 5' 9" 12st 7lbs
b: Alfreton, Derbyshire, 10 Feb 1889
d: 26 August 1947
QPR: May 1923
Football League: 12-0. **FAC:** 0-0. **FLC:** 0-0.
Other: 0-0. **Total:** 12-0.

It seemed that the capture of the Portsmouth captain in 1923 was a shrewd move by the then manager of QPR, Ned Liddell. He thought that Abbott would be a calming influence in the Rangers defence, having been the captain of the south coast team when they won the Southern League title in 1920. Now at the age of 33 he had the experience of playing in every defensive position including goalkeeper. Alas of the 12 matches that he was involved in not one was won and indeed 30 goals were conceded in the process. At the start of the following season he joined Chesterfield and became captain of the side until 1927, becoming trainer in 1928. While trainer, promotion was gained twice, in 1931 and again in 1936. Abbott held the job until May 1939 when he was sacked by the new manager Norman Bullock. Moving back south to Portsmouth he took a job in the dockyard and worked there throughout the Second World War. He died at the early age of 58.

Debut: 6 Oct 1923 v Swansea Town (A) 0-2 Div 3 (S).

ABEL Samuel Charles

(CF/RB) Striker/Def 5' 11" 12st 0lbs
b: Neston, Cheshire, 30 Dec 1908
d: London, 26 Sep 1959
QPR: (£400) May 1934
Football League: 36-6. **FAC:** 1-0. **FLC:** 0-0.
Other: 5-0. **Total:** 42-6.
Honours: Metropolitan Police v Royal Navy, 20 May 1942.

On joining the Loftus Road club, Sam suffered a most horrendous injury in a League match, which kept him out of the game for 18 months. When he was fully recovered he returned to the side as a right-back and found that he dominated in that position, until the end of the Second World War. Sam appeared in over 170 matches during the conflict turning out for Brighton & Hove Albion, Chelsea, Crystal Palace and Fulham. In between matches he played golf and during the summer, cricket. During the war, his days were spent as a Special Constable, for the Harlesden district of west London.

Debut: 15 Sep 1934 v Brighton & Hove Albion (H) 2-1 Div 3 (S).

ADAMS Ernest W

(OR) Wing
b: Willesden, 3 Apr 1922
QPR: Sep 1947
Football League: 5-0. **FAC:** 0-0. **FLC:** 0-0.
Other: 0-0. **Total:** 5-0.

A diminutive winger who played for the senior squad on two occasions during the latter part of the championship season of 1945. He appeared in the Second Division three times the following season but nothing was heard of him after 1950.

Debut: 24 Apr 1948 v Newport County (H) Div 3 (S).

ADDINALL Albert William

(CF) Striker 5' 11" 12st 1lb
b: Marylebone, London, 30 Jan 1921
QPR: 1943
Football League: 150-59. **FAC:** 6-2. **FLC:** 0-0.
Other: 0-0. **Total:** 156-61.

Bert was known as a rugged and fearless player, who was full of running and a firm favourite of the crowd. Representing Middlesex & London at school he was quickly snapped up by the club. Addinall made his debut for QPR in the latter stages of the Second World War, in which he served as a PT Instructor. Bert was soon representing the Army, playing against the Belgium Army in 1946. Perhaps his most memorable match for the club was their first home match in the Second Division after promotion. Leicester City were visiting Loftus Road when the Rangers played havoc with their defence, and during the first 45 minutes of the match Bert scored a hat-trick; Rangers won the match 4-1. In 1953 he was transferred, along with Harry Gilberg, to Brighton in exchange for centre-forward Ron Higgins and a four figure sum. In retirement he became a taxi driver in London and for a time was the landlord of the Ferry Inn in Shoreham, before returning once again to his cab.

Debut: 25 Sep 1946 v Bournemouth 3-0 Div 3 (S).

ADLAM Leslie William

(LH) Mid 5' 10" 12st 7lbs
b: Guildford, Surrey, 24 Jun 1897
QPR: Nov 1931
Football League: 56-0. **FAC:** 8-0. **FLC:** 0-0.
Other: 0-0. **Total:** 64-0.

The manager of the club at the time, Archie Mitchell, negotiated the transfer of the season when he secured the two half-backs from Oldham Athletic for £1,500 for the pair. One, Adlam, was a wholehearted player who had cost the Lancashire club the sum of £300 in 1923. Now at the age of 34 he was still worth his weight in gold for his experience alone. With these two players in the side, Adlam and Goodier, the team rose from bottom of the table in January to 13th place by the end of the season. Having done his job, Adlam was sold to Cardiff City for £100 in 1933. A year later he was coaching in France.

Debut: 14 Nov 1931 v Cardiff City (A) 4-0 Div 3 (S).

Patrick Agyemang

AGOGO Manuel (Junior)

Mid 5′ 11″ 11st 9lbs
b: Accra, Ghana, 1 Aug 1979
QPR: Mar 2002
Football League: 2-0. **FAC:** 0-0. **FLC:** 0-0.
Other: 0-0. **Total**: 2-0.

After spending two years in the USA, Manuel joined the club on a non-contract basis, where his time was spent mostly on the substitutes' bench. After his move to Barnet, he became one of the top Conference goalscorers in the 2002/03 season. He moved to Bristol Rovers, in the summer of 2003.

Debut: 6 Apr 2002 v Swindon Town (A) 1-0 Div 2.

AGYEMANG Patrick

Striker 6′ 1″ 14st 0lbs
b: Walthamstow, London, 29 Sep 1980
QPR: Jan 2008
Football League: 37-11. **FAC:** 2-0. **FLC:** 2-0.
Other: 0-0. **Total:** 41-11.
Honours: 3 Ghana caps.

Patrick could not have endeared himself more to the QPR faithful following his transfer from Preston. Scoring on his debut against Sheffield United, the striker found a rich vein of form and finished the 2007/08 season as the club's top scorer with eight goals in 17 League appearances. His scoring record at Wimbledon earned Patrick a call-up to the Ghana team, but he was left out of the final squad for the 2006 FIFA World Cup, a situation he aims to remedy for South Africa in 2010.

Debut: 12 Jan 2008 v Sheffield United (A) 1-2 Championship.

AINSWORTH Charles

(OL) Wing
b: Ashbourne, Derbyshire, 1885
d: 1955
QPR: 1908
Southern League: 2-2. **FAC:** 0-0. **FLC:** 0-0.
Other: 0-0. **Total:** 2-2.

Charlie was tall and well built for one who played on the wing, however, he earned glowing praise in the papers of his day. Ainsworth was a first-class player who had a rare turn of speed, scoring in both of the matches that he played in.

Debut: 25 Jan 1908 v Crystal Palace (H) 1-2 SL Div 1.

AINSWORTH Gareth

Mid 5′ 10″ 12st 5lbs
b: Blackburn, 10 May 1973
QPR: 2003
Football League: 140-20. **FAC:** 5-0. **FLC:** 3-1.
Other: 0-0. **Total:** 148-21.

Having been rejected as a trainee by Blackburn

Gareth Ainsworth

Rovers Gareth's professional career took off at Cambridge United under John Beck. Following the manager's dismissal from the Abbey Stadium Beck took over at Deepdale and promptly signed the midfielder for Preston. Spells at numerous clubs followed before Gareth signed for QPR at the start of the 2003/04 season and played a vital part in the club's promotion to the Championship. Injuries limited his appearances but Gareth turned his hand to coaching roles and was appointed caretaker manager following the dismissals of Iain Dowie and Paulo Sousa during the 2008/09 campaign.
Debut: 9 Aug 2003 v Blackpool (H) 5-0 Div 2.

ALBERTI Matteo

Mid 5' 11" 11st 9lbs
b: Brescia, Italy, 4 Aug 1988 Chievo Verona
QPR: 2008
Football League: 12-2. **FAC:** 1-0. **FLC:** 1-0.
Other: 0-0. **Total:** 14-2.
Debut: 9 Aug 2008 v Barnsley (H) 2-1 Championship.

ALLEN Bradley James

Striker 5' 8" 11st 0lbs
b: Harold Wood, Essex, 13 Sep 1971
QPR: Sep 1988
Premier/Football League: 81-27. **FAC:** 5-0.
FLC: 7-5.
Other: 0-0. **Total:** 93-32.
Honours: England schoolboy, Youth and U21caps.

Bradley forced his way into the QPR side at 20 years of age. He was a hard worker and was comfortable on the ball, showing good awareness in the opponents' penalty area. Perhaps his best period with Rangers was in October 1993 when he scored seven goals in six matches. In 1996 he was transferred to Charlton where he sustained many injuries which kept him out of the senior squad. Later, further moves took him to four clubs in the lower divisions.
Debut: 14 Jan 1989 v Wimbledon (A) 0-1 Div 1.

Bradley Allen

ALLEN Clive Darren

Striker 5' 10" 12st 3lbs
b: Stepney, London, 20 May 1961
QPR: Sep 1977
Football League: 49-32. **FAC:** 1-0. **FLC:** 5-2.
Other: 0-0. **Total:** 55-34.
QPR: (£700,000) Jun 1981
Football League: 87-40. **FAC:** 8-7. **FLC:** 7-2.
Other: 0-0. **Total:** 102-49.
Honours: England school caps. 15 youth caps. 3 U21 caps. 5 full caps. Football League cap. 2 FAC runner's-up medals. 2nd Div championship medal. FLC runner's-up medal. Footballer of the Year for 1987. Football Writers' Association Footballer of the Year 1987.

The son of the ex-QPR player-manager Les, Clive played for Havering, Essex and London schools before making his debut for Rangers. His prowess as a goalscorer was evident from an early age and all the major clubs were eager to sign him. Arsenal bought and sold him for over £1,000,000 in 1980 (at 19, he was the youngest seven-figure valued player) without his playing a match, within a 65-day period. Clive packed such a tremendous shot in either foot he broke Jimmy Greaves' scoring record at Spurs with 49 goals in the 1986/87 season. Clive's father played for Spurs and QPR, his uncle Dennis played for Reading, his cousin Martin for QPR and West Ham, his younger brother Bradley for QPR and his cousin Paul for West Ham, Spurs and Southampton.

Debut: 4 Jan 1978 v Chelsea (H) 0-0 Div 1.

ALLEN James

(RH) Def 5' 10"
b: Amble, Northumberland, 18 Aug 1913
d: London 1979
QPR: Apr 1935
Football League: 44-1. **FAC:** 1-0. **FLC:** 0-0.
Other: 1-0. **Total:** 46-1.

Jimmy Allen was a member of a very good team put together by manager Billy Birrell in 1935. They challenged for the Third Division (South) title a year later, but in the event QPR finished the season in fourth position and Allen moved across London in 1937.

Debut: 14 Sep 1935 v Aldershot 5-0 Div 3 (S).

ALLEN John C (Ian)

(OR) Wing
b: Elderslie, Scotland, 27 Jan 1932
QPR: 1952
Football League: 1-1. **FAC:** 0-0. **FLC:** 0-0.
Other: 0-0. **Total:** 1-1.

His only match for QPR was at Bournemouth in a Third Division (South) League match and the home team liked what they saw. John, or Ian as he was also known, had just finished his National Service and took to the sea air, scoring the only goal in a 1-0 victory for the Rangers. He was to enjoy a happy sojourn at the seaside town until he was sacked by the new manager in May 1956.

Debut: 7 Apr 1954 v Bournemouth & Boscombe Athletic 1-0 Div 3 (S).

ALLEN Joseph

(IR) Mid 5' 9" 11st 4lbs
b: Bilsthorpe, Notts, 30 Dec 1909
d: 29 Nov 1978
QPR: Apr 1933
Football League: 51-6. **FAC:** 3-1. **FLC:** 0-0.
Other: 4-0. **Total:** 58-7.

Joe played for Mansfield Town before they entered the League and went on to Spurs, scoring a goal in his only first team appearance. After a loan period at Northfleet, Mick O'Brien, the manager of QPR at the time, brought him to Loftus Road.

He became part of a very good side that finished the season fourth in the League in the early 1930s. Joe played cricket during the summer for Bilsthorpe and continued playing football for Mansfield Town during the Second World War.

Debut: 30 Sep 1933 v Exeter City (A) 1-1 Div 3 (S).

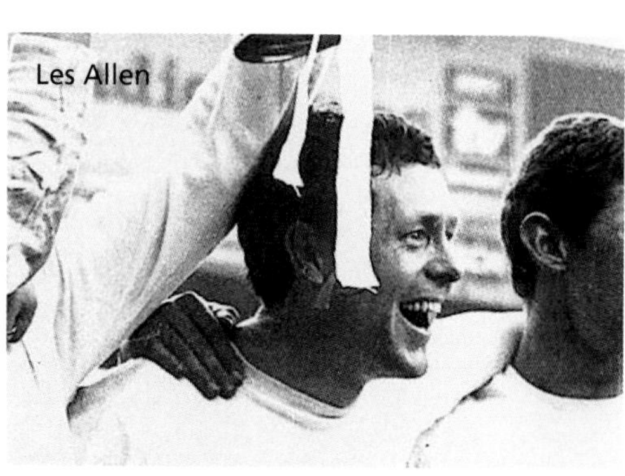
Les Allen

ALLEN Leslie

(IF) Mid/Striker 5' 10" 11st 5lb
b: Dagenham, Essex, 4 Sep 1937
QPR: (£21,000) Jul 1965
Football League: 128-55. **FAC:** 8-3. **FLC:** 15-4.
Other: 0-0. **Total:** 151-62.
Honours: England U23 cap. Football League cap. 1st Div championship medal. FAC winner's medal. FLC winner's medal. 3rd Div championship medal.

Les was a neat ball playing inside-forward with a quiet temperament. As a 16-year-old he was a member of the Briggs Sports team that reached the semi-final stages of the FA Amateur Cup in 1954. He joined Chelsea the following season but was never part of the set-up there. However, along came Bill Nicholson, the manager of Spurs, exchanged him for English international Johnny Brooks, and so the "Double" team of 1961 was formed. In the summer of 1965 he joined QPR where his experience was invaluable in bringing on a young side that rose to the First Division from the Third in successive seasons, including the winning of the League Cup.

After the brief and stormy appointment of Tommy Docherty as manager, for just 28 days, Les was to become the third manager within a month which lasted until 1971, when he resigned to become player-manager of Woodford Town. The managership of Swindon Town followed before he took a similar job in Greece for a time. In later life he worked as a model maker in the car industry.

Debut: 21 Aug 1965 v Brentford (A) 1-6 Div 3.

ALLEN Martin James

Mid 5' 10" 11st 0lbs
b: Reading, Berks, 4 Aug 1965
QPR: May 1983
Football League: 136-16. **FAC:** 10-1. **FLC:** 18-0.
Other: 3-1. **Total:** 167-18.
Honours: 3 England youth caps. 2 U21 caps.

Martin came from a long line of footballers related to the Allen family. His father Dennis played for Charlton Athletic, Reading and Bournemouth and his uncle Les and cousins Bradley and Clive have already been included. He was a vigorous, hard shooting, midfield player who loved to be involved in the match. Unfortunately Martin never saw eye to eye with the manager at the time, Trevor Francis, who quickly had him transferred. In 1999 an appeal to the League for unfair dismissal was granted to him, winning him the sum of £200,000 from Portsmouth. When his playing career finished he joined the coaching staff at Reading before becoming the Barnet manager.

Debut: 23 Mar 1985 v Luton Town (A) 0-2 Div 1.

ALLEN Reginald Arthur

Goal 6' 0" 12st 12lbs
b: Marylebone, London, 3 May 1919
d: London, 3 April 1976
QPR: May 1938
Football League: 183-0. **FAC:** 18-0. **FLC:** 0-0.
Other: 2-0. **Total:** 203-0.
Honours: Football League cap. 1st Div championship medal. 3rd Div (South) championship medal.

From the beginning it was obvious that Reg was to become a first-class goalkeeper, but the boy himself, modest to a fault, was lacking in confidence. Feeling that he let the side down in his first game for the club as an amateur at Clapton, he slipped off and made his own way to London instead of joining the arranged get-together after the match. However, the club invited him back to join the players in training. He was then asked to appear in the annual Brentford Hospital Cup match and played such a great game,

Martin Allen

Reg Allen

that the scouts of other clubs were soon buzzing around. The club decided to sign him – behind closed doors – the same evening. A few weeks later Reg made his debut as a professional in the reserve side at West Ham and their centre-forward scored six goals! West Ham won the game 7-1. What a sad debut for the young Allen but his worth was apparent to anyone in the game and he was soon to take over from Mason as the first team goalkeeper. Undoubtedly the best uncapped goalkeeper in the land during the post-war era. Matt Busby was relentlessly chasing him until the club gave way to their offer (the highest fee ever to be paid for a goalkeeper up until that time). Reg was cool under pressure and dealt with the most difficult crosses with ease. He played for the British Army twice during the war while serving as a commando. Allen was taken prisoner during a raid on the North African coast and spent three years in a POW camp.

Debut: 3 Dec 1938 v Newport County (A) 0-2 Div 3 (S).

ALLUM Albert

(OR) Wing

b: Notting Hill, London, 15 Oct 1930

QPR: Jun 1957

Football League: 1-0. **FAC:** 0-0. **FLC:** 0-0.

Other: 0-0. **Total:** 1-0.

Allum deputised for Longbottom who in turn took the injured Bobby Cameron's place in midfield. Albert's one match for Rangers was played before floodlights were made compulsory and the score at Layer Road, Colchester was 1-1 with just a minute to go. The afternoon was so gloomy that Springett in the Rangers goal claimed it was so dark that he never saw the match winner.

Debut: 2 Sep 1957 v Colchester United (A) 1-2 Div 3 (S).

ANDERSON Edward T

(IF) Mid

b: Scotland, 1881

QPR: 1906

Southern League: 19-3. **FAC:** 0-0. **FLC:** 0-0.

Other: 0-0. **Total:** 19-3.

Although Eddie stayed at Arsenal for just six weeks or so, he seemed to be a fast and skilful player. At Fulham he found himself included in the general clearout of players by the new manager. While at QPR he played in all three inside-forward positions, scoring on his debut.

Debut: 1 Sep 1906 v Luton Town (A) 1-1 SL Div 1.

ANDERSON George Edward

(OL) Wing 5' 8" 11st 4lbs

b: Sunderland, 1881

QPR: May 1912

Southern League: 3-1. **FAC:** 0-0. **FLC:** 0-0. **Other:** 0-0. **Total:** 3-1.

A very skilful player who supported his hometown club Sunderland but they never signed him. He usually played on his best form when he was pitted against them. His wife suffered from a long term illness and while he was reluctant to leave her at home in Sunderland (players rarely lived near their clubs) permission was granted to let Anderson visit his wife as often as he liked and to permit compassionate leave if her condition was to become much worse at anytime during the season. In fact he was forced to take some leave to visit his ailing wife. He then had his absence extended, by what was his own illness, followed by a leg injury. By this time he was just a shadow of himself and he was allowed to travel back to Scotland.

Debut: 7 Sep 1912 v Norwich City (H) 1-0 SL Div 1.

ANDERSON Thomas Cowan

(OR) Wing 5′ 9″ 11st 7lbs
b: Haddington, Scotland, 24 Sep 1934
QPR: Nov 1958
Football League: 10-3. **FAC:** 0-0. **FLC:** 0-0.
Other: 0-0. **Total:** 10-3.
Honours: Scottish schoolboy cap.

After finishing his National Service he was quickly snapped up by Watford. He was described as a very fast winger with blistering pace and nimble footwork, an attribute which brought him second place in the 1957 Powderhall Sprint race. Gradually, Tommy became known as "Soccer's Happy Wanderer". Eventually he is believed to have gone to South Africa, before finally settling down in Australia, becoming a Sydney soccer reporter and later hosted his own radio programme.

Debut: 29 Nov 1958 v Hull City (A) 0-1 Div 3.

ANDERTON Sylvan James

(HB) Mid 5′ 9″ 12st 0lbs
b: Reading, Berks, 23 Nov 1934
QPR: (£5,000) Jun 1962
Football League: 4-0. **FAC:** 0-0. **FLC:** 0-0.
Other: 0-0. **Total:** 4-0.

A product of Ted Drake's youth policy at Reading, it was the same man that captured him for Chelsea in 1959, when he was manager there. Anderton was a strongly built, hard tackling half-back. At QPR he deputised for Angell when he was out of the squad and stayed until the end of the season. He currently lives in Bideford, Devon, where he writes poetry and also scouts for Reading.

Debut: 20 Jan 1962 v Crystal Palace (H) 1-0 Div 3.

ANDREWS Cecil J

(LH) Def 5′ 11″ 13st 3lbs
b: Alton, Hampshire, 1 Nov 1930
QPR: Jun 1956
Football League: 58-1. **FAC:** 4-0. **FLC:** 0-0.
Other: 3-0. **Total:** 65-1.

Signed by the manager, Jack Taylor, he was a big, hefty old-fashioned defender, who gave no quarter nor did he ask for any. Alec Stock's arrival at Loftus Road heralded his departure. Nicknamed "Archie" after the popular radio ventriloquist at the time.

Debut: 18 Aug 1956 v Reading (A) 0-1 Div 3 (S).

ANDREWS James Patrick

(OL) 5′ 5″ 10st 10lbs
b: Invergordon, Scotland, 1 Feb 1927
QPR: Jun 1959
Football League: 82-16. **FAC:** 4-1. **FLC:** 1-0.
Other: 1-0. **Total:** 88-17.
Honours: Hertfordshire XI v FA XI, 22 May 1940.

Jimmy joined Alec Stock at QPR in 1959. At 32 years of age he was a fast and nimble winger, who was given the job of chief coach to the reserve team. It was to make a tremendous impact on the future of the club. Eventually Andrews became the team manager while Stock became the general manager. The set-up lasted just 77 days before Jimmy quit the job in 1965 to become a coach at Chelsea, then Luton Town in 1967, followed by Spurs five years later. Finally he took the job of coach at Cardiff City in 1973. Within four months he became the manager and stayed as such until he was sacked in November 1978. Since then Andrews has remained in Wales as chief scout to Southampton.

Debut: 22 Aug 1959 v Swindon Town (H) 2-0 Div 3.

ANGELL Brett

(F) Striker 6′ 2″ 13st 11lbs
b: Marlborough, Wiltshire, 20 Aug 1968
QPR: 2002
Football League: 13-0. **FAC:** 0-0. **FLC:** 0-0.
Other: 0-0. **Total:** 13-0.

Angell appeared an awkward looking player in possession of the ball, nevertheless he had the ability to be in the right place at the right time. Despite scoring over 160 goals in a long career he failed to notch one at Loftus Road.

Debut: 23 Nov 2002 v Luton Town (A) 0-0 Div 2.

ANGELL Peter F

(LH) Def 5′ 10″ 11st 2lbs
b: Chalvey, Berks, 11 Jan 1932
d: 1979
QPR: Jul 1953
Football League: 417-37. **FAC:** 27-1. **FLC:** 6-2.
Other: 7-0. **Total:** 457-40.

Peter was originally a left-winger at Slough Town when Charlton Athletic took an interest in him. But after a few games at the Valley in the London MidWeek League he was allowed to join QPR, where he signed professional forms in 1953. He was one of the most reliable players the club was to have in their post-war history. Noted as the best defender in the lower divisions during the 1950s and 1960s, he could in fact play in any position he was asked to and for several years was the club captain. Angell was also an expert penalty taker and seldom missed. He played week after week with almost boring consistency, and eventually totalled over 450 matches during his 12-year period at QPR. When his playing days were over he went to Charlton Athletic as a coach.

Debut: 12 Sep 1953 v Walsall (H) 2-0 Div 3 (S).

ARCHER Arthur

(RB) Def 5′ 9″ 12st 7lbs
b: Ashby-de-la-Zouch, Derbyshire 1874
d: 1940
QPR: Aug 1903
Southern League: 52-0. **FAC:** 1-0. **FLC:** 0-0.
Other: 0-0. **Total:** 53-0.
Honours: Staffordshire Cup winner's medal. Kettering & Bass Cup winner's medal.

One of the most colourful characters to come out of this period of football. A tough, uncompromising player with a huge kick and a fearless tackle. A big man in stature and in heart who was extremely popular wherever he went. He signed for QPR and Spurs simultaneously playing mid-week for the latter in the London League and for Rangers in the Southern League. Arthur retired in 1909 to coach in Germany and Belgium before the First World War and in Italy after it, finally becoming the Watford trainer in 1924.

Debut: 5 Sep 1903 v Brentford (H) 1-0 SL Div 1.

ARDILES Osvaldo Cesar

Mid 5′ 6″ 9st 10lbs
b: Cordoba, Argentina, 3 Aug 1952
QPR: Aug 1988
Football League: 8-0. **FAC:** 1-0. **FLC:** 1-0.
Other: 0-0. **Total:** 10-0.
Honours: Argentinean international and member of the World Cup squad in 1978 and 1982. UEFA Cup winner's medal. FAC winner's medal. FAC runner's-up medal.

A World Cup international who graced the game with his unique style of play, and his ability to ride tackles while he was running with the ball, he reached QPR at the age of 36 years on a free transfer. Ossie had moved to Spurs 10 years earlier along with Ricardo Villa, a centre-forward, the pair causing quite a sensation. After only a few matches for QPR, Ossie suffered a broken leg. Swindon Town then offered him the manager's chair, which he took and he soon guided them to promotion. In March 1991 he took over at Newcastle United but he was given the sack 12 months later, the same

Osvaldo Ardiles

fate awaited him at WBA in 1992 and at Spurs in 1993. Ossie has since tried his hand at management in Japan, Israel, Argentina and Paraguay.
Debut: 27 Aug 1988 v Manchester United (A) 0-0 Div 1.

ARMITAGE Stanley

(IL) Mid
b: Woolwich, London, 5 Jun 1919
QPR: 1946
Football League: 2-0. **FAC:** 0-0. **FLC:** 0-0.
Other: 0-0. **Total:** 2-0.

As happened with many young players in 1939, Stan was called to arms, losing the best part of his career during the conflict. He eventually played in non-League football but retired shortly afterwards.
Debut: 14 Sep 1946 v Reading (H) 2-0 Div 3 (S).

ARMSTRONG James Harris

(CH) Def 6′ 0″ 12st 2lbs
b: Lemington, near Newcastle, 8 Mar 1904
d: Watford 13 Apr 1971
QPR: May 1928
Football League: 122-5. **FAC:** 11-0. **FLC:** 0-0.
Other: 0-0. **Total:** 133-5.
Honours: Hertfordshire FA XI v FA XI, 22 May 1940.

Jimmy was ideally built for the role of centre-half and was a stalwart in the middle of the defence in the early 1930s. He became a casualty, when the new manager, Mick O'Brien, cleared out a lot of players when he arrived at the club. Watford immediately signed Jimmy and the club never regretted it, for he was on their books until 1941. When his career at Watford ended he took a job at Universal Asbestos and they employed him for the rest of his life.
Debut: 10 Nov 1928 v Exeter City (A) 1-1 Div 3 (S).

ASHFORD Herbert E

(LH) Mid
b: Southall, Middlesex
QPR: 1920
Football League: 10-0. **FAC:** 0-0. **FLC:** 0-0.
Other: 0-0. **Total:** 10-0.

Not much is known about this player. Bert was a reserve at Brentford and at QPR, standing in for either Mitchell or O'Brien when one or other of them was out of the team.
Debut: 12 Feb 1921 v Plymouth Argyle (A) 0-1 Div 3 (S).

ASHMAN Donald

(LB) Def 5′ 10″ 11st 12lbs
b: Staindrop, Durham, 9 Oct 1902
d: 1984
QPR: (£500) May 1932
Football League: 75-0. **FAC:** 5-0. **FLC:** 0-0.
Other: 4-0. **Total:** 84-0.
Honours: 2 2nd Div championship medals.

Cool, unruffled and undoubtedly the best full-back playing in the division at the time. When signed by Middlesbrough, Don was known as an inside-forward but turned out to be an excellent full-back and became an established part of their promotion winning side in the 1927 and 1929 seasons. He finally ended his playing career appearing for Darlington in the mid 1930s.
Debut: 27 Aug 1932 v Brentford (H) 2-3 Div 3 (S).

ASTON Charles Lane

(RB) Def
b: Bilston, Staffordshire, July 1875
d: Leytonstone, 9 Jan 1931
QPR: Jun 1901
Southern League: 25-1. **FAC:** 3-0. **FLC:** 0-0.
Other: 0-0. **Total:** 28-1.
Honours: 1st Div championship medal.

A very efficient player who was an expert at floating the ball down the line or across the pitch rather than giving it a hefty punt upfield. Charlie enjoyed going forward with the attack and seemed to have plenty of stamina to do so. At Aston Villa he was reserve to the great Howard Spencer and deputised for him on 14 occasions when they won the championship in 1899.
Debut: 7 Sep 1901 v Watford (H) 0-1 SL Div 1.

Simon Barker

B

BAIDOO Shabazz Kwame Kussie
BAILEY Dennis L
BAILEY Sidney
BAILEY Stefan
BAIN Kenneth
BAKER Peter R
BAKHOLT Kurt
BALANTA Angelo Jasiel
BALDOCK John William N
BALLANTYNE John
BALOGUN Jesilimi
BANKOLE Ademola
BANKS Reginald
BANNER William Henry
BANNISTER Gary
BARACLOUGH Ian R
BARBER Michael J
BARDSLEY David John
BARKER Christopher Andrew
BARKER Simon
BARLEY Derek Charles
BARNES Philip Kenneth
BARNES William Edwin
BARR Hamid
BARR John M
BARR William
BARRIE Walter B
BARRON Paul George
BARTLETT Frederick Leslie
BARTON Warren
BEAN Marcus
BEATS Edwin
BECK John Alexander
BECK Mikkel Venge
BEDFORD Noel Brian
BEDINGFIELD Frank
BEECHAM Ernest Cromwell
BELLINGHAM James
BEN ASKER Aziz
BENNETT Edward Ernest
BENSON George Herdman
BENSTEAD Graham Mark
BENTLEY Roy Frank Thomas
BERRY P
BEST Leon Julian
BEST Thomas H
BEVAN Frederick Edward T Walter
BIGNOT Marcus
BIRCH James
BIRCHAM Marc Stephen John
BLACK Samuel
BLACKMAN Frederick Ernest
BLACKMAN John James
BLACKSTOCK Dexter Anthony Titus
BLACKWOOD John
BLAKE Albert George
BLAKE F J C
BLAKE Sidney
BLIZZARD Leslie William B
BOLAM Robert C
BOLDER Adam
BONASS Albert Edward
BONNOT Alexandre
BOTT Wilfred E
BOTTOMS Michael C
BOWERS Alfred George W
BOWLES Stanley
BOWMAN John William
BOXSHALL Daniel
BRADSHAW James
BRADSHAW John Henry
BRADY Patrick J
BRADY T Raymond
BRANCO Serge
BRAZIER Matthew Ronald
BRAZIL Alan Bernard
BREACKER Timothy Sean
BREVETT Rufus Emanuel
BREWIS Robert
BRIDGES Barry John
BRINDLEY Horace
BROCK Kevin Stanley
BROOMES Marlon Charles
BROSTER John
BROWN Aaron Wesley
BROWN Albert Richard
BROWN Arthur F
BROWN Charles
BROWN Harold Archer
BROWN Harold Thomas
BROWN Wayne Lawrence
BROWN William Young
BROWNING Robert Ernest
BRUCE Paul Mark
BUBB Alvin Ryan
BULL Albert
BURGESS Daniel
BURGESS Oliver D
BURKE Steven James
BURNHAM John Robert
BURNS John Charles
BURRIDGE John
BUSBY Martyn G
BUSBY Walter
BUTLER Ernest
BUTTERWORTH Herbert
BUZSAKY Akos
BYRNE John Frederick

Shabazz Baidoo

BAIDOO Shabazz Kwame Kussie

Striker 5' 8" 10st 7lbs
b: Hackney, London, 13 Apr 1988
QPR: Jul 2004
Football League: 28-3. **FAC:** 2-1. **FLC:** 3-0.
Other: 0-0. **Total:** 33-3.

Shabazz showed great promise as a youngster on Arsenal's books but failed to make a first team appearance at Highbury. He signed for QPR in July 2004, making four appearances during the club's first season in the Championship. Shabazz only made sporadic appearances during his four years at Loftus Road but will always be remembered for his last-gasp equaliser against Leeds United during the 2006/07 campaign. After just three appearances for Dagenham & Redbridge, Shabazz drifted into non-League football with Lewes and then Croydon Athletic.
Debut: 5 Apr 2005 v Gillingham (H) 1-1 Championship.

BAILEY Dennis L

(CF) Striker 5' 10" 11st 6lbs
b: Lambeth, London, 13 Nov 1965
QPR: (£150,000) Jul 1991
Football/Premier League: 39-10. **FAC:** 5-3.
FLC: 2-1. **Other:** 2-0. **Total:** 48-14.
Honours: Leyland Daf Cup winner's medal.

His close ball control and ability to take on defenders in tight situations were decidedly the main factors for QPR buying him. Dennis proved the point when he scored the equaliser at Highbury on the opening day of the 1991/92 season. Scoring a hat-trick against Manchester United at Old Trafford on New Year's Day 1992 was the highlight of his career at the club, and the whole match was televised across the land. Yet after various loan periods he was finally transferred to Gillingham.
Debut: 17 Aug 1991 v Arsenal (A) 1-1 Div 1.

BAILEY Sidney

(LB) Def 5' 9" 11st 8lbs
b: London
QPR: 1921
Football League: 1-0. **FAC:** 0-0. **FLC:** 0-0.
Other: 0-0. **Total:** 1-0.

The only fact known about this player was that he was an amateur. Sid's sole outing in the senior squad was late in the season.
Debut: 22 Apr 1922 v Merthyr Town (H) 0-0 Div 3 (S).

BAILEY Stefan

Mid 5' 11" 12st 8lbs
b: Brent, London, 10 October 1987
QPR: Jul 2004
Football League: 18-0. **FAC:** 1-0. **FLC:** 3-0.
Other: 0-0. **Total:** 22-0.

Making his debut under Ian Holloway due to a long list of injuries, Stefan provided a composed performance against the Blades in April 2005 with a series of strong tackles, good turns and an array of impressive passes. Unfortunately, Stefan was never given a run in the first team and, despite showing promise, the tough tackling, hardworking midfielder was released at the end of the 2008/09 campaign.
Debut: Apr 2005 v Sheffield Utd (A) 2-3 Championship.

BAIN Kenneth

(LB) Def 5' 8" 11st 8lbs
b: Scotland
QPR: 1921
Football League: 91-0. **FAC:** 7.0. **FLC:** 0-0.
Other: 0-0. **Total:** 98-0.

Ken was the regular left-back in the early 1920s when the club ended the season bottom of Division 3 (South) in 1924, and he was included in the general clear-out of players by manager Ned Liddell.
Debut: 12 Nov 1921 v Aberdare Athletic (H) 1-0. Div 3 (S).

BAKER Peter R

(RB) Def
b: Walthamstow, London, 24 Aug 1934
QPR: Mar 1961
Football League: 27-0. **FAC:** 0-0. **FLC:** 1-0.
Other: 0-0. **Total:** 28-0.

Peter was the cousin of Peter Russell Baker, (hence both men shared the same initials), only Peter Russell played for the famous Spurs Double team in the early 1960s. The two of them both turned out for Spurs reserves in the 1950s as amateurs. However, unlike his famous cousin, the QPR Baker achieved few first team games wherever he played.
Debut: 4 Mar 1961 v Port Vale (H) 1-0 Div 3.

Stefan Bailey

BAKHOLT Kurt

Mid
b: Odense, Denmark, 12 Aug 1963
QPR: 1986
Football League: 1-0. **FAC:** 0-0. **FLC:** 0-0.
Other: 0-0. **Total:** 1-0.
Honours: Danish U21 international.

Kurt did not play a match for Aston Villa, instead he was given a contract at QPR. Coming on as a substitute at Maine Road in February 1986, replacing Robbie James in the second half. His contract was not renewed at the end of the season.

Debut: 8 Feb 1986 v Manchester City (A) 0-2 Div 1.

Ken Bain

BALANTA Angelo Jasiel

Striker 5' 10' 11st 11lbs
b: Santiago de Cali, Colombia, 1 Jul 1990
QPR: 2007
Football League: 21-2. **FAC:** 1-0. **FLC:** 3-1.
Other: 0-0. **Total:** 25-3.

Such has been the impact that Angelo has made at Loftus Road, he has been awarded a contract that ties him to the club until at least the summer of 2010. The Colombian teenager came through the ranks at QPR and signed his first professional contract in January 2008. By then, he had already made his first team debut and went on to register his first goal for the club the following month. An 11-match loan spell with Wycombe saw him notch three goals before he was recalled early to Loftus Road.

Debut: 4 Dec 2007 v Crystal Palace (H) 1-2 Championship.

Angelo Balanta

Gary Bannister

BALDOCK John William N
(LH) Mid
b: Shadwell, London, 1893
QPR: 1913
Southern/Football League: 57-8. **FAC:** 0-0. **FLC:** 0-0. **Other:** 0-0. **Total:** 57-8.

John was a somewhat clever player and made no fewer than 150 appearances for the club during the First World War. Drafted directly into the senior squad from the juniors, he caused a sensation by scoring on his debut. His early days were spent in the forward line but he settled down into a solid midfield player.

Debut: 6 Dec 1913 v Coventry City (H) 3-0 SL Div 1.

BALLANTYNE John
(IF) Mid 5′ 8″ 11st 0lbs
b: Glasgow, Scotland, 27 Oct 1899
QPR: 1935
Football League: 25-3. **FAC:** 1-0. **FLC:** 0-0. **Other:** 0-0. **Total:** 26-3.
Honours: Scottish League v Irish League. Scottish Cup runner's-up medal.

An experienced inside-left who had played some of his soccer in the USA in the 1920s while he was working there as an engineer. John rejoined Partick Thistle when he returned and played in the 1930 Scottish Cup final.

At QPR he was at the heart of a very good team that ended the season in fourth place in the title race.

Debut: 16 Nov 1935 v Northampton Town (A) 4-1 Div 3 (S).

BALOGUN Jesilimi
(CF) Striker
b: Nigeria, 27 Mar 1931
QPR: 1956
Football League: 13-3. **FAC:** 2-2. **FLC:** 0-0. **Other:** 1-2. **Total:** 16-7.

The competition for the place of centre-forward at the club was intense at this period in time. "Tesi" lasted the season, after scoring on his debut. His early career was marked by his refusal to wear anything on his feet during a match. On another occasion, while he was appearing in a reserve match, it snowed and not having encountered the stuff before, Balogun ran off the pitch refusing to go back until he was convinced that the cold powder was harmless!

Debut: 13 Oct 1956 v Watford (H) 3-1 Div 3 (S).

BANKOLE Ademola
Goal 6′ 3″ 12st 10lbs
b: Abeokuta, Nigeria, 9 Sep 1969
QPR: (£50,000) Jul 1998
Football League: 1-0. **FAC:** 0-0. **FLC:** 0-0. **Other:** 0-0. **Total:** 1-0.

A very unorthodox but agile goalkeeper who was released back to his former club in August 2000, where he became first choice.
Debut: 9 Oct 1999 v Tranmere Rovers (H) 2-1 Div 1.

BANKS Reginald

(OL)
QPR: 1935
Football League: 12-3. **FAC:** 0-0. **FLC:** 0-0.
Other: 0-0. **Total:** 12-3.
Honours: England Amateur cap v Wales.

Reg remained an amateur during the days he was with WBA, however, he never did appear in the senior squad for them. When he signed for QPR he became a professional.
Debut: 31 Aug 1935 v Millwall (H) 2-3 Div 3 (S).

BANNER William Henry

(LH) Def
b: Barnsley, Yorks, 1878
d: Holmeswood, 28 Jun 1936
QPR: 1903
Southern League: 4-0. **FAC:** 0-0. **FLC:** 0-0.
Other: 0-0. **Total:** 4-0.

A powerful, elegant and versatile player who was able to play anywhere in defence. However, he was only called upon to play in four matches, so after one season he returned to Saltergate. Retiring at the age of 30 he continued to play for Hardwick Colliery until the start of the First World War. Bill was quiet; an introspective man, who won many friends in the Holmeswood community for his services to local sport as a football and cricket coach.
Debut: 28 Dec 1903 v Northampton Town (A) 1-2 SL Div 1.

BANNISTER Gary

Striker 5′ 8″ 11st 10lbs
b: Warrington, Cheshire, 22 Jul 1960
QPR: (£200,000) Aug 1984
Football League: 136-56. **FAC:** 9-1. **FLC:** 23-9.
Other: 4-6. **Total:** 172-72.
Honours: 1 cap at U21 level. 2nd Div runner's-up medal. FLC runner's-up medal.

A product of Hollins Green, near Warrington, he made only 22 appearances for Coventry City prior to his £100,000 transfer to Sheffield Wednesday in 1981. However, Gary made an immediate impact by scoring 22 goals in his first season and 66 goals in all. QPR paid £200,000 for him in 1984 and he settled well at Loftus Road, scoring 72 goals before he returned to Coventry in 1988 for a substantial fee.

He was arguably the best signing made by Alan Mullery during his reign as manager at Loftus Road. Gary was rather short for a striker, nevertheless, he made up for this with his quick, intelligent play. Bannister was always on the lookout for mistakes made by opposing defenders and would punish them with his quick reflexes.
Debut: 25 Aug 1984 v WBA (H) 3-1 Div 1.

BARACLOUGH Ian R

(WB) 6′ 1″ 12st 2lbs
b: Leicester, 4 Dec 1970
QPR: (£50,000) Mar 1998
Football League: 125-1. **FAC:** 7-0. **FLC:** 7-0.
Other: 0-0. **Total:** 139-1.
Honours: England youth caps. 3rd Div championship medal.

A striker who was turned into an attacking full-back at Mansfield Town. He opened his scoring account with one of the most remarkable goals ever witnessed at Field Mill – a free-kick from fully 50 yards. A tall defender who liked to get forward as often as possible, Ian became a dead-ball specialist and was a favourite of the spectators during his three years at Loftus Road, where he operated on the left-hand side of the pitch. He moved to Notts County for the 2001/02 season and immediately established himself as a first team player.
Debut: 21 Mar 1998 v Stoke City (A) 1-2 Div 1.

BARBER Michael J

(OL) Wing
b: Kensington, London, 15 Aug 1941
QPR: Dec 1959
Football League: 63-11. **FAC:** 2-2. **FLC:** 4-0.
Other: 0-0. **Total:** 69-13.

A fast two-footed winger who indeed could play on both sides of the park. Mike would interchange with the opposite winger on several occasions during the course of a match.
Debut: 5 Sep 1960 v Coventry City (A) 4-4 Div 3.

Ian Baraclough

BARDSLEY David John

(WB) Def 5′ 10″ 10st 0lbs
b: Manchester, 11 Sep 1964
QPR: (£500,000) Sep 1989
Football League: 253-4. **FAC:** 19-0. **FLC:** 20-1. **Other:** 3-1. **Total:** 295-6.
Honours: 2 England youth caps. 2 England international caps. FAC runner's-up medal.

Dave was ever-present in the FA Cup run of Watford, which took them to Wembley. He scored the first two League goals of his career in his 100th appearance for the Vicarage Road club, as a substitute in a 5-1 victory at Chelsea. The England Youth manager Graham Taylor signed him for Watford, and nine years later capped him at senior level. After nearly four years in Hertfordshire, he moved on to Oxford United where he stayed for two seasons, before becoming a big signing at Loftus Road. An excellent full-back with a vast amount of pace and good attacking flair, who had the ability to cross the ball on the run, Dave was also very steady in his defensive role and although some of his tackling was somewhat crude at times, he was a huge asset to the team and gave very many fine performances. After nine years and nearly 300 appearances, Dave moved back to his first League club Blackpool, after an absence of 15 years.

Debut: 16 Sep 1989 v Derby County (H) 0-1 Div 1.

Dave Bardsley

BARKER Christopher Andrew

Def 5' 10" 13st 8lbs
b: Sheffield, 2 Mar 1980
QPR: 2007 **Football League:** 25-0. **FAC:** 1-0. **FLC:** 0-0. **Other:** 0-0. **Total:** 26-0.

Signed on a free transfer in the summer of 2007 after being released by Cardiff City, Chris quickly found his feet in the QPR defence and helped the club to a mid-table finish in his one and only campaign at Loftus Road. Having spent the previous season on loan at Championship newcomers Colchester United, the left-back made 25 League appearances for Rangers despite undergoing two hernia operations before a summer 2008 transfer to Plymouth Argyle.
Debut: 1 Sep 2007 v Southampton (H) 0-3 Championship.

BARKER Simon

Mid 5' 9" 11st 0lbs
b: Farnworth, Lancashire, 4 Nov 1964
QPR: (£400,000) Jul 1988
Football League: 315-33. **FAC:** 23-3. **FLC:** 31-5. **Other:** 7-0. **Total:** 376-41.
Honours: 4 England U21 caps. Football Milk Cup final medal.

In July 1988 QPR broke Blackburn Rovers' transfer record when they paid £400,000 for the midfielder. However, he initially found it difficult to break into the first team at Loftus Road, but once he had settled down, Simon developed a formidable partnership with Ray Wilkins. An attacking player who passed the ball intelligently and was capable of opening the tightest of defences, Simon was a good skilful player on his day and had an astute football brain. His stay at Loftus Road lasted 10 years, during which time he made close to 400 appearances (at a very high average of 38 per season in all first team matches), the most during the 1994/95 season. He enjoyed a benefit match v Jamaica in 1998, which produced record receipts for a QPR player, and later that year moved on to the Potteries, and Port Vale.
Debut: 27 Sep 1988 v Manchester United (A) 0-0 Div 1.

BARLEY Derek Charles

(CF) Striker
b: Highbury, London, 20 Mar 1932
QPR: May 1953
Football League: 4-0. **FAC:** 0-0. **FLC:** 0-0. **Other:** 0-0. **Total:** 4-0.

The son of a pre-war Arsenal player who seemed to be a very bright prospect indeed, reaching the East Anglian Cup final in 1952 and helping Arsenal win the London Midweek League in the following year. However, that was Derek's sole achievement in football, and he failed to make the grade at a high level.
Debut: 29 Aug 1953 v Aldershot (H) 0-2 Div 3 (S).

Chris Barker

BARNES Philip Kenneth

Goal 6'1" 11st 1lb
b: Sheffield, 2 Mar 1979
QPR: (Loan) 2006
Football League: 1-0. **FAC:** 0-0. **FLC:** 0-0.
Other: 0-0. **Total:** 1-0.
Debut: 4 Feb 2006 v Leeds United (A) 0-2 Championship.

BARNES William Edwin

(OL) Wing 5' 9" 10st 4lbs
b: West Ham, 20 May 1879
QPR: 1907
Southern League: 261-26. **FAC:** 15-1. **FLC:** 0-0.
Other: 3-0. **Total:** 279-27.
Honours: FAC winner's medal. 2 Southern League championship medals. Represented the Southern League v the Scottish League.

A very tricky and experienced winger who was made captain as soon as he arrived at the club, and gave good service for six years. Retiring from playing in 1915, William had to wait until after the hostilities of the First World War before he could take up a coaching appointment in Spain with Bilbao.

Debut: 2 Sep 1907 v Tottenham Hotspur (H) 3-3 SL Div 1.

BARR Hamid

Mid
b: London, 1980
QPR: Oct 2001
Football League: 0-0. **FAC:** 0-0. **FLC:** 0-0.
Other: 1-0. **Total:** 1-0.

Made one solitary substitute appearance, in the Associate Members' Cup before moving back into non-League football.

Debut: 16 Oct 2001 v Yeovil Town (A) 0-3 LDV Trophy.

BARR John M

(CH) CD 6' 0" 12st 7lbs
b: Glasgow, Scotland, 1917
QPR: 1939
Football League: 4-0. **FAC:** 0-0. **FLC:** 0-0.
Other: 0-0. **Total:** 4-0.

John was unfortunate, for the Second World War interrupted his career at QPR as soon as he joined the club. He was called up to join the army and was taken prisoner by the Germans in the Western Desert. John was forced to work in a concrete factory and had little chance of playing football. After arriving back in Britain at the end of the war, his transfer back to his native Scotland was his main concern.

Debut: 2 Nov 1946 v Notts County (A) 2-1 Div 3 (S).

BARR William

(CH) CD
QPR: 1925
Football League: 2-0. **FAC:** 0-0. **FLC:** 0-0.
Other: 0-0. **Total:** 2-0.
Honours: Amateur Cup winner's medal.

Billy Barr was the centre-half who turned out for the London Caledonians when they lifted the FA Amateur Cup by beating Evesham Town 2-1 in extra-time in 1923. At QPR he was released after the team finished last in the table with 21 points.

Debut: 5 Sep 1925 v Merthyr Town (H) 1-1 Div 3 (S).

BARRIE Walter B

(RB) Def. 5' 10" 11st 8lbs
b: Kirkcakly, Scotland, 9 Aug 1909
QPR: 1932
Football League: 157-1. **FAC:** 12-0. **FLC:** 0-0.
Other: 3-0. **Total:** 172-1.
Honours: London Challenge Cup winner's medal.

Walter was a part-time pro with Hibs and he was one of the many Scotsmen to sample soccer in the USA in the 1920s. At West Ham he remained a reserve for his two-year period there, but at QPR he was regarded as a first rate defender who became part of a very good squad that challenged for promotion just before the Second World War. After six years and 157 League appearances, he moved to the northwest and joined Third Division (North) Carlisle United in 1938. When not playing football he enjoyed a round of golf and sketching was another of his hobbies.

Debut: 24 Feb 1932 v Watford (H) 2-1 Div 3 (S).

BARRON Paul George

Goal 6' 2" 13st 5lbs
b: Woolwich, London, 16 Sep 1953
QPR: (£35,000) Mar 1985
Football League: 32-0. **FAC:** 1-0. **FLC:** 0-0.
Other: 0-0. **Total:** 33-0.
Honours: Charity Shield runner's-up medal. League Cup runner's-up medal.

A big, strong and very experienced goalkeeper who took over the Number 1 spot during Jim Smith's reign at the club. With the transfer of David Seaman as the first choice goalkeeper in 1986, Paul was made redundant and drifted into non-League football.

Debut: 28 Sep 1985 v Birmingham City (H) 3-1 Div 1.

BARTLETT Frederick Leslie

(CH) CD 6' 0" 12st 0lbs
b: Reading, Berks, 5 Mar 1913
d: 1968
QPR: 1933
Football League: 48-0. **FAC:** 2-0. **FLC:** 0-0.
Other: 1-0. **Total:** 51-0.

Fred was earmarked in the late 1930s as the

Paul Barron

best young player in the country. Tall and elegant he dominated the centre of the pitch. Over 200 wartime appearances were notched-up by him for the Orient club.
Debut: 3 Nov 1934 v Millwall (A) 0-2 Div 3 (S).

BARTON Warren

Def 5′ 11″ 12st 0lbs
b: Islington, London, 19 Mar 1969
QPR: 2003
Football League: 3-0. **FAC:** 0-0. **FLC:** 0-0.
Other: 0-0. **Total:** 3-0.
Debut: 4 Oct 2003 v Grimsby Town (A) 1-0 Div 2.

BEAN Marcus

Mid 5′ 11″ 11st 6lbs
b: Hammersmith, London, 2 Nov 1984
QPR: Schoolboy signing 2002
Football League: 67-2. **FAC:** 2-0. **FLC:** 3-0.
Other: 1-0. **Total:** 73-2.

Marcus joined the club at a professional level at the start of the 2002/03 season, and had the indignity of being sent off in his debut match! Not that he was alone though, as three other players found themselves taking early baths. Having been recruited to QPR as an 11 year old, it was no surprise to the youth coaching staff that he made the grade in the first team. With competition for places at a premium, however, Marcus took his talents and composure north to Blackpool in search of regular football.
Debut: 26 Aug 2002 v Wycombe Wanderers (A) 1-4 Div 2.

BEATS Edwin

(CF) Striker
QPR: 1927
Football League: 1-1. **FAC:** 0-0. **FLC:** 0-0.
Other: 0-0. **Total:** 1-1.
Honours: 2 England Schoolboy international caps.

An English Schoolboy international who played against Scotland and Wales in the 1920s. His only match for QPR was the 6-1 defeat at Millwall. Eddie scored the only goal for Rangers, the match report revealing: "That a rasping shot from the visitor's centre-forward was deflected off Len Graham, the Millwall left-half and beat the goalkeeper for the QPR goal."
Debut: 10 Mar 1928 v Millwall (A) 1-6 Div 3 (S).

Marcus Bean

BECK John Alexander

Mid 5′ 10″ 11st 9lbs
b: Edmonton, London, 25 May 1954
QPR: May 1972
Football League: 40-1. **FAC:** 5-0. **FLC:** 2-0.
Other: 0-0. **Total:** 47-1.

John was a dangerous midfield schemer who was an expert at dead ball situations and a specialist at crossing the ball. John Beck is well known as a manager for taking his club, Cambridge United, to the quarter-finals of the FA Cup in 1990 and to the brink of the Premiership in 1992. His impact as a manager can only be described as sensational, but his long ball style of play was not liked by the purists. Other manager positions included those at Preston North End in 1992, Lincoln City in 1995 and Barrow in 1998.

Debut: 26 Dec 1972 v Leyton Orient (H) 3-1 Div 2.

John Beck

BECK Mikkel Venge

Striker 6′ 2″ 12st 9lbs
b: Arhus, Denmark, 12 May 1973
QPR: (Loan) Feb 2000
Football League: 11-4. **FAC:** 0-0. **FLC:** 0-0.
Other: 0-0. **Total:** 11-4.
Honours: 19 Danish international caps. 2nd Div championship medal.

A striker who is willing, hard working and promising but never quite delivers the real thing. Helped B1909 to win promotion to the Danish First Division but was sold to solve a cashflow problem. Mikkel was transferred to Middlesbrough under the free "Bosman" ruling. After two loan periods, including that at QPR, he settled in French football with Lille. His father Carl played for the Danish side AGF.

Debut: 12 Feb 2000 v Stockport County (H) 1-1 Div 1.

BEDFORD Noel Brian

(CF) Striker 5′ 11″ 11st 8lbs
b: Ferndale, Wales, 24 Dec 1933
QPR: Jul 1959
Football League: 258-161. **FAC:** 16-13. **FLC:** 8-6.
Other: 1-0. **Total:** 283-180.

Alec Stock paid £750 to acquire his services from Bournemouth after he had scored 32 goals in 75 League games. At QPR he scored 180 goals in 294 matches, which repaid his fee many times over. A busy, bustling player, who was a handful for any opposing defender, Brian had a fierce shot and scored approximately 25 goals a season throughout his time at the "Bush". After short periods at Scunthorpe and Brentford, he moved across the Atlantic and joined Atlanta Chiefs. But on his return from the USA, in 1967, Brian found himself banned from playing by the FA due to the fact that the American Football Association was then not affiliated. It took a year for him to successfully appeal against the ban, however, in 1968 he was forced to retire owing to a severe knee injury. After his retirement from football he became a professional tennis coach. Bedford became the stadium manager at Loftus Road until 1992 when he was made redundant.

Debut: 22 Aug 1959 v Swindon Town (H) 2-0 Div 3.

Mikkel Beck

BEDINGFIELD Frank

(CF) Striker 5' 8" 12st 7lbs
b: Sunderland, 1877
d: Nov 1904
QPR: 1899
Southern League: 24-17. **FAC:** 8-4. **FLC:** 0-0. **Other:** 0-0. **Total:** 32-21.
Honours: County cap.

Short and stocky for a centre-forward, Frank was very fast off the mark and had a wholehearted attitude towards the game. At QPR he became the top goalscorer for the club in their first season in the Southern League. During the following season he played for Portsmouth and in 1901 he was tragically struck down with consumption. Cash was raised to send him to South Africa to recuperate in the sun but it was too late to avert his premature death.
Debut: 9 Sep 1899 v Tottenham Hotspur (A) 0-1 SL Div 1.

BEECHAM Ernest Cromwell

Goal 5' 9" 11st 7lbs
b: Hertford, 24 Aug 1896
d: Hertford, Aug 1985
QPR: May 1932

Aziz Ben Asker

Football League: 86-0. **FAC:** 9-0. **FLC:** 0-0. **Other:** 0-0. **Total:** 95-0.
Honours: Represented an English XI in Holland. Played for the Professionals v the Amateurs. London Combination winner's medal.

A fearless goalkeeper, short in stature but big in heart, who possessed a massive pair of hands and a huge kick. Ernest's career was renewed at QPR after he had suffered a particularly nasty spinal injury with his previous club. Then in 1934 he broke his arm and decided to retire, however, he was signed by Brighton & Hove Albion in 1935 but never played for them. He did turn out for Swindon Town, when their goalkeeper was injured. Ernest died in the same house as he was born in.
Debut: 27 Aug 1932 v Brentford (H) 2-3 Div 3 (S).

BELLINGHAM James

(RB) Def 6' 0" 13st 7lbs
b: Falkirk, Scotland, 1878
QPR: 1900
Southern League: 15-0. **FAC:** 2-0. **FLC:** 0-0. **Other:** 0-0. **Total:** 17-0.
Honours: Scottish inter-county player. Scottish Junior international trialist.

Bellingham had a fine knowledge of the game and was able to play anywhere in the defence. Although he was tall and heavy, he was very quick on his feet for a big man. James was a blacksmith by trade.
Debut: 8 Sep 1900 v Swindon Town (H) 7-1 SL Div 1.

BEN ASKER Aziz

CD 6' 2" 13st 5lbs
b: Chateau Gontier, France, 30 Mar 1976
QPR: (Loan) Aug 2001
Football League: 18-0. **FAC:** 0-0. **FLC:** 1-0. **Other:** 1-0. **Total:** 20-0.

Ben Asker came on a one year loan from France and was subsequently dropped from the squad after he received an injury, whereupon he returned to his club.
Debut: 11 Aug 2001 v Stoke City (H) 1-0 Div 2.

BENNETT Edward Ernest

Goal 5' 10" 10st 13lbs
b: Kilburn, London, 22 Aug 1925
QPR: Feb 1949
Football League: 2-0. **FAC:** 0-0. **FLC:** 0-0. **Other:** 0-0. **Total:** 2-0.
Honours: 11 England Amateur caps. Olympic winner's medal in 1952. FA tour of the West Indies.

The club were very lucky to have this man on their books when the regular goalkeeper, Reg Allen, was out of the squad, injured. Later Ted turned professional when he signed for Watford.
Debut: 19 Mar 1949 v West Ham United (A) 0-2 Div 2.

BENSON George Herdman

(OL) Wing 5' 8" 10st 9lbs
b: Garslang, Lancashire, 26 May 1893
d: Lancashire, 19 Dec 1974
QPR: 1923
Football League: 17-0. **FAC:** 0-0. **FLC:** 0-0. **Other:** 0-0. **Total:** 17-0.

George was just one of six players to be tried on the left wing during this re-election season. He was released halfway into the season and was given a one-month trial at Port Vale but failed to impress and moved into the Lancashire League.
Debut: 25 Aug 1923 v Brentford (H) 1-0 Div 3 (S).

BENSTEAD Graham Mark

Goal 6' 1" 13st 7lbs
b: Aldershot, Hants, 20 Aug 1963
QPR: Jul 1981
Football League: 0-0. **FAC:** 1-0. **FLC:** 0-0. **Other:** 0-0. **Total:** 1-0.
Honours: England Youth cap. 3 semi-pro caps.

A bricklayer by trade, Graham was a personable and bubbly character. Tommy Docherty first noticed the goalkeeper when QPR were playing a friendly against Southern League opponents Wimbledon in a floodlight match. Later he signed professional forms with Terry Venables.
Debut: 8 Jan 1983 v WBA (A) 2-3 FAC third round.

BENTLEY Roy Frank Thomas

(RB) Def 5' 10" 12st 0lbs
b: Bristol, 17 May 1924
QPR: Jun 1961
Football League: 45-0. **FAC:** 6-0. **FLC:** 1-0. **Other:** 0-0. **Total:** 52-0.
Honours: 12 English international caps. 2 B caps. 3 Football League caps. Great Britain v The Rest of Europe. Football League championship medal. 2 2nd Div promotion medals.

Roy was the son of a noted rugby player, who became one of the hottest properties of the post-war era. He started out as an inside-forward and became one of the first "roaming centre-forwards", of the 1950s. A fine header of the ball with a potent right-foot shot he became the most expensive signing to come out of the lower divisions. Eighteen months after Newcastle had signed him, Chelsea offered what was then a staggering fee for Bentley. He became their leading goalscorer for the next eight seasons, and was the club captain when they won the League championship.

At Fulham he resorted to centre-half for the next five years and covered that position with some success. At the age of 33, Bentley was persuaded by manager Alec Stock to continue his career and fill in at right-back and help to bring along the youngsters that QPR had at the time. Bentley later became

the Reading manager, until 1969, and in 1970 he took Swansea Town to promotion as their manager, where he stayed until 1972. Roy then took over the reins at Thatcham Town before becoming the secretary of Reading in 1977. His last job before he retired, was that of secretary of Aldershot in 1985.
Debut: 19 Aug 1961 v Brentford (H) 3-0 Div 3.

BERRY P

Goal
QPR: 1919
Southern League: 4-0. **FAC:** 0-0. **FLC:** 0-0.
Other: 0-0. **Total:** 4-0.

Berry played throughout the month of February 1920 during the club's last Southern League season, replacing the injured Merrick. Berry was never once on the winning side.
Debut: 14 Feb 1920 v Swansea Town (A) 1-3 SL Div 1.

BEST Leon Julian

Striker 6' 1" 12st 0lbs
b: Nottingham, 19 Sep 1986
QPR: (Loan) 2004
Football League: 5-0. **FAC:** 0-0. **FLC:** 0-0.
Other: 0-0. **Total:** 5-0.
Honours: 2 Republic of Ireland U21 caps.
Debut: 18 Dec 2004 v Reading (A) 1-0 Championship.

BEST Thomas H

(CF) Striker
b: Milford Haven, 23 Dec 1920
QPR: Dec 1949
Football League: 13-3. **FAC:** 1-0. **FLC:** 0-0.
Other: 0-0. **Total:** 14-3.

Tommy was built small and compact, like a pocket battleship, and he was never really in the running for a place in the senior side. He left at the end of the 1949/50 season moving into the non-League scene.
Debut: 10 Dec 1949 v Blackburn Rovers (A) 0-0 Div 2.

BEVAN Frederick Edward T Walter

(CF) Striker 5' 8" 12st 0lbs
b: Hackney, London, 27 Feb 1879
d: Hackney, 10 Dec 1935
QPR: May 1904
Southern League: 58-30. **FAC:** 1-0. **FLC:** 0-0.
Other: 0-0. **Total:** 59-30.
Honours: Lancashire Combination winner's medal. Western League championship medal.

Fred was a strong, burly player who was very bold and had a devastating shot in either foot. The 1905 edition of *Men Famous in Football*, noted him as a "clever dribbler". At Clapton Orient he was made captain as soon as he arrived there and was chosen as a reserve for the Football League v the Southern League in 1910. He retired during the Great War to become the coach at Clapton Orient where he stayed until 1923.
Debut: 3 Sep 1904 v Plymouth Argyle (H) 2-1 SL Div 1.

BIGNOT Marcus

CD 5' 10" 11st 2lbs
b: Birmingham, 22 Aug 1974
QPR: Mar 2001
Football League: 54-1. **FAC:** 1-0. **FLC:** 1-0.
Other: 1-0. **Total:** 57-1.
QPR: 2004
Football League: 128-0. **FAC:** 2-0. **FLC:** 6-0.
Other: 0-0. **Total:** 136-0.

Bignot followed his manager to the club from Bristol Rovers and played at the heart of the Rangers defence where his ball winning talents were much in evidence. Despite making over 50 appearances for the Rangers, Marcus became part of the general clearout at the club at the end of the 2001/02 season. After a one-month loan at Rushden & Diamonds, in August 2001, he subsequently signed a long-term contract with the Northants club but returned to Loftus Road where he made a further 136 appearances for Rangers.
Debut: 17 Mar 2001 v Grimsby Town (H) 0-1 Div 1.

BIRCH James

(IR) Striker 5' 7" 11st 2lbs
b: Blackwell, Derbyshire, 1888
d: 1940
QPR: 1912
Southern/Football League: 328-123. **FAC:** 29-19.
FLC: 0-0. **Other:** 0-0. **Total:** 357-142.

Jimmy was a somewhat compact player who was very stocky and was a natural successor to the captaincy after Archie Mitchell. Manager James Cowan signed the striker after he had scored 40 goals for Aston Villa reserves in 1912, and had also notched two goals in his first team debut standing in for Harry Hampton, the Villa regular centre-forward. He proved to be one of the finest servants the club ever had. Jimmy possessed a deceptive body swerve and could beat opponent after

Marcus Bignot

opponent without deviating from a straight line. For many years his deadly shooting made him the club's leading goalscorer from the inside-right position.
Debut: 5 Sep 1912 v Plymouth Argyle (H) 2-1 SL Div 1.

BIRCHAM Marc Stephen John

Mid 5' 10" 12st 4lbs
b: Wembley, Middlesex, 11 May 1978
QPR: 2002
Football League: 155-7. **FAC:** 3-0. **FLC:** 7-0.
Other: 0-0. **Total:** 165-7.
Honours: 17 Canada (full) caps & 1 U23 cap.

Marc supported the Rangers as a youngster, and became the first member of the QPR Loyal Supporters' Association to play for the club. However, he in fact joined the club from Millwall. The only two goals he scored in the 2002/03 season were both against Brentford. He is a hard working, strong running midfielder who always gives 100% in a match, which goes down well with the QPR fans. At one time he dyed his hair blue, white and black! Marc left for the West Country in 2007 but retired during the 2008/09 campaign due to a series of ankle injuries.
Debut: 10 Aug 2002 v Chesterfield (H) W 3-1 Div 2.

Marc Bircham

BLACK Samuel

(OL) Striker 5' 6" 11st 0lbs
b: Motherwell, Scotland, 18 Nov 1905
d: 1977
QPR: 1938
Football League: 5-0. **FAC:** 0-0. **FLC:** 0-0.
Other: 0-0. **Total:** 5-0.

A famous name in the history of Plymouth Argyle, so much so that he became something of a legend. His control was so good and Sammy was such a beautiful striker of the ball with either foot that he could find the back of the net from any angle which other players would consider impossible. During his Argyle career he scored 185 goals in 491 matches. At the age of 34, Black arrived at Loftus Road but he was all burnt out. He soon retired from the game, and went back to Plymouth where he found employment in the docks as a storekeeper and stayed there until after the Second World War.
Debut: 31 Dec 1938 v Bristol Rovers (A) 0-0 Div 3 (S).

BLACKMAN Frederick Ernest

(RB) Def 5' 10" 12st 7lbs
b: Brixton, London, 8 Feb 1884
QPR: 1919
Southern/Football League: 60-0. **FAC:** 2-0.
FLC: 0-0. **Other:** 0-0. **Total:** 62-0.
Honours: Southern League championship winner's medal. 2 caps for the Southern League v Football League. Played in an England trial match.

Fred was described in the *Athletic News* as quick on his feet, with a sound kick and a fearless tackle. During the First World War he played over 100 matches for Fulham, and played in the last London Victory Cup final of 1919. Fred retired in 1922 to pursue his trade as a carpenter and cabinet maker.
Debut: 30 Aug 1919 v Bristol Rovers (A) 2-0 SL Div 1.

BLACKMAN John James

(CF) Striker 5' 9" 12st 4lbs
b: Bermondsey, London, January 1911
QPR: 1932
Football League: 108-62. **FAC:** 8-7. **FLC:** 0-0.
Other: 4-2. **Total:** 120-71.

Blackman was snapped up by QPR after having won Cup and League medals in the Brixton Sunday League. He was a keen, bustling forward with a

sizzling shot whose scoring rate was approximately one in every other match. Jack, as he was known, was also noted as a good all-round athlete who had also won medals and trophies for boxing, running and jumping. He scored twice on his debut for the club and then five in the next six matches.
Debut: 13 Jan 1932 v Reading (A) 2-3 Div 3 (S).

Dexter Blackstock

BLACKSTOCK Dexter Anthony Titus

Striker 6′ 2″ 13st 0lbs
b: Oxford, 20 May 1986
QPR: £500,000 Aug 2006
Football League: 110-30. **FAC:** 4-1. **FLC:** 3-1.
Other: 0-0. **Total:** 117-32.
Honours: England U20 and U21 caps.

A teenage sensation once he burst into the Premiership with Southampton, Dexter Blackstock found the arrival of Bradley Wright-Phillips limited his first team opportunities and was signed by Gary Waddock in August 2006. The youngster repaid his manager's faith by notching 13 League goals that season including five in the last eight games to help the club preserve their Championship status. Despite a return to form after a quiet 2007/08, Dexter was loaned to Forest in March 2009 for the remainder of the season.
Debut: 12 Aug 2006 v Southend United (H) 2-0 Championship.

BLACKWOOD John

(CF) Striker 5′ 9″ 12st 0lbs
b: Maine, USA, 1875
QPR: 1902
Southern League: 46-33. **FAC:** 0-0. **FLC:** 0-0.
Other: 0-0. **Total:** 46-33.

John's parents happened to be living in the USA at the time of his birth, however, he came home in time to be educated in Scotland and joined Petershill FC at the age of 20. A keen, bustling player who had a hard shot and a nose for scoring, John was a real favourite of the spectators at Park Royal.
Debut: 29 Nov 1902 v Northampton Town (H) 0-0 SL Div 1.

BLAKE Albert George

(LH) Mid 5′ 8″ 11st 0lbs
b: Fulham, London, 1900
QPR: Aug 1933
Football League: 81-9. **FAC:** 5-0. **FLC:** 0-0.
Other: 3-1. **Total:** 89-10.

The latter part of Albert's career at Watford followed a strange pattern. He was re-engaged for the 1932/33 season after being given a free transfer, but not recalled until the final game of that season after two years out of the first team. He was then released again immediately afterwards, whereupon he signed for QPR. Albert was the product of the London amateur game, and looked very classy going forward. At defending however, it was another story. After four years service at Loftus Road, when William Birrell took over, Blake was one of those whose contract was ended.
Debut: 26 Aug 1933 v Brighton & Hove Albion (H) 2-0 Div 3 (S).

BLAKE F J C

(CF) Striker
QPR: 1913
Southern League: 2-0. **FAC:** 0-0. **FLC:** 0-0.
Other: 0-0. **Total:** 2-0.
Honours: Represented London League v London Combination. 2 Amateur Cup final winner's medals.

Blake remained an amateur throughout his career. He joined the army at the outbreak of

war and rose to the rank of captain and fought on the Western Front. On his return to civilian life he rejoined Ilford.
Debut: 26 Mar 1914 v Portsmouth (H) 1-0 SL Div 1.

BLAKE Sidney

(OL) Mid
b: Whitley Bay, near Newcastle
QPR: 1906
Southern League: 14-0. **FAC:** 0-0. **FLC:** 0-0. **Other:** 0-0. **Total:** 14-0.

This man was an outside-left when he appeared for QPR in 1906, but four years later after joining Newcastle United from South Shields, for the sum of £30, he had become a goalkeeper. Sid moved to Coventry in 1914 as a player but retired to become their trainer in 1918.
Debut: 1 Sep 1906 v Luton Town (A) 1-1 SL Div 1.

BLIZZARD Leslie William B

(RH) Def 6′ 0″ 12st 2lbs
b: Acton, Middlesex, 13 Mar 1923
d: Northampton, 1996
QPR: 1944
Football League: 5-0. **FAC:** 0-0. **FLC:** 0-0. **Other:** 0-0. **Total:** 5-0.
Honours: 3rd Div championship medal.

Les was with QPR during the war years and played alongside Alec Stock. Later when Stock became manager of Yeovil Town in 1948, Blizzard became part of the team, following him to Leyton Orient in 1950. Making a name for himself under the manager, Stock later spoke highly of the player, saying that Orient's promotion would not have been possible without Les's great efforts. Les was known as being a highly committed player.
Debut: 1 Mar 1947 v Norwich City (A) 1-0 Div 3 (S).

BOLAM Robert C

(OR) Mid 5′ 8″ 11st 7lbs
b: Birtley, County Durham, 1896
d: 1964
QPR: 1924
Football League: 2-0. **FAC:** 0-0. **FLC:** 0-0. **Other:** 0-0. **Total:** 2-0.

Ned Liddell's reign as manager of QPR ended in 1925 and Bob Hewison became the new boss. A general clear out of players was the order of the day. Bolam was one among many others to get his marching orders. It is believed that he immediately drifted out of the professional game.
Debut: 6 Dec 1924 v Bristol City (H) 3-0 Div 3 (S).

BOLDER Adam

Mid 5′ 9″ 10st 8lbs
b: Hull, 25 Oct 1980
QPR: Jan 2007
Football League: 41-2. **FAC:** 0-0. **FLC:** 1-0. **Other:** 0-0. **Total:** 42-2.

Brought in by John Gregory to shore up a side that was in danger of being relegated, Adam's tough tackling and composure on the ball helped alleviate those fears and steer QPR to mid-table safety in the 2007/08 campaign. He was made club captain for the following season but found himself being loaned out to Sheffield Wednesday before eventually signing for Millwall. Adam's younger brother Chris was also a professional footballer, plying his trade with Grimsby Town.
Debut: 30 Jan 2007 v Barnsley (A) 0-2 Championship.

Adam Bolder

BONASS Albert Edward

(OL) Wing 5' 8" 10st 7lbs
b: York, 1911
d: Tockwith, Yorkshire, 8 Oct 1945
QPR: Jun 1939
Football League: 0-0. **FAC:** 0-0. **FLC:** 0-0.
Other: 59-7. **Total:** 59-7.

Albert, like a lot of his team-mates, became a war reserve policeman shortly after war broke out. In 1943 he joined the RAF and served in Wellington bombers as a wireless operator, and he was forced to bale out of his aircraft over Manchester. He lost his life on active service, when the Stirling bomber in which he was a crew member crashed on a training flight. The trio of Football League matches that he was involved in were not recognised by the FA, the 1939/40 season being abandoned after three games, and therefore he had no Football League debut for the club, but he still merits inclusion for his 59 QPR matches that were all made during wartime.

BONNOT Alexandre

CD 5' 8" 11st 6lbs
b: Poissy, France, 31 Jul 1973
QPR: Aug 2001
Football League: 22-1. **FAC:** 1-0. **FLC:** 1-0.
Other: 1-0. **Total:** 25-1.

Alex arrived on a three-month contract in the summer of 2001. His contract was extended on a month by month basis until financial considerations led to him being released at the end of February 2002.
Debut: 11 Aug 2001 v Stoke City (H) 1-0 Div 2.

BOTT Wilfred E

(OL) Striker 5' 7" 11st 2lbs
b: Edlington, Yorkshire, 25 Apr 1907
QPR: (£750) May 1936
Football League: 75-34. **FAC:** 9-1. **FLC:** 0-0.
Other: 4-1. **Total:** 88-36.

Wilf was considered to be the fastest footballer in the country during the early 1930s. He was always among the top scorers at the end of each season and indeed headed the scoring list for QPR during the 1937/38 season. Wilf played in over 100 matches during the Second World War.
Debut: 29 Aug 1936 v Bristol City (A) 2-3 Div 3 (S).

BOTTOMS Michael C

(IL) Mid
b: Harrow, Middlesex, 11 Jan 1939
QPR: 1960
Football League: 2-0. **FAC:** 0-0. **FLC:** 1-0.
Other: 0-0. **Total:** 3-0.

Given a trial in the senior squad by manager Alec Stock, Mike never seemed to gel with the team, so he drifted out of the Football League scene.
Debut: 5 Sep 1960 v Coventry City (A) 4-4 Div 3.

BOWERS Alfred George W

(LH) Def 6' 1" 12st 6lbs
b: Canning Town, London, May 1895
QPR: May 1926
Football League: 1-0. **FAC:** 0-0. **FLC:** 0-0.
Other: 0-0. **Total:** 1-0.

Alf was an amateur until he signed for Charlton Athletic. He made just nine appearances in his entire career as a professional.
Debut: 2 Oct 1926 v Bournemouth (A) 2-6 Div 3.

BOWLES Stanley

(IL) Mid 5' 10" 11st 4lbs
b: Mosten, Manchester, 24 Dec 1948
QPR: (£110,000) Sep 1972
Football League: 255-71. **FAC:** 25-8. **FLC:** 27-7.
Other: 8-11. **Total:** 315-97.
Honours: 5 England international caps. 2nd Div runner's-up medals. 1st Div runner's-up medal.

Prior to his move to Loftus Road in September 1972, Stan played for Carlisle, where, despite only 11 months and 36 appearances at Brunton Park, he is still one of their best remembered players. At QPR, Stan was probably the brightest among a team of stars. With his magical feet and tremendous vision he was really a genius on the field of play; a class above the average player. However, off the pitch he was something of a wayward character with a weakness for gambling. He was always the most charismatic of players at all his clubs. Although there was always doubt about his temperament, Stan was indeed a wonderful player and left many magical moments for all supporters to savour over the years. At his last club, Brentford, he was a given a benefit match (the Bees v Rangers) in May 1987, and it is a mark of the respect that supporters had for "Mr Entertainment", that the attendance of 7,049 was the second highest at Griffin Park that season. In total Stan made 507 career League appearances, netting 127 goals.
Debut: 16 Sep 1972 v Nottingham Forest (H) 3-0 Div 2.

BOWMAN John William

(RH) Mid 5' 8" 12st 0lbs
b: Middlesbrough, 23 Apr 1879
d: Sudbury, 26 Jan 1943
QPR: Jun 1901
Southern League: 103-2. **FAC:** 7-0. **FLC:** 0-0.
Other: 0-0. **Total:** 110-2.

A good athlete and a strong swimmer. According to the *Bells* magazine (the sporting paper of the day), they wrote that he was "a brainy and intelligent player, who only makes for the good of the game". John became the club secretary in 1903, but in 1905 he took the job of manager of Norwich City. Bowman later became the Croydon Common manager until the start of the First World War, when the club had to close. After the war he owned a sports outfitters shop in the City of London as well as becoming a QPR director. Despite his ill-health, John took over as manager of the club for a short spell in 1931.
Debut: 7 Sep 1901 v Watford (H) 0-1 SL Div 1.

BOXSHALL Daniel

(OR) Striker
b: Bradford, Yorkshire, 2 Apr 1920
QPR: Jan 1944
Football League: 29-14. **FAC:** 8-3. **FLC:** 0-0.
Other: 0-0. **Total:** 37-17.
Honours: 3rd Div (South) championship medal.

Danny was a New Year's Day signing in 1944 and within three months he was in France winning the Military Medal. Boxshall was a very fast winger with a deadly shot whose favourite position was centre-forward. His tally of 11 goals in the championship side of 1948 was precious.
Debut: 26 Dec 1946 v Watford (A) 2-0 Div 3 (S).

BRADSHAW James

(IR) Striker 5' 7" 10st 7lbs
b: Burnley, Lancashire, 1880
QPR: 1910
Southern League: 2-2. **FAC:** 0-0. **FLC:** 0-0.
Other: 0-0. **Total:** 2-2.

Jimmy burst onto the scene at QPR by scoring two goals in his debut match, but almost immediately he was on his way to Southend United to become manager of the club. After military service in the Great War he became manager of Swansea Town in 1919 guiding them to promotion in 1925. Fulham in 1926 was his next club, followed by Bristol City in 1929. In 1932 he left the football scene to take up work in the insurance business.
Debut: 3 Sep 1910 v Coventry City (H) 5-0 SL Div 1.

BRADSHAW John Henry

(OR) Mid
b: Burnley, Lancashire, 28 Jun 1892
QPR: Aug 1921
Football League: 5-0. **FAC:** 0-0. **FLC:** 0-0.
Other: 0-0. **Total:** 5-0.

Small with red hair, Jack as he was known was just one member of a prominent footballing family. His manager at Southend United was his brother Joe and when Jack played for Watford, his father was manager there. His father also managed Woolwich Arsenal and Fulham, and was also secretary of the

Stan Bowles

Southern League. At Southend, Jack took the job of trainer, nevertheless there was still one appearance left for him in 1923, on the wing.
Debut: 24 Sep 1921 v Reading (A) 1-0 Div 3 (S).

BRADY Patrick J

(RB) Def 5′ 7″ 10st 6lbs
b: Dublin, Eire, 11 Mar 1936
QPR: 1963
Football League: 62-0. **FAC:** 5-0. **FLC:** 3-0.
Other: 0-0. **Total:** 70-0.
Honours: 4th Div championship medal.

Pat had a very cultured left foot and indeed was the brainy one of the two brothers, having studied at Dublin University for a BA in Science. He was a schoolboy international and it was something of a coup when Alec Stock captured the brothers in 1963.
Debut: 30 Oct 1963 v Hull City (A) 0-3 Div 3.

BRADY T Raymond

(CD) 6′ 0″ 12st 2lbs
b: Dublin, Eire, 3 Jun 1937
QPR: Jul 1963
Football League: 88-0. **FAC:** 6-1. **FLC:** 3-0.
Other: 0-0. **Total:** 97-1.

Honours: 6 caps for Eire. 4th Div championship medal.

Ray's rugged, uncompromising defending and fearless tackling proved an inspiration at Loftus Road. Brady tackled furiously, using his height splendidly and he was to show real constructive skill as he moved up field to supply a stream of smooth passes. One of the seven sons of a Dublin docker who produced three footballers, the third being Liam of Arsenal and Juventus. After his retirement from football Ray went on to run a public house in Kent.
Debut: 24 Aug 1963 v Oldham Athletic (A) 1-2 Div 3.

BRANCO Serge

Def
b: Douala, Cameroon, 11 Oct 1980
QPR: 2004
Football League: 7-0. **FAC:** 1-0. **FLC:** 1-0.
Other: 0-0. **Total:** 9-0.
Honours: 12 Cameroon caps.
Debut: 22 Sep 2004 v Aston Villa (A) 1-3 Carling Cup second round.

Serge Branco

BRAZIER Matthew Ronald

Mid 5′ 8″ 10st 7lbs
b: Whipps Cross, London 2 Jul 1976
QPR: Jul 1994
Football League: 49-2. **FAC:** 3-0. **FLC:** 5-1.
Other: 0-0. **Total:** 57-3.

A midfield player come defender who is at his best going forward. His battling

Alan Brazil

qualities soon enabled him to establish himself. Unfortunately, Matt found it difficult to live up to inflated expectations and at times he looked somewhat lightweight at his other clubs.
Debut: 28 Oct 1995 v Nottingham Forest (H) 1-1 PL.

BRAZIL Alan Bernard

For 5′ 11″ 13st 1lb
b: Glasgow, Scotland, 15 Jun 1959
QPR: Jun 1986
Football League: 4-0. **FAC:** 0-0. **FLC:** 2-1.
Other: 0-0. **Total:** 6-1.
Honours: Scottish Youth & U21 international caps. 13 Scottish international caps. 2 1st Div runner's-up medals. UEFA Cup winner's medal.

A powerfully built player with a rugged determined nature. However, Alan didn't quite seem able to capture the form at QPR that he had shown at his other League clubs. He suffered an unfortunate back injury in January 1987 while he was at the club and this forced his retirement from the fully professional game. He became the proprietor of the Black Adder Inn, in Ipswich.
Debut: 23 Aug 1986 v Southampton (A) 1-5 Div 1.

BREACKER Timothy Sean

(RB) Def 6′ 0″ 13st 0lbs
b: Bicester, Oxfordshire, 2 Jul 1965
QPR: (Loan) Oct 1998
Football League: 2-0. **FAC:** 0-0. **FLC:** 0-0.
Other: 0-0. **Total:** 2-0.
QPR: Feb 1999
Football League: 32-2. **FAC:** 2-0. **FLC:** 2-0.
Other: 0-0. **Total:** 36-2.
Honours: 2 England U21 caps. League Cup winner's medal.

A placid and unassuming man who was nevertheless a strong muscular player. Tim had a powerful attacking and adventurous nature and a liking to overlap. A leg injury, which he suffered in the middle of the 1999/2000 season unfortunately kept him out for the rest of the campaign, and led to his retirement from playing, whereupon he became the QPR reserve team coach.
Debut: 3 Oct 1998 v Grimsby Town (H) 1-2 Div 1.

BREVETT Rufus Emanuel

Def 5′ 8″ 11st 0lbs
b: Derby, 24 Sep 1969
QPR: (£250,000) Feb 1991
Premier/Football League: 152-1. **FAC:** 8-0.
FLC: 10-0. **Other:** 0-0. **Total:** 170-1.

Rufus is a stocky marauding left-sided wing-back, who is strongly committed and enjoys all he contributes to the game including taking the ball to the opposition when the opportunity occurs. He is a no nonsense defender who likes to go in where it hurts and although he may have lacked finesse or great passing ability, he was one of the best defenders at the club. However, at Fulham, in the flat back-four system, Rufus was less likely to cross the halfway line, especially in tight situations. A big

Tim Breacker

Rufus Brevett

money buy from Doncaster Rovers in 1991, Rufus enjoyed nearly eight years at Loftus Road, where he appeared in 170 first team matches, before a short journey took him to Fulham, and five years later to West Ham.

Debut: 23 Mar 1991 v Tottenham Hotspur (A) 0-0 Div 1.

BREWIS Robert

(CF) Striker
b: circa 1885
QPR: 1905
Southern League: 7-2. **FAC:** 0-0. **FLC:** 0-0.
Other: 0-0. **Total:** 7-2.

Not a lot is known about Brewis. However, his most successful period was at Lincoln City, where he notched 11 goals in 22 matches.

Debut: 7 Oct 1905 v Tottenham Hotspur (A) 1-2 SL Div 1.

BRIDGES Barry John

Striker 5′ 9″ 11st 3lbs
b: Horsford, Norfolk, 29 Apr 1941
QPR: (£50,000) Aug 1968
Football League: 72-31. **FAC:** 4-1. **FLC:** 6-3.
Other: 0-0. **Total:** 82-35.
Honours: 7 Schoolboy caps. 14 youth caps. 4 England caps. Football League cap. League Cup winner's medal.

Barry was the sprint champion at school, so one can imagine the pace of the player during a match. It was the most striking thing about him, whether he was in a good position or not when he received the ball. His prodigious turn of speed was quite phenomenal and he had good ball control and was a dangerous shot to boot. Bridges would drift from wing to wing during the course of a match and leave his marker completely bewildered. His ceaseless intelligent wandering to create space for others always gave the attack elbow room. At the end of his career he took the job of player/manager at St Patrick's Athletic in 1976, then Sligo Rovers manager in 1978. The manager's job at Dearham Town followed, then Kings Lynn and finally Horsford. He went on to run a hotel in Eastbourne.

Debut: 24 Aug 1968 v Manchester City (H) 1-1 Div 1.

Barry Bridges

BRINDLEY Horace

(OL) Mid 5′ 9″ 11st 9lbs
b: Knutton, Staffordshire, 1 Jan 1885
d: Stoke, Staffs, 1971
QPR: Aug 1910
Southern League: 17.0. **FAC:** 1-0. **FLC:** 0.0.
Other: 0-0.**Total:** 18-0.
Honours: Central League championship winner's medal.

The *East Anglian Football Gazette* wrote of Horace that he was a hard running, speedy winger, who packed a fierce shot.

Debut: 3 Sep 1910 v Coventry City (H) 5-0 SL Div 1.

Kevin Brock

BROCK Kevin Stanley

Mid 5′ 9″ 10st 2lbs
b: Bicester, Oxfordshire, 9 Sep 1962
QPR: Aug 1987
Football League: 40-2. **FAC:** 4-1. **FLC:** 6-0.
Other: 2-0. **Total:** 52-3.
Honours: 8 England youth caps. 4 U21 caps. 1 B cap. 3rd Div championship medal. 2nd Div championship medal. League Cup winner's medal.

Kevin followed manager Jim Smith on his journey from Oxford to QPR and on to Newcastle. Brock was a good solid all-round performer who scored on his debut for the club. He became manager of Banbury United in 1999.

Debut: 15 Aug 1987 v West Ham United (A) 3-0 Div 1.

Marlon Broomes

BROOMES Marlon Charles
Def 6' 0" 12st 12lbs
b: Birmingham 28 Nov 1977
QPR: (Loan) Oct 2000
Football League: 5-0. **FAC**: 0-0. **FLC:** 0-0.
Other: 0-0. **Total:** 5-0.
Honours: England school & youth caps. 2 U21 caps.

Marlon quickly became popular with the Loftus Road faithful in his short stay with the club. He put in some fine performances and a deal was underway but a transfer fee couldn't be agreed.
Debut: 25 Oct 2000 v Sheffield Wed (H) 1-2 Div 1.

BROSTER John
Def 5' 8" 11st 2lbs
b: Earlstone, Lancashire
QPR: 1913
Southern League: 68-3. **FAC:** 4-0. **FLC:** 0-0.
Other: 0-0. **Total:** 72-3.

John came to the fore during the war and plied his services throughout the 1914/18 conflict. Described as a serviceable intervener by a local paper he consequently served clubs in the north until he retired from the game.
Debut: 12 Mar 1914 v Swindon Town (H) 4-2 SL Div 1.

BROWN Aaron Wesley
Def 5' 10" 11st 11lbs
b: Bristol, 14 Mar 1980
QPR: Jul 2004
Football League: 3-0. **FAC:** 0-0. **FLC:** 1-0.
Other: 0-0. **Total:** 4-0.
Debut: 23 Apr 2005 v Wigan Athletic (A) 0-0 Championship.

BROWN Albert Richard
(OL) Striker 5' 5" 10st 0lbs
b: Pegswood, Northumberland, 14 Feb 1911
QPR: 1932
Football League: 60-20. **FAC:** 9-1. **FLC:** 0-0.
Other: 1-2. **Total:** 70-23.
Honours: Northumberland County schoolboy cap.

Bert was plucked out of the mines to become a pro for Rochdale in 1929. He became a very fast winger who had won prizes as a sprinter.
Debut: 27 Aug 1932 v Brentford (H) 2-3 Div 3 (S).

BROWN Arthur F
(CF) Striker 5' 11" 12st 10lbs
b: Tamworth, Staffordshire, 1879
QPR: Oct 1902
Southern League: 30-11. **FAC:** 1-1. **FLC:** 0-0.
Other: 0-0. **Total:** 31-12.
Honours: FA Cup runner's-up medal.

Known as the Tamworth Flyer, Arthur was a popular member of the team among the spectators in the early days of the club. At Southampton his scoring rate was phenomenal, netting 29 goals in 34 matches. However, he sustained an injury and during the summer of 1902 he was quickly transferred to QPR. Although Arthur's scoring rate was not as good as at Southampton, he nevertheless brought together what had been a very disorganised side, and introduced method into it. Plagued by injuries Brown became disenchanted with the club and the club with him, and he moved on in 1904.
Debut: 25 Oct 1902 v Reading (H) 1-3 SL Div 1.

Aaron Brown

BROWN Charles
(OR) Mid 5' 8" 10st 0lbs
b: Stakeford, Northumberland, 14 Jan 1898
d: Southampton, 2 Jan 1979
QPR: Aug 1924
Football League: 67-3. **FAC:** 6-0. **FLC:** 0-0.
Other: 0-0. **Total:** 73-3.
Honours: 3rd Div South championship medal.

Described as quick and crafty with subtle ball control, he had a way of unsettling his marker. Unfortunately, Charlie was a member of the team during that period in the history of the club when they were at their lowest. After retirement in 1936 he was employed by Vosper Thornycroft until 1967.
Debut: 30 Aug 1924 v Newport County (A) 0-0 Div 3 (S).

BROWN Harold Archer
(CF) Striker
b: Shildon, County Durham, 1897
QPR: 1924
Football League: 13-3. **FAC:** 0-0. **FLC:** 0-0.
Other: 0-0. **Total:** 13-3.

Nothing at all is known about this player, except that he was only on the winning side twice. It is not known where he went to after he left QPR.
Debut: 30 Aug 1924 v Newport County (A) 0-0 Div 3 (S).

BROWN Harold Thomas
Goal 6' 1" 12st 4lbs
b: Kingsbury, London, 9 Apr 1924
d: Abingdon, Jun 1982
QPR: 1942
QPR: Aug 1951
Football League: 189-0. **FAC:** 11-0. **FLC:** 0-0.
Other: 0-0. **Total:** 200-0.
Honours: Played for an FA XI in 1943 and 1944.

A wartime signing who made approximately 80 appearances for QPR during the hostilities of the 1939/45 war. Harry was a very alert and agile goalkeeper with a daring disposition. As a 17 year old, Brown was introduced to first team football on 15 November 1941 v Millwall in a wartime London League match at Loftus Road in which QPR won 4-1. With Reg Allen in the army he became the Number 1 for QPR. He was the man that mysteriously filled-in for Arsenal's Griffiths in the second half of the Moscow Dynamo match at a foggy White Hart Lane in which Arsenal lost 4-3.
Debut: 18 Aug 1951 v West Ham United (H) 2-0 Div 2.

BROWN Wayne Lawrence
CD 6' 0" 12st 6lbs

b: Barking, Essex, 20 Aug 1977
QPR: (Loan) Mar 2001
Football League: 2-0. **FAC:** 0-0. **FLC:** 0-0.
Other: 0-0. **Total:** 2-0.

Wayne joined the club on a loan deal on the transfer deadline day. Unfortunately he suffered injuries in only his second match for QPR so returned to Portman Road.

Debut: 24 Mar 2001 v Burnley (A) 1-2 Div 1.

BROWN William Young

(IR) Mid 5' 10" 12st 5lbs
b: South Inch, Jun 1889
QPR: May 1910
Southern League: 6-2. **FAC:** 0-0. **FLC:** 0-0.
Other: 0-0. **Total:** 6-2.

Billy was a regular scorer at Kettering but at QPR it all seemed to dry up. On being transferred to Chelsea he was so bad in one match that the crowd booed him off the field of play. At Bristol things improved and during the Great War of 1914/18 he won a medal for bravery when he was wounded in action. Billy fought his way back to fitness and played for Northampton Town until he retired.

Debut: 4 Mar 1911 v Brighton & Hove Albion (H) 0-0 SL Div 1.

BROWNING Robert Ernest

(IL) Mid 5' 10" 11st 11lbs
b: Kettering, Northamptonshire, July 1889
QPR: May 1910
Southern League: 51-20. **FAC:** 3-0. **FLC:** 0-0.
Other: 0-0. **Total.** 54-20.

The *Sports Echo* described Bob as a clever forward with an accurate shot. This was so until he received an injury from which he never recovered, losing his place in the first team, he played just eight times in the championship side. Southampton hoped that a change would help him but within a few months he was back in London playing for Brentford.

Debut: 8 Oct 1910 v Luton Town (H) 3-3 SL Div 1.

BRUCE Paul Mark

Mid 5' 11" 12st 0lbs
b: Lambeth, London, 18 Feb 1978
QPR: 1996
Football League: 5-1. **FAC:** 1-0. **FLC:** 0-0.
Other: 0-0. **Total:** 6-1.
QPR: Aug 1999
Football League: 32-2. **FAC:** 4-0. **FLC:** 2-0.
Other: 1-0 **Total:** 39-2.

Paul usually plays on the left hand side of midfield and has added defence to his style of play. He was one of 15 players to be released in 2001. However, Paul survived another season at QPR, and in 2002 was transferred to Dagenham & Redbridge.

Debut: 17 Jan 1998 v Tranmere Rovers (H) 0-0 Div 1.

BUBB Alvin Ryan

Striker 5' 6" 10st 7lbs
b: Paddington, London, 11 Oct 1980
QPR: Nov 1998
Football League: 1-0. **FAC:** 0-0. **FLC:** 0-0.
Other: 0-0. **Total:** 1-0.

Alvin preferred to play on the right hand side of the pitch. He shares the distinction of having the shortest career with QPR, at nine minutes! Along with 15 other players, he was released at the end of the 2001/02 season.

Debut: 6 May 2001 v Wolverhampton Wanderers (A) 1-1 Div 1.

BULL Albert

(LH) Mid. 5' 6" 10st 10lbs
b: Derby, Derbyshire, 1875
QPR: 1903
Southern League: 13-1. **FAC:** 2-0. **FLC:** 0-0.
Other: 0-0. **Total:** 15-1.

Bert was small in stature but big in heart, with a strong tackle he was a useful addition to any team. Mainly a reserve at QPR, but at Reading he was well liked and received a benefit before he left the club.

Debut: 19 Sep 1903 v Tottenham Hotspur (H) 2-0 SL Div 1.

BURGESS Daniel

(IR) Mid 5' 8" 11st 4lbs
b: Goldenhill, Staffordshire, 23 Oct 1896
QPR: 1925
Football League: 46-9. **FAC:** 4-0. **FLC:** 0-0.
Other: 0-0. **Total:** 50-9.

On his demobilisation from the Royal Artillery at the end of the Great War, Dan came to the notice of Arsenal while he was playing for Port Vale. His scoring rate while with Arsenal was phenomenal, 50 goals in 100 matches for the reserves. However, Dan couldn't turn it on in the senior squad. At QPR the side ended the season bottom of the table in 1926, yet he still managed to score eight goals.

Debut: 29 Aug 1925 v Gillingham (A) 0-3 Div 3 (S).

BURGESS Oliver D

Central Mid 5' 10" 11st 7lbs
b: Bracknell, Berks, 12 Oct 1981
QPR: 2000
Football League: 14-1. **FAC:** 3-0. **FLC:** 0-0.
Other: 1-0. **Total:** 18-1.

A promising defender who suffered a ligament injury in only his fourth match for the club. This resulted in Oliver missing the rest of the season, and he only made rare appearances during his Loftus Road career.

Debut: 7 Apr 2001 v Blackburn Rovers (H) 1-3 Div 1.

John Burnham

BURKE Steven James

(OL) Wing 5' 10" 11st 7lbs
b: Nottingham, 29 Sep 1960
QPR: (£125,000) Sep 1979
Football League: 67-5. **FAC:** 3-0. **FLC:** 7-0.
Other: 0-0. **Total:** 77-5.
Honours: English Youth international.

Steve attracted a large fee back in 1978, bearing in mind that he hadn't played a senior match for Nottingham Forest. Full of promise when he arrived at Loftus Road, he ended his football days being loaned out to all and sundry until his withdrawal from football.

Debut: 8 Sep 1979 v Fulham (H) 3-0 Div 2.

BURNHAM John Robert

(LH) Def 5' 11" 12st 8lbs
b: Sunderland, 1896
QPR: Aug 1921
Football League: 31-0. **FAC:** 2-0. **FLC:** 0-0.
Other: 0-0. **Total:** 33-0.

John was drafted into the side after Mick O'Brien moved to centre-half. Burnham was a big, burley player who could fit into any defensive position.

Debut: 26 Nov 1921 v Brighton & Hove Albion (H) 3-0 Div 3 (S).

BURNS John Charles

(IR) Mid 5' 10" 11st 7lbs
b: Fulham, London, 27 Nov 1906
QPR:1928
Football League: 117-29. **FAC:** 8-5. **FLC:** 0-0.
Other: 0-0. **Total:** 125-34.
Honours: Middlesex County schoolboy cap. The Rest v England. 12 English Amateur caps. 3rd Div (South) championship medal. 2nd Div championship medal. FA Amateur Cup winner's medal. FA Amateur Cup runner's-up medal.

A very fine all-round sportsman, who excelled at boxing, tennis and football. John was a headmaster who represented his country at football on the amateur field.

Debut: 14 Jan 1928 v Southend United (H) 3-2 Div 3 (S).

John Burridge

BURRIDGE John

Goal 5′ 11″ 11st 0lbs
b: Workington, Cumbria, 3 Dec 1951
QPR: Dec 1980
Football League: 39-0. **FAC:** 2-0. **FLC:** 4-0.
Other: 0-0. **Total:** 45-0.
Honours: Anglo-Italian Cup winner's medal. 2nd Div championship medal. 2nd Div runner's-up medal. League Cup winner's medal. Scottish Cup winner's medal.

A great character who was a fitness fanatic, John had a very quick reaction to any situation that was in store for him, which obviously made him a good pro. Over 700 appearances were made by Burridge throughout his career, which saw him play for a multitude of clubs both sides of the border.
Debut: 26 Dec 1980 v West Ham United (H) 3-0 Div 2.

BUSBY Martyn G

Mid 6′ 1″ 12st 5lbs
b: Slough, Berks, 24 May 1953
QPR: Jul 1970
Football League: 80-6. **FAC:** 1-0. **FLC:** 10-0.
Other: 1-0. **Total:** 92-6.
QPR: Sep 1977
Football League: 66-11. **FAC:** 6-3. **FLC:** 0-0.

Martyn Busby

Other: 0-0. **Total:** 72-14.
Honours: England youth cap. 2nd Div runner's-up medal.

Martyn was an effective member of the senior squad throughout the 1970s, except for an 18-month period in the middle of it. He retired in 1980 after receiving a severe injury and later went into pub management. He then became the manager of Beaconsfield United.
Debut: 18 Apr 1970 v Leicester City (A) 1-2 Div 2.

BUSBY Walter

(OL) Wing 5′ 5″ 11st 3lbs
b: Wellingborough, Northamptonshire, 1882
QPR: 1902
Southern League: 14-3. **FAC:** 1-0. **FLC:** 0-0.
Other: 0-0. **Total:** 15-3.
Honours: Represented the United League and the North Hants League. North Hants Cup medal. United League championship medal. South Eastern League championship medal. London League championship medal.

Walter was noted in the *Athletic News*, as a very useful and sterling player, a fast and direct winger who was just as good as a centre-forward; however his small stature was against him in the early years of football.
Debut: 3 Sep 1902 v Wellingborough (H) 2-0 SL Div 1.

BUTLER Ernest

(OR) Wing 5′ 6″ 10st 6lbs
b: Stillington, County Durham, 17 Jun 1896
QPR: 1922
Football League: 34-0. **FAC:** 1-0. **FLC:** 0-0.
Other: 0-0. **Total:** 35-0.

The fact that Ernie could play on both wings lengthened his career at QPR. However, when the club ended the season bottom of the League in 1924 he was one of those that were released at the end of the season.
Debut: 7 Oct 1922 v Swindon Town (H) 0-2 Div 3 (S).

BUTTERWORTH Herbert

(WH) Mid 5′ 6″ 11st 4lbs
b: Unsworth, Manchester, 1 Jan 1885
QPR: Aug 1910
Southern League: 40-0. **FAC:** 1-0. **FLC:** 0-0.
Other: 0-0. **Total:** 41-0.
Honours: 2nd Div runner's-up medal. Southern League championship medal.

Bert was noted as a wholehearted player who could fill both wing-half positions when necessary and ended his days coaching in Holland after the 1914/18 war.
Debut: 26 Nov 1910 v Crystal Palace (A) 1-2 SL Div 1.

Akos Buzsaky

BUZSAKY Akos

Mid 5′ 11″ 11st 9lbs
b: Budapest, Hungary, 7 May 1982
QPR: 2007
Football League: 38-11. **FAC:** 1-0. **FLC:** 2-0.
Other: 0-0. **Total:** 41-11.
Honours: 13 Hungary caps.

The signing of Akos Buzsaky – initially on loan – from Plymouth Argyle brought a player with outstanding individual ability to Loftus Road. A Hungarian international since 2005, Buzsaky scored six goals in his first 13 appearances, and ended the campaign with 10 goals to his name. He failed to find the net as regularly during his first full season with Rangers but "Buzz" (as he has been nicknamed) looks set to be a popular fixture in hoops for the near future.
Debut: 3 Nov 2007 v Hull City (H) 2-0 Championship.

BYRNE John Frederick

For 6′ 0″ 12st 4lbs
b: Manchester, 1 Feb 1961
QPR: (£100,000) Oct 1984
Football League: 126-30. **FAC:** 9-2. **FLC:** 13-4.
Other: 1-0. **Total:** 149-36.
Honours: 23 caps for the Republic of Ireland. 4th Div championship medal. 2 League Cup runner's-up medals.

John was recommended to the York City boss by a taxi driver who spotted him playing in a Manchester park. A naturally gifted player who impressed with his fine ball control, he won the first of his 23 caps with QPR. John became the top scorer at Le Havre until he broke a leg. At Sunderland he became a huge success when he scored in every round of the 1992 FA Cup except the final.
Debut: 27 Oct 1984 v Norwich City (A) 0-2 Div 1.

Lee Camp

C

CABLE Thomas Harry
CAESAR Gus Cassius
CAIN Thomas
CAMERON James
CAMERON Kenneth
CAMERON Robert
CAMP Lee Michael John
CAMPBELL Charles J
CAMPBELL Dougauld
CANNON Frank
CAPE John Phillips
CAREY Peter Richard
CARLISLE Clarke
CARR William Patterson
CERNY Radek
CHALLIS Trevor Michael
CHANDLER Arthur Clarence Hillier
CHANNING Justin Andrew
CHAPMAN Reginald F J
CHARLES Jeremy Melfyn
CHARLES Lee
CHARLESWORTH George W
CHARLTON William
CHEETHAM Thomas Miles
CHESTER Albert
CHIVERS Gary Paul Steven
CHRISTIE David
CINI Joseph
CLARK Clive
CLARK William
CLARKE Charles
CLARKE Colin John
CLARKE Frank James
CLARKE George B
CLARKE Leon
CLAYTON Horace Leonard
CLAYTON Lewis
CLEMENT David
CLIPSHAM
CLUTTERBUCK Henry James
COCHRANE Justin Vincent
COCKBURN William Old
COCKELL David J
COGGINS William Herbert
COLE Jake
COLE John E
COLGAN Walter
COLLIER John C
COLLINS Harry
COLLINS James Henry
COLLINS John W
COLVIN Robert
CONEY Dean Henry
CONNER Robert
CONNOLLY Karl Andrew
CONNOLLY Matthew Thomas
COOK Lee
COOPER Gary J
CORBETT Walter Samuel
COWAN James
COWARD William C
COWIE Andrew
CRANIE Martin James
CRAWFORD Gavin
CRAWFORD John Forsyth
CRIBB Stanley Roy
CRICKSON Gerry E
CROMPTON Norman
CROSS John
CROSS William
CROUCH Peter James
CULKIN Nicolas James
CULLIP Danny
CUNNINGHAM Joel
CUNNINGHAM Thomas E
CURETON Jamie
CURRIE Anthony William
CURTIS John Charles Keyworth
CZERKAS, Adam

CABLE Thomas Harry

(CH) CD 5' 10" 11st 0lbs
b: Barking, Essex, 27 Nov 1900
d: Southend, 23 May 1986
QPR: Nov 1925
Football League: 18-2. **FAC:** 0-0. **FLC:** 0-0.
Other: 0-0. **Total:** 18-2.
Honours: 1 English Amateur cap. The Rest v England. 4 Amateur Cup winner's medals.

Tommy was a hard tackling, uncompromising player who kept his amateur status until he joined Spurs. At the end of his career he became the Kettering Town player/manager, later on the Leyton manager and in 1950 the Grays Athletic boss.
Debut: 25 Dec 1925 v Charlton Athletic (H) 2-2 Div 3 (S).

CAESAR Gus Cassius

(RB) Def 6' 0" 12st 7lbs
b: Tottenham, London, 5 Mar 1966
QPR: (Loan) Nov 1990
Football League: 5-0. **FAC:** 0-0. **FLC:** 0-0.
Other: 0-0. **Total:** 5-0.
Honours: 3 U21 caps for England. League Cup runner's-up medal. Makita Tournament winner's medal. Charity Shield runner's-up medal. Football Combination championship medal. Scottish FA Cup runner's-up medal.

Gus was (perhaps unfairly) never forgiven for making a mistake in the Arsenal v Luton Town League Cup final at Wembley which led to the Hatters' equaliser and left his club under a dark cloud. He was loaned to QPR with the option to buy but had the propensity for making errors under pressure so his transfer was never completed.
Debut: 1 Dec 1990 v Manchester City (A) 1-2 Div 1.

CAIN Thomas

(HB) Def 5' 8" 11st 0lbs
b: Ealing, Middlesex
QPR: 1919
Southern League: 6-0. **FAC:** 0-0. **FLC:** 0-0.
Other: 0-0. **Total:** 6-0.

A reserve who was used as a substitute for Archie Mitchell and sometimes stood in for Broster. He was also a reserve at Brentford where he stayed until 1926.
Debut: 22 Mar 1920 v Luton Town (A) 1-2 SL Div 1.

CAMERON James

(LH) Def 5' 6" 10st 7lbs
b: Inverness, Scotland
QPR: 1923
Football League: 24-0. **FAC:** 1-0. **FLC:** 0-0.
Other: 0-0. **Total:** 25-0.

Twelve players were recruited at the beginning of the season of which Jimmy was one; eight others appeared in the senior squad. By the end of the season, six players had gone to pastures new, including Jimmy, who had moved to the States.
Debut: 25 Aug 1923 v Brentford (H) 1-0 Div 3 (S).

CAMERON Kenneth

(IF) Mid 5' 9" 11st 2lbs
b: Hamilton, Scotland, 1905
QPR: Aug 1936
Football League: 8-1. **FAC:** 0-0. **FLC:** 0-0.
Other: 0-0. **Total:** 8-1.

Ken was the substitute for Alex James when he was at PNE. However, at QPR 10 years later, he seemed to be a player of fitful brilliance who never seemed to carry it off.
Debut: 29 Aug 1936 v Bristol City (A) 2-3 Div 3 (S).

CAMERON Robert

(IL) Mid 5' 8" 11st 0lbs
b: Greenock, Scotland, 23 Nov 1932
QPR: Jun 1950
Football League: 256-54. **FAC:** 19-3. **FLC:** 0-0.
Other: 4-0. **Total:** 279-57.
Honours: Scottish schoolboy caps. Represented the Army during his National Service. London FA v Basle. London Challenge Cup winner's medal.

Bobby played the game with a somewhat casual attitude that made him appear almost too nonchalant, however, this was when he was at his most dangerous. He would demand the ball at every opportunity and almost run the match on his own. Bobby first came to the fore in the 1952/53 season when he made 34 Football League appearances. He finally became a long-serving player at Loftus Road, with nearly 300 first team games to his credit in his nine-year period at the club. After a further three years, at Leeds United, he dropped down into non-League football, and emigrated in 1964 to Australia where he finished his playing career.
Debut: 13 Jan 1951 v Coventry City (H) 3-1 Div 2.

CAMP Lee Michael John

Goal 5' 11" 11st 11lbs
b: Derby, 22 Aug 1984
QPR: (Loan) 2004
Football League: 12-0. **FAC:** 0-0. **FLC:** 0-0.
Other: 0-0. **Total:** 12-0.
QPR: (Loan) 2007
Football League: 11-0. **FAC:** 0-0. **FLC:** 0-0.
Other: 0-0. **Total:** 11-0.
QPR: (£300,000) 2007
Football League: 50-0. **FAC:** 1-0. **FLC:** 2-0.
Other: 0-0. **Total:** 53-0.

Lee's first stint at Loftus Road ensured him hero status when his dynamic displays in the final dozen games of the 2003/04 season helped his temporary employers gain promotion to the Championship. A second loan spell followed in February 2007 before the move was made permanent five months later.

Clarke Carlisle

Lee was ever-present during the 2007/08 League campaign but found himself loaned out to fellow Championship side Nottingham Forest in late 2008.
Debut: 13 Mar 2004 v Hartlepool United (A) 4-1 Div 2.

CAMPBELL Charles J

(CF) Striker
b: Blackburn, Lancashire, 1903
QPR: 1925
Football League: 4-1. **FAC:** 0-0. **FLC:** 0-0.
Other: 0-0. **Total:** 4-1.
Charlie scored his only League goal for QPR against Reading and that is probably why they bought him, however he only ever played one match for the Berkshire side, at left-half.
Debut: 29 Aug 1925 v Gillingham (A) 0-3 Div 3 (S).

CAMPBELL Dougauld

(OR) Wing 5' 0" 11st 6lbs
b: Kirkintilloch, Scotland, 14 Dec 1922
QPR: Mar 1948
Football League: 0-0. **FAC:** 1-0. **FLC:** 0-0.
Other: 0-0. **Total:** 1-0.

Doug started as an amateur at QPR and turned pro in 1948. He made just a single appearance for the club in an FA Cup replay at Huddersfield, the side losing 5-0.
Debut: 8 Jan 1949 v Huddersfield Town (A) 0-5 FA Cup third round.

CANNON Frank

(IR) Mid 5' 9" 11st 11lbs
b: Ware, Hertfordshire, 8 Jan 1885
d: France, Feb 1916
QPR: 1907
Southern League: 27-0. **FAC:** 0-0. **FLC:** 0-0.
Other: 2-1. **Total:** 29-1.
Honours: Represented Hertfordshire in numerous county matches and won several gold medals with Hitchin Town. Southern League championship medal. Staffordshire Cup winner's medal. Birmingham Cup winner's medal.

Frank began his football career at the age of 15 with Hitchin Town in 1900, and worked as a solicitor's clerk. He continued in that capacity after turning professional with QPR in 1907. Frank was a dashing player and a fine dribbler, with a blistering shot. Sadly he was one of the many footballers to lose his life on the Western Front during the Great War of 1914/18.
Debut: 29 Feb 1908 v Millwall Athletic (A) 0-0 SL Div 1.

CAPE John Phillips

(OR) Wing 5' 8" 11st 0lbs
b: Carlisle, Cumberland, 16 Nov 1910
d: St Johns School, Carlisle, 6 Jun 1994
QPR: Jun 1937
Football League: 61-12. **FAC:** 3-1. **FLC:** 0-0.
Other: 1-0. **Total:** 65-13.
Honours: 2nd Div championship medal.

John captained his school at both football and rugby before joining his home town club Carlisle United at the age of 17. Moving to Newcastle United for what was a hefty fee in those days, (£1,750), Carlisle used the money to construct a roof on the Brunton Park stand. Johnny Cape was a very fast winger with the ball at his feet and very direct, he also had a powerful shot. Manchester United bought him after John had scored a hat-trick in a 7-4 victory at St James' Park. He moved to Loftus Road in 1937, and during the Second World War he worked as an electrician while continuing to play football. He finished his career back at Carlisle, and resided in his home town for the rest of his life, after retiring from the game in 1947.
Debut: 28 Aug 1937 v Brighton & Hove Albion (H) 2-1 Div 3 (S).

CAREY Peter Richard

Def
b: Barking, Essex, 14 Apr 1933
QPR: Jul 1960
Football League: 15-1. **FAC:** 1-0. **FLC:** 1-0.
Other: 0-0. **Total:** 17-1.
Honours: Represented Essex FA.

A play anywhere utility player that followed Alec Stock from Orient to QPR in the early 1960s. After his playing days were over, he managed a number of non-League sides, including Walthamstow Avenue in the early 1970s.
Debut: 20 Aug 1960 v Bournemouth & Boscombe Athletic 0-1 Div 3.

CARLISLE Clarke

Def 6' 1" 12st 7lbs
b: Preston, Lancashire, 14 Oct 1979
QPR: May 2000
Football League: 98-6. **FAC:** 6-0. **FLC:** 5-0.
Other: 0-0. **Total:** 109-6.
Honours: 3 England U21 caps.

A strong central defender with good pace, and able to read the game, Clarke became a favourite of the Loftus Road faithful after producing some fine performances. He suffered a ligament injury halfway through the 2000/01 season which prevented further appearances and a long layoff, but he came back to record a near ever-present record for 2002/03. In 2002, Clarke was adjudged to be "Britain's Brainiest Footballer" in a TV programme run by ITV. His contract was not renewed in 2004 and Clarke was allowed to join Leeds United on a free transfer.
Debut: 12 Aug 2000 v Birmingham City 0-0 Div 1.

CARR William Patterson

(RH) Def 5′ 9″ 12st 0lbs
b: Cambois, Cumberland, 6 Nov 1901
d: 1990
QPR: 1935
Football League: 28-0. **FAC:** 0-0. **FLC:** 0-0.
Other: 0-0. **Total:** 28-0.
Honours: 1st Div runner's-up medal.

A very experienced full-back who was past his prime (aged 35 years) when he joined the club, nevertheless Bill played with a high degree of defensive knowledge, on either flank.
Debut: 31 Aug 1935 v Millwall (H) 2-3 Div 3 (S).

CERNY Radek

Goal 6′ 1″ 13st 10lbs
b: Prague, Czechoslovakia, 18 Feb 1974
QPR: 2008
Football League: 42-0. **FAC:** 2-0. **FLC:** 3-0.
Other: 0-0. **Total:** 47-0.
Honours: 3 Czech caps.

A very experienced goalkeeper who has played at the highest level, Radek found his first team opportunities limited at Spurs so opted to sign for QPR in May 2008. The Czech international had been unable to oust Paul Robinson from between the posts but has staked his claim at Loftus Road with a string of solid performances. Radek's father was also a goalkeeper – who started out as a youth at Slavia before playing in the Czech Third and Fourth Divisions – as was his older brother Petr.
Debut: 9 Aug 2008 v Barnsley (H) 2-1 Championship.

CHALLIS Trevor Michael

Def 5′ 8″ 11st 0lbs
b: Paddington, London, 23 Oct 1975
QPR: Jul 1994
Football League: 13-0. **FAC:** 2-0. **FLC:** 0-0.
Other: 0-0. **Total:** 15-0.
Honours: England U21 captain.

Trevor was noted for his strength in the tackle and he earned praise for his measured distribution and willingness to get forward. But after four years, and only a handful of QPR appearances, he moved to the West Country.
Debut: 19 Nov 1995 v Coventry City (H) 1-1 PL.

CHANDLER Arthur Clarence Hillier

(CF) Striker 5′ 8″ 11st 7lbs
b: Paddington, London, 27 Nov 1895
d: 18 Jun 1984
QPR: Sep 1920
Football League: 78-16. **FAC:** 8-2. **FLC:** 0-0.
Other: 0-0. **Total:** 86-18.
Honours: 2 caps for the Rest v England. The North v South. FA tour of South Africa. 2nd Div championship medal. 1st Div runner's-up medal. Football League v Scottish League.

Arthur was a legend throughout the city of Leicester for his prodigious goalscoring, notching 273 goals in 419 matches. A hard and courageous player with a dynamic shot, Chandler was feared by all defenders alike, yet at the same time he was always admired for his fair play. But unfortunately he somewhat lost his goalscoring touch after his transfer to QPR.
Debut: 1 Jan 1921 v Crystal Palace (A) 0-0 Div 3.

CHANNING Justin Andrew

(RB) Def 5′ 11″ 11st 7lbs
b: Reading, Berks, 19 Nov 1968
QPR: Aug 1986
Football League: 55-5. **FAC:** 3-0. **FLC:** 4-0.
Other: 5-0. **Total:** 67-5.
Honours: England Youth & U20 caps.

Graduating through the apprentice ranks, he made his first team debut at the age of 17. Justin was a versatile player who could fill-in at full-back, midfield or wing-forward. He was a hard worker both on and off the ball and was blessed with a powerful shot. With his contract at an end at Leyton Orient, he was released in 1998 and he moved in to non-League football.
Debut: 1 Nov 1986 v Luton Town (A) 0-1 Div 1.

CHAPMAN Reginald F J

(CH) CD
b: Shepherds Bush, 7 Sep 1921
d: Seaford, Sussex, 4 Jul 1992
QPR: 1940
Football League: 93-3. **FAC:** 4-0. **FLC:** 0-0.
Other: 0-0. **Total:** 97-3.
Honours: 3rd Div (South) championship medal.

A loyal club player who filled the centre-half spot with natural ability, Reg joined the club in 1940 and played a few matches during the war, turning part-time pro in 1946 and so keeping his job as an accountant. The hostilities robbed him of his early Football League playing years, but he remained with QPR for six post-war seasons. Never an automatic choice in the first team he nonetheless notched

Radek Cerny

up nearly 100 appearances for the club before dropping down to non-League level.
Debut: 14 Sep 1946 v Reading (H) 2-0 Div 3 (S).

CHARLES Jeremy Melfyn

(CF) Striker 6' 1" 13st 11lbs
b: Swansea, Wales, 26 Sep 1959
QPR: (£100,000) Nov 1983
Football League: 12-5. **FAC:** 1-0. **FLC:** 0-0.
Other: 0-0. **Total:** 13-5.
Honours: 3 Welsh youth caps. 3 U21 caps. 19 full caps for Wales. League Cup winner's medal. 2 Welsh Cup winner's medals and championship medals with Swansea City.

A famous name in Welsh soccer, the son of Mel and the nephew of the legendary John Charles, Jeremy was a member of the Swansea City side that rose from the Fourth Division to the First in four years. He was forever plagued by injuries at QPR and lasted at Loftus Road for just 18 months.
Debut: 10 Dec 1983 v WBA (A) 2-1 Div 1.

CHARLES Lee

Striker 5' 11" 12st 4lbs
b: Hillingdon, Middlesex, 20 Jan 1971
QPR: (£67,500) Aug 1995
Football League: 16-1. **FAC:** 0-0. **FLC:** 1-0.
Other: 0-0. **Total:** 17-1.
Honours: England semi-professional international.

The scorer of 45 goals for Chertsey Town, the reason why such a high fee was paid for him, Lee was a confident, speedy forward, with a good first touch on the ball, but he was released in the summer of 1998 for personal reasons. He became a regular goalscorer once more in non-League football.
Debut: 25 Nov 1995 v West Ham United (A) 0-1 PL.

CHARLESWORTH George W

(OR) Wing 5' 10" 12st 10lbs
b: Bristol, 29 Nov 1901
d: 1965
QPR: May 1926
Football League: 23-3. **FAC:** 0-0. **FLC:** 0-0.
Other: 0-0. **Total:** 23-3.

George, an outside-right, joined Kettering Town from QPR when the legendary Eddie Hapgood was just starting out on his career. Eventually, after a famous FA Cup run, over half the Kettering team, including Charlesworth, was snapped up by Crystal Palace, he had scored 40 goals in 105 matches for Kettering Town.
Debut: 4 Sep 1926 v Coventry City (H) 1-1 Div 3 (S).

CHARLTON William

(CF) Striker
b: South Stoneham, 4 Jun 1912

Jeremy Charles

QPR: 1936
Football League: 20-10. **FAC:** 1-0. **FLC:** 0-0.
Other: 0-0. **Total:** 21-10.
Honours: 4 Amateur international caps. Played twice for the Oxford Blues. Played for the Corinthians and the Middlesex Wanderers.

Bill was a gifted amateur of the old school who turned out for the club while he was at college. After the Second World War he became the headmaster of a London school and lived in Barnes.
Debut: 19 Dec 1936 v Bristol Rovers (A) 1-1 Div 3 (S).

CHEETHAM Thomas Miles

(CF) Striker 5' 10" 11st 8lbs
b: Byker, Newcastle-upon-Tyne, 11 Oct 1910
d: 1993
QPR: Aug 1935
Football League: 115-81. **FAC:** 10-10. **FLC:** 0-0.
Other: 4-1. **Total:** 129-92.
Honours: Represented the Army in India. Played in an England trial match.

A scoring sensation who exploded on to the scene in 1935, Tommy broke the club scoring record in his first season. After being sold to Brentford in 1939 he was soon called-up into the army, being on the reserve list. Wounded at Dunkirk in 1940, Tommy was rescued and continued his football career during and after the Second World War. In September 1949, he became the coach to Willesden FC (a QPR nursery side).
Debut: 4 Sep 1935 v Brighton & Hove Albion (A) 1-1 Div 3 (S).

CHESTER Albert

(OR) Wing
b: Hexham, Northumberland
QPR: 1919
Southern League: 1-0. **FAC:** 0-0. **FLC:** 0-0.
Other: 0-0. **Total:** 1-0.

Turning out just once for QPR, Bert had played for most London clubs in the First World War period, during which time Croydon Common (for which he had played) closed down.
Debut: 15 Nov 1919 v Brighton & Hove Albion (A) 3-2 SL Div 1.

CHIVERS Gary Paul Steven

Def 5' 11" 13st 1lb
b: Stockwell, London, 15 May 1960
QPR: Feb 1984
Football League: 60-0. **FAC:** 2-0. **FLC:** 6-0.
Other: 1-0. **Total:** 69-0.
Honours: Represented the London schools. 3rd Div runner's-up medal.

Gary joined Chelsea at the age of 18, however, five years later when he went to Swansea, injuries prevented him from playing. Arriving at QPR, Chivers showed that he could play right across the back four when required to do so. At Brighton he finished up as captain before later taking over the player/manager job at Worthing. Later he became a chauffeur with the hope of eventually becoming a taxi driver.
Debut: 7 Nov 1984 v Partizan Belgrade (A) 0-4 UEFA Cup second round second leg.

CHRISTIE David

(IF) Mid 5' 7" 11st 4lbs
b: Forfar, Scotland, 1867
QPR: 1900
Southern League: 10-1. **FAC:** 1-0. **FLC:** 0-0.
Other: 0-0. **Total:** 11-1.

David was an experienced Scot who covered for Frank Downing whenever he was out of the side. Despite his age, he was still playing at 37!
Debut: 1 Sep 1900 v Bristol Rovers (A) 1-2 SL Div 1.

CINI Joseph

(OR) Wing
b: Malta, 29 Nov 1936
QPR: 1959
Football League: 7-1. **FAC:** 0-0. **FLC:** 0-0.
Other: 0-0. **Total:** 7-1.
Honours: Maltese international.

Joe was the first Maltese player to make the grade in the English League, remaining an amateur throughout the season he was at Loftus Road.
Debut: 22 Aug 1959 v Swindon Town (H) 2-0 Div 3.

CLARK Clive

(OL) Striker 5' 7" 10st 6lbs
b: Leeds, Yorkshire, 14 Dec 1940
QPR: Aug 1958
Football League: 58-7. **FAC:** 3-0. **FLC:** 2-0.
Other: 0-0. **Total:** 63-7.
QPR: (£70,000) Jun 1969
Football League: 8-1. **FAC:** 0-0. **FLC:** 2-0.
Other: 0-0. **Total:** 10-1.
Honours: English U23 cap. FA Cup winner's medal. League Cup runner's-up medal. 3rd Div championship medal.

Clive was a fast, direct and courageous winger, who was a supreme goalscorer. The son of a professional boxer he was the first player to score in every round of the League Cup. Ironically it was Clive who scored West Brom's two goals against QPR in the 1967 League Cup final. Clark retired from playing after sustaining a groin injury in the USA. Although he did some coaching, he worked in the building industry in Lytham for a time, before moving to Filey.
Debut: 6 Sep 1958 v Bournemouth & Boscombe Athletic (A) 0-2 Div 3.

CLARK William

(CF) Striker 6' 0" 13st 0lbs
b: Larkhall, Scotland, 25 Feb 1932
QPR: 1954
Football League: 95-32: **FAC:** 1-0. **FLC:** 0-0.
Other: 0-0. **Total:** 96-32.

Billy's deft touches and subtle flicks made him the ideal partner for Bobby Cameron. Unnoticed interchanging between the two of them confused the opposing defence and brought the side plenty of goals. Despite a near ever-present, his time at Loftus Road was limited to around two years for, never having really settled in London, he was homesick, and he moved back to Scotland, to Berwick Rangers.
Debut: 6 Feb 1954 v Shrewsbury Town (H) 0-0 Div 3 (S).

CLARKE Charles

(IR) Mid
b: Fleet, Lincolnshire
d: 1943
QPR: 1936
Football League: 6-0. **FAC:** 0-0. **FLC:** 0-0.
Other: 0-0. **Total:** 6-0.

Charlie was a reserve, filling in at inside-right, before an exchange deal, for R F Stevens, took him to Luton Town. Sadly Charlie Clarke was killed on active service during the Second World War.
Debut: 21 Jan 1937 v Brighton & Hove Albion (H) 2-3 Div 3 (S).

CLARKE Colin John

(CF) Striker 6' 0" 13st 6lbs
b: Newry, Northern Ireland, 30 Oct 1962
QPR: (£750,000) Mar 1989
Football League: 46-11. **FAC:** 7-2. **FLC:** 3-1.
Other: 0-0. **Total:** 56-14.
Honours: 39 caps for Northern Ireland.

Rejection by Bobby Robson, the manager of Ipswich Town, and a free transfer from Peterborough United did nothing to suggest the young Irishman had a rosy future, however, in 1986 he became a World Cup hero with many European clubs wishing to sign him. At Loftus Road, Colin became a very popular player and the supporters were very sad to see him transferred to Portsmouth.
Debut: 11 Mar 1989 v Newcastle United (A) 2-1 Div 1.

CLARKE Frank James

(CF) Striker 6' 0" 11st 0lbs
b: Willenhall, Staffordshire, 15 Jul 1942
QPR: (£35,000) Feb 1968
Football League: 67-17. **FAC:** 4-2. **FLC:** 5-5.
Other: 0-0. **Total:** 76-24.
Honours: 2nd Div runner's-up medal.

An Alec Stock acquisition during the 1968 promotion season, Frank was a hard working and unselfish player who liked to supply his team-mates with deft passes and little side flicks. He was the brother of Alan Clarke, the Leeds United and England striker of the 1970s. Frank continued playing football until 1977.
Debut: 24 Feb 1968 v Bolton Wanderers (A) 1-1 Div 2.

CLARKE George B

(OR) Wing 5' 9" 11st 9lbs
b: Bolsover, Derbyshire, 24 Jul 1900
d: 11 Feb 1977
QPR: Jul 1933
Football League: 15-6. **FAC:** 0-0. **FLC:** 0-0.
Other: 1-0. **Total:** 16-6.
Honours: Mansfield Hospital Cup winner's medal. 2 3rd Div (South) runner's-up medals.

George was a fast and tricky winger, who attracted a lot of interest in his younger days. Aston Villa snapped him up as a cover for Arthur Dorrell but he was called upon just once in six years. Clarke showed his value at Crystal Palace (who got him on a free transfer), by scoring 100 goals in 300 matches in eight seasons.
Debut: 26 Aug 1933 v Brighton & Hove Albion (H) 2-0 Div 3 (S).

CLARKE Leon

Striker 6' 2" 14st 2lbs
b: Wolverhampton, 10 Feb 1985
QPR: (Loan) 2006
Football League: 1-0. **FAC:** 0-0. **FLC:** 0-0.
Other: 0-0. **Total:** 1-0.
Debut: 4 Feb 2006 v Leeds United (A) 0-2 Championship.

CLAYTON Horace Leonard

(IR) Mid
b: Hackney, London, 4 Jul 1898
d: 1985
QPR: 1920
Football League: 6-1. **FAC:** 0-0. **FLC:** 0-0.
Other: 0-0. **Total:** 6-1.

Horace was a reserve and usually played in the side when Jimmy Birch was absent.
Debut: 17 Mar 1921 v Plymouth Argyle (H) 4-0 Div 3.

CLAYTON Lewis

(WH) Mid 5′ 8″ 11st 2lbs
b: Royston, Yorkshire, 7 Jun 1924
QPR: Aug 1950
Football League: 91-5. **FAC:** 2-0. **FLC:** 0-0.
Other: 0-0. **Total:** 93-5.

Lewis was noted as an organiser rather than a destroyer. A dour but dependable half-back who could play on both sides of the park. He had a career at Loftus Road that lasted five years, during which time he notched up a creditable 91 League games.

Debut: 9 Sep 1950 v Coventry City (A) 0-3 Div 2.

CLEMENT David

(RWB) 6′ 0″ 12st 5lbs
b: Battersea, London, 2 Feb 1948
d: Putney, London, 31 Mar 1982

Dave Clement

QPR: Jul 1965
Football League: 407-21. **FAC:** 29-2. **FLC:** 34-3.
Other: 6-1. **Total:** 476-27.
Honours: Youth caps. 5 England caps. 2 2nd Div runner's-up medals. 1st Div runner's-up medal.

Dave was a keen and dedicated player who possessed a great amount of stamina and was as strong as a bull in the tackle. His distribution was excellent when he moved upfield with the attack, yet he was a fairly rare goalscorer. He signed for QPR as a 17 year old, and made five appearances for England during his time at Loftus Road. During a career that lasted 14 years he notched up over 400 appearances, which included two ever-present seasons in the League, in 1970/71 and the following year. Yet after such valuable service, and aged 31, he was valued at £170,000 by Bolton Wanderers. His son, Neil, played for Chelsea but made his name at West Brom where he was noted for his long range free kicks. Tragically, Dave was found stabbed to death in his father-in-law's flat in Putney, at the age of 34.

Debut: 8 Apr 1967 v Scunthorpe United (H) 5-1 Div 3.

CLIPSHAM

(HB) Mid
QPR: 1902
Southern League: 2-0. **FAC:** 1-0. **FLC:** 0-0.
Other: 0-0. **Total:** 3-0.

Clipsham played for Wandsworth before he moved to QPR but that is all is known of this player whose further details are lost in the mists of time.

Debut: 1 Nov 1902 v Luton Town (H) 0-3 FA Cup.

CLUTTERBUCK Henry James

Goal 5′ 10″ 12st 4lbs
b: Wheatenhurst, Gloucestershire, 1873
d: 19 Dec 1948
QPR: May 1899
Southern League: 56-0. **FAC:** 14-0. **FLC:** 0-0.
Other: 0-0. **Total:** 70-0.

Clutterbuck started his career at the same time and in the same team as the Sharpe brothers, one of whom was destined to represent England at both cricket and football. Henry became the Rangers' first professional goalkeeper and although he was rather short for a man who stood between the sticks, he made up for this with his physique and a sound cool agility. He did not miss a competitive match in the two years he was with the club. He retired in 1905 at the age of 32.

Debut: 9 Sep 1899 v Tottenham Hotspur (A) 0-1 SL Div 1.

COCHRANE Justin Vincent

Mid 6′ 0″ 11st 8lbs
b: Hackney, London, 26 Jan 1982
QPR: Jul 1999
Football League: 1-0. **FAC:** 0-0. **FLC:** 0-0.
Other: 0-0. **Total:** 1-0.

A member of the successful QPR U19 team, Justin was a promising player who had the misfortune to receive a harsh red card just 17 minutes after coming on in his first senior match. Released in the summer of 2002 he was signed by Hayes. (He moved to Crewe Alexandra for a five figure fee in July 2003.)

Debut: 28 Apr 2001 v Stockport County (H) 0-3 Div 1.

COCKBURN William Old

(CH) CD 6′ 0″ 12st 0lbs
b: Willington Quay, Northumberland, 1899
d: Rosehill, 27 Dec 1958
QPR: Jul 1928
Football League: 57-0. **FAC:** 5-0. **FLC:** 0-0.
Other: 0-0. **Total:** 62-0.

Bill was a gritty player who was coming to the end of his career when he moved to Rangers. At Liverpool he took over from Wadsworth after he was transferred to Bristol City. Cockburn was a player with an excellent disposition and he finished his career at Swindon Town.

Debut: 25 Aug 1928 v Torquay United (A) 4-3 Div 3.

COCKELL David J

(RH) Def
b: Ashford, Middlesex, 1 Feb 1939
QPR: 1960
Football League: 9-0. **FAC:** 1-0. **FLC:** 0-0.
Other: 0-0. **Total:** 10-0.

Dave was the substitute for either Angell or Keen, therefore he rarely got a look in. He opted to spend the rest of his footballing career in the non-League football scene.

Debut: 19 Nov 1960 v Shrewsbury Town (H) 1-1 Div 3.

COGGINS William Herbert

Goal 5′ 11″ 11st 8lbs
b: Bristol, 16 Sep 1901
d: Somerset, 7 Jul 1958
QPR: 1935
Football League: 6-0. **FAC:** 0-0. **FLC:** 0-0.
Other: 0-0. **Total:** 6-0.
Honours: 3rd Div (South) championship medal. 2nd Div championship medal.

Billy played six matches for QPR when the regular goalkeeper, Bill Mason, was injured. Coggins had played nearly 200 matches for Bristol City and over 50 for Everton. He retired to his native Bristol and died at West Town, Somerset aged 57.

Debut: 28 Dec 1935 v Millwall (A) 0-2 Div 3 (S).

Jake Cole

COLE Jake

Goal 6′ 3″ 13st 0lbs
b: Hammersmith, London, 11 Sep 1985
QPR: 2003
Football League: 6-0. **FAC:** 0-0. **FLC:** 2-0.
Other: 0-0. **Total:** 8-0.
Debut: 19 Dec 2005 v Coventry City (H) 0-1 Championship.

COLE John E

(RB) Def
b: Wales
QPR: 1900
Southern League: 1-0. **FAC:** 0-0. **FLC:** 0-0.
Other: 0-0. **Total:** 1-0.

John came from the same stable as Henry Clutterbuck, the goalkeeper. However, he stayed just a short time at the club, playing in the first match of the season.

Debut: 1 Sep 1900 v Bristol Rovers (A) 1-2 SL Div 1.

COLGAN Walter

(RH) Def
b: Castleford, Yorkshire, 3 Apr 1937
QPR: 1954
Football League: 3-0. **FAC:** 0-0. **FLC:** 0-0.
Other: 0-0. **Total:** 3-0.

A regular defender in the London Combination reserve side, Walter was a replacement for Pat Woods, so he was only rarely called upon to play in the side as the regular player was very seldom injured.

Debut: 28 Dec 1957 v Southend United (H) 1-1 Div 3 (S).

COLLIER John C

(RH) Def 5′ 9″ 11st 10lbs
b: Dysart, Scotland, 1 Feb 1897
d: 28 Dec 1940
QPR: Jul 1926
Football League: 36-1. **FAC:** 1-0. **FLC:** 0-0.
Other: 0-0. **Total:** 37-1.

This canny Scot played with vigour and dash, being a hard tackler who always commanded respect from the opposition. In 1928 he was appointed player/manager of the York City club, who were at the time playing in the Midland League. However, in only his second match, John broke his ankle and so ended the playing part of his contract. Nevertheless he continued to manage the side until they were elected to the Football League. He left at the end of the season to become a publican, only to return to York in 1933 to take up the manager's job again.

In March 1937 he announced that he was giving up the job to go into business with one of his brothers. Ill health overcame him suddenly and he died at the early age of 43.

Debut: 28 Aug 1926 v Crystal Palace (A) 1-2 Div 3.

COLLINS Harry

Goal 6′ 0″ 11st 12lbs
b: Wynlaton, County Down, Ireland, 1876
QPR: 1901
Southern League: 115-0. **FAC:** 6-0. **FLC:** 0-0.
Other: 0-0. **Total:** 121-0.

The *Athletic News* wrote of Harry "He is a quick and clever custodian". On his transfer to QPR Harry was elected club captain of the Latimer Road side. His stay lasted four seasons

during which time he was more or less a regular in the first team.
Debut: 7 Sep 1901 v Watford (H) 0-1 SL Div 1.

COLLINS James Henry

(IR) Mid 5' 8" 12st 3lbs
b: Bermondsey, London, 30 Jan 1911
d: 10 Jul 1983
QPR: 1931
Football League: 22-4. **FAC:** 0-0. **FLC:** 0-0.
Other: 0-0. **Total:** 22-4.
Honours: Welsh Cup runner's-up medal.

A muscular player, Jimmy was strong and adaptable who played for several clubs during the 1930s. He played for Swindon Town and Aberman during the Second World War.
Debut: 7 Nov 1931 v Luton Town (H) 3-1 Div 3 (S).

COLLINS John W

(IL) Mid 5' 9" 10st 10lbs
b: Chiswick, 10 Aug 1942
QPR: Aug 1959
Football League: 218-46. **FAC:** 15-6. **FLC:** 6-4.
Other: 0-0. **Total:** 239-56.

John displayed a terrific amount of stamina as well as having a flair for scoring important goals. At one time he completed an unusual hat-trick against Hull City, all the goals being scored with his head. A local boy he was signed by Rangers as a 17 year old in 1959, and his seven year career at Loftus Road encompassed over 200 games and 56 first team goals. In October 1966 he moved north to Boundary Park where his goalscoring continued and included netting six in a match for Oldham Athletic, just two days after joining them from QPR in a friendly game versus the Swiss club FC Thun. He also had an excellent time at Reading where he managed 29 goals in 96 matches and finished as the Reading top scorer in 1969. John returned to Loftus Road in the early 1970s to become a member of the coaching staff.
Debut: 30 Apr 1960 v Barnsley (H) 1-0 Div 3.

COLVIN Robert

(OR) Wing 5' 5" 10st 0lbs
b: Dumfries, Scotland, 5 Dec 1876
QPR: 1902
Southern League: 11-0. **FAC:** 0-0. **FLC:** 0-0.
Other: 0-0. **Total:** 11-0.

A tiny and experienced winger who proved he was skilful during the club's early days. Apparently Bob suffered from ill health while he was at QPR so he was allowed to recuperate in Scotland and the club sacked him the following season, however, this didn't deter him from carrying on playing elsewhere.
Debut: 3 Sep 1902 v Wellingborough (H) 2-0 SL Div 1.

CONEY Dean Henry

(CF) Striker 6' 0" 12st 6lbs
b: Dagenham, Essex, 18 Sep 1963
QPR: (£200,000) Jun 1987
Football League: 48-7. **FAC:** 5-0. **FLC:** 6-0.
Other: 3-2. **Total:** 62-9.
Honours: 4 England caps at U21 level.

Dean made his League debut at the age of 17 while he was at Fulham and manager Trevor Francis secured his transfer. However, Coney remained disappointed with the style of play at QPR. Being basically a front man he was told to play midfield by Trevor Francis. So when the offer came to sign for Norwich City he jumped at the chance "to play for a footballing side".
Debut: 15 Aug 1987 v West Ham United (A) 3-0 Div 1.

CONNER Robert

(OL) Wing 5' 7" 11st 7lbs
b: Newcastle, 1913
QPR: 1935
Football League: 5-0. **FAC:** 0-0. **FLC:** 0-0.
Other: 1-0. **Total:** 6-0.

Bob played just a handful of matches during the 1935/36 season, and he was one of the players released at the end of that campaign.
Debut: 26 Nov 1935 v Brighton & Hove Albion (A) 1-5 Div 3 (S).

Dean Coney

CONNOLLY Karl Andrew

Mid 5' 10" 11st 2lbs
b: Prescot, Lancashire, 9 Feb 1970
QPR: May 2000
Football League: 73-12. **FAC:** 6-0. **FLC:** 1-0.
Other: 2-0. **Total:** 82-12.
Honours: Welsh Cup winner's medal.

Karl was on Tranmere Rovers' books as a schoolboy but was not offered an apprenticeship. He continued to play for the "Prentonians" on a casual basis while still working in a chip shop! He then drifted into local football playing for the "Rockies", in the St Helens Combination, and also Napoli in the Warrington Sunday League. He eventually signed for Wrexham in May 1991 and QPR a year later. Karl is an attacking midfield player creating numerous opportunities for the front men, through his ability to hold on to the ball and beat defenders. He was, however, never a true regular in the first team after his initial season. He moved to Swansea City in August 2003.
Debut: 12 Aug 2000 v Birmingham City (H) 0-0 Div 1.

Karl Connolly

CONNOLLY Matthew Thomas

Def 6' 2" 13st 3lbs
b: Barnet, 24 Sep 1987
QPR: 2008
Football League: 55-0. **FAC:** 1-0. **FLC:** 4-0.
Other: 0-0. **Total:** 60-0.
Honours: England Youth.

Matthew – a graduate of Arsenal's youth academy who played in a couple of Carling Cup matches for the Gunners during the 2006/07 campaign – signed a three-and-a-half year deal with Rangers in January 2008 and earned rave reviews for his performances to the end of the season. Indeed, his form earned him a call up to the England Under-21 squad and he has since established himself in the first team at Loftus Road.
Debut: 12 Jan 2008 v Sheffield United (A) 1-2 Championship.

Lee Cook

COOK Lee

Mid 5' 9" 10st 12lbs
b: Hammersmith, London, 3 Aug 1982
QPR: (Loan) Dec 2002
Football League: 13-1. **FAC:** 0-0. **FLC:** 0-0.
Other: 0-0. **Total:** 13-1.
QPR: (£150,000) Jul 2004
Football League: 119-9. **FAC:** 4-0. **FLC:** 4-1.
Other: 0-0. **Total:** 127-10.
QPR: (£850,000) Aug 2008
Football League: 34-1. **FAC:** 1-0. **FLC:** 3-0.
Other: 0-0. **Total:** 38-1.

Initially signed on loan in December 2002 as a possible solution to one of Ian Holloway's problems – a lack of natural wide players – Lee settled in well at Loftus Road but it would be another 18 months before Rangers finally got their man. A big-money move to Fulham, however, dissected the left-winger's time with QPR but he failed to secure a first team place and the fans' favourite returned (originally on loan) during the 2008/09 season.
Debut: Dec 2002 v Brentford (H) 1-1 League 1.

COOPER Gary J

Mid 5' 8" 11st 3lbs
b: Hammersmith, London, 20 Nov 1965
QPR: Jun 1983
Football League: 1-0. **FAC:** 0-0. **FLC:** 2-0.
Other: 1-0. **Total:** 4-0.
Honours: England youth caps. 3 England U17 caps. AutoWindscreen Shield winner's medal. 2nd Div championship medal.

After his QPR days he was converted into a very consistent defender playing at left-back.
Debut: 2 Mar 1985 v Norwich City (H) 2-2 Div 1.

Matthew Connolly

CORBETT Walter Samuel

(RB) Def
b: Wellington, Shropshire, 26 Nov 1880
d: Birmingham, 1955
QPR: Sep 1907
Southern League: 1-0. **FAC:** 0-0. **FLC:** 0-0.
Other: 0-0. **Total:** 1-0.
Honours: 18 English Amateur caps. 3 English Professional caps. Great Britain Olympic Gold Medal for soccer. Captain of the Birmingham & District Juniors v Scotland on 3 occasions. Represented an Amateur/Professional XI on a continental tour.

Walter was the manager of an export house in the Midlands, this took him all over the world, and he spoke several languages. He suffered from polio as a lad and always carried a handkerchief in his withered left hand. The *Sports Argus* wrote about this great full-back in 1906, saying that, "He was one of the most gentlemanly players one could hope to meet". Walter was a wonderful footballer who it was rumoured, never did a dirty trick or ever conceded a penalty on the field of play. He had a fine turn of speed and showed infinite resource.
Debut: 7 Sep 1907 v New Brompton (H) 2-2 SL Div 1.

COWAN James

(CH) CD 5′ 6″ 12st 3lbs
b: Jamestown, Scotland, 17 Oct 1868
d: Scotland, 12 Dec 1918
QPR: Dec 1906
Southern League: 1-1. **FAC:** 0-0. **FLC:** 0-0.
Other: 0-0. **Total:** 1-1.
Honours: 3 Scottish caps. 2 FA Cup winner's medals. 5 League championship medals. A runner's-up medal.

Jimmy was an untiring and energetic tackler and the mainstay of the famous Villa defence throughout the 1890s. As a centre-half he was of immense value to the club, being undismayed and uncomplaining after the hardest of matches. Known as the prince of half-backs, Cowan was a shrewd tactician, surprisingly quick and certainly one of the all time greats who eventually became the first manager of QPR. Under his management the club won two Southern League titles. In 1896, Jimmy entered the famous Powderhall Sprint Handicap, doing so under an assumed name, winning the race and collecting £80 prize money. However, he was later fined four weeks pay by a furious Villa committee.
Debut: 16 Dec 1905 v Northampton Town (H) 6-1 SL Div 1.

James Cowan

Peter Crouch

COWARD William C

(OL) Wing 5′ 6″ 10st 4lbs
b: Windsor, Berkshire
QPR: 1927
Football League: 126-22. **FAC:** 12-4. **FLC:** 0-0.
Other: 0-0. **Total:** 138-26.

Billy was a neat and tricky player who joined the club mid-season, and scored in his first two matches for the Rangers. He turned professional on his transfer from Wycombe Wanderers, and was a regular first team player during his four-plus years. For a winger he scored a reasonable number of goals. In 1932, Billy was transferred to Walsall along with the goalkeeper Cunningham.

Debut: 31 Mar 1928 v Torquay United (H) 2-3 Div 3 (S).

COWIE Andrew

(OL) Wing 5′ 6″ 10st 11lbs
b: Lockee, Scotland, 1879
QPR: 1899
Southern League: 11-2. **FAC:** 5-0. **FLC:** 0-0.
Other: 0-0. **Total:** 16-2.

Andy was a member of the QPR side that defeated Brighton United 6-0 in their very first Southern League fixture. He scored a hat-trick in the match. However, it was deleted from the record books, on account of the later demise of their opponents.

Debut: 9 Sep 1989 v Tottenham Hotspur (A) 0-1 SL Div 1.

CRANIE Martin James

Def 6' 0" 12st 4lbs
b: Yeovil, 23 Sep 1986
QPR: (Loan) 2007
Football League: 6-0. **FAC:** 0-0. **FLC:** 0-0.
Other: 0-0. **Total:** 6-0.
Honours: England U20 and U21 caps.
Debut: 8 Oct 2007 v Norwich City (H) 1-0 Championship.

CRAWFORD Gavin

(RH) Def 5' 9" 12st 0lbs
b: Galston, Scotland, 1867
d: March 1955
QPR: 1899
Southern League: 24-1. **FAC:** 9-0. **FLC:** 0-0.
Other: 0-0. **Total:** 33-1.

Gavin was the ex-captain of Arsenal and he immediately became the skipper of QPR. Retiring in 1899 he later became the groundsman at the Valley, Charlton, keeping his job until 1947.

Debut: 9 Sep 1899 v Tottenham Hotspur (A) 0-1 SL Div 1.

CRAWFORD John Forsyth

(Wing) Striker 5' 2" 8st 6lbs
b: Jarrow, County Durham, 26 Sep 1896
d: 27 Sep 1975
QPR: May 1934
Football League: 53-15. **FAC:** 2-1. **FLC:** 0-0.
Other: 4-2. **Total:** 59-18.
Honours: 1 England cap.

Known as "Jackie", he was a tricky little winger with intricate footwork, who could cross the ball with either foot and would shoot at goal on numerous occasions during a match. Jackie came to Loftus Road in the role of player/coach and stayed until the outbreak of the Second World War. Upon leaving the club, Crawford worked in a munitions factory in Essex and remained there until after the hostilities had ceased, becoming the part-time coach of Maldon Town.

Debut: 25 Aug 1934 v Swindon Town (A) 1-3 Div 3 (S).

CRIBB Stanley Roy

(OL) Wing 5' 8" 11st 0lbs
b: Gosport, Hampshire, 11 May 1905
d: Gosport, 13 Jan 1989
QPR: Jun 1931
Football League: 28-12. FAC: 4-6. **FLC:** 0-0.
Other: 0-0. **Total:** 32-18.
Honours: County representative before his 17th birthday.

Stan was a very fast moving winger who became a solid penalty taker. After six years at Southampton he was transferred to West Ham United but he never made an appearance for them and after a year he moved to QPR. When his playing days were over he continued to be involved in football by helping with the formation of Gosport Borough FC and became their manager from 1944 until 1967. He then scouted for the Saints until he died in 1989.

Debut: 29 Aug 1931 v Brentford (A) 0-1 Div 3 (S).

CRICKSON Gerry E

(RH) Def
b: Dover, Kent, 21 Sep 1934
QPR: Sep 1951
Football League: 5-0. **FAC:** 1-0. **FLC:** 0-0.
Other: 0-0. **Total:** 6-0.
Honours: English School and Youth international.

Gerry played just six matches in four years for the QPR first 11, before opting to return to his home side Dover.

Debut: 6 Apr 1953 v Millwall (H) 1-3 Div 3 (S).

CROMPTON Norman

(CH) CD 5' 10" 11st 10lbs
b: Farnworth, Lancashire, 1905
QPR: May 1928
Football League: 1-0. **FAC:** 0-0. **FLC:** 0-0.
Other: 0-0. **Total:** 1-0.

In 1932 at Denbeigh he scored 18 goals including 13 penalties from centre-half while he was captain of the side. However, it was at Darwin later in his career that Norman was to become famous, as captain of the side that lost to Arsenal, 11-1 in the FA Cup at Highbury in 1932.

Debut: 3 May 1928 v Norwich City (H) 0-0 Div 3 (S).

CROSS John

(LH) Def 5' 11" 11st 7lbs
b: Scotland, 1879
QPR: 1903
Southern League: 23-0. **FAC:** 1-0. **FLC:** 0-0.
Other: 0-0. **Total:** 24-0.

The 1903 edition of *Men Famous in Football* wrote of John that "He is brilliant in defence and attack, he has good resources and a fine command of the ball, he places it well to his forward".

Debut: 5 Sep 1903 v Brentford (H) 1-0 SL Div 1.

CROSS William

(OR) Wing 5' 7" 10st 7lbs
b: Scotland, 1883
QPR: 1903
Southern League: 32-4. **FAC:** 1-0. **FLC:** 0-0.
Other: 0-0. **Total:** 33-4.

Billy was the younger brother of John. Both playing for QPR in the 1904/05 season, John returned to Scotland while Billy moved on to play for Brentford.

Debut: 10 Sep 1904 v West Ham United (A) 3-1 SL Div 1.

CROUCH Peter James

(CF) Striker 6' 7" 11st 12lbs
b: Macclesfield, Cheshire, 30 Jan 1981
QPR: (£60,000) Jul 2000
Football League: 42-10. **FAC:** 3-2. **FLC:** 2-0.
Other: 0-0. **Total:** 47-12.
Honours: 33 England caps.

Gerry Francis had coached this player as a junior at Spurs, where he stayed for two years. With QPR, Peter quickly became a first team regular and finished the 2000/01 season as the top scorer. But he soon became a big money mover, when the giant centre-forward was transferred to Portsmouth, where he showed tremendous ball control and the ability to run at and beat defenders. He was eventually sold on to Aston Villa in March, thus becoming the tallest striker in the Premiership at that time. He scored on his debut for Villa against Newcastle, but was voted as Pompey's "Player of the season", despite his earlier departure that season. Crouch signed for Spurs in July 2009 .

Debut: 12 Aug 2000 v Birmingham City (H) 0-0 Div 1.

CULKIN Nicolas James

Goal 6' 2" 13st 7lbs
b: York, 6 Jul 1978
QPR: 2002
Football League: 22-0. **FAC:** 0-0. **FLC:** 0-0.
Other: 0-0. **Total:** 22-0.

Nick was a solid young goalkeeper who possessed a good pair of hands and bore a passing resemblance to Peter Schmeichel. He never made the grade at Manchester United, and after a series of loan deals Nick eventually signed for QPR in the summer of 2002. His career was prematurely ended, however, when he had to retire from football in 2005 due to a longstanding knee injury.

Debut: 10 Aug 2002 v Chesterfield (H) W 3-1 Div 2.

CULLIP Danny

Def 6' 1" 12st 7lbs
b: Bracknell, Berks, 17 Sep 1976
QPR: Jan 2007
Football League: 19-0. **FAC:** 0-0. **FLC:** 1-0.
Other: 0-0. **Total:** 20-0.

QPR completed the signing of Danny on a free transfer on the final day of the January 2007 transfer window and the experienced centre-half played a pivotal role in Rangers' survival that season, leading by example at the heart of the R's defence. His performances were duly noted by manager John Gregory, who labelled his arrival as "the turning point" in the club's quest to avoid relegation. Following the appointment of Luigi De Canio as manager, however, Danny was

deemed surplus to requirements. His contract was terminated and he went on to play for Gillingham and Lewes.
Debut: 3 Feb 2007 v Burnley (H) 3-1 Championship.

Danny Cullip

CUNNINGHAM Joel

Goal 6′ 0″ 11st 7lbs
b: Lockie, Dundee, Scotland, 1905
QPR: Jun 1926
Football League: 168-0. **FAC:** 6-0. **FLC:** 0-0.
Other: 0-0. **Total:** 174-0.

Not finding a permanent place in a Scottish club side, Joel decided to try south of the border and he gradually built up a reputation as being one of the best goalkeepers in the Third Division. Cunningham stayed six years with the club becoming a favourite of the spectators with his antics, of swinging on the cross bar like a trapeze artist and making sliding tackles on the opposing forwards. Joel kept goal for Walsall in 1933 when they knocked Arsenal out of the FA Cup and at Dartford he enjoyed the limelight again in 1936 when they sensationally beat Cardiff City at Ninian Park.
Debut: 30 Oct 1926 v Northampton Town (H) 4-2 Div 3 (S).

Tommy Cunningham

Jamie Cureton

CUNNINGHAM Thomas E

(CH) CD 6′ 1″ 11st 3lbs
b: Bethnal Green, London, 7 Dec 1955
QPR: May 1975
Football League: 30-2. **FAC:** 3-0. **FLC:** 2-0.
Other: 0-0. **Total:** 35-0.

Tommy joined QPR on a free transfer from Chelsea and was a big strong centre-half who was somewhat over enthusiastic and accrued a not too impressive disciplinary record, he always gave 100% effort in a match. Becoming captain at Orient he was later chief coach, and then assistant

Tony Currie

manager at Barnet. In July 2001 he was appointed manager of Wingate & Finchley, the Ryman League club.
Debut: 2 Oct 1976 v Arsenal (A) 2-3 Div 1.

CURETON Jamie

Striker 5' 8" 10st 7lbs
b: Bristol, 28 Aug 1975
QPR: 2004
Football League: 43-6. **FAC:** 1-0. **FLC:** 2-1.
Other: 0-0. **Total:** 46-7.

Despite a lucrative deal with Busan I'cons, Jamie never settled in Korea, and sought the council of his former manager Ian Holloway who was determined to bring the striker to Rangers. The cause was aided by the supporters group OUR QPR and the funds needed to make the transfer possible were gratefully provided. Unfortunately, Jamie never found his true scoring form at Loftus Road and found the net just seven times in 46 games for the club before moving on to Swindon Town.
Debut: 7 Feb 2004 v Notts County (H) 3-2 Championship.

CURRIE Anthony William

Mid 5' 11" 12st 9lbs
b: Edgware, Middlesex, 1 Jan 1950
QPR: (£400,000) Aug 1979
Football League: 81-5. **FAC:** 9-0. **FLC:** 8-1.
Other: 0-0. **Total:** 98-6.
Honours: 3 England youth caps. 13 U23 caps. 17 full England caps. A Football League cap. 2nd Div championship medal. 2nd Div runner's-up medal. FA Cup runner's-up medal.

Tony was one of the most gifted players during the 1970s, he was an artist on the ball being blessed with great vision, his close ball control was equal to anyone past or present. He could strike the ball with accuracy but preferred to spray passes to colleagues with the most delectable ease and timing.

Strong in possession and difficult to dispossess, he was flamboyant and arrogant. Tony was the team captain in the 1982 FA Cup final replay, and now works as a community officer for Sheffield United.
Debut: 8 Sep 1979 v Fulham (H) 3-0 Div 2.

CURTIS John Charles Keyworth

Def 5' 10" 11st 7lbs
b: Nuneaton, 3 Sep 1978
QPR: 2007
Football League: 4-0. **FAC:** 0-0. **FLC:** 1-0.
Other: 0-0. **Total:** 5-0.
Honours: England U20 and B caps.
Debut: 11 Aug 2007 v Bristol City (A) 2-2 Championship.

CZERKAS Adam

Striker 6' 1" 11st 11lbs
b: Sokołów Podlaski, Poland, 13 Jul 1984
QPR: (Loan) 2006
Football League: 3-0. **FAC:** 0-0. **FLC:** 1-0.
Other: 0-0. **Total:** 4-0.
Debut: 5 Aug 2006 v Burnley (A) 0-2 Championship.

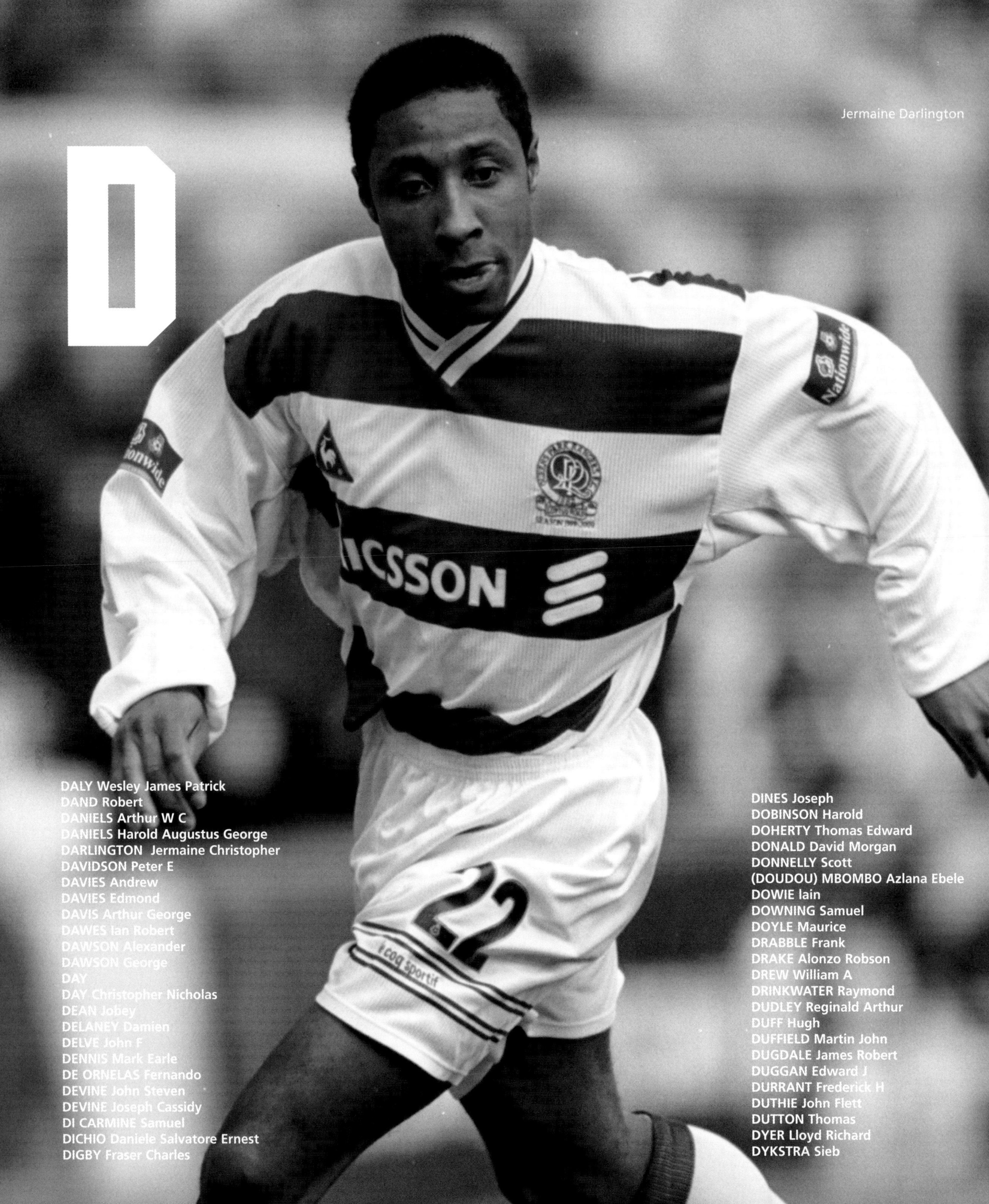

Jermaine Darlington

D

DALY Wesley James Patrick
DAND Robert
DANIELS Arthur W C
DANIELS Harold Augustus George
DARLINGTON Jermaine Christopher
DAVIDSON Peter E
DAVIES Andrew
DAVIES Edmond
DAVIS Arthur George
DAWES Ian Robert
DAWSON Alexander
DAWSON George
DAY
DAY Christopher Nicholas
DEAN Jobey
DELANEY Damien
DELVE John F
DENNIS Mark Earle
DE ORNELAS Fernando
DEVINE John Steven
DEVINE Joseph Cassidy
DI CARMINE Samuel
DICHIO Daniele Salvatore Ernest
DIGBY Fraser Charles
DINES Joseph
DOBINSON Harold
DOHERTY Thomas Edward
DONALD David Morgan
DONNELLY Scott
(DOUDOU) MBOMBO Azlana Ebele
DOWIE Iain
DOWNING Samuel
DOYLE Maurice
DRABBLE Frank
DRAKE Alonzo Robson
DREW William A
DRINKWATER Raymond
DUDLEY Reginald Arthur
DUFF Hugh
DUFFIELD Martin John
DUGDALE James Robert
DUGGAN Edward J
DURRANT Frederick H
DUTHIE John Flett
DUTTON Thomas
DYER Lloyd Richard
DYKSTRA Sieb

DALY Wesley James Patrick
Mid 5' 9" 11st 2lbs
b: Hammersmith, London 7 Mar 1984
QPR: 2001
Football League: 8-0. **FAC:** 1-0. **FLC:** 0-0.
Other: 0-0. **Total:** 9-0.

A young midfield player who came up through the ranks at the club. Wesley spent much of his time in the reserves and made only a handful of first team appearances before dropping down into non-League football.
Debut: 16 Mar 2002 v Colchester United (A) 1-3 Div 2.

DAND Robert
(HB) Def 5' 7" 11st 0lbs
b: Ilford, Essex, 1900
QPR: 1924
Football League: 1-0. **FAC:** 0-0. **FLC:** 0-0.
Other: 0-0. **Total:** 1-0.
Honours: 1 English Amateur cap.

A successful amateur career that included an England appearance against Ireland, Reggie was persuaded to give up his job as a stockbroker's clerk to become a footballer at Reading. At QPR he reverted back to the City of London and ended up playing for Margate.
Debut: 25 Dec 1924 v Norwich City (H) 1-2 Div 3 (S).

DANIELS Arthur W C
(OL) Wing 5' 10" 10st 7lbs
b: Mossley, Manchester
QPR: Jun 1930
Football League: 14-3. **FAC:** 0-0. **FLC:** 0-0.
Other: 0-0. **Total:** 14-3.

A fast and tricky winger, Arthur lacked consistency and never relished rough play. He shared the wing with five others during his season at QPR.
Debut: 30 Aug 1930 v Thames (H) 3-0 Div 3 (S).

DANIELS Harold Augustus George
(WH) Mid 5' 9" 11st 0lbs
b: Kensington, London, 25 Jun 1920
QPR: Oct 1943
Football League: 14-0. **FAC:** 5-0. **FLC:** 0-0.
Other: 0-0. **Total:** 19-0.
Honours: Represented the Royal Artillery during the war.

Harry was a very reliable player who was especially able to rectify slip-ups made by any members of the team. Wounded in the North African campaign he nevertheless made around 70 wartime appearances for QPR.
Debut: 31 Aug 1946 v Watford (H) 2-1 Div 3 (S).

DARLINGTON Jermaine Christopher
WB 5' 7" 10st 10lbs
b: Hackney, London, 11 Apr 1974
QPR: (£25,000) Mar 1999
Football League: 71-2. **FAC:** 6-0. **FLC:** 2-0.
Other: 0-0. **Total:** 79-2.

Jermaine became a firm favourite with the spectators, because of his surging runs out of defence, operating with equal effectiveness from either flank. However, after just over two years at Loftus Road, he was signed by Wimbledon during the close season of 2001 for £200,000. Jermaine was comfortable with the ball at his feet, and he fitted in to the side at both left and right-back. As he had previously played in midfield he liked to push forward and join the attack and his speed and vision made him a handful to control.
Debut: 10 Apr 1999 v WBA (H) 2-1 Div 1.

DAVIDSON Peter E
Mid 5' 10" 11st 1lb
b: Newcastle, 31 Oct 1956
QPR: (£40,000) Jul 1979
Football League: 1-0. **FAC:** 0-0. **FLC:** 0-0.
Other: 0-0. **Total:** 1-0.

Peter joined QPR in the summer of 1979 but failed to grasp the opportunity. He soon returned to Berwick Rangers and stayed with them until 1987.
Debut: 25 Aug 1979 v Leicester City (H) 1-4 Div 2.

DAVIES Andrew
Def 6' 2" 12st 3lbs
b: Stockton-on-Tees, 17 Dec 1984
QPR: (Loan) 2005
Football League: 9-0. **FAC:** 0-0. **FLC:** 0-0.
Other: 0-0. **Total:** 9-0.
Debut: 14 Jan 2005 v Stoke City (H) 1-0 Championship.

Andrew Davies

DAVIES Edmond

(CF) Striker
b: Oswestry, Shropshire, 5 Jun 1927
QPR: Apr 1950
Football League: 1-1. **FAC:** 0-0. **FLC:** 0-0.
Other: 0-0. **Total:** 1-1.

Eddie scored in his only senior match for the club. But his potential was never realised at Loftus Road or elsewhere, and he finished up playing for his non-League home town club.
Debut: 27 Jan 1951 v Brentford (H) 1-1 Div 2.

DAVIS Arthur George

(IF) Striker 5′ 10″ 11st 12lbs
b: Birmingham, July 1900
d: Birmingham, 1955
QPR: Aug 1922
Football League: 62-21. **FAC:** 5-1. **FLC:** 0-0.
Other: 0-0. **Total:** 67-22.

Arthur managed a goal on his debut and he was one of the three main scorers at the club at the time, along with Birch and Parker. Unfortunately during his time with Rangers, they had to apply for re-election to the League and this hastened his downfall.
Debut: 28 Aug 1922 v Norwich City (A) 1-1 Div 3 (S).

DAWES Ian Robert

(LB) Def 5′ 10″ 11st 10lbs
b: Croydon, Surrey, 22 Feb 1963
QPR: Dec 1980
Football League: 229-3. **FAC:** 8-0. **FLC:** 28-1.
Other: 5-0. **Total:** 270-4.
Honours: 8 England schoolboy caps.
2nd Div championship medal. League Cup runner's-up medal.

Ian was under 18 when he signed for Rangers, and during his long career at Loftus Road, one period included 198 consecutive appearances before he missed a match through injury. This run embraced the four seasons 1982/83 to 1985/86 when he was an ever-present in Football League matches.

He consistently put in faultless performances week after week for QPR, and he was eventually transferred to Millwall. Despite 270 first-team appearances for Rangers, he went on to become one of Millwall's longer serving players, consistently putting in faultless performances at either right or left-back. He was equally adept whether defending or assisting the attack. At The Den he added another 258 first-team games to his record. In 1995 he moved into the non-League scene, at Bromley, and the following year played for Dorking. But he soon had to retire due to a recurring knee injury. Ian later became the manager of Carshalton Athletic and coach at Charlton and Millwall, before taking over as manager of Redhill in 2002.
Debut: 27 Mar 1982 v Rotherham United (A) 0-1 Div 2.

Ian Dawes

DAWSON Alexander

(OR) Wing
b: Glasgow, Scotland, 21 Oct 1933
QPR: Feb 1957
Football League: 59-5. **FAC:** 5-2. **FLC:** 0-0.
Other: 3-0. **Total:** 67-7.

Alex's best match was at Accrington where he notched two of the four goals that were scored that day. Just after this he was sacked by then manager Taylor. His career at Loftus Road only lasted three seasons, during which time he made 67 first-team appearances, including notably 33 League outings in the 1957/58 season.

Debut: 13 Apr 1957 v Brighton & Hove Albion (H) 0-0 Div 3 (S).

DAWSON George

(LB) Mid
b: Glasgow, Scotland, 13 Sep 1930
QPR: May 1955
Football League: 1-0. **FAC:** 0-0. **FLC:** 0-0.
Other: 0-0. **Total:** 1-0.

The only occasion that George played in the senior squad resulted in a 6-2 victory for the team.

Debut: 10 Mar 1956 v Colchester United (H) 6-2 Div 3 (S).

DAY

(CF) Striker
QPR: 1912
Football League: 4-0. **FAC:** 0-0. **FLC:** 0-0.
Other: 0-0. **Total:** 4-0.

The season after winning the Southern League title, an injury to the regular centre-forward left the side bereft of a striker. Day was the sixth man to be tried in that position during the season.

Debut: 8 Mar 1913 v Portsmouth (H).1-1 SL Div 1.

DAY Christopher Nicholas

Goal 6' 3" l3st 6lbs
b: Walthamstow, London, 28 Jul 1975
QPR: Jul 2001
Football League: 75-0. **FAC:** 2-0. **FLC:** 6-0.
Other: 1-0. **Total:** 84-0.
Honours: 6 England U21 caps. UEFA-U18s youth caps.

Chris quickly became a favourite of the Shepherds Bush fans after he signed from Watford. However, he unfortunately suffered a fracture of the right leg in November 2001 which kept him out of action for the rest of the season, but he made a successful comeback towards the end of 2002/03 after his long lay-off. Although he remained at Loftus Road until the summer of 2005, Chris found himself behind Lee Camp and Simon Royce in the battle for the keeper's jersey and moved to Oldham.

Debut: 11 Aug 2001 v Stoke City (H) 1-0 Div 2.

DEAN Jobey

(RH) Mid
b: Chesterfield, 25 Nov 1934
QPR: Nov 1952
Football League: 16-0. **FAC:** 1-0. **FLC:** 0-0.
Other: 0-0. **Total:** 17-0.

The stand-in for Petchey, who was very seldom injured, Jobey was eventually transferred to Bradford PA, but he only became an important reserve team man there.

Debut: 30 Aug 1955 v Brentford (A) 0-2 Div 3 (S).

Chris Day

Damien Delaney

DELANEY Damien

Def 6' 3" 14st 0lbs
b: Cork, Ireland, 20 Jul 1981
QPR: Jan 2008
Football League: 54-2. **FAC:** 2-0. **FLC:** 3-1.
Other: 0-0. **Total:** 59-3.
Honours: 2 Republic of Ireland caps.

Damien was brought to England by Peter Taylor, having begun his footballing career at local club Cork City but he made just eight Premiership appearances for Leicester City before signing for Hull City in October 2002. The midfielder-turned-centre-back spent more than five years with the Tigers and made history as the last Hull City player to score a goal at Boothferry Park prior to the club's move to the Kingston Communications Stadium. Damien moved to Loftus Road in January 2008 and his versatility has made him a key asset to the Rangers squad as well as earning him a call up to Giovanni Trapattoni's Republic of Ireland squad. Damien signed for Ipswich Town in July 2009.
Debut: 19 January 2008 v Barnsley (H) 2-0 Championship.

DELVE John F

Mid 5' 7" 11st 0lbs
b: Isleworth, London, 27 Sep 1953
QPR: Jul 1971
Football League: 15-0. **FAC:** 1-0. **FLC:** 1-0.
Other: 0-0. **Total:** 17-0.
Honours: 2nd Div runner's-up medal. 3rd Div runner's-up medal.

John was a terrier-like player who was always looking for the ball and played a small part in the promotion of the club in 1973. However, he is known mainly as an Exeter City stalwart who captained them to a grand FA Cup run in 1981. In 1988 Delve took the job of caretaker/manager until the end of the season.
Debut: 9 Dec 1972 v Luton Town (A) 2-2 Div 2.

DENNIS Mark Earle

(LB) Def 5' 9" 10st 8lbs
b: Streatham, London, 2 May 1961
QPR: (£50,000) May 1987
Football League: 28-0. **FAC:** 2-0. **FLC:** 2-0.
Other: 3-0. **Total:** 35-0.
Honours: 8 England youth caps. 3 U21 caps. 1st Div runner's-up medal.

An exciting talented player who could send teasing centres across the goal mouth from the wing-back position. Mark had a potential talent that was never realised owing to his fiery temper. He was ordered off over a dozen times and received over 70 yellow card cautions. Nevertheless his enthusiasm made him a popular character with the Loftus Road crowd. Mark eventually became the manager of Fleet Town and later assisted at Eastleigh.
Debut: 15 Aug 1987 v West Ham United (A) 3-0 Div 1.

DE ORNELAS Fernando

Mid 6' 0" 11st 10lbs
b: Caracas, Venezuela, 29 Jul 1976
QPR: Oct 2001
Football League: 2-0. **FAC:** 0-0. **FLC:** 0-0.
Other: 0-0. **Total:** 2-0.
Honours: 27 caps for Venezuela.

Fernando was a right-sided midfield player who joined QPR on a monthly basis, but after just a month or so made a move to Portugal.
Debut: 27 Oct 2001 v Oldham Athletic (H) 1-1 Div 2.

DEVINE John Steven

(IR) Striker
b: Aberdeen, Scotland
QPR: 1938
Football League: 7-1. **FAC:** 0-0. **FLC:** 0-0.
Other: 1-0. **Total:** 8-1.

This young player from Scotland couldn't settle in London. At the beginning of the 1939/40 season

Mark Dennis

Samuel Di Carmine

all contracts were cancelled owing to the outbreak of the Second World War. It is not known what happened to John from that time on.
Debut: 27 Aug 1938 v Reading (A) 4-2 Div 3 (S).

DEVINE Joseph Cassidy

(IL) Mid 5′ 9″ 10st 9lbs
b: Motherwell, Scotland, 8 Sep 1905
d: Chesterfield, 9 May 1980
QPR: (£2,500) May 1933
Football League: 57-9. **FAC:** 6-1. **FLC:** 0-0.
Other: 2-0. **Total:** 65-10.
Honours: 1 Football League cap.

Joe was the engine room of the side in the early 1930s, controlling the ball excellently and reading the game in an instant was no bother to him. He was given the captaincy of the club as soon as he arrived. After his retirement from playing football, Joe became a Scottish referee in the Highland League. Later in life he ran a successful sports outfitters shop in London.
Debut: 26 Aug 1933 v Brighton & Hove Albion (H) 2-0 Div 3 (S).

DI CARMINE Samuel

Striker 6′ 2″ 12st 3lbs
b: Florence, Italy, 20 Sep 1988
QPR: (Loan) 2008
Football League: 27-2. **FAC:** 2-1. **FLC:** 4-0.
Other: 0-0: **Total:** 33-3.

Rangers' strike force was bolstered during the 2008/09 campaign by the season-long loan signing of Italian hot-shot Samuel Di Carmine. The teenager, highly rated in his home country, had only made two League appearances for his home town club, Fiorentina, before arriving in the UK but notched his first goal for his new employers against Birmingham in October 2008. Not a prolific but a powerful striker, the experience will have done Samuel no harm whatsoever.
Debut: 12 Aug 2008 v Swindon Town (A) 3-2 Carling Cup first round.

DICHIO Daniele Salvatore Ernest

Striker 6′ 3″ 12st 3lbs
b: Hammersmith, London, 19 Oct 1974
QPR: May 1993
Football League: 76-20: **FAC:** 4-1. **FLC:** 6-2.
Other: 0-0. **Total:** 86-23.
Honours: England school caps. U21 cap. 1st Div championship medal.

Danny Dichio

Fraser Digby

Tall, excellent in the air and possessing a fierce shot, that is Daniele Dichio, always proving a handful for the marking defender. Danny scored on his QPR League debut while substituting for Les Ferdinand and the following weekend he appeared as a substitute against Newcastle and scored again. A local boy, Danny formed an excellent partnership with Bradley Allen in the reserves. After a few loan periods he was a big money signing for Sunderland in 1998 and, in 2001, he commanded an even bigger fee when he made a move to The Hawthorns.
Debut: 29 Oct 1994 v Aston Villa (H) 2-0 PL.

DIGBY Fraser Charles

Goal 6′ 2″ 13st 10lbs
b: Sheffield, Yorkshire, 23 Apr 1967
QPR: Oct 2001
Football League: 19-0: **FAC:** 1-0. **FLC:** 0-0.
Other: 0-0. **Total:** 20-0.
Honours: School & youth cap. 5 England U21 caps.

An experienced goalkeeper who was the replacement for Day, who broke his leg. Fraser was a regular in the line-up until he became an injury victim himself in February 2002. One year later he signed for Third Division club Kidderminster Harriers.
Debut: 3 Nov 2001 v Notts County (A) 2-0 Div 2.

DINES Joseph

(LH) Def
b: Kings Lynn, Norfolk, 12 Apr 1886
d: 27 Sep 1918
QPR: 1909
Southern League: 1-0. **FAC:** 0-0. **FLC:** 0-0.
Other: 0-0. **Total:** 1-0.
Honours: 27 England Amateur caps. Olympic Gold medal.

A schoolmaster whose father was a blacksmith, Joe was reputed to be a gentleman, with mild manners and a charming character. Gaining a commission in the army, Dines travelled to all parts of the country on his duties, hence his solitary appearance for QPR and for Liverpool. Sadly, Joe was a casualty in the Great War and was killed on the western front.

Debut: 16 Apr 1910 v West Ham United (H) 3-3 SL Div 1.

DOBINSON Harold

(CF) Striker 5' 10" 12st 3lbs
b: Darlington, 2 Mar 1898
d: 1990
QPR: 1923
Football League: 2-0. **FAC:** 0-0. **FLC:** 0-0.
Other: 0-0. **Total:** 2-0.
Honours: FA Amateur Cup winner's medal.

Harold was at the end of a long and successful career, and did not turn professional until after the Great War. At QPR he was a reserve and was not retained at the end of the 1923/24 season.

Debut: 20 Oct 1923 v Northampton Town (A) 0-3 Div 3 (S).

DOHERTY Thomas Edward

Mid 5' 8" 9st 13lbs
b: Bristol, 17 Mar 1979
QPR: 2005
Football League: 15-0. **FAC:** 0-0. **FLC:** 0-0.
Other: 0-0. **Total:** 15-0.
Debut: 6 August 2005 v Hull City (A) 0-0 Championship.

DONALD David Morgan

(OL) Wing 5' 7" 10st 0lbs
b: Coatbridge, Scotland, 29 Dec 1878
d: Derby, Jan 1932
QPR: 1914
Southern League: 97-10. **FAC:** 4-0. **FLC:** 0-0.
Other: 0-0. **Total:** 101-10.
Honours: Represented the London League v London Combination.

Dave dominated the left wing from 1914 to 1920. A substantial fee had been paid for him in 1910 by Derby County, but Chesterfield got him on a free. A £100 sum had been placed on him, but there was no regulating of transfers between the Football League and the Midland League, in which the Spireites then played. At 36 years old he moved to QPR but still managed over 100 appearances.

Debut: 12 Sep 1914 v Southampton (A) 0-3 SL Div 1.

DONNELLY Scott

Striker 5' 8" 11st 10lbs
b: Hammersmith, London, 25 Dec 1987

Doudou

QPR: 2004
Football League: 13-0. **FAC:** 1-0. **FLC:** 0-0.
Other: 0-0. **Total:** 14-0.
Debut: 19 Oct 2004 v Preston NE (A) 1-2 Championship.

(DOUDOU) MBOMBO Aziana Ebele

For 5' 5" 9st 11lbs
b: Kinshasha, Zaire, 11 Sep 1980
QPR: Aug 2001
Football League: 46-3. **FAC:** 1-0. **FLC:** 1-0.
Other: 2-0. **Total:** 50-3.

A speedy player, who became a favourite with the crowd having watched his wholehearted efforts during a match. With the club in administration, two supporters agreed to finance his wages, but after playing a handful of games during the 2002/03 season he was released during the summer.

Debut: 25 Aug 2001 v Reading (H) 0-0 Div 2.

DOWIE Iain

Striker 6' 1" 13st 11lbs
b: Hatfield, Hertfordshire, 9 Jan 1965
QPR: Jan 1998
Football League: 30-2. **FAC:** 2-0. **FLC:** 1-0.
Other: 0-0. **Total:** 33-2.
Honours: 59 caps for Northern Ireland. U21 cap. U23 cap.

Iain came to the club in 1998 in a part exchange deal for Trevor Sinclair. After playing centre-half principally in the reserves he became the chief coach, and was later appointed manager of Oldham Athletic. Dowie returned to QPR in 2008 as manager but was sacked after just 15 games.

Debut: 31 Jan 1998 v Stockport County (A) 0-2 Div 1.

DOWNING Samuel

(LH) Mid 5' 10" 13st 0lbs
b: Willesden, Middlesex, 19 Jan 1883
d: Cuckfield, Mar 1974
QPR: 1900
Southern League: 179-22: **FAC:** 9-1. **FLC:** 0-0.
Other: 2-0. **Total:** 190-23.
Honours: Southern League championship medal. 2nd Div runner's-up medal.

According to some contemporary writers, Sam lacked the pace that would have given him wider recognition, while others wrote that he was an artistic and constructive player who was noted for his accurate and long-range shooting. Nevertheless he was renowned for his scrupulously fair play. After his retirement from football he coached cricket at a college in Maidenhead.

Debut: 1 Sep 1900 v Bristol Rovers (A) 1-2 SL Div 1.

Iain Dowie

DOYLE Maurice

Mid 5' 8" 10st 7lbs
b: Ellesmere Port, 17 Oct 1969
QPR: (£120,000) Apr 1989
Premier League: 6-0. **FAC:** 0-0. **FLC:** 0-0.
Other: 0-0. **Total:** 6-0.

Maurice had all the ingredients of a first class player; stamina, tenacity and fine ball control, yet he was never able to demonstrate these attributes in a match. Good in the air for such a small man, his worth was never realised, for amazingly he played in more than 170 reserve matches, yet was unable to make it in the first team.

Debut: 9 Feb 1993 v Ipswich Town (A) 1-1 PL.

DRABBLE Frank

Goal 5' 10" 12st 0lbs
b: Southport, Lancashire, 8 Jul 1888
d: Staines, 29 Jul 1964
QPR: Mar 1924
Football League: 2-0. **FAC:** 0-0. **FLC:** 0-0.
Other: 0-0. **Total:** 2-0.

Frank was a vastly experienced goalkeeper who stood between the sticks for QPR on two occasions when they were without custodians. He became an estate agent in later life, having previously had a short spell as a bookmaker. Frank was a useful cricketer playing for Southport & Birkdale Cricket club. He died of a heart attack just after his 76th birthday.

Debut: 1 Mar 1924 v Bournemouth & Boscombe Athletic (H) 0-1 Div 3 (S).

DRAKE Alonzo Robson

(IL) Mid 5' 10" 12st 0lbs
b: Parkgate, Rotherham, 16 Apr 1884
d: Huddersfield, 14 Feb 1919
QPR: Aug 1908
Southern League: 19-5. **FAC:** 1-0. **FLC:** 0-0.
Other: 0-0. **Total:** 20-5.
Honours: Represented Sheffield City v Glasgow City.

Known as a hardworking and dashing player, embracing soccer in the winter and cricket in the summer, although Alonzo was better known as the latter. His career was blighted by ill-health which led to his untimely death at the early age of 34.

Debut: 1 Sep 1908 v West Ham United (A) 0-2 SL Div 1.

DREW William A

(OR) Wing
b: London
QPR: 1926
Football League: 1-0. **FAC:** 0-0. **FLC:** 0-0.
Other: 0-0. **Total:** 1-0.
Honours: English Schoolboy international.

Bill was one of five right-wingers to be tried in the first team during the 1926/27 season.

Debut: 18 Sep 1926 v Charlton Athletic (A) 0-2 Div 3 (S).

DRINKWATER Raymond

Goal
b: Jarrow, Co Durham, 18 May 1931
d: 24 Mar 2008
QPR: 1957
Football League: 199-0. **FAC:** 12-0. **FLC:** 3-0.
Other: 1-0. **Total:** 215-0.

Ray was a tall, agile and very reliable goalkeeper who stood between the sticks for some five seasons, and was the successor to Ron Springett. He was ever-present until the amateur Mike Pinner joined the club along with Alec Stock as manager. The newcomer was good enough to keep Drinkwater out of the side for almost half the season until Pinner joined the RAF for his period of National Service.

Ray enjoyed a career at Loftus Road which extended over six years, during which time he made well over 200 first-team appearances, before he moved west to the non-League scene when he joined Bath City.

Debut: 15 Mar 1958 v Coventry City (A) 1-1 Div 3 (S).

DUDLEY Reginald Arthur

(RB) Def
b: Hemel Hempstead, 3 Feb 1915
d: Cambridge, Feb 1994
QPR: Dec 1946
Football League: 58-0. **FAC:** 4-0. **FLC:** 0-0.
Other: 0-0. **Total:** 62-0.
Honours: English Amateur cap. 3rd Div (South) championship medal.

Reg was a player full of class who came to Loftus Road in an exchange deal with Wilf Heathcote. In November 1947 he suffered a double fracture of his leg, plus a broken nose during a match. In the summer of 1950 he was transferred to Watford for a token £200 to captain the reserves. Later in his career he was dismissed as the Hemel Hempstead Town (formerly Apsley) manager, in light of financial irregularities in connection with which he had been acquitted previously.

Debut: 7 Dec 1946 v Port Vale (H) 2-0 Div 3 (S).

DUFF Hugh

(RH) Mid
QPR: 1908
Southern League: 20-0. **FAC:** 2-0. **FLC:** 0-0.

Other: 0-0. **Total:** 22-0.
Honours: Kent League championship medal.

Hugh played over 100 matches and scored some 60 goals for Arsenal reserves. At QPR he was the substitute for Archie Mitchell.

Debut: 7 Sep 1908 v Watford (H) 2-0 SL Div 1.

DUFFIELD Martin John

Mid 5' 8" 11st 3lbs
b: Park Royal, Middlesex, 28 Feb 1964
QPR: Jan 1982
Football League: 1-0. **FAC:** 0-0. **FLC:** 0-0.
Other: 0-0. **Total:** 1-0.
Honours: English youth cap.

Martin made his only appearance for the club on the last day of the 1982/83 season, when he came on as a substitute. He became a well known name in semi-pro football, and also became a long distance lorry driver.

Debut: 14 May 1983 v Grimsby Town (A) 1-1 Div 2.

DUGDALE James Robert

(CH) CD 5' 10" 11st 6lbs
b: Liverpool, 15 Jan 1932
QPR: Oct 1962
Football League: 10-0. **FAC:** 3-0. **FLC:** 0-0.
Other: 0-0. **Total:** 13-0.
Honours: 3 England B caps. 1 Football League cap. 2 FA Cup winner's medals. 1 League Cup winner's medal.

Jimmy was a cool commanding centre-half who kept the opposing centre-forward well under control. He was troubled with a knee injury which eventually forced him to retire, whereupon he became a publican and had many public houses. Sadly he had to have his leg amputated in 1990 and was forced to retire.

Debut: 22 Oct 1962 v Hull City (H) 4-1 Div 3.

DUGGAN Edward J

(IF) Mid
b: West Ham, London, 27 Jun 1922
d: 1982
QPR: 1949
Football League: 47-5. **FAC:** 1-0. **FLC:** 0-0.
Other: 0-0. **Total:** 48-5.

The best part of this player's career was lost due to the war, but during the hostilities Ted played in over 100 matches. He was used as a schemer rather than a goalscorer at QPR.

Debut: 5 Feb 1949 v Grimsby Town (H) 1-2 Div 2.

DURRANT Frederick H

(CF) Striker
b: Dover, Kent, 19 Jun 1921
QPR: (£5,000) Sep 1946
Football League: 51-26. **FAC:** 2-0. **FLC:** 0-0.
Other: 0-0. **Total:** 53-26.
Honours: 3rd Div (South) championship medal.

This big, burley centre-forward made the most of his size on the football pitch. Fred was the capture of manager Dave Mangnall who was without a centre-forward at the time and a marked contribution was made by the newcomer for the club to clinch promotion. Durrant was another player whose career was blighted by the war, for he was a 1939 Brentford signing, but joined Rangers in 1946. In just over two years he made 53 first-team appearances for QPR before moving west to Exeter City.

Debut: 28 Sep 1946 v Torquay United 0-0 Div 3 (S).

Ted Duggan

DUTHIE John Flett

(WH) Def 5' 8" 11st 3lbs
b: Fraserburgh, Scotland, 7 Jan 1903
d: Fraserburgh, 30 Sep 1969
QPR: Sep 1927
Football League: 11-0. **FAC:** 0-0. **FLC:** 0-0.
Other: 0-0. **Total:** 11-0.

A contemporary writer, wrote about John, "He is a clever player who prefers to pass the ball on the ground, however he is inclined to play the game too close." John was reputed to be working as a herring fisherman, who was out at sea, when QPR offered him a trial in 1927.

Debut: 22 Oct 1927 v Crystal Palace (A) 1-1 Div 3 (S).

DUTTON Thomas

(IL) Mid 5' 8" 10st 7lbs
b: Southport, Lancashire, 11 Nov 1906
d: Rochdale, 1982
QPR: 1934
Football League: 23-6. **FAC:** 1-0. **FLC:** 0-0.
Other: 2-0. **Total:** 26-6.
Honours: 3rd Div (North) runner's-up medal. Notts FA County Cup winner's medal.

Tommy was predominately a left-footed player, who would roam anywhere in the middle of the park. He guested for Southport and Watford during the war, but the hostilities in effect curtailed his football playing career.

Debut: 25 Aug 1934 v Swindon Town (A) 1-3 Div 3 (S).

DYER Lloyd Richard

Mid 5' 8" 10st 2lbs
b: Aston, 13 Sep 1982
QPR: (Loan) 2005
Football League: 15-0. **FAC:** 0-0. **FLC:** 0-0.
Other: 0-0. **Total:** 15-0.
Debut: 27 Sep 2005 v Millwall (A) 1-1 Championship.

DYKSTRA Sieb

Goal 6' 5" 14st 7lbs
b: Kerkrade, Holland, 20 Oct 1966
QPR: (£250,000) 1994
Football League: 11-0. **FAC:** 0-0. **FLC:** 1-0.
Other: 0-0. **Total:** 12-0.

Sieb was a big money signing by QPR but remained at Loftus Road for only two years or so. Despite just a handful of first-team appearances, he moved north to Scotland and became a huge favourite of the Dundee crowd. He featured in every first team match for Dundee United in 1997/98.

Debut: 22 Oct 1994 v Norwich City (A) 2-4 PL.

E

EASTOE Peter Robert
EATON Frank
EDGHILL Richard
EDGLEY Harold Horace
EDWARDS Albert
EDWARDS John
EDWARDS Joseph H
EGGLETON James Arthur Edward
ELSEY Karl W
EMBLETON Sidney W
EMMERSON George Arthur Heads
EPHRAIM Hogan Phillip
EVANS Bernard
EVANS Charles
EVANS Ian Peter
EVANS J Lloyd
EVANS Rhys Karl
EVANS Roger
EVANS William
EVANS William B
EVATT Ian Ross

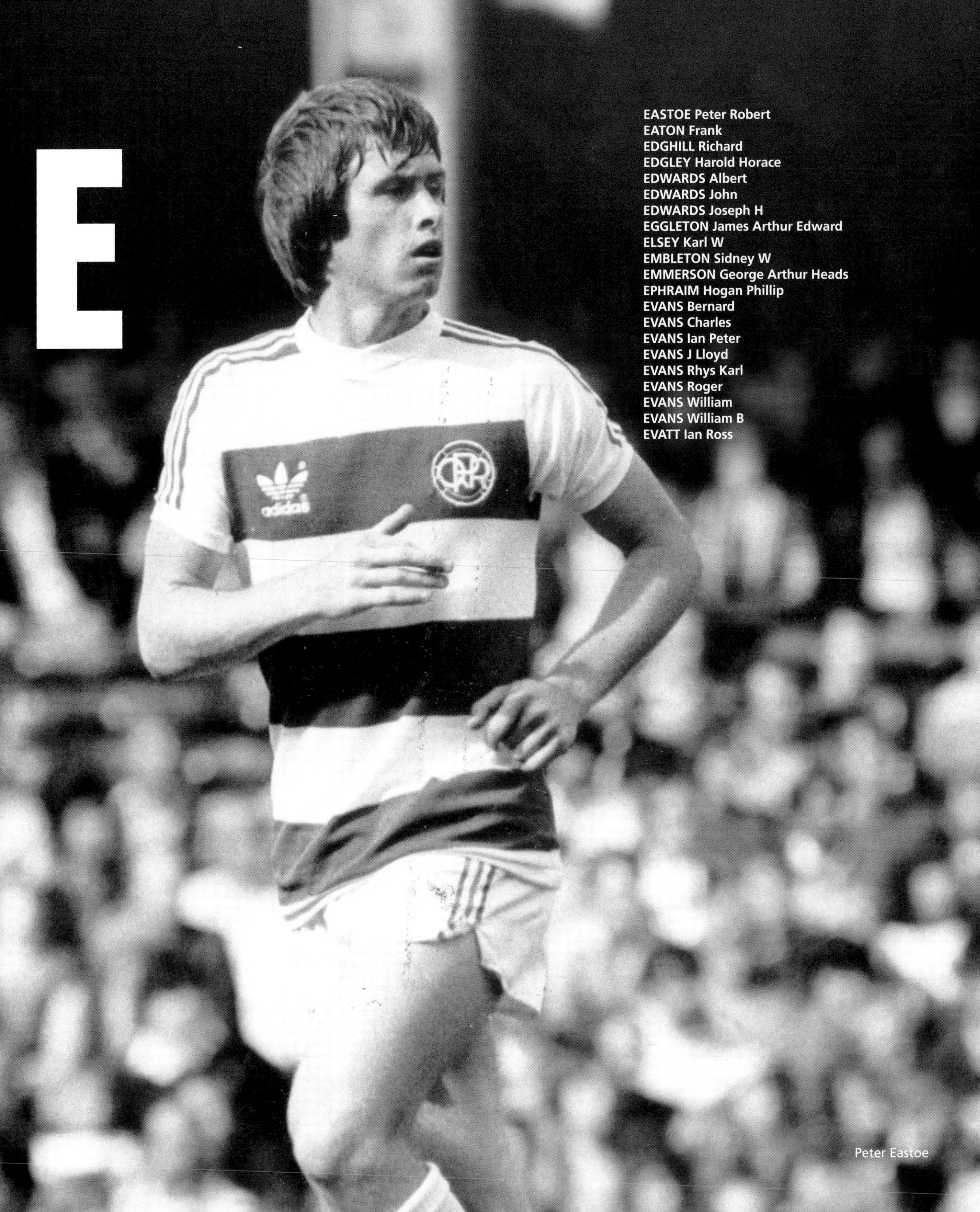

Peter Eastoe

EASTOE Peter Robert

Striker 5' 9" 11st 0lbs
b: Tamworth, Staffordshire, 2 Aug 1953
QPR: (£80,000) Mar 1976
Football League: 72-15. **FAC:** 3-0. **FLC:** 8-5.
Other: 2-0. **Total:** 85-20.
Honours: 8 England youth caps.

When Peter arrived at Loftus Road, he displayed intelligence and skill, unsettling most teams with his precise lay-offs, dummy-runs and neat ball control. Eastoe had the technique to shield the ball and the strength to ride his opponents' tackles. Swapped with Everton's Micky Walsh in 1979, he was in turn exchanged for Andy King and £250,000 in 1982 by WBA.

Peter became a frequent loan signing until he moved into non-League football, and subsequently the player/manager of Alvechurch in 1991. Two years later he took on the post of assistant manager at Nuneaton Borough.

Debut: 16 Oct 1976 v Manchester City (A) 0-0 Div 1.

EATON Frank

(IR) Striker 5' 9" 11st 2lbs
b: Stockport, Lancashire, 12 Nov 1902
d: 1979
QPR: Jul 1933
Football League: 15-2. **FAC:** 2-0. **FLC:** 0-0.
Other: 2-0. **Total:** 19-2.

Frank was a long-striding, slim forward, who once scored five goals for Barnsley in a League match in 1927. He was unfortunate to receive a severe injury in a Third Division South game at Torquay in September 1933, and although he played a few more matches, Eaton decided to retire at the end of that season.

Debut: 26 Aug 1933 v Brighton & Hove Albion (H) 2-0 Div 3 (S).

EDGHILL Richard

Def 5' 9" 11st 5lbs
b: Oldham, 23 Sep 1974
QPR: 2003
Football League: 40-0. **FAC:** 1-0. **FLC:** 3-0.
Other: 0-0. **Total:** 44-0.
Honours: 1 England B and 3 U21 caps.

Richard made his name at Manchester City but found the manager's preference of Shaun Wright-Phillips as the right-sided wing-back limited the number of appearances he made at Maine Road. Despite this, he registered more than 200 games for City before joining Wigan Athletic in 2002. His arrival at Loftus Road added experience to the defence and coincided with the promotion campaign of 2003/04. He played in almost half of Rangers' League games the following season but was soon on his way to Bradford City.

Debut: 30 Aug 2003 v Chesterfield (H) 3-0 Div 2.

EDGLEY Harold Horace

(OL) Wing 5' 10" 11st 6lbs
b: Crewe, January 1892
d: Nottingham, March 1966
QPR: Aug 1921
Football League: 69-6. **FAC:** 6-0. **FLC:** 0-0.
Other: 0-0. **Total:** 75-6.

A useful winger, well built and surprisingly quick, Harry was at home on either flank. He had the misfortune to break his leg just three weeks before Aston Villa were due to meet Huddersfield Town in the FA Cup final in 1920. As he had played in all the other rounds, the club had a special medal minted for him. During his two seasons at QPR, Harry was a regular in the first team, before his move north to Stockport County in 1923. He finally retired in 1927, and later became a director of Notts County.

Debut: 27 Aug 1921 v Swindon Town (H) 0-0 Div 3 (S).

EDWARDS Albert

(HB) Def 5' 7" 11st 0lbs
d: in First World War 1914/18
QPR: 1902
Southern League: 17-1. **FAC:** 0-0. **FLC:** 0-0.
Other: 0-0. **Total:** 17-1.

Bert was a defender of undoubted ability, frail but very cultured. He had a deceptive raking stride and sound positional sense. Sadly he was a casualty of the Great War of 1914/18.

Debut: 29 Nov 1902 v Northampton Town (H) 0-0 SL Div 1.

EDWARDS John

(LB) Def 5' 9" 12st 7lbs
b: Staffordshire, 1875
QPR: 1901
Southern League: 28-2. **FAC:** 1-0. **FLC:** 0-0.
Other: 0-0. **Total:** 29-2.

Richard Edghill

John was a strong but somewhat erratic player who had a tremendous and honest attitude to the game, with a liking to going forward with the attack.
Debut: 3 Sep 1902 v Wellingborough Town (H) 2-0 SL Div 1.

EDWARDS Joseph H
(OR) Wing
QPR: 1925
Football League: 3-0. **FAC:** 0-0. **FLC:** 0-0.
Other: 0-0. **Total:** 3-0.

Joe was one of seven wingers to be tried in the side during the 1926/27 season but to no avail. This was the second time that the club had to apply for re-election.
Debut: 2 Apr 1926 v Bournemouth & BA (H) 2-2 Div 3 (S).

EGGLETON James Arthur Edward
(CH) CD 6' 0" 12st 0lbs
b: Heston, Middlesex, 29 Aug 1897
d: Hillingdon, 13 Jan 1963
QPR: (£500) Oct 1926
Football League: 42-0. **FAC:** 1-0. **FLC:** 0-0.
Other: 0-0. **Total:** 43-0.
Honours: Represented Middlesex & London schools. 13 caps for the Army. 2 London Challenge Cup winner's medals.

Jimmy was a strong tackling centre-half until he was very badly injured in a match which prevented him ever playing again. His promising start in professional football extended over only approximately two seasons. Nevertheless he did stay at the club for another 30 years as a trusted backroom man in many spheres, including trainer, scout and confidant.
Debut: 27 Dec 1926 v Watford (A) 2-1 Div 3 (S).

ELSEY Karl W
Mid 5' 10" 11st 6lbs
b: Swansea, Wales, 20 Nov 1958
QPR: Jan 1979
Football League: 7-0. **FAC:** 0-0. **FLC:** 0-0.
Other: 0-0. **Total:** 7-0.

The son of a Swansea Town professional, Karl was a tough-tackling defender or a solid midfield man but whatever role he played he proved himself to be a versatile player of ability. However, he did have a tendency to be inconsistent. Elsey was a relatively late starter, taking up the game at the age of 17, preferring fishing as a sport. Signing for QPR after just one Combination match, he moved from the Welsh League to the English First Division in four months.
Debut: 24 Mar 1979 v WBA (A) 1-2 Div 1.

Hogan Ephraim

EMBLETON Sidney W
(OR) Wing
b: Poplar, London
QPR: 1930
Football League: 2-0. **FAC:** 0-0. **FLC:** 0-0.
Other: 0-0. **Total:** 2-0.

One of the many amateurs drafted into the side during the period between the two World Wars. Sid was the substitute to Coward during this period.
Debut: 7 Mar 1931 v Brentford (H) 3-1 Div 3 (S).

EMMERSON George Arthur Heads
(OR) Wing 5' 8" 10st 7lbs
b: Bishop Auckland, 15 May 1906
d: Melton Mowbray, 6 Dec 1966
QPR: 1933
Football League: 52-13. **FAC:** 5-3. **FLC:** 0-0.
Other: 3-0. **Total:** 60-16.
Honours: 3 Durham County Amateur Badges. Welsh Senior Cup winner's medal.

Emmerson was a fast and tricky winger from Cardiff City, who had come to Loftus Road in an exchange deal with another winger named Marcroft. George had a fabulous season with the club until he was injured in April 1934.
Debut: 26 Aug 1933 v Brighton & Hove Albion (H) 2-0 Div 3 (S).

EPHRAIM Hogan Phillip
Mid 5' 9" 11st 0lbs
b: Archway, London, 31 Mar 1988
QPR: 2007
Football League: 56-3. **FAC:** 3-0. **FLC:** 0-0.
Other: 0-0. **Total:** 59-3.

A graduate of the successful West Ham United academy, Hogan found his first team opportunities limited at Upton Park so – after just one League Cup appearance – agreed to be loaned to Colchester. He starred in 21 League games for United before joining Rangers, initially on loan, in August 2007. The youngster impressed during this spell and was rewarded with a three-and-a-half year contract with QPR in January 2008. His form continued into the 2008/09 season and Hogan is widely considered one of the county's brightest prospects.
Debut: 11 Aug 2007 v Bristol City (A) 2-2 Championship.

EVANS Bernard
(CF) Striker 6' 1" 13st 6lbs
b: Chester, Cheshire, 4 Jan 1937
QPR: (£2,000) Nov 1960
Football League: 78-35. **FAC:** 4-4. **FLC:** 2-0.
Other: 0-0. **Total:** 84-39.
Honours: Welsh Cup winner's medal.

Bernard started his Football League career at Wrexham where as a 17 year old he made an impressive start by scoring in 27 seconds from

the kick-off. He was a big hefty centre-forward, recommended to Alec Stock by the chief scout in Wales. However, his League career ended in 1964 while he was playing for Crewe, when he received a bad injury. In 1966 Bernard set up an industrial cleaning business in Chester.
Debut: 19 Nov 1960 v Shrewsbury Town (H) 1-1 Div 3.

EVANS Charles
(IF) Mid
b: Luton, Bedfordshire
QPR: 1929
Football League: 1-0. **FAC:** 0-0. **FLC:** 0-0.
Other: 0-0. **Total:** 1-0.

A reserve who turned out for the senior squad on just one occasion in the absence of J C Burns.
Debut: 1 Feb 1930 v Southend United (H) 2-5 Div 3 (S).

EVANS Ian Peter
(CH) CD 6' 2" 11st 2lbs
b: Egham, Surrey, 30 Jan 1952
QPR: Jan 1970
Football League: 39-2. **FAC:** 4-0. **FLC:** 3-0.
Other: 0-0. **Total:** 46-2.
Honours: 2 Welsh U23 caps. 13 full Welsh caps. 2nd Div runner's-up medal. 3rd Div runner's-up medal.

A dominating figure at the heart of the QPR defence in the early 1970s, Ian was a tall slim defender who was particularly accomplished in the air. Unfortunately he was struck down by a severe injury in October 1977 which kept him out of the game for two years. He was made coach at Barnsley in September 1981 but was relieved of the post in August 1983. After that Ian became assistant manager to Steve Coppell at Crystal Palace until February 1989 when he succeeded Terry Yorath as manager at Swansea City, which lasted until March 1990. Ian became the reserve team coach at Millwall, and was the assistant manager to Mick McCarthy's Republic of Ireland side.
Debut: 6 Apr 1971 v Sheffield Wednesday (H) 1-0 Div 2.

EVANS J Lloyd
(OR) Wing
QPR: 1904
Southern League: 1-0. **FAC:** 0-0. **FLC:** 0-0.
Other: 0-0. **Total:** 1-0.

Just one of seven wingers to be tried during the 1904/05 season.
Debut: 25 Feb 1905 v Millwall (H) 1-1 SL Div 1.

EVANS Rhys Karl
Goal 6' 1" 12st 2lbs
b: Swindon, Wiltshire, 27 Jan 1982
QPR: (Loan) Nov 2001
Football League: 11-0. **FAC:** 0-0. **FLC:** 0-0.
Other: 0-0. **Total:** 11-0.
Honours: England school & youth caps.

Rhys was originally signed as the reserve team goalkeeper, but he came into the picture when Fraser Digby was injured and hence stepped up into the first team. He then moved across London to Leyton Orient where he made a handful of first team appearances during the 2002/03 season. He later signed for Swindon Town, Blackpool, Millwall and Bradford City.
Debut: 26 Feb 2002 v Wigan Athletic (H) 1-1 Div 2.

EVANS Roger
(CF) Striker
b: Bangor, Wales, 17 Nov 1879
d: Swanage, Dorset, 25 Apr 1974
QPR: 1901
Southern League: 1-0. **FAC:** 0-0. **FLC:** 0-0.
Other: 0-0. **Total:** 1-0.
Honours: Represented Middlesex & London. Won London Challenge Cup winner's medals in 1901, 02, 03 and 04. Capped for Wales in 1902.

Roger was an amateur, an ex-public schoolboy who was taught his serious football at Ilford. He was the subject of an approach by Liverpool in November 1899 which caused outrage among the Essex club's fans. The Liverpool officials were reported to the FA and found guilty of an illegal approach and the secretary, John McKenna, was suspended for a month. Roger's work as an insurance manager made demands on his time but, during 1904, Evans signed for Baron Von Reiffenstein's new club, Southern United, who hoped to challenge the best clubs in the south, but in the end nothing came of the idea. Roger remained on Clapton's books.
Debut: 15 Mar 1902 v Bristol Rovers (H) 0-0 SL Div 1.

EVANS William
(IR) Mid 5' 7" 10st 8lbs
b: Llansaintffraid, Wales
QPR: 1897
QPR: 1899
Southern League: 9-3. **FAC:** 4-3. **FLC:** 0-0.
Other: 0-0. **Total:** 13-6.
Honours: Represented London & Middlesex.

His business took him to London regularly and it was there that Bill played most of his football. He retired in 1901 due to a serious injury he sustained while playing for Lincoln City.
Debut: 7 Oct 1899 v Bristol City (A) 3-5 SL Div 1.

EVANS William B
(RB) Def 5' 10" 12st 0lbs
b: Llanidloes, Wales
QPR: 1924
Football League: 17-0. **FAC:** 0-0. **FLC:** 0-0.
Other: 0-0. **Total:** 17-0.

"Billy B", was the least famous of the three Evans players who were on the books of Southend United at the time. The other two were Jimmy who represented Wales and moved on to Burnley, and Tommy who came from Rotherham County.
Debut: 20 Sep 1924 v Swansea Town (H), 0-0 Div 3 (S).

EVATT Ian Ross
Def 6' 3" 13st 12lbs
b: Coventry, 19 Nov 1981
QPR: (£150,000) 2005
Football League: 27-0. **FAC:** 0-0. **FLC:** 1-0.
Other: 0-0. **Total:** 28-0.

Spotted by Derby County scouts at the age of 10, Ian signed his first professional contract on his 17th birthday but could not establish himself in the Rams' first team. A loan spell at Northampton Town preceded a move to Chesterfield where he became club captain and won the 2003/04 Player of the Season award. His form persuaded Ian Holloway to bring him to Loftus Road in June 2005 and he made 28 appearances the following season before being transfer-listed in April 2006.
Debut: 23 Aug 2005 v Northampton Town (A) 0-3 Carling Cup first round.

Ian Evatt

Mark Falco

F

FALCO Mark Peter
FALLON Peter D
FARMER Alexander
FARROW Desmond A
FAULKNER Robert
FENWICK Harrison
FENWICK Terrence William
FERDINAND Leslie
FEREDAY Wayne
FERGUSON Christopher
FERGUSON J
FERGUSON Michael Kevin
FIDLER Joseph Edward
FIDLER Thomas G
FIELD William H
FILLERY Michael C
FINCH Robert J
FINNEY Charles William Thomas
FITZGERALD Brian Maurice
FITZGERALD Michael Alfred
FLANAGAN Michael Anthony
FLEMING Mark J
FLETCHER Jack
FLETCHER Jack
FOLEY Dominic Joseph
FORBES Terrell
FORD Ewart L
FORTUNE James J
FOSTER Cyril James
FOX George F
FOX T S
FOXALL Abraham
FRANCIS George E
FRANCIS Gerald Charles
FRANCIS Trevor John
FREEMAN Benjamin
FRY Robert P
FURLONG Paul Anthony

FALCO Mark Peter

Striker 6' 0" 12st 0lbs
b: Hackney, London, 22 Oct 1960
QPR: (£350,000) Jan 1988
Football League: 87-27. **FAC:** 10-2. **FLC:** 6-4.
Other: 3-0. **Total:** 106-33.
Honours: 4 England youth caps. UEFA Cup winner's medal.

Tall with a strapping physic, Mark appeared to be somewhat cumbersome and lacking in pace but when he ran on to a through-ball it took a good man to stop his surge on goal. A constant menace in the air with a fearless attitude, Mark was effective at retaining the ball and too frequently he took the knocks, but contributed the legwork that paved his side's way to goal. He retired in 1992, having sustained a nasty injury. Mark continued in the semi-pro game and was still playing in 1996 when he was turning out for Worthing as player/manager.

Debut: 5 Dec 1987 v Manchester United (H) 0-2 Div 1.

FALLON Peter D

(LB) Def
b: Dublin, Eire, 19 Oct 1922
QPR: 1953
Football League: 1-0. **FAC:** 0-0. **FLC:** 0-0.
Other: 0-0. **Total:** 1-0.

Peter was the brother of the League of Ireland player Willie Fallon. On being demobbed from the RAF, he joined Exeter City and turned out for them in over 100 matches. At Loftus Road, Peter was mainly used for training the youngsters.

Debut: 19 Sep 1953 v Shrewsbury Town (A) 1-1 Div 3 (S).

FARMER Alexander

(WH) Mid 5'11" 12st 0lbs
b: Lochgelly, Scotland, 9 Oct 1908
QPR: 1933
Football League: 81-10. **FAC:** 4-2. **FLC:** 0-0.
Other: 8-0. **Total:** 93-12.

Alex was known as a utility player, for although his main position was at centre-half, he could also play at wing-half or inside-forward, and either left or right. Eventually he was taken on the training staff, staying on the payroll of the club until well into the 1950s.

Debut: 3 Feb 1934 v Torquay United (A) 1-1 Div 3 (S).

FARROW Desmond A

(LH) Def 5' 8" 10st 2lbs
b: Peterborough, Cambs, 11 Feb 1926
QPR: 1944
Football League: 118-7. **FAC:** 3-0. **FLC:** 0-0.
Other: 0-0. **Total:** 121-7.

Terry Fenwick

Des was a fine left-footed player who could defend with notable ability. A wartime signing, he played over 120 senior matches for the Rangers up to 1952. Then, one of the first moves taken by Jack Taylor when he took over the manager's job from Dave Mangnall, was to sell Farrow for a good sum to Stoke City plus a player.

The replacement was once the substitute for Stanley Matthews at the Victoria Ground, but as things transpired the deal was a complete failure on both sides.

Debut: 9 Oct 1948 v Brentford (H) 2-0 Div 2.

FAULKNER Robert

(OR) Wing 5' 9" 11st 0lbs
b: Paisley, Glasgow, Scotland, Aug 1897
QPR: 1920
Football League: 50-1. **FAC:** 2-0. **FLC:** 0-0.
Other: 0-0. **Total:** 52-1.
Honours: 3 caps for Canada.

Robert was a very fast winger who could "centre the ball on a sixpence". However, he had much more success in Canada where he played three times for that country against the USA in 1925.

Debut: 28 Aug 1920 v Watford (H) 1-2 Div 3.

FENWICK Harrison

(HB) Def 5' 8" 11st 0lbs
b: Washington, Co Durham, Oct 1900
QPR: 1924
Football League: 19-0. **FAC:** 0-0. **FLC:** 0-0.
Other: 0-0. **Total:** 19-0.

Harrison worked in the coal mines before he decided to go south after the First World War. QPR signed him for a season, where he played in any of the three half-back positions.

Debut: 4 Dec 1924 v Merthyr Town (H) 1-1 Div 3 (S).

FENWICK Terrence William

Def 5' 10" 10st 11lbs
b: Seaham, Co Durham, 17 Nov 1959
QPR: (£110,000) Dec 1980
Football League: 256-33. **FAC:** 18-6. **FLC:** 29-6.
Other: 5-0. **Total:** 308-45.
Honours: England youth caps. 11 U21 caps. 20 Senior caps. 2 2nd Div championship winner's medals. FA Cup runner's-up medal. League Cup runner's-up medal.

Capable of playing in any defensive or midfield slots, Terry was probably one of the best defenders

Les Ferdinand

the club has ever possessed, and made many of his England appearances while with the club. Terry's versatility saw him playing full-back, in central defence, in midfield, and in a continental style sweeper's role, at Spurs, where his ability to read the game and his confidence on the ball was used to good effect. He was at Loftus Road for eight seasons, during which time he appeared in over 300 senior games.

Normally a first team regular, his least number of seasonal League matches totalled 21, in 1986/87. He followed his manager, Terry Venables, from Crystal Palace to QPR in 1980 where he played in over 300 matches. Terry broke his leg in 1989 and then his ankle in 1991, which virtually ended his career. Moving to Swindon Town in 1993 he then took the job of player/manager of Portsmouth in 1994, which lasted until 1998.
Debut: 19 Dec 1980 v Bolton Wanderers (A) 2-1 Div 2.

FERDINAND Leslie

Striker 5' 11" 13st 5lbs
b: Acton, Middlesex, 18 Dec 1966
QPR: (£15,000) Mar 1987
Football League: 162-80. **FAC:** 7-3: **FLC:** 13-7.
Other: 1-0. **Total:** 183-90.
Honours: England B cap. 17 full English caps. Football League Cup winner's medal. Turkish Cup winner's medal.

It was some years before Les made his mark at QPR. Signed from just down the road at Hayes, he cost a reasonable fee for a non-League player (some sources incorrectly quote £30,000), but made only a handful of appearances in his first three seasons at Loftus Road.

During this time, two loan periods included a month at Brentford, whose fans considered that he would never make the grade! But Les gradually found a regular spot in the Rangers' First/Premier Division team, and after eight seasons he had become a highly sought after player. Nicknamed "Sir Les" by the QPR fans, he adopted this title for his autobiography. A fine centre-forward with great heading abilities and a sizzling shot to go with it, Les spread his play wide before getting into position himself for a cross into the middle. His power and pace made him difficult to contain. A record £6m transfer fee took him to Newcastle United for two years before the same sum brought him back to London, and Spurs. 2001/02 was undoubtedly his best season at White Hart Lane, where he looked lean, sharp and athletic, and instilled a real threat into the attack. Les was consistently the team's most formidable player and netted a total of 15 goals in all competitions. He also developed a fine partnership with Teddy Sheringham. In January 2003 he made another move, this time to West Ham and became a near regular in the latter part of that season. Les moved on to Leicester, Bolton, Reading and Watford before retiring in 2006.
Debut: 20 Apr 1987 v Coventry City (A) 1-4 Div 1.

Wayne Fereday

FEREDAY Wayne

Mid 5' 9" 11st 8lbs
b: Warley, Yorkshire, 16 Jun 1963
QPR: 1980
Football League: 196-21. **FAC:** 14-0. **FLC:** 29-3.
Other: 5-1. **Total:** 244-25.
Honours: 5 U21 caps. Football League appearance.

Lithe and extremely fast, Wayne was one of the quickest players on the circuit and was probably at his best on the left wing. He was easily able to take on defenders and get in a dangerous cross. It was during 1980/81, his first season, that Wayne made a name for himself by scoring twice on his Football League debut. After nine seasons, and playing in 244 competitive matches for QPR he headed north before teaming-up with his ex-manager, Jim Smith, at Newcastle. Further moves brought him back south and to the Midlands, before he finally joined the non-League scene in 1995. He moved to Poole, Dorset later that year.
Debut: 19 Aug 1980 v Bristol Rovers (H) 4-0 Div 2.

FERGUSON Christopher

(IR) Mid 5' 6" 10st 12lbs
b: Kirkconnel, Dumfries & Galloway, Scotland
QPR: May 1930
Football League: 15-1. **FAC:** 0-0. **FLC:** 0-0.
Other: 0-0. **Total:** 15-1.

Chris was the younger brother of Bill who played full-back for Chelsea in the early 1920s, and turned out mainly for the reserves at Stamford Bridge. Another brother, Pearson, played for Carlisle United.
Debut: 13 Mar 1930 v Brighton & Hove Albion (H) 4-1 Div 3 (S).

FERGUSON J

(OR)
QPR: 1909
Southern League: 2-0. **FAC:** 0-0. **FLC:** 0-0.
Other: 0-0. **Total:** 2-0.

A player who made just two appearances for QPR, Ferguson never played a Southern League match, for both of his games were in the FA Cup, at West Ham and in the replay.
Debut: 19 Feb 1910 v West Ham United (A) 1-1 FA Cup third round.

FERGUSON Michael Kevin

Mid 5' 10" 11st 4lb
b: Burnley, Lancashire, 9 Mar 1943
QPR: (£15,000) Nov 1969
Football League: 68-2. **FAC:** 6-1. **FLC:** 3-0.
Other: 0-0. **Total:** 77-3.

Mike was a well built, strong running player, who would beat an opponent, wait for him to recover and beat him all over again. Unfortunately he had a very temperamental nature which brought about many altercations on the pitch. He was capable of playing full-back, midfield or orthodox winger. His wide football career saw him initially travelling throughout the country, which started at Plymouth, and included Accrington Stanley (he was with the club when they dropped out of the League). His stay at Loftus Road lasted four years before he was on his travels again. While at Rochdale he spent the summer in the USA, and late in 1975 went to manage IA Akranes in Iceland. He then coached Rossendale, briefly made a comeback as a player, with Halifax, before returning to Rochdale as manager, but was fired when the club were relegated from Division 3. After coaching around the world he managed Enfield for a time in 1989. Later living in Burnley, Mike acted as a players' agent and attended many matches for the England management.
Debut: 22 Nov 1969 v Leicester City (H) 1-1 Div 2.

FIDLER Joseph Edward

(LB) Def 5' 9" 11st 12lbs
b: Sheffield, Yorkshire, 1885

QPR: 1906
Southern League: 172-0. **FAC:** 11-0. **FLC:** 0-0.
Other: 2-0. **Total:** 185-0.
Honours: Played for the Southern League v Scottish League. Southern League championship medal.

A strong, tough, stalwart defender, who was one of the old school, who had a long and successful period at QPR. After seven years and nearly 200 games for the Rangers, he moved across London, and played in the last 13 League matches for Woolwich Arsenal in the 1913/14 season. Another move was soon made, to the Potteries where he started off as a regular first team player at left-back, but then lost his position to the newly signed England international Bob Benson. In 1915, and unable to gain a place in the Port Vale team, he decided to join the army.
Debut: 29 Sep 1906 v Clapton Orient (A) 0-3 SL Div 1.

FIDLER Thomas G

(CF) Striker
b: Hounslow, Middlesex, 4 Sep 1933
QPR: 1954
Football League: 12-2. **FAC:** 2-2. **FLC:** 0-0.
Other: 0-0. **Total:** 14-4.

Tommy was the reserve striker to Willie Clark, and was released by manager Taylor at the end of the 1954/55 season.
Debut: 24 Aug 1954 v Southend United (A) 2-2 Div 3 (S).

Mike Fillery

FIELD William H

Goal 5' 11" 12st 5lbs
b: Oxford, Oxfordshire
QPR: 1923
Football League: 29-0. **FAC:** 0-0. **FLC:** 0-0.
Other: 0-0. **Total:** 29-0.

Bill became the Number 1 goalkeeper when Les Hill left the club. However, he reverted back to the reserves when Hebden arrived and Billy Hill was "given his cards" after the club had to apply for re-election in 1926.
Debut: 19 Jan 1924 v Brighton & Hove Albion (H) 1-0 Div 3 (S).

FILLERY Michael C

Mid 5' 10" 11st 2lbs
b: Mitcham, Surrey, 17 Sep 1960
QPR: (£200,000) Aug 1983
Football League: 97-9. **FAC:** 5-0. **FLC:** 11-1.
Other: 4-0. **Total:** 117-10.
Honours: Schoolboy international. 7 English youth caps.

Mike was a highly talented and stylish player who always appeared casual and disinterested in the match. Despite nearly 100 League games over a four year period, he somehow lacked the consistency and application to do justice to himself. After several moves around the Football League, in 1991 he moved to Crawley Town as the assistant manager.
Debut: 27 Aug 1983 v Manchester United (A) 1-3 Div 1.

FINCH Robert J

(RH) Def 5' 9" 11st 0lbs
b: Camberwell, London, 24 Aug 1948
d: South Africa, 1978
QPR: 1967
Football League: 5-0. **FAC:** 0-0. **FLC:** 0-0.
Other: 0-0. **Total:** 5-0.

Bobby actually wrote a letter to the club asking for a trial and by April 1968 he was in the senior squad covering for Dave Clement. In 1970 Bobby emigrated to South Africa.
Debut: 16 Apr 1968 v Cardiff City (A) 0-1 Div 2.

FINNEY Charles William Thomas

(CF) Striker 5' 9" 10st 6lbs
b: Stoke-on-Trent, 5 Sep 1931
QPR: May 1957
Football League: 10-1. **FAC:** 0-0. **FLC:** 0-0.
Other: 0-0. **Total:** 10-1.

Charlie caused something of a sensation on his debut in the Football League, scoring at Old Trafford for Stoke City, in what was described as a "perfect left foot shot". He was capable of playing in any of

Mike Flanagan

the inside-forward positions but could not turn it on at Loftus Road.
Debut: 24 Aug 1957 v Brentford (H) 1-0 Div 3 (S).

FITZGERALD Brian Maurice

Mid 5' 9" 12st 2lbs
b: Perivale, Middlesex, 23 Oct 1983
QPR: Oct 2000
Football League: 1-0. **FAC:** 0-0. **FLC:** 0-0.
Other: 0-0. **Total:** 1-0.
Honours: Republic of Ireland youth caps.

Following several good performances in the reserves, Brian made his senior debut as a substitute in 2002. But he never made the grade at Loftus Road and was released during the close season of 2003.
Debut: 12 Jan 2002 v Bury (H) 3-0 Div 2.

FITZGERALD Michael Alfred

(IL) Striker
b: Conisbrough, Yorkshire, 25 Jan 1911
d: Brighton, 1981
QPR: 1936
Football League: 94-43. **FAC:** 5-7. **FLC:** 0-0.
Other: 4-2. **Total:** 103-52.

Just one of the legendary goalscorers that have turned out for the club. Mike headed the scoring list in 1937 and 1938 (scoring 17 goals on both occasions, plus another nine in the 1938/39 season). Undoubtedly the 1939 to 1946 period badly disrupted his football career, as it did so many other players in their prime. During the Second World War he volunteered to serve in submarines, and remained there until 1946. When the war ended he joined Aldershot and played another 60 odd matches for the Shots. He ended his playing days at non-League Tonbridge, having joined them in 1948.
Debut: 7 Nov 1936 v Newport County (A) 2-1 Div 3 (S).

FLANAGAN Michael Anthony

Mid 5' 10" 12st 4lbs
b: Ilford, Essex, 9 Nov 1952
QPR: (£150,000) Aug 1980
Football League: 78-20. **FAC:** 12-0. **FLC:** 3-2.
Other: 0-0. **Total:** 93-22.
Honours: 3 England Amateur youth caps. 2 England B caps. FA Youth Cup winner's medal. FA Cup runner's-up medal. 2nd Div championship medal.

The transfer fee of £650,000 between Charlton Athletic and Crystal Palace was a record deal between London clubs at that time when Mike switched between the two. He was a fiery character who had an exquisite left foot shot, and teamed up with Clive Allen in what became known as the "Flanagan & Allen Show"; between them they scored some 60 goals in four years. Mike returned to Charlton (twice) before moving down to football at non-League level.
Debut: 19 Dec 1980 v Bolton Wanderers (A) 2-1 Div 2.

FLEMING Mark J

Def 5' 9"10st 11lbs
b: Hammersmith, London, 11 Aug 1969
QPR: 1987
Football League: 3-0. **FAC:** 1-0. **FLC:** 0-0.
Other: 1-0. **Total:** 5-0.
Honours: England Youth international. Southern Floodlight Junior Cup medal.

Mark played as a defender at Loftus Road but was turned into a midfield player at his last club. He was a keen sportsman, embracing golf, tennis and swimming.
Debut: 27 Feb 1988 v Wimbledon (H) 1-0 Div 1.

FLETCHER Jack

(IL) Striker 5' 8" 11st 5lbs
QPR: 1905
Southern League: 38-13. **FAC:** 3-0. **FLC:** 0-0.
Other: 0-0. **Total:** 41-13.

Not a lot is known about this player, except that

he scored a hat-trick against Northampton Town in November 1906.
Debut: 23 Dec 1905 v Bristol Rovers (A) 1-2 SL Div 1.

FLETCHER Jack

(IF) Mid 5′ 8″ 11st 5lbs
b: Tyne Docks, South Shields, 1910
QPR: 1935
Football League: 21-0. **FAC:** 0-0. **FLC:** 0-0.
Other: 0-0. **Total:** 21-0.

As soon as Billy Birrell took over at QPR he snapped up Fletcher from Bournemouth. Birrell wanted a playmaker and he certainly found one in Jack, as it turned out that he became the engine-room of the attack. Although he didn't score any goals himself he laid on quite a few for Cheetham. The Rangers rose from the middle of the table in 1935 to fourth in 1936.
Debut: 4 Sep 1935 v Brighton & Hove Albion 1-1 Div 3 (S).

FOLEY Dominic Joseph

Striker 6′ 1″ 12st 8lbs
b: Cork, Eire, 7 Jul 1976
QPR: (Loan) Oct 2001
Football League: 1-0. **FAC:** 0-0. **FLC:** 0-0.
Other: 0-0. **Total:** 1-0.
QPR: (Loan) Mar 2002
Football League: 4-1. **FAC:** 0-0. **FLC:** 0-0.
Other: 0-0. **Total:** 4-1.
Honours: 7 caps for the Republic of Ireland. 8 U21 caps.

Dominic played Gaelic football before he turned to soccer and scored a hat-trick on his debut for Ethnikos. His first loan period at QPR was curtailed by a torn ligament, but in the second spell he scored on his debut. His fairly short playing career in England was punctuated with short loan periods both before and after his time at Loftus Road.
Debut: 27 Oct 2001 v Oldham Athletic (H) 1-1 Div 2.

FORBES Terrell

Def 6′ 0″ 12st 8lbs
b: Southwark, London, 17 Aug 1981
QPR: Jul 2001
Football League: 115-0. **FAC:** 3-0. **FLC:** 6-0.
Other: 1-0. **Total:** 125-0.
Honours: FA Youth Cup.

A right sided defender with a liking to join in with the attack, Terrell soon became another favourite of the Loftus Road crowd.

With his runs down the right wing invariably followed by the delivery of a good cross, Terrell was voted Player of the Year by one of the club's supporters' associations for 2001/02. His first two seasons at Loftus Road saw him as a near ever-present yet he failed to score a goal for the team before being released at the end of the 2003/04 campaign.
Debut: 11 Aug 2001 v Stoke City (H) 1-0 Div 2.

Terrell Forbes

Gerry Francis

FORD Ewart L

Mid
b: Bedworth, Nuneaton, 1910
QPR: 1924
Football League: 55-4. **FAC:** 9-0. **FLC:** 0-0.
Other: 0-0. **Total:** 64-4.

A regular on the left flank until manager Bob Hewison arrived at Loftus Road. Spottiswoode was bought from Swansea Town to replace Ford and Ewart was transferred to Merthyr Town at the end of the season.
Debut: 30 Aug 1924 v Newport County (A) 0-0 Div 3 (S).

FORTUNE James J

(OL) Wing
b: Dublin, Eire, 1890
QPR: 1913
Southern League: 8-0. **FAC:** 5-0. **FLC:** 0-0.
Other: 0-0. **Total:** 13-0.

The Irishman was a reserve wherever he went. At QPR he stood in for Ben Ives.
Debut: 11 Oct 1913 v Plymouth Argyle (H) 0-0 SL Div 1.

FOSTER Cyril James

(RH) Def 5' 8" 10st 7lbs
b: Aylesbury, Buckinghamshire, 1903
QPR: Jun 1928
Football League: 5-0. **FAC:** 0-0. **FLC:** 0-0.
Other: 0-0. **Total:** 5-0.

Cyril usually played at half-back and he had a vigorous style of play but was used mainly as a reserve.
Debut: 20 Oct 1928 v Bournemouth (H) 0-0 Div 3 (S).

FOX George F

(OL) Wing
QPR: 1916
Southern League: 8-0. **FAC:** 0-0. **FLC:** 0-0.
Other: 0-0. **Total:** 8-0.

Not a lot is known about George, but he did make over 200 appearances scoring some 29 goals during the First World War.
Debut: 27 Sep 1919 v Gillingham (A) 1-0 SL Div l.

FOX T S

(LB) Def
QPR: 1905
Southern League: 1-0. **FAC:** 0-0. **FLC:** 0-0.
Other: 0-0. **Total:** 1-0.
Honours: FA Amateur Cup runner's-up medal.

Fox was still an amateur when he turned out for QPR in his only match for the club.
Debut: 11 Apr 1906 v Fulham (A) 0-1 SL Div 1.

FOXALL Abraham

(OL) Wing
b: Sheffield, Yorkshire, 1874
QPR: 1900
Southern League: 27-2. **FAC:** 4-2. **FLC:** 0-0.
Other: 0-0. **Total:** 31-4.

Abe was the mainstay in the QPR forward line in the early days of the Southern League. He missed just one match during the entire season.
Debut: 8 Sep 1900 v Bristol Rovers (A) 1-2 SL Div 1.

FRANCIS George E

(CF) Striker 5' 9" 12st 0lbs
b: Acton, Middlesex, 4 Feb 1934
QPR: May 1961
Football League: 2-1. **FAC:** 0-0. **FLC:** 1-2.
Other: 0-0. **Total:** 3-3.

In George's short stay at Loftus Road, he scored three goals in three matches, but he found it difficult to settle at the club. He was the typical centre-forward of his day, quick and opportunistic. At Brentford he was known as one half of "The Terrible Twins", the other half being Jim Towers who also moved over to QPR.
Debut: 13 Sep 1961 v Crystal Palace (H) 5-2 League Cup first round.

FRANCIS Gerald Charles

Mid 5' 10" 10st 8lbs
b: Chiswick, Middlesex, 6 Dec 1951
QPR: Jun 1969
Football League: 295-61. **FAC:** 18-0. **FLC:** 21-5.
Other: 1-2. **Total:** 335-68.
QPR: Feb 1981
Football League: 21-4. **FAC:** 0-0. **FLC:** 0-0.
Other: 0-0. **Total:** 21-4.
Honours: 6 England U23 caps. 12 full caps (8 as captain). 2nd Div runner's-up medal. 1st Div runner's-up medal. 3rd Div championship medal as manager. Leyland Daf runner's-up medal as manager.

The son of Roy Francis, a reserve team player who used to play for Brentford, Gerry made his League

Trevor Francis

debut at the age of 17 years. He was a midfield player of dash and quality who would have won many more caps had he not been injured, but he is the only QPR player to captain England while at Loftus Road. Gerry's first of two periods at Loftus Road lasted 10 years and took in nearly 300 League games. He was valued at £150,000 by Crystal Palace, but returned to QPR less than two years later, and after only 20 plus League games he was on the move again, this time to Coventry City, and another £150,000 fee! Frequent moves followed in the next few years before he finally hung his boots up after a playing career that had spanned a notable 16 years. Gerry has had a wide managerial career, which began at Exeter City, then at Bristol Rovers, on to QPR in 1991, Spurs in 1994, then – as in his playing days – he returned to QPR in 1998 until 2001. He then managed Bristol Rovers again for a short period.
Debut: 29 Mar 1969 v Liverpool (H) 1-2 Div 1.

FRANCIS Trevor John

Striker 5′ 10″ 11st 7lbs
b: Plymouth, Devon, 19 Apr 1954
QPR: Mar 1988
Football League: 32-12. **FAC:** 1-0. **FLC:** 8-3.
Other: 1-0. **Total:** 42-15.
Honours: England youth caps. 5 U23 caps. 52 Senior caps. 2 2nd Div runner's-up medals. European Cup winner's medal. 2 League Cup runner's-up medals. Italian Cup winner's medal. Scottish League Cup winner's medal.

Trevor had acceleration and style in tight situations and was very dangerous around the penalty box. Intricate ball control, powerful shooting and amazing self confidence was his trade-mark. The first 16 year old to score four goals in a League match and the first £1,000,000 footballer. Trevor had an unhappy spell as the player/manager of QPR. However, his career took a huge upturn when he took the same post at Sheffield Wednesday, for they reached two domestic Cup finals and finished in a respectable position in the League. As manager of Birmingham City he failed to gain any trophies and moved on to take charge of Crystal Palace.
Debut: 26 Mar 1988 v Portsmouth (A) 1-0 Div 1.

FREEMAN Benjamin

(LH) Mid 5′ 11″ 11st 7lbs
b: Small Heath, Birmingham, 1878
QPR: 1901
Southern League: 51-1. **FAC:** 2-0. **FLC:** 0-0.
Other: 0-0. **Total:** 53-1.

Ben was an ex-soldier who served in the Warwickshire Regiment and was invalided out in 1897. He took up football and was signed by Small Heath. Unable to get a game with the senior squad he was transferred to Grays United and it was from there that QPR secured him.
Debut: 7 Sep 1901 v Watford (H) 0-1 SL Div 1.

FRY Robert P

Goal
b: Pontypridd, Wales, 29 Jun 1935
QPR: 1957
Football League: 1-0. **FAC:** 0-0. **FLC:** 0-0.
Other: 1-0. **Total:** 2-0.

Bob's actual first team debut came in the Southern Professional Floodlight Cup, a competition which could be considered as a forerunner to, even though regionalised, the League Cup.
Debut: 6 Nov 1957 v Reading (A) 2-5 SPF Cup first round replay.

FURLONG Paul Anthony

Striker 6′ 0″ 13st 8lbs
b: Wood Green, London, 1 Oct 1968
QPR: (Loan) Aug 2000
Football League: 3-1. **FAC:** 0-0. **FLC:** 0-0.
Other: 0-0. **Total:** 3-1.
QPR: Aug 2002
Football League: 171-57. **FAC:** 3-0. **FLC:** 4-0.
Other: 1-0. **Total:** 179-57.

A big, strong striker who holds the ball up well and shoots with power and accuracy, Paul unfortunately injured the tendon to his patella (knee), which led to the premature end of his loan period. After a return to Birmingham City and then a further loan period, he signed permanently for QPR, and became a near ever-present before being released in May 2007.
Debut: 20 Aug 2000 v Crystal Palace (A) 1-1 Div 1.

Paul Furlong

Kevin Gallen

G

GALLEN Kevin Andrew
GARDNER Andrew
GARDNER William
GAUL W
GAYLARD Hugh H
GERMAN Antonio
GIBBONS John William
GIBBS Derek William
GILBERG Harold
GILFILLAN John E
GILHOOLEY Michael
GILLARD Ian Terrance
GILLESPIE J
GILMORE Henry Patrick
GITTINS Alfred G
GIVENS Daniel Joseph
GLOVER Allan Richard
GNOHERE Arthur
GODDARD George
GODDARD Paul
GOFTON George
GOLDIE William
GOLDING Norman James
GOODIER Edward
GOODMAN William R
GOODRIDGE Gregory St Clair
GORKSS Kaspars
GOUGH Claude William McKinley
GOULD Harry L
GRAHAM Malcolm
GRAHAM Mark Roland
GRAHAM Richard Stephen
GRANT George M
GRAY Andrew A
GRAY Thomas
GREEN Thomas
GREER William H O
GREGORY Clarence
GREGORY John (Jack)
GREGORY John Charles
GRETTON Thomas
GRIFFITHS Leroy
GRIMSDELL Ernest Frederick
GULLAN Stanley K
GUY-WATSON H

GALLEN Kevin Andrew

Striker 5' 11" 12st 10lbs
b: Chiswick, Middlesex, 21 Sep1975
QPR: Sep 1992
Football League: 171-36. **FAC:** 8-2. **FLC:** 12-2.
Other: 0-0. **Total:** 191-40.
QPR: Nov 2001
Football/Premier League: 197-54. **FAC:** 3-0.
FLC: 8-3. **Other:** 0-0. **Total:** 208-57.
Honours: England school & youth caps.
4 U21 caps.

Kevin had a phenomenal scoring rate as a youth player when he netted 126 goals in two seasons, which even surpassed the earlier record of Jimmy Greaves. Kevin became a strong, quick and natural striker with a hard shot. He was with QPR initially, from a 17 year old, for eight years, and appeared in nearly 200 senior matches. He then moved to Huddersfield under the Bosman ruling. But he was plagued by injuries, and similarly at Barnsley, before manager Steve Parkin brought him back to QPR, where he was a near ever-present between 2002/03 and 2004/05. A great servant to the club, Kevin was released in the summer of 2007 and went on to help the MK Dons to promotion to League One.
Debut: 20 Aug 1994 v Manchester United (A) 0-2 PL.

GARDNER Andrew

(OL) Wing 5' 8" 11st 7lbs
b: Milton, Glasgow, Scotland, 17 Apr 1877
QPR: 1905
Southern League: 5-0. **FAC:** 0-0. **FLC:** 0-0.
Other: 0-0. **Total:** 5-0.

Andy was a fleet-footed sharp-shooter but it didn't happen at QPR. He finished up as a left-wing reserve player, although once he played at half-back.
Debut: 2 Sep 1905 v New Brompton (H) 4-0 SL Div 1.

GARDNER William

(IF) Mid 5' 7" 12st 0lbs
b: Langley Moor, Durham, 7 Jun 1893
QPR: Mar 1923
Football League: 2-0. **FAC:** 0-0. **FLC:** 0-0.
Other: 0-0. **Total:** 2-0.
Honours: 2 England Amateur caps. Amateur Cup runner's-up medal. Represented the North Eastern League.

Wally was a top class forward who was much sought after by the big clubs. Chunky and powerful he played in all three inside-forward berths, and he certainly turned it on after leaving QPR, scoring some 80 goals in 150 matches. In 1933 Wally retired from football to help run the family business.
Debut: 7 Apr 1923 v Merthyr Town (H) 1-1 Div 3 (S).

GAUL W

(CF) Striker
QPR: 1912
Southern League: 14-7. **FAC:** 0-0. **FLC:** 0-0.
Other: 0-0. **Total:** 14-7.

It is known that this man was an amateur and joined the "Footballers Battalion" during the latter part of 1914. Nothing else is known about him except that he was the sixth centre-forward to be tried during his single season.
Debut: 21 Dec 1912 v Crystal Palace (H) 2-0 SL Div 1.

GAYLARD Hugh H

(RB) Defender
QPR: 1899
Southern League: 4-0. **FAC:** 3-0. **FLC:** 0-0.
Other: 0-0. **Total:** 7-0.

Hugh was an amateur who regularly played for Uxbridge but turned-out for QPR when the usual right-back was unable to play.
Debut: 16 Dec 1899 v Bristol Rovers (H) 3-0 SL Div 1.

GERMAN Antonio

Striker
QPR: Mar 2009
Football League: 3-0. **FAC:** 0-0. **FLC:** 0-0.
Other: 0-0. **Total:** 3-0.
Debut: 14 Mar 2009 v Southampton (A) 0-0 Championship.

GIBBONS John William

(CF) Striker
b: Charlton, London, 8 Apr 1925
QPR: Dec 1947
Football League: 8-2. **FAC:** 0-0. **FLC:** 0-0.
Other: 0-0. **Total:** 8-2.

George Smith, who was the captain of QPR during their championship season of 1947/48, became the manager of Ipswich Town upon retirement from playing, and Johnny was his first capture on the transfer market as a manager. The centre-forward was unsuccessful at Portman Road and he ended his career coaching the youngsters at White Hart Lane.
Debut: 23 Oct 1948 v West Ham United (H) 2-1 Div 2.

GIBBS Derek William

(WH) Def 5' 10" 11st 7lbs
b: Fulham, London, 22 Dec 1934
QPR: Aug 1963
Football League: 27-0. **FAC:** 2-0. **FLC:** 0-0.
Other: 0-0. **Total:** 29-0.

Alec Stock, who had acquired Gibbs' services for Leyton Orient in 1960, had been so keen to sign him for QPR that he had forgotten to register him before he played. The club was fined £40 for this misdemeanour. Derek was a dependable player who could be, and was, utilised in any position.
Debut: 24 Aug 1964 v Oldham Athletic (A) 1-2 Div 3.

GILBERG Harold

(IF) Mid 5' 7" 11st 2lbs
b: Tottenham, London, 27 Jun 1923
d: Torquay, 16 Sep 1994
QPR: Aug 1951
Football League: 66-12. **FAC:** 4-0. **FLC:** 0-0.
Other: 0-0. **Total:** 70-12.

His father played for Tunbridge Wells Rangers but Harry was taken on by the Spurs ground staff as a 14 year old in 1937 while still at school. He served the club's junior team for five years and made his first team debut in a wartime fixture. However, in the 10 years he was at the club, Harry played just 16 times. During the war, Warrant Officer Gilberg served with Lancaster bombers and completed more than 30 operational flights. After his transfer to QPR he settled into a fine partnership with Bert Addinall and continued with it at Brighton & Hove Albion where they were both transferred together. Harry suffered from repeated knee problems, which brought about his enforced retirement in 1956.

He lived in Broxbourne, Herts, but while on holiday in Torquay in 1994, he suddenly collapsed and died.
Debut: 18 Aug 1951 v West Ham United (H) 2-0 Div 2.

GILFILLAN John E

Goal 6' 0" 12st 0lbs
b: Townhill, Cowdenbeath, Scotland, 29 Jun 1896
d: Portsmouth, 2 Jan 1976
QPR: 1937
Football League: 21-0. **FAC:** 2-0. **FLC:** 0-0.
Other: 0-0. **Total:** 23-0.
Honours: Scottish Cup runner's-up medal. 2 FA Cup runner's-up medals.

John, who is something of a legend in Portsmouth, kept goal at QPR in 1937 at the age of 41, sharing the Number 1 spot with Billy Mason. John's grandson Steve Mills, carried on the tradition and kept goal for Southampton from 1972 until 1976. John died in St Mary's Hospital, Portsmouth in 1976.
Debut: 16 Oct 1937 v Reading (A) 0-1 Div 3 (S).

GILHOOLEY Michael

(CH) CD 6' 0" 12st 11lbs
b: Glencraig, Fife, Scotland, 26 Nov 1896
QPR: May 1927
Football League: 9-0. **FAC:** 0-0. **FLC:** 0-0.
Other: 0-0. **Total:** 9-0.
Honours: 1 cap for Scotland.

An outstanding talented central defender,

Mike was signed by Celtic at the age of 16. He was so dominating in the air at Hull City that he earned the nickname of "Rubberneck" among his colleagues and spectators alike. Mike's next club, Sunderland, broke the transfer record to secure him, paying £5,250. However, dogged by injuries which undoubtedly prevented him enjoying a longer period of success, he arrived at QPR but was only to play a few matches.
Debut: 27 Aug 1927 v Newport County (H) 4-2 Div 3 (S).

GILLARD Ian Terrance

(LB) Def 6' 0" 13st 5lbs
b: Hammersmith, London, 9 Oct 1950
QPR: Oct 1968
Football League: 408-9. **FAC:** 36-1. **FLC:** 33-1.
Other: 8-0. **Total:** 485-11.
Honours: 5 England caps at U23 level. 3 full England caps. 1st Div runner's-up medal. FA Cup runner's-up medal.

Ian was a strong and flexible defender who on the ball was confident at going forward with the attack and constructive as well. He joined QPR as a 16 year old apprentice, making his first team debut at 18. He began to carve out a regular place in the team during the 1969/70 season. Ian eventually made the third most appearances in the club's history, over a period of almost 14 years. In nearly 500 matches he filled the left-back position magnificently, and scored several fine goals, a memorable one being a 30 yard drive from a Stan Bowles free-kick in the League Cup at Southend United. His last appearance for the club was, fittingly, the FA Cup final replay in 1982. He then moved to Aldershot, initially as player-coach, before hanging up his boots in 1986.
Debut: 23 Nov 1968 v Nottingham Forest (H) 2-1 Div 1.

Ian Gillard

GILLESPIE J

(RB) Def
b: Scotland, 1886
QPR: 1908
Southern League: 1-0. **FAC:** 0-0. **FLC:** 0-0.
Other: 0-0. **Total:** 1-0.
Gillespie appeared just once in the side when John McDonald was absent.
Debut: 5 Dec 1908 v Millwall (H) 2-2 SL Div 1.

GILMORE Henry Patrick

(LH) Def 5' 11" 12st 0lbs
b: West Hartlepool, Co Durham, 1913
QPR: May 1937
Football League: 6-0. **FAC:** 1-0. **FLC:** 0-0.
Other: 3-0. **Total:** 10-0.

At QPR he stood in for Dickie March on several occasions. Although Pat was at Hull City twice, he never appeared in a League or Cup match for them, although on the second occasion he played in the wartime league.
Debut: 24 Dec 1938 v Reading (H) 2-2 Div 3 (S).

GITTINS Alfred G

(IL) Striker 5' 9" 11st 4lbs
b: Manchester, July 1886
QPR: 1907
Southern League: 42-17. **FAC:** 2-0. **FLC:** 0-0.
Other: 2-0. **Total:** 46-17.
Honours: Southern League championship medal.

Alf was recognised as one of the most dangerous men in the country at going forward. Nowhere at his other clubs was he so successful at scoring goals, finishing as top marksman in the club's first championship winning season.
Debut: 2 Sep 1907 v Tottenham Hotspur (H) 3-3 SL Div 1.

GIVENS Daniel Joseph

Striker 5' 11" 11st 2lbs
b: Dublin, Eire, 9 Aug 1949
QPR: (£40,000) Jul 1972

Don Givens

Football League: 242-77. **FAC:** 24-10. **FLC:** 20-6. **Other:** 8-7. **Total:** 294-100.
Honours: 56 Eire International caps. 2nd Div runner's-up medal. 1st Div runner's-up medal. 2nd Div promotion medal. Swiss League championship medal.

Despite his given name of Daniel, he has always been known as "Don" in the football world. The son of a champion jockey hurdler, Don was a potent, intelligent and dangerous finisher and an aggressive, mobile front-runner. He won the first of his many international caps three months before his debut for Manchester United.

Don topped the goalscorers list for QPR on four separate occasions and was the leading marksman when the club achieved their best ever League place in 1976. Don played for several clubs both before and after his six years with QPR.

At Manchester United he made only five first team appearances before his first move, to Luton Town for a moderate fee. He finished his playing career in Switzerland, playing for Xamax forsix years, winning a championship medal (the club's first such victory), before becoming the club coach.

Debut: 12 Aug 1972 v Swindon Town (A) 2-2 Div 2.

GLOVER Allan Richard

Mid 5' 9" 11st 2lbs
b: Staines, Middlesex, 21 Oct 1950
QPR: Mar 1968
Football League: 6-0. **FAC:** 1-0. **FLC:** 0-0. **Other:** 0-0. **Total:** 7-0.

Allan joined WBA in a deal involving Clive Clark returning to Loftus Road. A clever and witty winger-cum-midfielder who was unlucky enough to receive

a bad ankle injury in 1974 which halted his career and he subsequently never shrugged off the injury. His loan spell at Southend United was the shortest on record, for it lasted all of 30 seconds, before he was carried off injured.
Debut: 11 Jan 1969 v West Ham United (H) 1-1 Div 1.

GNOHERE Arthur

Def 6′ 0″ 13st 7lbs
b: Yamoussoukro, Ivory Coast, 20 Nov 1978
QPR: 2003
Football League: 21-0. **FAC:** 0-0. **FLC:** 1-0. **Other:** 0-0. **Total:** 22-0.

A strong central defender who is commanding in the air and who boasts vast experience, Arthur became popular among the players and coaching staff for his committed displays. Signed, initially on loan, from Burnley for whom he had made around 100 appearances, the defender proved adequate cover for injuries. He fast became admired by the Rangers faithful, as he proved a solid defensive partner in a number of different combinations but his future ultimately lay away from Loftus Road and he moved on in 2005.
Debut: 6 Sep 2003 v Colchester United (A) 2-2 Championship.

GODDARD George

(CF) Striker 5′ 10″ 11st 7lbs
b: Gomshall, Surrey, 20 Dec 1903
d: 24 Mar 1987
QPR: 1926
Football League: 243-174. **FAC:** 16-12. **FLC:** 0-0. **Other:** 0-0. **Total:** 259-186.
Honours: 1 county cap as an amateur.

Arthur Gnohere

Paul Goddard

George is the club's top goalscorer by far, leading the list of Loftus Road centre-forwards, and it is highly unlikely that his total will ever be exceeded. A butcher by trade, although at the time of his signing for QPR, he worked in a bus garage. He signed for the club after scoring over 200 goals in two years for Redhill. George was the QPR top marksman for seven consecutive years, and he headed the Third Division Southern section scoring list in 1930 with 39. Although he played in less than 20 matches for Wolves, he scored a dozen goals in that brief spell, all of them coming in the 1933/34 season. On his retirement from football he took over a butcher's shop in the centre of London and later ran a successful cafe. George died in 1987 at Kingston-upon-Thames.
Debut: 11 Sep 1926 v Brentford (A) 2-4 Div 3 (S).

GODDARD Paul

Striker 5′ 8″ 11st 8lbs
b: Harlington, Middlesex, 12 Oct 1959
QPR: Jul 1977
Football League: 70-23. **FAC:** 0-0. **FLC:** 5-0.
Other: 0-0. **Total:** 75-23.
Honours: 8 England U21 caps. 1 England B cap. 1 full cap. 2nd Div championship medal. League Cup runner's-up medal. Football League championship medal.

Paul was not a tall powerful centre-forward in the traditional sense but a small man who knew how to control and shield the ball. He had a poacher's instinct in front of goal and a willingness to play for the team. Paul won his only cap for his country when he came on as a substitute and scored. After his playing days were over he became coach to Ipswich Town in May 1994, caretaker manager in December of the same year, and finally became assistant coach in 1995.
Debut: 11 Apr 1978 v Arsenal (H) 2-1 Div 1.

GOFTON George

(CF) Striker
b: Hartlepool, 28 Feb 1912
QPR: 1932
Football League: 7-8. **FAC:** 4-0. **FLC:** 0-0.
Other: 0-0. **Total:** 11-8.

George was just one of four centre-forwards to be tried in the senior squad during the season. This was the period when the club moved to the White City and Archie Mitchell took over as manager, experimenting with two centre-forwards. Goddard was the main striker along with Gofton between October and December. Collins was then tried in place of Gofton between January and March and finally Blackman came into the side until the season's end. Mitchell was sacked in May 1933 and Gofton stayed with the club for another two years but he never played first team football again.
Debut: 22 Oct 1932 v Coventry City (H) 3-3 Div 3 (S).

GOLDIE William

(CF) Striker
b: Scotland
QPR: 1900
Southern League: 5-1. **FAC:** 4-2. **FLC:** 0-0.
Other: 0-0. **Total:** 9-3.

Goldie followed Bedingfield, after the latter

was snapped up by Portsmouth at the end of the previous season.
Debut: 8 Sep 1900 v Swindon Town (H) 7-1 SL Div 1.

GOLDING Norman James

(OR) Wing
b: Southwark, London, 23 Jan 1937
QPR: Aug 1959
Football League: 30-6. **FAC:** 1-0. **FLC:** 0-0.
Other: 1-0. **Total:** 32-6.

One of Alec Stock's first signings for QPR, Norman shared the outside-right spot with Pat Kerrins. Astonishingly he scored five goals in his first five matches.
Debut: 14 Sep 1959 v York City (H) 0-0 Div 3.

GOODIER Edward

(CH) CD 6′ 1″ 12st 8lbs
b: Farnworth, Lancs, 15 Oct 1902
d: Farnworth, 4 Nov 1967
QPR: Nov 1931
Football League: 139-2. **FAC:** 13-0. **FLC:** 0-0.
Other: 4-0. **Total:** 156-2.

Ted left Oldham Athletic because of a disagreement over a benefit payment and both he and Adlam joined QPR for a combined fee of £1,500. When Goodier arrived at the club, this tall, elegant player started as a wing-half but after a season he was turned into a successful centre-half. After five seasons he was transferred to Watford for a fee plus a player. The following year he was introduced to managerial duties during which he served Rochdale for five years. During the Second World War he became the caretaker/manager of Birmingham City and in June 1952 took over the manager's job at Wigan Athletic. Finally he ended up as the manager of Oldham Athletic from May 1956 until June 1958.
Debut: 14 Nov 1931 v Cardiff City (A) 4-0 Div 3 (S).

GOODMAN William R

(CH) CD
b: Islington, London, 1894
QPR: 1923
Football League: 1-0. **FAC:** 0-0. **FLC:** 0-0.
Other: 0-0. **Total:** 1-0.

Goodman was signed originally as a centre-half but he made just a single appearance for QPR on the left wing, in a rare victory during the season of the club's first re-election year.
Debut: 18 Apr 1924 v Norwich City (H) 2-1 Div 3 (S).

GOODRIDGE Gregory St Clair

(OL) Mid 5′ 6″ 10st 2lbs
b: Barbados, 10 Jul 1971

Kaspars Gorkss

QPR: (£350,000) Aug 1995
Premier League: 7-1. **FAC:** 1-0. **FLC:** 1-0.
Other: 0-0. **Total:** 9-1.
Honours: Barbados international.

Greg was a skilful and exciting winger with a tremendously long throw-in. The captain of the Barbados international side, he never played a full match for QPR always coming on as a substitute. He was predominately a left-sided player who liked to run full-backs ragged.
Debut: 14 Oct 1995 v Newcastle United (H) 2-3 PL.

GORKSS Kaspars

Def 6′ 3″ 13st 5lbs
b: Riga, Latvia, 6 Nov 1981
QPR: (£250,000 + player) 2008
Football League: 31-0. **FAC:** 2-0. **FLC:** 2-0.
Other: 0-0. **Total:** 35-0.
Honours: 12 Latvia U21 caps. 21 full caps.

Rangers ended their search for a centre-half with the capture of Kaspars Gorkss in late July 2008. The Latvian international had impressed during his first campaign in English football and was allegedly

the interest of numerous Championship clubs plus Scottish giants Rangers. As it was, the Rangers that Kaspars signed for were the ones at Loftus Road and the defender quickly slotted into the Rangers defence, making more than 30 League appearances during his first season in London.
Debut: 9 Aug 2008 v Barnsley (H) 2-1 Championship.

GOUGH Claude William McKinley

(LH) Def
b: South Cerney, Gloucestershire, 17 Oct 1901
d: South Cerney, 16 May 1963
QPR: 1926
Football League: 19-0. **FAC:** 0-0. **FLC:** 0-0.
Other: 0-0. **Total:** 19-0.

Much was expected of Gough as a youngster, but it never materialised. He was given an extended run in the side but his form was sporadic and he was released at the end of the 1926/27 season.
Debut: 28 Aug 1926 v Crystal Palace (A) 1-2 Div 3 (S).

GOULD Harry L

Goal
b: London
QPR: 1920
Football League: 2-0. **FAC:** 0-0. **FLC:** 0-0.
Other: 0-0. **Total:** 2-0.

Gould was a policeman who was an amateur goalkeeper and filled in when the other regulars were out injured.
Debut: 26 Mar 1921 v Newport County (H) 2-0 Div 3.

GRAHAM Malcolm

(IL) Striker
b: Hall Green, Wakefield, Yorkshire, 26 Jan 1934
QPR: Jul 1963
Football League: 21-7. **FAC:** 1-1. **FLC:** 1-0.
Other: 0-0. **Total:** 23-8.
Honours: 2nd Div runner's-up medal.

Mal was a short and bustling forward. Some spectators loved him, some disliked him. Some talked of his "Puskas-like left foot". Alec Stock acquired him from his old club, Leyton Orient, however, he was the second choice at all his other clubs.
Debut: 24 Aug 1963 v Oldham Athletic (A) 1-2 Div 3.

GRAHAM Mark Roland

Mid 5' 7" 10st 8lbs
b: Newry, Northern Ireland, 24 Oct 1974
QPR: May 1993
Premier League: 18-1. **FAC:** 2-0. **FLC:** 3-0.
Other: 0-0. **Total:** 23-1.
Honours: School, Youth and B level for Northern Ireland.

Mark, after a lengthy period at QPR, soon moved out of League football and became settled at the non-League level where he moved around quite frequently. He signed for Billericay (in February 2003) along with his brother, and former QPR player, Richard.
Debut: 20 Aug 1994 v Manchester United (A) 0-2 PL.

GRAHAM Richard Stephen

Mid 5' 8" 10st 6lbs
b: Newry, Northern Ireland, 5 Aug 1979
QPR: Aug 1996
Football League: 2-0. **FAC:** 0-0. **FLC:** 0-0.
Other: 0-0. **Total:** 2-0.
Honours: Youth and 2 U21 caps for Northern Ireland.

Richard is the younger brother of Mark and he can perform equally as well, either on the wing or in the central midfield. He was given a free transfer in the summer of 2002, when he moved to Chesham United, and the following February, along with his brother signed on for Billericay Town.
Debut: 29 Sep 1998 v Wolverhampton Wanderers (A) 2-1 Div 1.

GRANT George M

(RH) Mid
b: Plumstead, London, 1891
QPR: 1920
Football League: 69-1. **FAC:** 3-0. **FLC:** 0-0.
Other: 0-0. **Total:** 72-1.
Honours: London Challenge Cup runner's-up medal.

George was an ever-present in the QPR team in their first Football League season. He played in 54 League games for Arsenal from 1913 to 1915.
Debut: 28 Aug 1920 v Watford (H) 1-2 Div 3.

GRAY Andrew A

Mid 5' 11" 13st 3lbs
b: Brixton, London, 22 Feb 1964
QPR: (£400,000) Feb 1989
Football League: 11-2. **FAC:** 0-0. **FLC:** 0-0.
Other: 0-0. **Total:** 11-2.
Honours: 1 full England cap. 2 England U21 caps. 2nd Div runner's-up medal.

Andy was a forceful player, with a good all-round technique that encompassed a fierce shot and a long throw in. He was a hard working, muscular midfielder who was a late entry into the professional ranks.
Debut: 4 Feb 1989 v Millwall (H) 1-2 Div 1.

GRAY Thomas

(OR) Wing 5' 7" 11st 6lbs
b: Grimsby, Lincolnshire, 1876
QPR: 1900
Southern League: 28-8. **FAC:** 4-2. **FLC:** 0-0.
Other: 0-0. **Total:** 32-10.

Tommy was noted in the *Football Chat* magazine as a sharp forward who was not afraid of being in a scrimmage. Ever-present in his only season with the club, he was a firm favourite with the crowd.
Debut: 1 Sep 1900 v Bristol Rovers (A) 1-2 SL Div 1.

GREEN Thomas

(CF) Striker 5' 8" 11st 7lbs
b: Rock Ferry, Cheshire, 25 Nov 1883
QPR: 1906
Southern League: 37-2. **FAC:** 2-0. **FLC:** 0-0.
Other: 0-0. **Total:** 39-2.
Honours: Lancashire Combination championship medal.

Tommy was a very fast forward with a furious shot from either foot. Outside-right was his natural position but he preferred to play at centre-forward.
Debut: 1 Sep 1906 v Luton Town (A) 1-1 SL Div 1.

GREER William H O

(IF) Mid
b: County Derry, Ireland
QPR: 1908
Southern League: 32-7. **FAC:** 2-0. **FLC:** 0-0.
Other: 0-0. **Total:** 34-7.
Honours: 3 Irish international caps.

Bill was one of the first players to win a cap for his country while with QPR. He played the game with terrific zest and a terrier-like attitude.
Debut: 25 Dec 1908 v Norwich City (H) 2-2 SL Div 1.

GREGORY Clarence

(OL) Wing
b: Willinghall, Warwickshire
QPR: 1922
Football League: 24-1. **FAC:** 0-0. **FLC:** 0-0.
Other: 0-0. **Total:** 24-1.

Clarence joined QPR to be with his brother Jack but he only stayed with the club for one season, before stepping down to non-League level.
Debut: 26 Aug 1922 v Watford (H) 1-2 Div 3 (S).

GREGORY John (Jack)

(IF) Mid
b: Willinghall, Warwickshire
QPR: 1912
Southern/Football League: 199-44. **FAC:** 12-4.
FLC: 0-0. **Other:** 0-0. **Total:** 211-48.

Jack was – presumably the older – brother of Clarence, who came to the notice of the club while he was playing for Willenhall Swifts in the Birmingham League, where he was selected to play in a Junior international match against Scotland. He scored 19 goals for Willenhall in 1912 before the Rangers signed him.

John Gregory

Jack played for QPR for 10 years making over a century of appearances in wartime football and together with his peacetime games he totalled over 300. Along with his brother Clarence, the pair played together at QPR for one season, before moving into non-League football in 1923.

Debut: 7 Dec 1912 v Watford (H) 2-0 SL Div 1.

GREGORY John Charles

Mid 6′ 1″ 11st 5lbs
b: Scunthorpe, Lincolnshire, 11 May 1954
QPR: (£300,000) Jun 1981
Football League: 161-36. **FAC:** 9-1. **FLC:** 16-4.
Other: 4-1. **Total:** 190-42.
Honours: 6 England caps. FA Cup runner's-up medal. 2 2nd Div championship medals.

The son of a professional footballer, John was a highly versatile player who brought a good deal of experience to the young Loftus Road starlets. Gregory had a proper "apprenticeship" in football, after appearing in approximately 350 matches before he came to QPR in 1981. A Terry Venables buy, John spent four years at Loftus Road, appearing in the losing FA Cup final against Spurs in 1982, and he was ever-present in the team that won the Second Division title in 1982/83.

John also appeared for England during his Loftus Road period. He was a neat passer of the ball, able to dictate the tempo of the game and had a lot of stamina. He was an elegant type of player, upright and controlled, and an uncompromising tackler who would get "stuck-in". After his playing days were over he took up coaching at Portsmouth, followed by the manager's job, but this ended with dismissal 12 months later. John worked with Brian Little at Leicester City and accompanied him to Aston Villa in 1994. He was appointed manager of Wycombe Wanderers in 1996, and then the same at Aston Villa followed by the Derby County hot seat in 2002. John was appointed manager at Loftus Road in September 2006 but was sacked just over a year later despite keeping Rangers in the Championship the previous May.

Debut: 29 Sep 1981 v Wrexham (A) 3-1 Div 2.

GRETTON Thomas

Goal 6′ 0″ 12st 0lbs
b: Walsall, Staffordshire
QPR: 1929
Football League: 4.0. **FAC:** 0-0. **FLC:** 0-0.
Other: 0-0. **Total:** 4-0.

Tom was the reserve team goalkeeper at all of his three clubs. At QPR he deputised for Cunningham who was injured at the time but was released at the end of the season.

Debut: 7 Dec 1929 v Swindon Town (A) 2-2 Div 3 (S).

GRIFFITHS Leroy

Striker 5′ 11″ 13st 5lbs
b: London, 30 Dec 1976
QPR: (£40,000) May 2001
Football League: 36-3. **FAC:** 1-0. **FLC:** 0-0.
Other: 0-0. **Total:** 37-3.

A striker who could also play in a wide position, Leroy was noted by the fans after scoring a spectacular goal against Chelsea in a pre-season friendly in August 2001. He featured regularly in the senior squad in the 2001/02 season, but only made a few appearances in the next, and negotiated a termination of his contract during the summer of 2003 when he signed for Farnborough Town.

Debut: 11 Aug 2001 v Stoke City (H) 1-0 Div 2.

GRIMSDELL Ernest Frederick

(LB) Def 6′ 1″ 12st 10lbs
b: Watford, Hertfordshire, 1892
d: Bushy, Hertfordshire, Sept 1947
QPR: Aug 1920
Football League: 20-0. **FAC:** 1-0. **FLC:** 0-0.
Other: 0-0. **Total:** 21-0.
Honours: 2 England Amateur caps.
Represented the Army v Royal Navy and the FA v Cambridge University.

An accomplished full-back who turned professional at QPR (he had a famous brother, Arthur, who played for Spurs). Unfortunately Ernie was so badly injured in the 1922/23 season that he subsequently took up refereeing and became a Football League linesman.

Debut: 4 Sep 1920 v Watford (A) 2-0 Div 3.

GULLAN Stanley K

Goal 5′ 10″ 12st 2lbs
b: Edinburgh, Scotland, 20 Jan 1920
QPR: Jul 1949
Football League: 48-0. **FAC:** 0-0. **FLC:** 0-0.
Other: 0-0. **Total:** 48-0.

Stan was solid in frame and a very good shot stopper. Barry Hugman's *A-Z of Players Records* gives his birthplace as Edinburgh, while Rothmans Annual for 2000/01 gives it as Southend, Essex. Stan was a civil servant who apparently played most of his football in Scotland.

Debut: 6 Sep 1950 v Bury (A) 1-0 Div 2.

GUY-WATSON H

Goal
QPR: 1905
Southern League: 1-0. **FAC:** 0-0. **FLC:** 0-0.
Other: 0-0. **Total:** 1-0.
An amateur who played in the very last match of the 1905/06 season, during which QPR tried no fewer than five keepers.
Debut: 28 Apr 1906 v Bristol Rovers (H) 7-0 SL Div 1.

H

HAGGAN John
HALEY William Thomas
HALL Ernest W
HALL Fitzroy Benjamin
HAMILTON John Eley
HAMILTON John Haggarty
HAMILTON Lewis
HAMILTON William R
HAMMOND Joseph Henry
HANDFORD Thomas W
HANNAH James
HARKOUK Rachid
HARPER Lee Charles Phillip
HARRIS Allan J
HARRIS Bernard
HARRIS George T
HARRIS Neil
HARRISON James H
HART Ernest
HART George
HARTBURN John H
HARTWELL Ambrose Walter
HASTY Patrick Joseph
HATELEY Mark Wayne
HATTON Cyril
HAWKINS Bertram W
HAWLEY Frederick W
HAYWOOD Adam B
HAZELL Anthony Phillip
HAZELL Robert Joseph
HEATH William J
HEATHCOTE Wilfred
HEBDEN George Horace Robert
HEINOLA Antti Juhani
HELGUSON Heidar
HELLAWELL Michael Stephen
HERRERA Roberto
HIGGINS Alexander John
HIGGINS Dennis
HIGGINS Ronald Valentine
HILL Charles John
HILL Gordon Alexander
HILL Joseph
HILL Leonard G
HILL William L
HIRST Henry
HISLOP Matthew
HITCH Alfred
HITCHCOCK Ernest
HODGE Steven Brian
HOLD Oscar
HOLLINS John William
HOLLOWAY Ian Scott
HOOPER Harold
HOTEN Ralph Vincent
HOWE Ernest James
HOWE Harold G
HOWELL Andrew
HOWES Arthur
HUCKER Peter I
HUDSON Stanley R
HUMPHREYS Percy
HUNT Ronald G
HURRELL William P
HURST William

Fitz Hall

HAGGAN John

(CH) CD
b: Chester-le-Street, Durham, 16 Dec 1896
d: 1982
QPR: 1919
Southern League: 1-0. **FAC:** 0-0. **FLC:** 0-0.
Other: 0-0. **Total:** 1-0.

John replaced Archie Mitchell in the side, the latter being absent from the senior squad on the very last day of the season.

Debut: 26 Apr 1920 v Southend United (A) 2-2 SL Div 1.

HALEY William Thomas

(IF) Mid 5′ 8″ 10st 8lbs
b: Woolwich, London, 16 Feb 1904
d: Rochester, 20 Jan 1960
QPR: May 1931
Football League: 17-5. **FAC:** 0-0. **FLC:** 0-0.
Other: 0-0. **Total:** 17-5.

Bill was in dispute with Charlton Athletic and it took around one year before he was paid the wages owing to him. For his transfer, Derby County paid £1,000 plus the gate receipts of a match between the two clubs played at the Valley during the 1926/27 season. He scored on his debut for QPR but Billy soon left the professional football scene at the age of 27 to concentrate on running a sweetshop in Woolwich, until 1933. He left the district to take over a public house in Sheerness called The Goat, later he kept licensed premises in Edenbridge. At the time of his death he was the proprietor of The Gore Court Arms in Sittingbourne.

Debut: 31 Aug 1931 v Bristol Rovers (A) 1-1 Div 3 (S).

HALL Ernest W

(LB) Def 6′ 1″ 12st 10lbs
b: Barnsdale, Coventry
QPR: 1931
Football League: 61-0. **FAC:** 9-0. **FLC:** 0-0.
Other: 0-0. **Total:** 70-0.

Ernie was a big, tough defender who formerly worked in an iron foundry before signing for QPR. He finally left for Chester FC and turned out for them in over a hundred matches, until the start of the Second World War, becoming the assistant trainer and finally trainer.

Debut: 9 Oct 1931 v Swindon Town (H) 1-2 Div 3 (S).

HALL Fitzroy Benjamin

Def 6′ 4″ 13st 0lbs
b: London, 20 Dec 1980
QPR: 2008
Football League: 38-2. **FAC:** 2-0. **FLC:** 2-0.
Other: 0-0. **Total:** 42-2.

When Rangers signed Fitz on a four and a half year deal in the January 2008 transfer window they captured not just a central defender with vast Premiership experience from his time with Crystal Palace and Wigan Athletic, they also added a player who has the versatility to play in central midfield to their squad. Fitz began his career as a West Ham United youth player but was released at the age of 15 – on the same day as Paul Konchesky, Bobby Zamora and Jlloyd Samuel – and was once told that he wasn't good enough to become a professional footballer. Luckily for QPR, that prophecy has proved untrue…

Debut: 5 Jan 2008 v Chelsea (A) 0-1 FAC third round.

Fitz Hall

HAMILTON John Eley

(OR) Wing
b: Nottingham, 23 Jan 1902
d: Nottingham, 16 Jan 1980
QPR: Jun 1926
Football League: 10-0. **FAC:** 0-0. **FLC:** 0-0.
Other: 0-0. **Total:** 10-0.

After playing under a pseudonym and scoring twice in a benefit match in March 1921, John joined Watford. He only played two matches however, before moving north to Blackpool. At QPR he was one of five wingers to be tried in 1926 and he was never able to impress.

Debut: 28 Aug 1926 v Crystal Palace (A) 1-2 Div 3 (S).

HAMILTON John Haggarty

(OR) Wing 5′ 6″ 11st 0lbs
b: Glasgow, Scotland, 1880
QPR: 1902
Southern League: 47-3. **FAC:** 3-0. **FLC:** 0-0.
Other: 0-0. **Total:** 50-3.

In common with many others, John travelled the soccer circuit in those early football days. Along with John Blackwood, he was transferred to West Ham United just before Boxing Day, 1904. It was to no avail however, for the Hammers lost their next four matches, although Blackwood did at least get on the scoresheet.

Debut: 3 Sep 1902 v Wellingborough (H) 2-0 SL Div 1.

HAMILTON Lewis

Def 6′ 0″ 11st 8lbs
b: Derby, 21 Nov 1984
QPR: 2004
Football League: 1-0. **FAC:** 0-0. **FLC:** 0-0.
Other: 0-0. **Total:** 1-0.
Debut: 19 Apr 2005 v Burnley (A) 0-2 Championship.

Lee Harper

HAMILTON William R

Striker 6' 1" 12st 0lbs
b: Belfast, Northern Ireland, 9 May 1957
QPR: (£25,000) Apr 1978
Football League: 12-2. **FAC:** 1-0. **FLC:** 0-0.
Other: 0-0. **Total:** 13-2.
Honours: 41 Northern Ireland international caps. 1 U21 cap. Cup & League double of Northern Ireland. 3rd Div championship medal. 2nd Div championship medal.

Billy was capped at full level within a month of his arrival at Loftus Road but he was not at the club very long before being transferred to Burnley. He was not the quickest of forwards from a standing start but nevertheless a tireless campaigner who never stopped running, although Clive Allen was the preferred striker. Hamilton played over 250 matches for Burnley in a little under five years and upon retirement he took over the managership of Limerick in 1988, followed by the same job at Distillery in 1991.

Debut: 2 Dec 1978 v Bolton Wanderers (H) 1-3 Div 1.

HAMMOND Joseph Henry

(OR) Wing 5' 10" 11st 0lbs
b: West Ham, London, 1909
QPR: 1934
Football League: 18-6. **FAC:** 1-0. **FLC:** 0-0.
Other: 2-1. **Total:** 21-7.

Joe came to prominence with his work team, the London Paper Mills, who won their League in the 1932/33 season, and he was instantly signed by Leytonstone. At QPR, he remained an effective reserve to Emmerson, however, with the arrival of manager Billy Birrell to the club, Joe was soon released.

Debut: 14 Apr 1934 v Southend United (A) 2-0 Div 3 (S).

HANDFORD Thomas W

(OL) Wing
QPR: 1894
QPR: 1900
Southern League: 3-0. **FAC:** 0-0. **FLC:** 0-0.
Other: 0-0. **Total:** 3-0.
Honours: London Cup winner's medal.

Tommy played for the club before they turned pro but kept his amateur status throughout his career. In retirement he became a referee and he was prominent in the minor leagues throughout England, as well as acting as an occasional Football League linesman.

Debut: 14 Sep 1901 v Tottenham Hotspur (A) 0-2 SL Div 1.

HANNAH James

(OL) Wing
b: Glasgow, Scotland
QPR: 1899
Southern League: 17-2: **FAC:** 3-0. **FLC:** 0-0.
Other: 0-0. **Total:** 20-2.
Honours: 1 Scottish international cap. 1 Scottish Cup winner's medal. 3 Football League championship medals.

Jimmy was a fine dribbler and wily wingman, he could play in any frontline position and knew exactly when to part with the ball.

Debut: 25 Nov 1899 v Sheppey (A) 1-3 SL Div 1.

HARKOUK Rachid

For 6' 0" 12st 5lbs
b: Chelsea, London, 19 May 1956
QPR: (£100,000) Jun 1978
Football League: 20-3. **FAC:** 1-0. **FLC:** 3-0.
Other: 0-0. **Total:** 24-3.
Honours: Algerian international. 2nd Div runner's-up medal.

After only a modest number of appearances for QPR, Rachid moved on to Notts County where he made over 150 appearances, until injury forced him to retire.

Debut: 26 Aug 1978 v Nottingham Forest (H) 0-0 Div 1.

HARPER Lee Charles Phillip

Goal 6' 1" 13st 11lbs
b: Chelsea, London, 30 Oct 1971
QPR: (£125,000) Jul 1997
Football League: 118-0. **FAC:** 4-0. **FLC:** 9-0.
Other: 0-0. **Total:** 131-0.

A shot stopper who commands the penalty area with assurance. This earned him the runner-up spot in the supporters' Player of the Year award in 1999/2000. A well built goalkeeper who shared the top spot with Tony Roberts, but then lost it to Ludek Miklosko. However, when the latter was injured, Lee took his chance and never looked back. He was released in the summer of 2001 after four years at Loftus Road, during which time he made over 130 first team appearances. He was unable to command a regular first team place at First Division Walsall and moved on to Northampton after a year, where he was more successful.

Debut: 9 Aug 1997 v Ipswich Town (H) 0-0 Div 1.

HARRIS Allan J

(LB) Def 5' 8" l0st 7lbs
b: Hackney, London, 28 Dec 1942
QPR: (£30,000) Jul 1967
Football League: 94-0. **FAC:** 1-0. **FLC:** 3-0.
Other: 0-0. **Total:** 98-0.
Honours: 3 England school caps. England youth caps. FA Cup runner's-up medal.

Allan was sold to Coventry City without playing a match for Chelsea. When he was transferred back to them in 1966, he played alongside his brother Ron, before moving on to QPR. After his playing days were over he became assistant manager to Terry Venables at Crystal Palace, QPR, Spurs and Barcelona, eventually becoming manager himself at the Spanish club.

Debut: 10 Aug 1967 v Portsmouth (A) 1-1 Div 2.

HARRIS Bernard

(FB) Def 5' 9" 11st 0lbs
b: Sheffield, Yorkshire, 14 Mar 1901

QPR:1929
Football League: 60-0. **FAC:** 7-0. **FLC:** 0-0.
Other: 0-0. **Total:** 67-0.

Bernard was a very useful defender for he could operate at right or left-back. Although playing for several other clubs during a reasonable length Football League career, it was with QPR that he spent the longest period.

Debut: 31 Aug 1929 v Crystal Palace (A) 1-1 Div 3 (S).

HARRIS George T

(LH) Mid 5' 9" 11st 10lbs
b: High Wycombe, 1898
QPR: 1924
Football League: 38-0. **FAC:** 5-0. **FLC:** 0-0.
Other: 0-0. **Total:** 43-0.

George was a reserve player wherever he went, except at QPR where he had a two year stint in the senior squad. At his final League club, Fulham, he scored the only goal of his professional career.

Debut: 10 Sep 1924 v Watford (A) 0-1 Div 3 (S).

HARRIS Neil

(CF) Striker
b: Glasgow, Scotland, 9 Feb 1920
QPR: 1946
Football League: 1-1. **FAC:** 1-1. **FLC:** 0-0.
Other: 0-0. **Total:** 2-2.

Mark Hateley

On 4 December 1946, Neil scored in his debut match for QPR. Three days later he was on the goalscorers' list again, only this time he cracked his head against a goalpost, knocking himself unconscious, fracturing his skull and breaking his pelvis in the process. He never played competitive football again. On his recovery, Neil was made assistant to Dave Mangnall, however, with the leaving of the manager, he moved back to Wales to run an import/export business.

Debut: 4 Dec 1946 v Poole Town (A) 6-0 FA Cup first round replay.

HARRISON James H

(CF) Striker
b: Hammersmith, London, 31 Jul 1928
QPR: 1952
Football League: 6-1. **FAC:** 0-0. **FLC:** 0-0.
Other: 0-0. **Total:** 6-1.

Spotted by a scout playing football on Wormwood Scrubs, Jimmy was given an extended trial, first for Willesden (the QPR nursery side), and then for the senior squad. He was not retained at the end of the 1952/53 season.

Debut: 3 Jan 1953 v Coventry City (A) 0-2 Div 3 (S).

HART Ernest

(IL) Mid
b: Huddersfield, Yorkshire
QPR: 1922
Football League: 5-2. **FAC:** 0-0. **FLC:** 0-0.
Other: 0-0. **Total:** 5-2.

Ernie occasionally came into the 1922/23 side to replace Arthur Chandler when he was out injured. The following season, he left to play for Guildford United (later named City).

Debut: 4 Nov 1922 v Aberdare Athletic (A) 0-0 Div 3 (S).

HART George

(RH) Mid
b: Gosforth, Northumberland
QPR: 1923
Football League: 6-1. **FAC:** 0-0. **FLC:** 0-0.
Other: 0-0. **Total:** 6-1.

George was a reserve, filling in at either wing-half or inside-left for two seasons. The club finished bottom of the division at the end of his first season, yet he was one of the lucky ones to be retained for another campaign.

Debut: 27 Oct 1923 v Northampton Town (H) 3-2 Div 3 (S).

HARTBURN John H

(OL) Wing 5' 2" 10st 4lbs
b: Houghton-le-Spring, Durham, 20 Dec 1920
QPR: Mar 1947
Football League: 58-11. **FAC:** 6-2. **FLC:** 0-0.
Other: 0-0. **Total:** 64-13.
Honours: 2 3rd Div (South) championship medals.

Johnny was a very fast, tiny winger, who came with the full recommendation of Alec Stock, his manager at Yeovil Town. He could centre the ball "on a sixpence" and had one of the deadliest shots in the Third Division. At Leyton Orient he hit one of the fastest hat-tricks in the history of the game, by scoring all three in three minutes. On his retirement from playing, Johnny spent four years as the commercial manager at Leyton Orient. He then had a further nine years in the same capacity at Fulham, and finally spent five years as the secretary of Barnet FC, before retiring in 1987.

Debut: 23 Aug 1947 v Norwich City (H) 3-1 Div 3 (S).

HARTWELL Ambrose Walter

(CH) CD 5' 11" 12st 7lbs
b: Exeter, Devon, 26 Jun 1883
QPR: Aug 1909
Southern League: 57-2. **FAC:** 7-0. **FLC:** 0-0.
Other: 0-0. **Total:** 64-2.
Honours: Represented the Southern League v the Football League on 2 occasions.

Regarded as a "good man" and a "thorough trier" to have in the team. Ambrose was renowned for his prodigious kicking; it was once said that he fired a penalty shot clear out of the ground!

Debut: 1 Sep 1909 v Watford (H) 4-3 SL Div 1.

HASTY Patrick Joseph

(CF) Striker
b: Belfast, Northern Ireland, 17 Mar 1932
QPR: Oct 1959
Football League: 1-0. **FAC:** 0-0. **FLC:** 0-0.
Other: 0-0. **Total:** 1-0.
Honours: Northern Ireland Amateur international cap.

Paddy made just one appearance turning out for QPR on the last day of the 1959/60 season.

Debut: 4 May 1960 v Wrexham (A) 1-1 Div 3.

HATELEY Mark Wayne

Striker 6' 1" 11st 7lbs
b: Liverpool, 7 Nov 1961
QPR: (£1,500,000) Nov 1995
Premier/Football League: 27-3. **FAC:** 5-2.
FLC: 1-0. **Other:** 1-0. **Total:** 34-5.
Honours: 7 England youth caps. 10 U21 caps. 32 full caps. 5 Scottish championship medals. 1 runner's-up medal. 3 Scottish Cup medals. 3 Scottish League Cup medals. 1 French championship medal.

The son of the ex Liverpool player, Tony Hateley, Mark had been groomed for England stardom. QPR chased him in 1983 along with Portsmouth, but

Bob Hazell

the latter club won his signature. The nickname of "Attilla" was born in Italy, during his debut for AC Milan when he was sent off. He scored five goals early on in his career and his headwork was reminiscent of his father. After injuries and lost form, things started to come together with the Rangers – Glasgow version – as Mark hammered in 113 goals in 220 matches. However, at his next club, QPR, he was a great disappointment, as he was at Hull City, both as player and manager, and he was sacked in 1999.
Debut: 29 Nov 1995 v Aston Villa (A) 1-1 Football League Cup fourth round.

HATTON Cyril

(IL) Striker 5′ 8″ 11st 0lbs
b: Grantham, 14 Sep 1918
d: Grantham, 3 Jul 1987
QPR: (£1,000 + Player) Apr 1946
Football League: 162-64. **FAC:** 15-7. **FLC:** 0-0.
Other: 0-0. **Total:** 177-71.
Honours: 3rd Div (South) championship medal. 3rd Div (South) runner's-up medal.

Cyril was a schemer and scorer of goals who was at the heart of the 1949 championship side. The general of the team he was an excellent servant of the club for seven years. Hatton was introduced to QPR during the war years and when normal football resumed he was exchanged for goalkeeper Harry Brown plus a small transfer fee. His last post was that of player/manager plus secretary of Grantham Town. He later bought a shop and became a newsagent in his home town.
Debut: 31 Aug 1946 v Watford (H) 2-1 Div 3 (S).

HAWKINS Bertram W

(CF) Striker
b: Bristol, 29 Sep 1923
QPR: Jun 1953
Football League: 8-3. **FAC:** 0-0. **FLC:** 0-0.
Other: 0-0. **Total:** 8-3.

Bert enjoyed a brief but spectacular spell at Upton Park, but it came to an end at QPR. He started with a pre-season injury in a practice match, and after three matches and one goal, he sustained another injury. Without a reserve centre-forward, manager Jack Taylor was put on the spot. After four weeks Hawkins rejoined the squad but his return did not solve the centre-forward problem. During the 1954 close season he was transferred to Cheltenham Town.
Debut: 19 Aug 1953 v Brighton & Hove Albion (H) 1-2 Div 3 (S).

HAWLEY Frederick W

(CH) CD 5′ 10″ 12st 0lbs
b: Alverston, Derbyshire, 27 Aug 1890
d: 1954
QPR: May 1926
Football League: 29-1. **FAC:** 0-0. **FLC:** 0-0.
Other: 0-0. **Total:** 29-1.

Fred was a well built pivot who entered professional football with Sheffield United before the First World War. During hostilities he worked in a munitions factory guesting for various clubs, notably Coventry City, Birmingham City, Derby County and both Nottingham teams.
Debut: 28 Aug 1926 v Crystal Palace (A) 1-2 Div 3 (S).

HAYWOOD Adam B

(IR) Mid 5′ 5″ 10st 10lbs
b: Burton-on-Trent, 23 Mar 1875
d: 1932
QPR: 1899
Southern League: 17-3. **FAC:** 10-6. **FLC:** 0-0.
Other: 0-0. **Total:** 27-9.
Honours: Represented the United League v Thames & Medway Combination. Represented the North v South.

A much travelled player who not only played in all the forward positions but right and left-half as well. Adam had all the qualities that these positions demanded, and had a keen eye for half a chance, plus a fierce shot, and could rough it with the biggest and strongest in the game. Haywood became the Crystal Palace player/coach and then retired from the game in 1912.
Debut: 9 Sep 1899 v Tottenham Hotspur (A) 0-1 SL Div 1.

HAZELL Anthony Phillip

Def 5′ 9″ 12st 7lbs
b: High Wycombe, 19 Sep 1947
QPR: Oct 1964
Football League: 369-4. **FAC:** 18-0. **FLC:** 28-1.
Other: 0-0. **Total:** 415-5.
Honours: 5 England youth caps. 3rd Div championship medal. League Cup winner's medal. 2 Div 2 runner's-up medals.

A loyal and dedicated defender who was both solid and skilful. Tony was a fast and skilful defender who added steel to the Ranger's defence and was a hard ball-winner. Tony joined the club at 15 years of age, and gave outstanding service to QPR over a period of 10 years, during which time he made no less than 415 first team appearances. His least number of League games was during his final season at Loftus Road (12), but on four occasions he made over 40, being ever-present three times and missing just one match in the 1972/73 season. Remarkably he was on the playing staff of Millwall, Crystal Palace and Charlton Athletic when they each won promotion. After three years at the Valley, he retired from football and became an insurance salesman, before working for BT.
Debut: 3 Oct 1964 v Gillingham (A) 2-2 Div 3.

HAZELL Robert Joseph

CD 6′ 1″ 14st 7lbs
b: Kingston, Jamaica, 14 Jun 1949

QPR: (£240,000) Sep 1979
Football League: 106-8. **FAC:** 6-1. **FLC:** 11-0.
Other: 0-0. **Total:** 123-9.
Honours: 2 England youth caps. 1 U21 cap. 1 B cap. 2nd Div championship medal. FA Cup runner's-up medal.

For such a big man, Bob's delicate control of the ball during a match was a surprise. His performance in the 1982 FA Cup semi-final when he nullified the effects of West Brom's Cyrille Regis, is generally regarded as his best performance for the Rangers. Bob was very popular with the spectators at Loftus Road but unfortunately he had a disagreement off the pitch over training tactics and his contract was annulled after four years. The same thing happened at Leicester and he was again transferred. Bob's final club, Port Vale, released him when he fell victim to a back injury in January 1989, and he was given a free transfer in June that year. Hazell moved to Walsall, and started working for the Birmingham Social Services in 1999.

Debut: 5 Sep 1979 v Bradford City (A) 2-0 FL Cup.

HEATH William J

b: Stepney, London, 26 Jun 1920
QPR: Sep 1945
Football League: 96-3. **FAC:** 5-0. **FLC:** 0-0.
Other: 0-0. **Total:** 101-3.

Although Bill played in many positions, he was noted mainly as a defender. During the war years he played in any position he was asked to and therefore became known, in modern terms, as a utility player. Bill carried out each task with a certain aplomb and was the first reserve for whoever was injured.

Debut: 14 Sep 1946 v Reading (H) 2-0 Div 3 (S).

HEATHCOTE Wilfred

(CF) Striker
b: Hemsworth, Dewsbury, 29 Jun 1911
QPR: 1943
Football League: 5-1. **FAC:** 0-0. **FLC:** 0-0.
Other: 0-0. **Total:** 5-1.

Wilf was a schoolteacher by profession who played football for a hobby. He was a great favourite of the spectators and became the top scorer for QPR during the war years, scoring some 90 goals in approximately 105 appearances. Wilf also played many wartime representative matches, in a goalscoring role. He moved on to Millwall at the end of the war in exchange for Reg Dudley, but soon faded out of League football.

Debut: 31 Aug 1946 v Watford (H) 2-1 Div 3 (S).

Heidar Helguson

HEBDEN George Horace Robert

Goal 5' 10" 12st 2lbs
b: West Ham, London, 2 Jun 1900
d: Leicester, 16 Aug 1973
QPR: May 1925
Football League: 59-0. **FAC:** 4-0. **FLC:** 0-0.
Other: 0-0. **Total:** 63-0.
QPR: Nov 1929
Football League: 1-0. **FAC:** 0-0. **FLC:** 0-0.
Other: 0-0. **Total:** 1-0.
Honours: 2 schoolboy caps.

George's future was severely jeopardised by wartime service during his teens. He was first in the Royal Navy and then in the Merchant Marines, and reported as being torpedoed on four occasions. After the First World War he was elevated from London amateur football to the professional level with Leicester City. By 1922 he had made the senior squad with a string of instinctively fearless performances. His sojourn at QPR was not so good, with the club having to apply for re-election. When he retired, in 1930, he initially ran his own garage business in Ilford, Essex.

Debut: 29 Aug 1925 v Gillingham (A) 0-3 Div 3.

HEINOLA Antti Juhani

(LB) Def 5' 10" 12st 6lbs
b: Helsinki, Finland, 20 Mar 1973
QPR: (£150,000) Jan 1998
Football League: 34-0. **FAC:** 1-0. **FLC:** 3-0.
Other: 0-0 **Total:** 38-0.
Honours: 8 Senior caps for Finland. U21 caps.

Antti had good pace going forward while remaining sound at the back. A fractured cheekbone and serious head injury in the second half of 1998/99 put paid to the rest of the season and he struggled to win his place back in the senior squad. Suddenly, in 2001, Antti announced his retirement from the game and returned to Finland to study for an Economics degree at Helsinki University.

Debut: 24 Jan 1998 v Nottingham Forest (H) 0-1 Div 1.

HELGUSON Heidar

Striker 5' 10" 12st 1lbs
b: Dalvík, Iceland, 22 Aug 1977
QPR: 2008
Football League: 20-5. **FAC:** 1-0. **FLC:** 0-0.
Other: 0-0. **Total:** 21-5.

The signing of Heidar in January 2009 – following a loan spell at Loftus Road – brought a wealth of experience to Rangers' strike force. The Icelander has spent 10 seasons in English football, both in the Premiership and the Championship, with clubs such as Fulham, Watford and Bolton Wanderers. Known

for his aerial prowess despite being only 5'10", Heidar's giant leap and positioning skills make him a lethal header of the ball. He also has a sharp finish and is a good penalty taker.
Debut: 6 Dec 2008 v Wolverhampton W (H) 1-0 Championship.

HELLAWELL Michael Stephen

(OR) Wing
b: Keighley, Yorkshire, 30 Jun 1938
QPR: Aug 1955
Football League: 45-7. **FAC:** 3-1. **FLC:** 2-0.
Other: 0-0. **Total:** 50-8.
Honours: 2 England caps. Fairs Cup runner's-up medal. Football League Cup winner's medal. Represented a Div 3 XI.

A red haired winger with an astonishing turn of speed over the first 20 to 25 yards, Mike Hellawell was also a fine cricketer and played a match for Warwickshire. At QPR he was exchanged for Bill Finney, another winger. When retirement came in May 1971, he set himself up in business, running a shop in his home town of Keighley.
Debut: 25 Feb 1956 v Exeter City (H) 1-0 Div 3 (S).

HERRERA Roberto

(LB) Def 5' 7" 10st 6lbs
b: Torbay, Devon, 12 Jun 1970
QPR: Mar 1988
Football League: 6-0. **FAC:** 0-0. **FLC:** 3-0.
Other: 2-0. **Total:** 11-0.

Roberto is a flamboyant character whose pace and control made him a firm favourite of the crowd at his various clubs. An unusual QPR post-war sequence that Roberto holds is the 145 reserve matches that he played for the club, second only in number to Maurice Doyle.
Debut: 14 Jan 1989 v Wimbledon (A) 0-1 Div 1.

HIGGINS Alexander John

Mid 5' 9" 11st 6lbs
b: Sheffield, Yorkshire, 22 Jul 1981
QPR: Mar 2001
Football League: 1-0. **FAC:** 0-0. **FLC:** 0-0.
Other: 0-0. **Total:** 1-0.

Alex played in the last nine minutes of the last game of the 2000/01 season at Molineux. This being the only QPR appearance makes his the second shortest career with the club. He became out of contract that summer and was released.
Debut: 6 May 2001 v Wolverhampton W (A). 1-1 Div 1.

HIGGINS Dennis

(RB) Def
QPR: 1913

Gordon Hill

Southern League: 26-0. **FAC:** 4-0. **FLC:** 0-0.
Other: 0-0. **Total:** 30-0.
Honours: Represented the South v the North.

Dennis was an amateur who joined the "Sportsmen Battalion" during the First World War, and became a captain. Unfortunately he was so badly injured at Ypres, in Flanders, that he never played again.
Debut: 21 Mar 1913 v Reading (A) 0-1 SL Div 1.

HIGGINS Ronald Valentine

(CF) Striker
b: Silvertown, East Ham, London, 14 Feb 1923
QPR: Jan 1953
Football League: 3-1. **FAC:** 0-0. **FLC:** 0-0.
Other: 0-0. **Total:** 3-1.

Ron was a fitter in a London shipyard and was a part-time professional, who was part of the deal that took Addinall and Gilberg to Brighton. Developing into a prolific goalscorer at Tonbridge, in 1951, he became the subject of many clubs fighting for his signature. Ron didn't enjoy the best of luck at any of his Football League clubs and soon returned to the non-League scene.
Debut: 28 Feb 1953 v Brighton & Hove Albion (H) 3-3 Div 3 (S).

HILL Charles John

(LH) Mid
b: Cardiff, Wales, 6 Sep 1918
d: Dec 1998
QPR: Mar 1949
Football League: 21-1. **FAC:** 0-0. **FLC:** 0-0.
Other: 0-0. **Total:** 21-1.

Charlie, nicknamed "midge", was such of small stature that he was lost when played as a centre-forward, nevertheless he scored his goal from this position. His time was during the period of the "utility player".
Debut: 2 Apr 1949 v WBA (A) 1-1 Div 2.

HILL Gordon Alexander

(OL) Wing 5' 7" 10st 12lb
b: Sunbury, Middlesex, 1 Apr 1954
QPR: (Trial) 1960s
QPR: (£175,000) Nov 1979
Football League: 14-1. **FAC:** 1-0. **FLC:** 1-0.
Other: 0-0. **Total:** 16-1.
Honours: England Amateur cap. Youth, U21, England B. 6 full England caps. FA Cup runner's-up medal. FA Cup winner's medal.

At home on either wing he was tricky, fast and possessed a shot that was like a thunderbolt. Rejected by QPR in the early 1960s for refusing to get his hair cut, the club had to pay a substantial sum to acquire him in the late 1970s. Gordon was something of a flamboyant character and temperamental. Tommy Docherty bought him on three occasions, first when manager of Manchester United, then Derby County, and lastly at Loftus Road for a short period. Gordon was later heard of

Len Hill

living and working in Tampa, Florida, as a tennis and football coach.
Debut: 1 Dec 1979 v Cambridge United (A) 1-2 Div 2.

HILL Joseph

(IR) Mid
b: Sheffield, Yorkshire, 1906
QPR: 1932
Football League: 15-1. **FAC:** 1-0. **FLC:** 0-0.
Other: 0-0. **Total:** 16-1.
Honours: Notts Senior Cup winner's medal. 3rd Div (North) Cup winner's medal. 3rd Div (North) League championship medal.

Joe had the ability to find space and was a clever dribbler, possessing a truly splendid shot. He enjoyed the most successful period of his career at Stockport County where he hit a hat-trick on his debut for the club in that famous 13-0 thrashing of Halifax Town. When Joe retired from football he worked as an assistant to a bookmaker in Yorkshire for many years.
Debut: 1 Sep 1932 v Aldershot (H) 2-2 Div 3 (S).

HILL Leonard G

Goal 5' 11" 12st 0lbs
b: Islington, London, 15 Feb 1899
d: Southend, 1979
QPR: 1920
Football League: 162-0. **FAC:** 14-0. **FLC:** 0-0.
Other: 0-0. **Total:** 176-0.
Honours: League v The Army. FA XI v Oxford University.

A survivor of the Great War, Hill cheated death on a couple of occasions before he was invalided out of the army with a suspected fractured skull. Len then embarked on a somewhat safer occupation, that of a goalkeeper, proving to be a fine and reliable custodian. On his retirement from football, in 1930, he worked as a cricket coach at Watford Grammar school, and in 1933 he was reported to be coaching at the Hercules sports club in Utrecht, Holland.
Debut: 4 Sep 1920 v Watford (A) 2-0 Div 1.

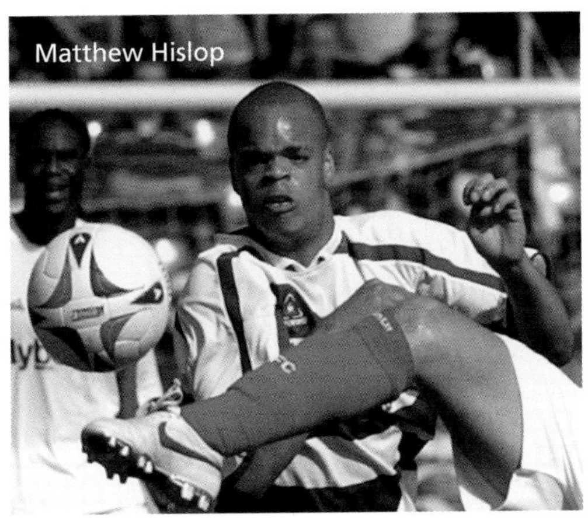
Matthew Hislop

HILL William L

(OR) Wing
b: Uxbridge, Middlesex, 9 Jun 1930
QPR: 1951
Football League: 10-1 **FAC:** 1-0. **FLC:** 0-0.
Other: 0-0. **Total:** 11-1.

William's one season at QPR was that when they were relegated from the Second Division to the Third Division (South). Billy seemed to excel in the reserves but couldn't seem to pull it off in the senior squad. He was released at the end of the season.
Debut: 1 Dec 1951 v Leicester City (A) 0-4 Div 2.

HIRST Henry

(HB) Mid 5' 8' 11st 7lbs
b: Horbury, Yorkshire, 24 Oct 1899
QPR: May 1925
Football League: 26-0. **FAC:** 4-1. **FLC:** 0-0.
Other: 0-0. **Total:** 30-1.

At QPR, Henry had the longest spell of first team football than at any of his other clubs. He filled in at centre-half as well as at wing-half during the club's second re-election season.
Debut: 5 Sep 1925 v Merthyr Town (H) 1-1 Div 3 (S).

HISLOP Matthew

Def 5' 11" 12st 0lbs
b: Wolverhampton, 31 Jan 1987
QPR: 2005
Football League: 1-0. **FAC:** 0-0. **FLC:** 0-0.
Other: 0-0. **Total:** 1-0.
Debut: 24 Sep 2005 v Leicester City (A) 2-1 Championship.

HITCH Alfred

(CH) CD 5' 8" 11st 3lbs
b: Walsall, Staffordshire, 1878
d: Uxbridge, 1962
QPR: May 1899
Southern League: 49-4. **FAC:** 12-3. **FLC:** 0-0.
Other: 0-0. **Total:** 61-7.
QPR: May 1902
Southern League: 118-13. **FAC:** 4-0. **FLC:** 0-0.
Other: 0-0. **Total:** 122-13.
Honours: North v South England trial match.

Alf was a very astute and clever player who in the days when heading the ball was classed as "not fashionable", was noted in the football paper of the time, *Bells Weekly*, as a, "Greatly gifted player when heading the ball out of defence."

The England selectors took note of him, however, honours eluded him, probably because of his unconventional style of playing the game. With his retirement from football he opened a tobacconist shop in St Albans, which he had for many years.
Debut: 7 Oct 1899 v Bristol City (A) 3-5 SL Div 1.

HITCHCOCK Ernest

(CF) Striker
QPR: 1907
Southern League: 2-2. **FAC:** 0-0. **FLC:** 0-0.
Other: 0-0. **Total:** 2-2.

Ernie played and scored in the opening two matches of the 1907/08 season, but never played again. The arrival of Walker put paid to that, for the newcomer made the position his own.
Debut: 2 Sep 1907 v Tottenham Hotspur (H) 3-3 SL Div 1.

HODGE Steven Brian

Mid 5' 7" 10st 3lbs
b: Nottingham, 25 Oct 1962
QPR: £300,000) Oct 1994
Premier League: 15-0. **FAC:** 1-0. **FLC:** 0-0.
Other: 0-0. **Total:** 16-0.
Honours: 24 England caps. 8 U21 caps. 2 League Cup winner's medals. FA Cup winner's medal. 1st Div championship medal.

Steve was a left-sided defensive midfield player who had a striker's instinct around the penalty area. He had a fierce shot and the gift of slipping away from defenders.
Debut: 29 Oct 1994 v Aston Villa (H) 2-0 PL.

Steve Hodge

HOLD Oscar

(CF) Striker 5' 9" 11st 0lbs
b: Carlton, Barnsley, 19 Oct 1918
QPR: Feb 1952
Football League: 5-1. **FAC:** 0-0. **FLC:** 0-0.
Other: 0-0. **Total:** 5-1.

Oscar had a delicate one touch style of play which was his hallmark, although he was known more as a manager and a coach in his later football life. When his playing days were over he became the manager of March Town, then Gainsborough Trinity and finally Wisbech Town. In 1960 Oscar became the FA coach in Nigeria, then the manager of Cambridge City a year later. The following year he took over the managership of Doncaster Rovers, and in 1964 the same at Fenerbahce, Istanbul before becoming coach to Ankara. His next job was that of coach to the National Sporting Club, Jeddah in 1967, followed by the same role at Apollon, Cyprus in 1972. Oscar also coached in Kuwait in 1974 and finally in Apollon, Cyprus, again, in 1982. He retired to Cyprus.

Debut: 8 Mar 1952 v Southampton (H) 2-1 Div 2.

HOLLINS John William

(RH) Mid 5' 8" 11st 7lbs
b: Guildford, Surrey, 16 Jul 1946
QPR: (£80,000) Jun 1975
Football League: 151-6. **FAC:** 11-1. **FLC:** 13-0.
Other: 8-0. **Total:** 183-7.
Honours: 8 England youth caps. 4 Football League caps. 6 B caps. 12 U23 caps. 1 England Senior cap. FA Cup winner's medal. FA Cup runner's-up medal. League Cup runner's-up medal. European Cup winner's medal. European Cup runner's-up medal. FA Charity Shield runner's-up medal. 2nd Div championship medal.

John Hollins

John came from a family of four brothers, three of whom played League football, as did his father and grandfather. His brother Dave was a Welsh international and his father played in goal for Stoke City and Wolves. John was an outstanding attacking wing-half whose running, tackling and passing was always crisp. A totally dedicated player who would always give 100% in whatever match he was playing in. In 1985, he became the manager of Chelsea until 1988. In 1995 he became the reserve team coach at QPR until taking on the manager's job at Swansea in 1998.

Debut: 16 Aug 1975 v Liverpool (H) 2-0 Div 1.

HOLLOWAY Ian Scott

Mid 5' 7" 10st 0lbs
b: Kingswood, Gloucestershire, 12 Mar 1963
QPR: (£230,000) Aug 1991
Football League: 147-4. **FAC:** 8-1. **FLC:** 13-0.
Other: 2-0. **Total:** 170-5.
Honours: 3rd Div championship medal. Leyland Daf Trophy runner's-up medal.

The son of Bill Holloway, a well respected local amateur footballer, young "Ollie" broke into the Bristol Rovers side during the 1983 season. He was never far from the centre of the action and his enthusiasm and commitment caused much interest from elsewhere. Eventually, Ian was tempted to Loftus Road and rejoined Gerry Francis at QPR, where he played alongside a number of former Bristol Rovers team-mates including Dennis Bailey, Gary Penrice, Devon White and Steve Yates. Ian was a grafter with an aggressive tackle and he was also a good distributor of the ball. Holloway became the manager of Bristol Rovers in 1996, before following Gerry Francis as manager at QPR in February 2001. Ian is a great credit to his profession, on and off the field, and remains one of the club's most popular former players. There can be no finer example for any young player to emulate than that of Ian Holloway.

Debut: 17 Sep 1991 v Arsenal (A) 1-1 Div 1.

HOOPER Harold

(RB) Def 5' 8" 12st 0lbs
b: Brierley Hill, 18 Aug 1900
QPR: May 1926
Football League: 16-0. **FAC:** 0-0. **FLC:** 0-0.
Other: 0-0. **Total:** 16-0.

A dour and resolute defender who was mainly a reserve wherever he went, Harold was the cousin of Charlie Roberts, the Manchester United and England defender.

Debut: 28 Aug 1926 v Crystal Palace (A) 1-2 Div 3 (S).

HOTEN Ralph Vincent

(IL) Mid 5' 11" 12st 4lbs

Ian Holloway

b: Pinxton, Nottinghamshire, 27 Dec 1896
d: Wellingborough, Feb 1978
QPR: 1930
Football League: 9-4. **FAC:** 0-0. **FLC:** 0-0.
Other: 0-0. **Total:** 9-4.
Honours: Represented the Southern League v the Welsh League.

A respected, good, all-round Third Division player who spent his last football days at QPR. Ralph scored on his debut for the club and in his last match.

Debut: 30 Aug 1930 v Thames Association (H) 3-0 Div 3 (S).

HOWE Ernest James

(CH) CD 6'1" 12st 12lbs
b: Chiswick, Middlesex, 15 Feb 1953
QPR: (£50,000) Dec 1977
Football League: 89-3. **FAC:** 12-3. **FLC:** 5-0.
Other: 0-0. **Total:** 106-6.

Ernie was one of the first players to have his transfer fee set by a tribunal, being valued at £50,000, which was far below Fulham's estimation. Portsmouth also paid a £50,000 transfer fee for his signature. He was an excellent header of the ball and very tricky on the ground, while memorable goals were scored by him from set-pieces. Injury forced him prematurely into coaching, initially at Wokingham. Later Ernie joined Farnham Town and then Woking, before becoming the Basingstoke manager in 1994.

Debut: 17 Dec 1977 v Liverpool (A) 0-1 Div 1.

HOWE Harold G

(OL) Wing 5′ 6″ 11st 2lbs
b: Hemel Hempstead, 9 Apr 1906
d: 1976
QPR: 1929
Football League: 68-13. **FAC:** 6-1. **FLC:** 0-0.
Other: 0-0. **Total:** 74-14.

Harold was a left-footed player with a phenomenal shot. Plucked out of the Watford reserve team and sharing the left-wing spot with about half-a-dozen others, he helped the club to third position in the League.
Debut: 19 Oct 1929 v Clapton Orient (H) 1-1 Div 3 (S).

HOWELL Andrew

Def 5′ 11″ 12st 1lbs
b: Great Yarmouth, 18 Mar 1989
QPR: 2006
Football League: 0-0. **FAC:** 0-0. **FLC:** 1-0.
Other: 0-0. **Total:** 1-0.
Debut: 22 Aug 2006 v Northampton Town (H) 3-2 Carling Cup first round.

HOWES Arthur

Goal 5′ 11″ 13st 0lbs
b: Leicester, 1876
QPR: 1904
Football League: 49-0. **FAC:** 4-0. **FLC:** 0-0.
Other: 0-0. **Total:** 53-0.

Alert and agile, Arthur was usually the reserve to the first team keepers, Collins and then Kingsley. Finally, on earning the role as first choice keeper, he was so severely injured that he never played in a first class game again.
Debut: 12 Nov 1904 v Luton Town (A) 1-1 SL Div 1.

HUCKER Peter I

Goal 6′ 4″ 13st 0lbs
b: Hampstead, London, 28 Oct 1959
QPR: Jul 1977

Ernie Howe

Andrew Howell

Football League: 160-0. **FAC:** 11-0. **FLC:** 12-0.
Other: 4-0. **Total:** 187-0.
Honours: 2 England U21 caps. 2nd Div championship medal. FA Cup runner's-up medal.

Early in his career, at QPR, he found his way blocked, in turn by Phil Parkes, Derek Richardson and Chris Woods. But Peter finally made his League debut in the last game of the 1980/81 season. Named Man of the Match in the Cup final of 1982, he won two England U21 caps as an over-aged player in 1984. Hucker was a sound and solid goalkeeper who was ever-present in the QPR side from 2 January 1982 until 21 September 1985, apart for one FA Cup match. After several loan periods and other brief moves, he switched to the non-League circuit in 1991 and now has several successful soccer schools for children.
Debut: 2 May 1981 v Shrewsbury Town (A) 3-3 Div 2.

HUDSON Stanley R

(OL) Wing
b: Fulham, London, 10 Feb 1923
d: 1951
QPR: 1948
Football League: 22-7. **FAC:** 1-0. **FLC:** 0-0.
Other: 0-0. **Total:** 23-7.

A fast and tricky winger who by his direct play and shooting became the darling of the fans. Sadly he died prematurely at the age of 28.
Debut: 10 Sep 1948 v Brentford (H) 2-0 Div 2.

HUMPHREYS Percy

(IL) Mid 5′ 7″ 12st 6lbs
b: Cambridge, 3 Dec 1880
d: Stepney, London, 13 Apr 1959
QPR: May 1900
Southern League: 27-9. **FAC:** 4-3. **FLC:** 0-0.
Other: 0-0. **Total:** 31-12.
Honours: 1 England cap. 1 Football League cap.

A strongly built player described as full of class and dash. Percy was a probing and thrustful forward with a dexterous dribble and a dangerous shot. At the beginning of the First World War, he was due to take up an appointment as a player/coach with a Swiss club, however, this role didn't materialise, so he returned to England and played just three games as an adieu to the senior game, with Norwich City in 1915. Percy's death was registered as suicide.
Debut: 8 Sep 1900 v Swindon Town (1-1) 7-1 SL Div 1.

HUNT Ronald G

(CH) CD 5′11″ 11st 10lbs
b: Paddington, London, 19 Dec 1945
QPR: Mar 1963
Football League: 219-1. **FAC:** 14-0. **FLC:** 22-0.
Other: 0-0. **Total:** 255-1.
Honours: League Cup winner's medal. 3rd Div championship medal. 2 2nd Div runner's-up medals.

Ron was a ground staff boy with West Ham United and later, after moving to Slough, in Berkshire, he joined Reading FC. He was recommended to QPR by Dave Dorman of the Pathfinders club, in Slough, a nursery team for young talent. Ron turned out to be a loyal club man and a very fine central defender, and his time at Loftus Road spanned 10 years during which time he made over 250 first team appearances. A knee injury shortened his career and he retired in 1973. Ron Hunt is probably best remembered for his foray into the West Brom penalty area towards the end of the League Cup final in 1967. Following his collision with the Albion goalkeeper, the ball ran loose to Mark Lazarus who netted that famous winning goal.
Debut: 28 Dec 1964 v Bristol Rovers (H) 3-1 Div 3.

HURRELL William P

(IF) Mid
b: Dundee, Scotland, 28 Jan 1920
QPR: Jul 1953
Football League: 6-1. **FAC:** 3-2. **FLC:** 0-0.
Other: 0-0. **Total:** 9-3.

Bill came to QPR as a stop gap, being 33 years old and at the end of his career. He played mostly in the reserves and filled in, in the senior squad, when injuries required. He was a skilful and tricky player.
Debut: 16 Sep 1953 v Southampton (H) 1-3 Div 3 (S).

HURST William

(CF) Striker
b: Newcastle
QPR: 1924
Football League: 8-4. **FAC:** 0-0. **FLC:** 0-0.
Other: 0-0. **Total:** 8-4.

Bill was a reserve centre-forward and scored two goals on his debut for the club. After such a bright start he gradually faded from the picture and left at the same time as manager, Ned Liddell, during the 1924 close season.
Debut: 7 Mar 1925 v Luton Town (H) 3-1 Div 3 (S).

G H I

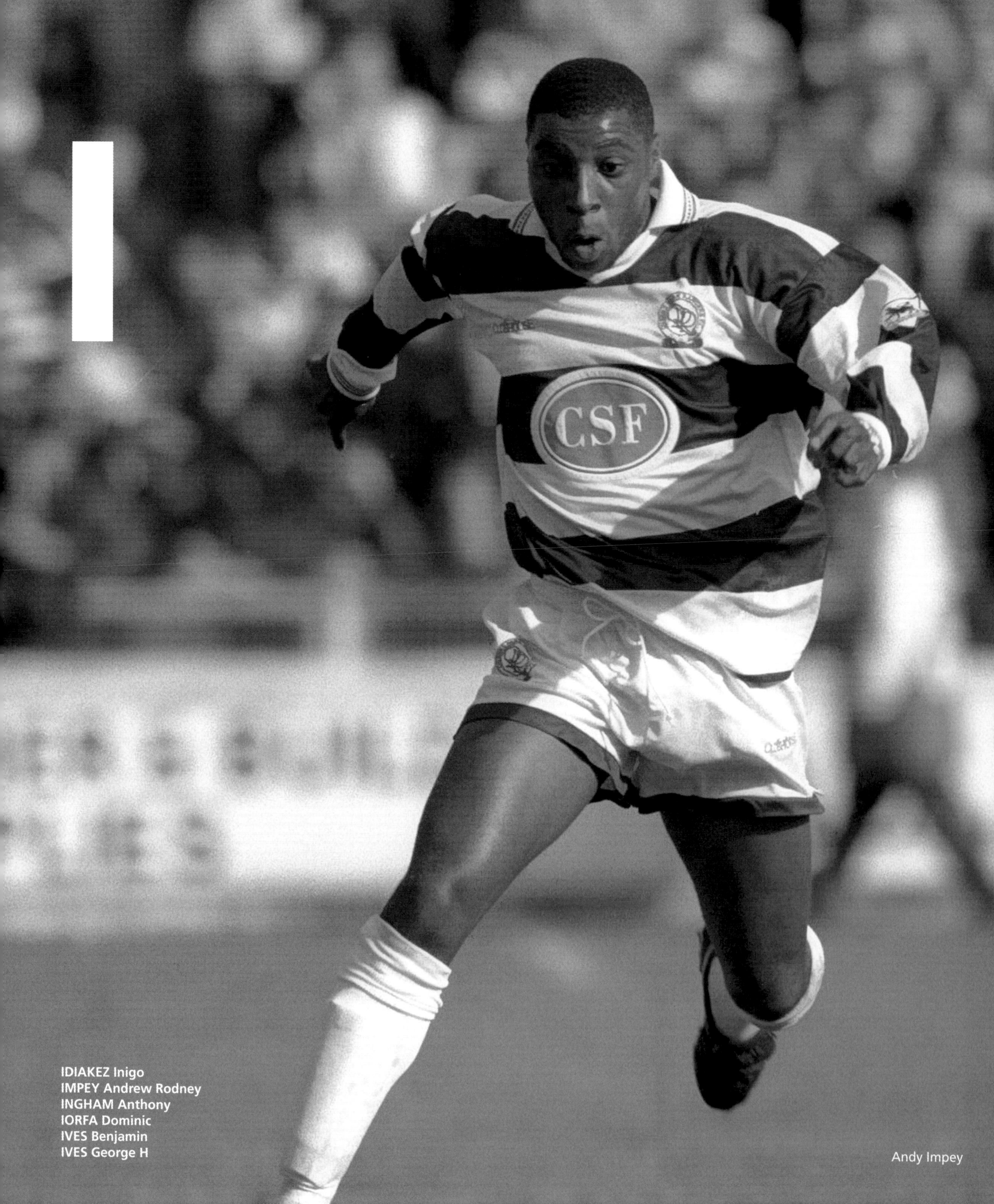

I

IDIAKEZ Inigo
IMPEY Andrew Rodney
INGHAM Anthony
IORFA Dominic
IVES Benjamin
IVES George H

Andy Impey

IDIAKEZ Inigo

Mid 6' 0"
b: San Sebastian, Spain, 8 Nov 1973
QPR: (Loan) 2007
Football League: 5-1. **FAC:** 0-0. **FLC:** 0-0.
Other: 0-0. **Total:** 5-1.
Debut: 10 Mar 2007 v Sheffield Wednesday (H) 1-1 Championship.

IMPEY Andrew Rodney

RWB 5' 8" 11st 2lbs
b: Hammersmith, London, 13 Sep 1971
QPR: (£35,000) Jun 1990
Football League: 187-13. **FAC:** 10-1. **FLC:** 16-3.
Other: 2-1. **Total:** 215-18.
Honours: England U21 cap.

Andy is an outstandingly good player, reflected in the transfer fees that he has twice commanded, who is aggressive, strong and very quick, and able to play on either flank. He was popular with the fans being voted the Player of the Year in 1995. He was a fairly regular first team player for five of his six playing seasons at Loftus Road.

During the 1992/93 season he missed appearing in just one League match (including one as substitute). Andy moved on to West Ham in 1997, after a toe injury delayed his transfer, for a £1 million plus fee, but after only 25 League matches soon became a Leicester City player, at an even higher cost.
Debut: 23 Oct 1991 v Norwich City (A) 2-1 Full Members' Cup second round.

INGHAM Anthony

(LB) Def 5' 10" 11st 5lbs
b: Harrogate, Yorkshire, 18 Dec 1925
QPR: (£5,000) Jun 1950
Football League: 514-3. **FAC:** 30-0. **FLC:** 4-0.
Other: 7-0. **Total:** 555-3.
Honours: Represented the 3rd Div (South) v 3rd Div (North).

Tony turned out to be arguably the best buy that manager Mangnall bought for the club. He turned out to be a fine captain and a first class defender who became a favourite of the crowd at Loftus Road. Tony was ever-present from 25 February 1956 until 17 September 1961, a total of 274 matches, and played in the senior squad from 1950 until 1963. With his 514 League matches, and a staggering 555 matches in total he comfortably holds the club record for the most appearances. With QPR as a player he played League football for 13 seasons, during which time his least number of appearances was "only" 17 in 1951/52.

Tony made his last QPR appearance in 1963, playing in 41 League matches that season and epitomising the term "one club" man (despite his earlier time at Leeds United for three years or so and just three League appearances). Apart from his activities on the pitch he also served the club as that of commercial manager, when his playing days were over, and for a short period acted as club secretary. He finally became a director of the club.
Debut: 25 Nov 1950 v Doncaster Rovers (H) 1-2 Div 2.

Inigo Idiakez

IORFA Dominic

For 6' 1" 12st 12lbs
b: Lagos, Nigeria, 1 Oct 1968
QPR: (£145,000) Mar 1990
Football League: 8-0. **FAC:** 0-0. **FLC:** 1-0.
Other: 0-0. **Total:** 9-0.
Honours: 3 Nigerian caps.

A tall, gangly, Nigerian international who failed to make any impression at the club. Dominic was released and moved onto several clubs on free transfers.
Debut: 5 May 1990 v Wimbledon (H) 2-3 Div 1.

IVES Benjamin

(OL) Wing
b: Tottenham, London, 1889
QPR: 1913
Southern League: 36-3. **FAC:** 0-0. **FLC:** 0-0.
Other: 0-0. **Total:** 36-3.

Ben made a promising start to his career with the club by scoring two goals on his debut. However, he soon appears to have faded from the team completely.
Debut: 19 Apr 1913 v Merthyr Tydfil (H) SL Div 1.

IVES George H

(OR) Wing
b: Barton, Lincolnshire
QPR: 1937
Football League: 0-0. **FAC:** 0-0. **FLC:** 0-0.
Other: 1-0. **Total:** 1-0.

George played just one match for the club and that was in the third round of the Division 3 (South) Cup.
Debut: 1 Mar 1938 v Watford (H) 2-3 Div 3 (S) Cup third round.

Leighton James

J

JACKMAN V
JACKS George Charles
JACKSON Matthew Alan
JAMES Leighton
JAMES Norman Leslie
JAMES Robert Mark
JARRETT Jason Lee
JEANNE Leon Charles
JEFFERIES M
JEFFERSON Arthur
JOBSON John Thomas
JOHN Reginald
JOHNS Nicholas Paul
JOHNSON Henry Edward
JOHNSON John Henry
JOHNSON Richard
JONES Charles H
JONES Paul Steven
JONES Raymond Barry Bankote
JONES Vincent Peter
JORDAN Frank
JORDAN Harry

JACKMAN V

(OL) Wing
QPR: 1912
Southern League: 3-0. **FAC:** 0-0. **FLC:** 0-0.
Other: 0-0. **Total:** 3-0.

Jackman used to fill in when a player was absent from the team.

Debut: 21 Mar 1913 v Reading (A) 0-1 SL Div 1.

JACKS George Charles

(IL) Mid 5' 6" 10st 8lbs
b: Stepney, London, 14 Mar 1946
QPR: Jan 1964
Football League: 1-0. **FAC:** 0-0. **FLC:** 0-0.
Other: 0-0. **Total:** 1-0.
Honours: 3rd Div runner's-up medal. 4th Div runner's-up medal.

George was a tireless player with boundless energy who became a footballer of some repute. He was given a free transfer by QPR and was quickly snapped up by Millwall where manager Benny Fenton developed Jacks into a first class midfield man-to-man marker. He went on to work for the Kent Messenger group and still lives locally.

Debut: 24 Apr 1965 v Exeter City (H) 0-0 Div 3.

JACKSON Matthew Alan

(RB) Def 6' 1" 12st 12lbs
b: Leeds, Yorkshire, 19 Oct 1971
QPR: (Loan) Aug 1996
Football League: 7-0. **FAC:** 0-0. **FLC:** 0-0.
Other: 0-0. **Total:** 7-0.
Honours: English Schools international. 10 U21 caps. FA Cup winner's medal.

Matt is a polished defender, renowned for his excellent positional play and composure under pressure. He is comfortable on the ball and strikes it well. QPR tried to sign him permanently, but couldn't agree a fee, and Norwich City snapped him up, where he subsequently became team captain.

Debut: 23 Aug 1996 v Portsmouth (A) 2-1 Div 1.

JAMES Leighton

(OL) Wing 5' 9" 12st 6lbs
b: Llwchwyr, Wales, 16 Feb 1953
QPR: (£180,000) Oct 1977
Football League: 28-4. **FAC:** 5-2. **FLC:** 0-0.
Other: 0-0. **Total:** 33-6.
Honours: 12 Welsh youth caps. 7 U23 caps. 54 full Welsh caps. 2nd Div championship medal. FA Charity Shield winner's medal. Texaco Cup runner's-up medal. Anglo Scottish Cup winner's medal. Sherpa Van Trophy runner's-up medal.

Leighton had tremendous ability, pace, two good feet, a teasing centre and an eye for a goal. He was one of the youngest players to gain full international honours, being 18 years and 238 days old when he won his first cap. In 1987 he became the manager of the Burnley youth team, the Bradford City coach in 1990 and in the same year the manager of Gainsborough Trinity. In 1993 the Morecombe managership followed, then the same job at Netherfield in 1995. In the same year he managed Darwin as well as Ilkeston Town.

Debut: 29 Oct 1977 v WBA (H) 2-1 Div 1.

JAMES Norman Leslie

(CH) CD 6' 2" 13st 0lbs
b: Bootle, Lancashire, 25 Mar 1908
d: October 1985
QPR: 1936
Football League: 68-1. **FAC:** 5-0. **FLC:** 0-0.
Other: 3-0. **Total:** 76-1.

At Liverpool Norman was the reserve for Bradshaw and showed fine promise when he appeared. He didn't make it as a first team player at Bradford City, but at QPR he was the centre of a very fine defence put together by Billy Birrell. The team challenged strongly for promotion in 1938 and nearly made it.

Debut: 31 Oct 1936 v Gillingham (H) 0-1 Div 3 (S).

JAMES Robert Mark

Mid 5' 11" 13st 11lbs
b: Gorseinon, Wales, 23 Mar 1957
d: Llanelli, 19 Feb 1998
QPR: (£100,000) Oct 1984
Football League: 87-4. **FAC:** 5-1. **FLC:** 9-0.
Other: 0-0. **Total:** 101-5.
Honours: 11 Welsh youth caps. 3 U21 caps. 47 full caps for Wales. 4 Welsh Cup winner's medals. League Cup runner's-up medal. 4th Div promotion medal. 3rd Div promotion medal. 2nd Div promotion medal.

A barrel-chested midfield player who was turned into a defender by QPR, Robbie's enthusiasm and pace led him to prompt the attack with subtle balls from out of defence. After playing for Cardiff City he managed non-League Merthyr before returning to playing with Barry Town. He then went on to manage Weston-Super-Mare and finally Llanelli. Robbie finally took over the managership of a notable Swansea city centre public house, before his untimely death in 1998.

Debut: 17 Nov 1984 v Arsenal (A) 0-1 Div 1.

JARRETT Jason Lee

Mid 6' 0" 13st 1lbs
b: Bury, 14 Sep 1979
QPR: (Loan) 2007
Football League: 2-0. **FAC:** 0-0. **FLC:** 0-0.
Other: 0-0. **Total:** 2-0.
Debut: 3 Oct 2007 v Colchester United (A) 2-4 Championship.

JEANNE Leon Charles

Mid 5' 8" 10st 10lbs
b: Cardiff, Wales, 17 Nov 1980
QPR: Nov 1997
Football League: 12-0. **FAC:** 0-0. **FLC:** 0-0.
Other: 0-0. **Total:** 12-0.
Honours: Youth caps for Wales. 8 U21 caps. Welsh Cup winner's medal.

Early in his career, Leon showed among other things that he is a very pacey player. Not only very fast but also able to play as a wide front man. Somewhat undisciplined, he was released and signed up by Cardiff City in the summer of 2001, but he failed to make his mark there and drifted into non-League football.

Debut: 20 Feb 1999 v Watford (H) 1-2 Div 1.

JEFFERIES M

Goal
b: Bristol
QPR: 1913
Southern League: 1-0. **FAC:** 0-0. **FLC:** 0-0.
Other: 0-0. **Total:** 1-0.

He made just a single appearance for QPR in their early Park Royal days.

Debut: 27 Sep 1913 v West Ham United (H) 2-2 SL Div 1.

JEFFERSON Arthur

(LB) Def 5' 8" 13st 6lbs
b: Goldthorpe, Yorkshire, 14 Dec 1916
d: 1997
QPR: Feb 1936
Football League: 211-1. **FAC:** 23-0. **FLC:** 0-0.
Other: 5-0. **Total:** 239-1.
Honours: 3rd Div (South) runner's-up medal. 3rd Div (South) championship medal.

After impressive displays in the reserves, Arthur, who had been with Peterborough United, accepted a contract – and so began his long association with the club. He was a fearless character for whom personal safety counted little when the interests of his side were at stake. He suffered a broken collarbone and in the first match after recovery suffered concussion. In his initial season with QPR a broken leg resulted in three months absence. He had a cartilage removed and a few seasons later, suffered a broken arm.

Arthur was a favourite of the spectators at Loftus Road, a good old fashioned full-back was how he can be described. He was an expert at the sliding tackle, (which is not allowed in the modern game) and an expert at the first time volley. After leaving Rangers he notched-up another 180 matches for Aldershot. On retiring from football, at the age of 36 years, he, along with team-mate Bert Smith opened a fish and chip shop near Loftus Road.

Debut: 31 Aug 1936 v Millwall (A) 0-2 Div 3 (S).

JOBSON John Thomas

(CH) CD
b: Hebburn, Durham, 8 Aug 1903
QPR: Jun 1932
Football League: 4-0. **FAC:** 0-0. **FLC:** 0-0.
Other: 0-0. **Total:** 4-0.
Honours: 2 3rd Div runner's-up medals.

Jack (as he was known) was a very experienced player who was used as a reserve at QPR. At Hartlepool he was the mainstay of their defence for three years and at Stockport for a further five. Jobson was a totally committed player who could be relied upon until the final whistle of every match.
Debut: 27 Aug 1932 v Brentford (H) 2-3 Div 3 (S).

Reg John

JOHN Reginald

(RH) Mid 5' 10" 11st 0lbs
b: Aberdare, Wales, 27 Jul 1899
QPR: Aug 1920
Football League: 131-1. **FAC:** 14-0. **FLC:** 0-0.
Other: 0-0. **Total:** 145-1.

Reg was a strong, fast and determined tackler who had sound defensive qualities. After a six year spell of fairly regular first team football at QPR, where he notched up over 140 first team games, Reg failed to make a big impact in his one season with Charlton Athletic, when he played just six senior matches. During his time at the Valley he was the victim of a case of mistaken identity, when it was reported that John had been booked for misconduct in a reserve match. However, the manager informed the FA that he had not been cautioned or even spoken to by the referee and that the player who actually offended was someone else! He played in all three half-back positions before his move to Folkestone in August 1927.
Debut: 6 Nov 1920 v Southampton (A) 2-2 Div 3.

JOHNS Nicholas Paul

Goal 6' 2" 11st 5lbs
b: Bristol, 8 Jun 1957
QPR: (£40,000) Dec 1987
Football League: 10-6. **FAC:** 3-0. **FLC:** 2-0.
Other: 1-0. **Total:** 16-0.
Honours: 2nd Div runner's-up medal.

Nicky was on occasions an outstandingly brilliant goalkeeper who played throughout the 1980s for Charlton Athletic, and QPR bought him as the reserve to their regular keeper, David Seaman. Johns was last heard of as being employed as a Football in the Community officer based at Crystal Palace.
Debut: 21 Dec 1987 v Reading (H) 1-3 Full Members' Cup first round.

JOHNSON Henry Edward

(CF) Striker 5' 7" 11st 6lbs
b: Birmingham, 1897
QPR: Feb 1924
Football League: 50-15. **FAC:** 5-0. **FLC:** 0-0.
Other: 0-0. **Total:** 55-15.
Honours: Junior international. British Army representative.

Harry was secured on a free transfer by Southampton where he started well but faded badly. On arriving at QPR he played through the two re-election campaigns before finally leaving in 1926.
Debut: 16 Feb 1924 v Reading (H) 1-4 Div 3 (S).

JOHNSON John Henry

(IL) Mid 5' 8" 11st 11lbs
b: Bristol, 25 May 1897
d: 1974
QPR: 1927
Football League: 18-7. **FAC:** 1-1. **FLC:** 0-0.
Other: 0-0. **Total:** 19-8.

John was the usual substitute for Goddard whenever the latter was injured. He scored in his first two matches, so he was tried as a twin centre-forward, alongside Goddard, however, this plan failed completely.
Debut: 3 Sep 1927 v Swindon Town (A) 2-0 Div 3 (S).

JOHNSON Richard

Mid 5' 11" 12st 0lbs
b: Kurri Kurri, Australia, 27 Apr 1974
QPR: Feb 2003
Football League: 17-0. **FAC:** 0-0. **FLC:** 1-0.
Other: 0-0. **Total:** 18-0.
Debut: 20 Feb 2004 v Peterborough United (H) 1-1 Div 2.

JONES Charles H

(IF) Mid 5' 10" 11st 7lbs
b: Swansea, Wales, 1911
QPR: 1932
Football League: 16-0. **FAC:** 0-0. **FLC:** 0-0.
Other: 0-0. **Total:** 16-0.

Charlie was used as a replacement for George Rounce whenever George was out of the side, injured, or otherwise.
Debut: 10 Sep 1932 v Crystal Palace (H) 2-1 Div 3 (S).

JONES Paul Steven

Goal 6' 3" 14st 0lbs
b: Chirk, Wrexham, Wales, 16 Apr 1967
QPR: Feb 2006
Football League: 26-0. **FAC:** 0-0. **FLC:** 0-0.
Other: 0-0. **Total:** 26-0.
Honours: 50 Wales caps.

A reliable goalkeeper who began his long professional career by racking up around 250 appearances for Kidderminster Harriers, Paul played at the highest level. He starred in the Premiership for Southampton and Liverpool and won 50 caps for his country. Paul – who became the first substitute goalkeeper used in an FA Cup final when Saints lost to Arsenal in 2003 – joined Rangers in February 2006 and played a vital part in preserving the club's Championship status. Paul is currently the goalkeeping coach at Hereford United.
Debut: 11 Feb 2006 v Millwall (H) 1-0 Championship.

JONES Raymond Barry Bankote

Striker 6' 4"14st 2lbs
b: Newham, London, 28 Aug 1988
d: East Ham, London, 25 Aug 2007
QPR: 2006
Football League: 33-5. **FAC:** 2-0. **FLC:** 2-1.

Other: 0-0. **Total:** 37-6.
Honours: 1 England U19 cap.

Ray was a talented footballer – praised for his intelligence with the ball at his feet and more than capable in the air – who made his Rangers debut at the latter end of the 2005/06 season. A teenager with bags of potential, Ray's life and professional career were tragically cut short in the early hours of 25 August 2007 when the car in which he was travelling collided with a bus. As a mark of respect, QPR postponed their next League game and decided to retire the number 31 shirt in memory of Ray, who wore the shirt during his time at Loftus Road.

Debut: 22 Apr 2006 v Watford (H) 1-2 Championship.

Ray Jones
(congratulating Shabazz Baidoo)

Vinnie Jones

JONES Vincent Peter

Mid 6' 0" 11st 12lbs
b: Watford, Herts, 5 Jan 1965
QPR: (£500,000) Mar 1998
Football League: 7-1. **FAC:** 0-0. **FLC:** 0-0.
Other: 0-0. **Total:** 7-1.
Honours: 9 caps for Wales. FA Cup winner's medal. 2nd Div championship medal.

A midfield player who was a great motivator on the field and hated to lose. Vinnie always gave 100% effort and was well known for his intimidating style. He was a transfer deadline signing and was brought into the team as the player/coach. Jones was well known for his dangerous set-pieces and long throw-ins. He now has many interests outside football, including that of film star, and appears in television game and chat shows.

Debut: 28 Mar 1998 v Huddersfield Town (A) 1-1 Div 1.

JORDAN Frank

(OR) Wing
QPR: 1899
Southern League: 2-0. **FAC:** 0-0. **FLC:** 0-0.
Other: 0-0. **Total:** 2-0.

A reserve team player, Frank had been a member of the club in its formative years.

Debut: 14 Sep 1901 v Tottenham Hotspur (A) 0-2 SL Div 1.

JORDAN Harry

(OR) Wing
QPR: Jun 1899
Southern League: 1-0. **FAC:** 1-0. **FLC:** 0-0.
Other: 0-0. **Total:** 2-0.

He was the brother of Frank, and the pair turned pro at QPR. Harry had been an amateur at Watford.

Debut: 7 Oct 1899 v Bristol City (A) 3-5 SL Div1.

K

KANYUKA Patrick
KEECH William
KEEN James Frederick
KEEN Michael Thomas
KEETCH Robert
KELLARD Thomas
KELLY Edward Patrick
KELLY Michael John
KELLY William Brian
KENNEDY Mark
KERR Andrew
KERRINS Patrick Michael
KERSLAKE David
KING A
KING Andrew Edward
KING Arthur
KING R
KINGSLEY Matthew
KIWOMYA Christopher Mark
KNIGHT Frederick C
KNOWLES Frank
KNOWLES Joseph
KOEJOE Samuel
KULCSAR George
KUS Marcin Robert

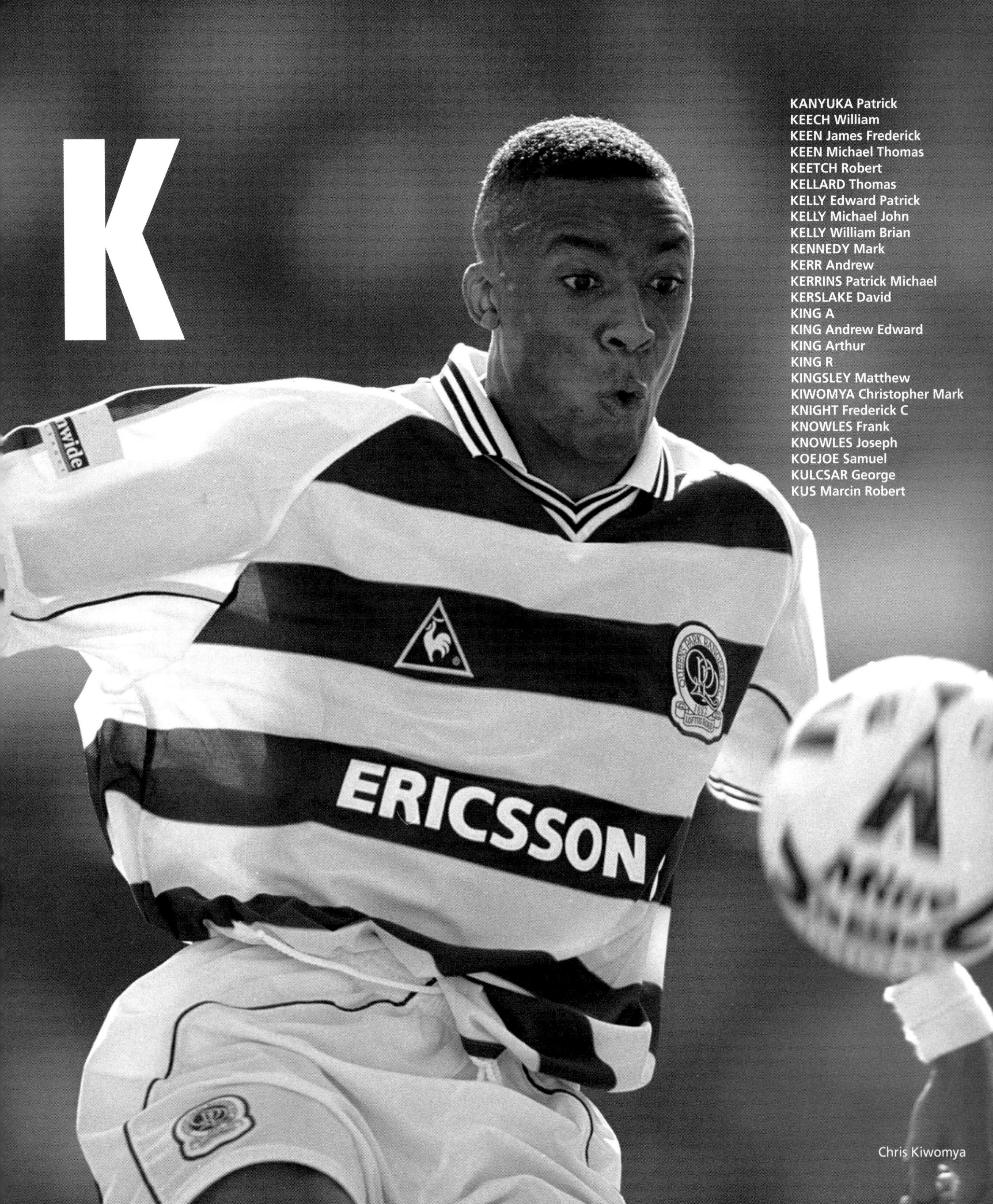

Chris Kiwomya

KANYUKA Patrick

Def 6′ 0″ 12st 6lbs
b: Kinshasa, DR Congo, 19 Jul 1987
QPR: 2005
Football League: 12-0. **FAC:** 1-0. **FLC:** 2-0.
Other: 0-0. **Total:** 15-0.
Debut: 19 Apr 2005 v Burnley (A) 0-2 Championship.

KEECH William

(WH) Mid 5′ 9″ 12st 7lbs
b: Irthlingborough, Northamptonshire, 1872
QPR: Aug 1899
Southern League: 55-3. **FAC:** 14-3. **FLC:** 0-0.
Other: 0-0. **Total:** 69-6.
Honours: Northamptonshire County representative. Sheffield & Hallamshire Cup winner's medal. Represented the Southern League.

By all accounts William was a very good athlete, winning three handicaps and numerous boxing titles. He was also the holder of the Royal Humane Society's gold medal. Football-wise he was a very good midfield man whose brother Ben played for QPR also, but in the reserves. After retirement William came back to the club as a member of the training staff.
Debut: 9 Sep 1899 v Tottenham Hotspur (A) 0-1 SL Div 1.

KEEN James Frederick

(OR) Wing 5′ 7″ 10st 6lbs
b: Newcastle, 25 Nov 1897
d: 1980
QPR: May 1923
Football League: 31-0. **FAC:** 1-0. **FLC:** 0-0.
Other: 0-0. **Total:** 32-0.

A product of the Welbeck Road school in Newcastle's East-End, Jimmy could play on both wings, however, speed was the major asset of his game for he was a professional sprinter of some repute and held many titles. Jimmy was not retained at the end of the 1923/24 season and later returned to the Newcastle area to play in minor football.
Debut: 25 Aug 1923 v Brentford (H) 1-0 Div 3 (S).

KEEN Michael Thomas

(RH) Mid 6′ 1″ 11st 8lbs
b: High Wycombe, 19 Mar 1940
QPR: Jun 1958
Football League: 393-39. **FAC:** 25-2. **FLC:** 21-3.
Other: 0-0. **Total:** 439-44.
Honours: 2nd Div runner's-up medal. League Cup winner's medal. 3rd Div runner's-up medal. Isthmian League championship medal as the manager.

As a tall, stylish all-round wing-half he captained the side to a unique double, of League Cup winners and Third Division champions, in 1967. Mike was a tough, skilful, no compromise wing-half of the old fashioned school, he was perceptive and also a strong tackler and was ever-present from 16 March 1963 until 14 September 1968. His time in the first team at Loftus Road extended over 10 season, that of 1964/65 being the most successful so far as goals were concerned, when he notched up a very creditable 13 in League matches. After turning out for Watford on over a hundred occasions he became manager in 1973, then the same at Northampton Town in 1978. Mike had retired as a player after making a career total of 664 League appearances, half-way through his spell as the Watford manager, when the club dropped into the Fourth Division. However he did lead Wycombe Wanderers to the Isthmian League championship.

Five years later, in 1985, he became the boss of Marlow, and in 1995 the same at Flackwell Heath. Mike later took up coaching one night a week at the West Ham school of excellence in Slough.
Debut: 7 Sep 1959 v York City (A) 1-2 Div 3.

KEETCH Robert

CD 5′ 10″ 11st 7lbs
b: Tottenham, London, 25 Oct 1941
d: 29 Jun 1996
QPR: Nov 1966
Football League: 52-0. **FAC:** 2-0. **FLC:** 2-0.
Other: 0-0. **Total:** 56-0.
Honours: 2nd Div runner's-up medal.

Bobby was a typical footballer of the swinging 60s after the abolition of the maximum wage. A somewhat paradoxical character off the pitch but very tough and uncompromising on it, he would arrive at the ground, more often than not in a Rolls Royce wearing a pinstripe suit and a fob-watch in his waist-coat pocket. He was a star in the middle of the defence and played a big part in the rise of the club from the Third to the First Division in successive seasons. He retired at the age of 27, in 1968, to spend more time with his business. This involved flying all over the world, buying and selling. Bobbie died of a stroke in 1996.
Debut: 11 Mar 1967 v Peterborough United (H) 0-0 Div 3.

KELLARD Thomas

(IF) Mid 5′ 9″ 10st 4lbs
b: Oldham, Lancashire, 1905
QPR: May 1928
Football League: 5-1. **FAC:** 0-0. **FLC:** 0-0.
Other: 0-0. **Total:** 5-1.

A first-class reserve who won many honours in the lower leagues of professional football, Tom was a keen sprinter in his younger days and he was a regular scorer in the reserve team, however, he was rarely in line for a first team place. Tom came to the club from Oldham Athletic, along with Norman Crompton.
Debut: 25 Dec 1928 v Swindon Town (H) 4-2 Div 3 (S).

KELLY Edward Patrick

Mid 5′ 7″ 12st 0lbs
b: Glasgow, Scotland, 7 Feb 1951
QPR: (£80,000) Sep 1976
Football League: 28-1. **FAC:** 0-0. **FLC:** 3-0.
Other: 2-0. **Total:** 33-1.
Honours: 5 Scottish youth caps. 3 U23 caps. Combination Cup winner's medal. 2 Combination League winner's medals. London Challenge Cup winner's medal. European Fairs Cup winner's medal. League championship winner's medal. FA Cup winner's medal. League runner's-up medal. 2nd Div championship medal.

Eddie had been the captain of Arsenal in the early 1970s but at QPR, although he was tough in the tackle and gave the impression of strength and skill, he seemed to lack a certain pace. He left after a season and thereafter changed clubs constantly. Eddie became the manager of Barnstaple in 1995, before moving into the double glazing industry in Paignton, Devon.
Debut: 11 Sep 1976 v Aston Villa (H) 2-1 Div 1.

KELLY Michael John

Goal 6′ 0″ 12st 7lbs
b: Northampton, 18 Oct 1942
QPR: (£3,000) Mar 1966
Football League: 54-0. **FAC:** 4-0. **FLC:** 5-0.
Other: 0-0. **Total:** 63-0.
Honours: 3 English Amateur caps. FA Amateur Cup winner's medal. 2 Isthmian League championship medals. 2nd Div runner's-up medal.

Mike was a highly efficient goalkeeper who had turned out in over 200 matches for Wimbledon as an amateur before turning professional at QPR. Apt to communicate (in a loud voice) with defenders during the course of a match, he had the unusual pre-match ritual of kicking the base of both goalposts and touching the crossbar in the centre before the start of every match. In 1976 he became the manager of the Minnesota Kicks in the USA. A year later he was in charge of Plymouth Argyle and then the Fulham assistant manager in 1978. This was followed by becoming the Crystal Palace coach in 1981, then a year later the same at Portsmouth, followed by WBA in 1983. In 1985 he was given the job at the FA School of Excellence as chief coach, then the England goalkeeping coach in 1987. Mike was last heard of at Liverpool in 1991 – as the coach!
Debut: 29 Aug 1967 v Bristol City (H) 3-1 Div 2.

KELLY William Brian

(CF) Striker
b: Isleworth, London, 25 Sep 1937
QPR: Nov 1958
Football League: 6-0. **FAC:** 0-0. **FLC:** 0-0.
Other: 0-0. **Total:** 6-0.

Andy King

Bill was one of seven players to be tried during the 1958/59 season in an effort to cure the centre-forward problem. All were failures until George Whitelaw came along the following season.
Debut: 13 Dec 1958 v Swindon Town (A) 0-2 Div 3.

KENNEDY Mark
(OL) Wing 5′ 11″ 11st 9lbs
b: Dublin, Eire, 15 May 1976
QPR: (Loan) Jan 1998
Football League: 8-2. **FAC:** 0-0. **FLC:** 0-0.
Other: 0-0. **Total:** 8-2.
Honours: 34 Republic of Ireland international caps. Youth caps. School caps and 7 caps at U21 level.
Mark is a highly talented left-footed player who was on loan to QPR with a view to a permanent transfer, but the deal fell through.
Debut: 31 Jan 1998 v Stockport County (A) 0-2 Div 1.

KERR Andrew
(CF) Striker 5′ 8″ 11st 7lbs
b: Falkirk, Scotland, 1900
QPR: Mar 1926
Football League: 2-0. **FAC:** 0-0. **FLC:** 0-0.
Other: 0-0. **Total:** 2-0.
Andrew was successful at Luton Town and Reading where he topped the reserve team goalscorers, but he couldn't pull it off at QPR.
Debut: 20 Mar 1926 v Crystal Palace (1-1) 1-3 Div 3 (S).

KERRINS Patrick Michael
(CF) Striker 5′ 11″ 11st 2lb
b: Fulham, London, 13 Sep 1936
QPR: Dec 1953
Football League: 146-30. **FAC:** 9-0. **FLC:** 0-0.
Other: 2-1. **Total:** 157-31.
Pat was a product of the juniors. He was very fast and could play on either wing as well as at centre-forward. When he first appeared as a striker it must have seemed to all and sundry at the club that this problem position had been solved, for he scored five goals in four matches. He was given an extended run leading the attack the following season but to no avail. However, he effectively kept the club in the Third Division when the regional Leagues were split to form the new Third and Fourth Divisions in 1958. At this time he scored another crucial five goals in four late season matches from the centre-forward position. Pat ended his days as a half-back at Romford.
Debut: 13 Feb 1954 v Exeter City (A) 0-0 Div 3 (S).

KERSLAKE David
Mid 5′ 8″ 11st 0lb
b: Stepney, London, 19 Jun 1966
QPR: Jun 1983
Football League: 58-6. **FAC:** 4-0. **FLC:** 8-4.
Other: 4-0. **Total:** 74-10.
Honours: 10 English school caps. 29 youth caps. 3 U17 youth caps. 1 U21 cap. 2nd Div play-off medal.
David was a very good midfield player, who at the time was the most capped Youth international. He was later turned into a defender although he was happier going forward. Although at Loftus Road for over six years, he only made 74 appearances in the senior squad, but was snapped up by Swindon Town for a sizeable fee, which was considerably increased when he subsequently moved on. He ended his career back at Swindon Town in 2000.
Debut: 19 Apr 1985 v Newcastle United (A) 0-1 Div 1.

KING A
For
QPR: 1911
Southern League: 3-0. **FAC:** 1-0. **FLC:** 0-0.
Other: 0-0. **Total:** 4-0.
Nothing is known about this player, except that he played most of his games in the reserve team.
Debut: 26 Dec 1911 v Crystal Palace (A) 0-3 SL Div 1.

KING Andrew Edward
Mid 5′ 9″ 10st 13lbs
b: Luton, Bedfordshire, 14 Aug 1956
QPR: (£425,000) Sep 1980
Football League: 30-9. **FAC:** 2-0. **FLC:** 1-0.
Other: 0-0. **Total:** 33-9.
Honours: 2 England U21 caps. League Cup final runner's-up medal. 4th Div promotion medal.
Andy was a hugely gifted player but at the same time an erratic and inconsistent one. Yet if he had harnessed his undoubted talent with a degree of self discipline, he would almost certainly have gone on to full England honours. His masterful control and deft distribution was on show, yet he never really fitted into the set-up as one would have liked, so he left the club. His most notable achievement at QPR was to score the first ever goal on the Loftus Road artificial pitch! He became the Waterford player manager in 1988, before playing for Southport a year later. He then took over the managership at Mansfield Town in 1993.
Debut: 20 Sep 1980 v Sheffield Wednesday (A) 0-1 Div 2.

KING Arthur
For
QPR: 1901
Southern League: 21-2. **FAC:** 1-0. **FLC:** 0-0.
Other: 0-0. **Total:** 22-2.
Arthur took over the centre-forward position when the regular player, Millar, was injured in 1902. However, he played the majority of his matches at outside-right.
Debut: 7 Sep 1901 v Watford (H) 0-1 SL Div 1.

KING R

(IR) Mid
QPR: 1908
Southern League: 3-0. **FAC:** 0-0. **FLC:** 0-0.
Other: 0-0. **Total:** 3-0.

A reserve player who was briefly tried unsuccessfully, in the first team.
Debut: 21 Nov 1908 v Swindon Town (A) 1-3 SL Div 1.

KINGSLEY Matthew

Goal 5′ 11″ 14st 5lbs
b: Turton, Lancashire, 1876
d: 27 Mar 1960
QPR: 1905
Southern League: 20-0. **FAC:** 0-0. **FLC:** 0-0.
Other: 0-0. **Total:** 20-0.
Honours: 1 England cap. 3 Football League caps.

Matt was a reliable goalkeeper who usually fisted the ball away instead of catching it, so as not to be bundled into the net as was the practice in those far off days. He also had the habit of continually swinging his arms to and fro as he was waiting for action. He was sacked by West Ham United in 1904 following a fracas on the pitch with Herbert Lyon of Brighton, when the ex-England goalkeeper kicked him. The crowd spilled onto the pitch, ugly scenes developed, before Kingsley was sent off, and Lyon was carried off to the dressing room for treatment.
Debut: 2 Sep 1905 v New Brompton (H) 4-0 SL Div 1.

KIWOMYA Christopher Mark

Striker 5′ 9″ 11st 2lbs
b: Huddersfield, Yorkshire, 2 Dec 1969
QPR: Aug 1998
Football League: 86-25. **FAC:** 5-3. **FLC:** 5-2.
Other: 0-0. **Total:** 96-30.
Honours: 2nd Div championship medal. European Cup Winners' Cup runner's-up medal.

Much of Chris' career was spent at Ipswich, until he was signed by Arsenal for a large fee. But he was unable to justify the expenditure and after less than two years and only a few appearances for the Gunners he was loaned out. He finally signed on a free transfer for Rangers and spent three years at Loftus Road. A swift-footed striker Chris can play on the left hand side of the field or in a central role, and is able to get behind defences without breaking the offside rule. After nearly 100 appearances he moved on, first to Le Havre (France) and then to Grimsby Town.
Debut: 29 Aug 1998 v Bury (H) 0-0 Div 1.

KNIGHT Frederick C

(CF) Striker
QPR: 1921
Football League: 2-1. **FAC:** 0-0. **FLC:** 0-0.
Other: 0-0. **Total:** 2-1.

Fred stood in for the centre-forward J W Smith when he was injured, and scored on his debut. However, he was never heard of again.
Debut: 12 Nov 1921 v Aberdare Athletic (H) 1-0 Div 3 (S).

KNOWLES Frank

(CD) CD 5′ 11″ 11st 12lbs
b: Hyde, Cheshire, 1891
QPR: Feb 1924
Football League: 35-0. **FAC:** 5-0. **FLC:** 0-0.
Other: 0-0. **Total:** 40-0.

Frank proved himself at Manchester United by being the stand-in for the great Charlie Roberts and he was first choice whenever he was absent. Frank had a very fortunate escape in 1912, when he was one of six passengers in a car, which crashed and overturned near Rudyard Lake in Staffordshire. Two of the passengers were killed instantly but Knowles escaped with no more than a severe shaking. During the First World War, Frank guested for Hyde, Arsenal and Oldham Athletic, but at QPR he could not stop the club from having to seek re-election for the first time in their history.
Debut: 23 Feb 1924 v Reading (A) 0-4 Div 3 (S).

Sammy Koejoe

KNOWLES Joseph

(RB) Def 5′ 6″ 11st 6lbs
b: Monkwearmouth, Sunderland, 1872
QPR: 1899
Southern League: 22-0. **FAC:** 7-0. **FLC:** 0-0.
Other: 0-0. **Total:** 29-0.

Joe was noted as a safe and sturdy player, as well as a brilliant defender. He was one of the first players to join QPR when they embraced professionalism and was a good capture for the fledgling club in their first season in the Southern League.
Debut: 9 Sep 1899 v Tottenham Hotspur (A) 0-1 SL Div 1.

KOEJOE Samuel

Striker 6′ 1″ 12st 2lbs
b: Paramaribo, Surinam, 17 Aug 1974
QPR: (£250,000) Nov 1999
Football League: 34-3. **FAC:** 5-0. **FLC:** 3-0.
Other: 0-0. **Total:** 42-3.

Sammy was a big, bustling striker with good pace whose contract was cancelled by mutual agreement at the end of August 2002.
Debut: 4 Dec 1999 v Huddersfield Town (A) 0-1 Div 1.

KULCSAR George

Mid 6′ 2″ 13st 4lbs
b: Budapest, Hungary, 12 Aug 1967
QPR: (£250,000) Dec 1997
Football League: 56-1. **FAC:** 2-0. **FLC:** 2-0.
Other: 0-0. **Total:** 60-1.
Honours: 3 Australian caps.

Ray Harford's first buy during the short period he was with the club as manager. George never seemed to stop running, and was a strong ball winning player with control over the centre of the park. His single goal for the club was a valuable one, for it was one of six scored at Crystal Palace in May 1969, which saved the Rangers from relegation. He was released from his contract by mutual consent in May 2001.
Debut: 21 Dec 1997 v Bradford City (H) 1-0 Div 1.

KUS Marcin Robert

Def 6′ 0″ 11st 7lbs
b: Warsaw, Poland, 2 Sep 1981
QPR: 2006
Football League: 3-0. **FAC:** 0-0. **FLC:** 0-0.
Other: 0-0. **Total:** 3-0.
Debut: 4 Feb 2006 v Leeds United (A) 0-2 Championship.

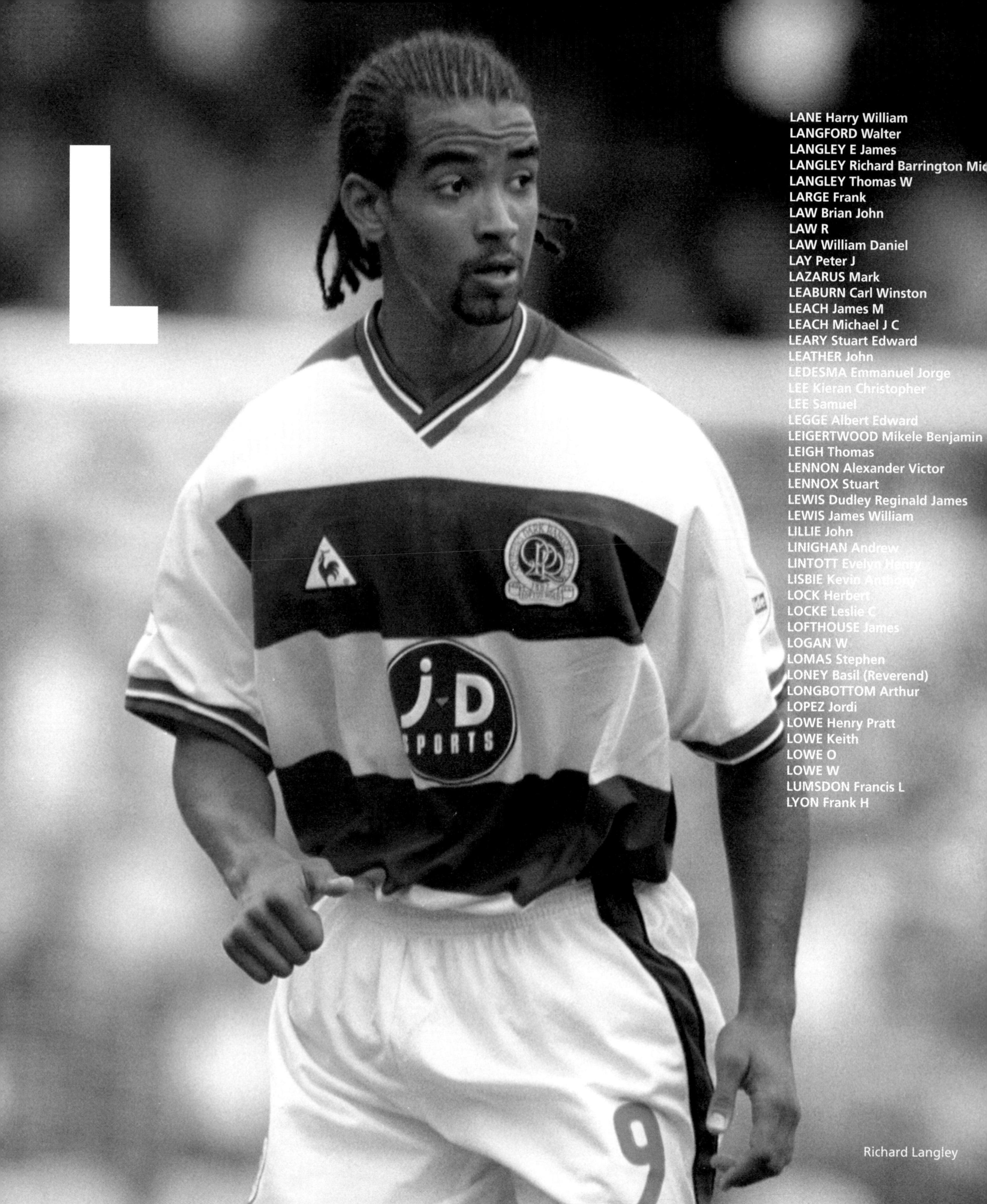

L

LANE Harry William
LANGFORD Walter
LANGLEY E James
LANGLEY Richard Barrington Mic
LANGLEY Thomas W
LARGE Frank
LAW Brian John
LAW R
LAW William Daniel
LAY Peter J
LAZARUS Mark
LEABURN Carl Winston
LEACH James M
LEACH Michael J C
LEARY Stuart Edward
LEATHER John
LEDESMA Emmanuel Jorge
LEE Kieran Christopher
LEE Samuel
LEGGE Albert Edward
LEIGERTWOOD Mikele Benjamin
LEIGH Thomas
LENNON Alexander Victor
LENNOX Stuart
LEWIS Dudley Reginald James
LEWIS James William
LILLIE John
LINIGHAN Andrew
LINTOTT Evelyn Henry
LISBIE Kevin Anthony
LOCK Herbert
LOCKE Leslie C
LOFTHOUSE James
LOGAN W
LOMAS Stephen
LONEY Basil (Reverend)
LONGBOTTOM Arthur
LOPEZ Jordi
LOWE Henry Pratt
LOWE Keith
LOWE O
LOWE W
LUMSDON Francis L
LYON Frank H

Richard Langley

LANE Harry William

Def 5' 11" 11st 4lbs
b: Stoney Stanton, Leicestershire, 23 Oct 1894
QPR: Jul 1922
Football League: 5-0. **FAC:** 0-0. **FLC:** 0-0.
Other: 0-0. **Total:** 5-0.

Harry was a school teacher by profession, and therefore an amateur and mainly a reserve at his various clubs. During the Great War he served in the Army and the Air Force. He was a versatile player appearing in defence or attack, but at QPR he was used mainly as a defender.

Debut: 4 Nov 1922 v Aberdare Athletic (A) 0-0 Div 3 (S).

LANGFORD Walter

(IL) Mid 5' 9" 11st 5lbs
b: Wolverhampton, 24 Mar 1905
d: Wolverhampton, 7 Jan 1996
QPR: Aug 1933
Football League: 11-0. **FAC:** 1-0. **FLC:** 0-0.
Other: 1-0. **Total:** 13-0.

Tommy Langley

Walter was a reserve who stood in for the captain of the side, Joe Devine, he could also fill in at half-back and did so during his time at Loftus Road. Walter was one of the first signings of manager Mick O'Brien and was part of a very good side put together by him.

Debut: 9 Sep 1933 v Luton Town (H) 2-1 Div 3 (S).

LANGLEY E James

(LB) Def 5' 10" 11st 12lbs
b: Kilburn, London, 7 Feb 1929
QPR: Jul 1965
Football League: 87-8. **FAC:** 8-1. **FLC:** 10-1.
Other: 0-0. **Total:** 105-10.
Honours: 3 England caps. 1 Football League cap. 3 B caps. 4 caps for the FA XI. Went on the tour of the West Indies and South Africa. 2nd Div runner's-up medal. Championship medal. League Cup winner's medal.

Jim became the favourite of the Loftus Road crowd with his wholeheartedness and tough but legal tackling. He was always noted for his fairness in the game, and was given license to roam the field.

Jim would use a wide range of tricks, such as a bicycle-kick, the overhead-kick, he had an enormous throw-in and his sliding tackle, which were all superb. Jim played in over 50 matches during the successful 1966/67 campaign, including the League Cup final. At Hillingdon Borough, as player/manager, he made another trip to Wembley, when he took his team in 1971 to the FA Challenge Trophy final.

Debut: 21 Aug 1965 v Brentford (A) 1-6 Div 3.

LANGLEY Richard Barrington Michael

Mid 5' 10" 11st 4lbs
b: Harlesden, London, 27 Dec 1979
QPR: Dec 1996
Football League: 134-19. **FAC:** 7-0. **FLC:** 6-2.
Other: 1-0. **Total:** 148-21.
QPR: 2005
Football League: 33-3. **FAC:** 1-0. **FLC:** 0-0.
Other: 0-0. **Total:** 34-3.
Honours: England youth. 12 caps for Jamaica.

A central midfield player from the QPR youth academy who could pass, shoot, tackle and play his way out of tight situations, rather than hoofing the ball up the pitch. A lot of injuries have passed Richard's way, including a broken hand, keyhole surgery on his knee, a kidney and a cartilage operation. Richard made around 100 appearances at Loftus Road in over five years, however, during the 2002/03 season he was a big influence in the side, when he missed few games during the season. Crucial goals, including a hat-trick helped to ensure QPR a promotion play-off place that season. Richard left for Cardiff City in 2003 before returning to Loftus Road two year later. This time, though, his stay lasted just one campaign before signing for Luton Town.

Debut: 31 Oct 1998 v Swindon Town (A) 1-3 Div 1.

LANGLEY Thomas W

(CF) Striker 5' 11" 10st 7lbs
b: Lambeth, London, 8 Feb 1958
QPR: (£425,000) 1980
Football League: 25-8. **FAC:** 0-0. **FLC:** 3-1.
Other: 0-0. **Total:** 28-9.
Honours: England schoolboy caps. 8 youth caps. 1 U21 cap. 3 B caps.

Associated with Chelsea at the age of 10 years old, Tommy played for the Colts team at the age of 12. He made his Football League debut at the age of 16 and he was a fast and totally committed player who showed his enthusiasm throughout the match.

Debut: 28 Mar 1980 v Swansea City (H) 0-0 Div 2.

JKL

LARGE Frank

(CF) Striker 5' 10" 13st 2lbs
b: Leeds, Yorkshire, 26 Jan 1940
QPR: (£7,500) Jun 1962
Football League: 18-5. **FAC:** 3-2. **FLC:** 1-0.
Other: 0-0. **Total:** 22-7.
Honours: 2 3rd Div championship medals.

A bustling centre-forward who could terrify goalkeepers just by looking in their direction, Frank scored a career total of 209 goals in 569 competitive matches. He was an Alec Stock acquisition, but it was Northampton Town that seemed to get the best out of him. After less than a year at Loftus Road he made frequent moves, and after his retirement from the game he became a charge hand in a factory in Northampton. In the mid-1980s he moved to County Mayo, Ireland, to run a bed and breakfast business combined with working in a nearby estate as a handyman/gamekeeper.

Debut: 18 Aug 1962 v Brighton & Hove Albion (H) 2-2 Div 3.

LAW Brian John

CD 6' 2" 13st 12lbs
b: Merthyr Tydfil, Wales, 1 Jan 1970
QPR: Aug 1987
Football League: 20-0. **FAC:** 3-0. **FLC:** 3-0.
Other: 1-0. **Total:** 27-0.
Honours: 2 U21 caps. 1 full Welsh cap.

A powerful youngster who was very quick, but Brian was forced to retire in 1992 with foot ligament injuries. He embarked on a back-packing holiday around the world and when he returned he resurrected his career with Wolves, who put him through a rigorous trial which lasted a month. After two and a half years, Brian was transferred to

Millwall, where he became captain of the side until 2000 when he was released from his contract.
Debut: 23 Apr 1988 v Sheffield Wednesday (H) 1-1 Div 1.

LAW R
(OR) Wing
QPR: 1910
Southern League: 1-0. **FAC:** 0-0. **FLC:** 0-0.
Other: 0-0. **Total:** 1-0.

A young trialist who played for the senior squad in the last match of the 1910/11 season.
Debut: 29 Apr 1911 v Plymouth Argyle (H) 1-0 SL Div 1.

LAW William Daniel
(OL) Wing 5′ 7″ 11st 7lbs
b: Pleck, Walsall, March 1882
d: 1952
QPR: May 1908
Southern League: 4-1. **FAC:** 1-0. **FLC:** 0-0.
Other: 0-0. **Total:** 5-1.

A clever little winger who could centre the ball with accuracy while on the run. Billy was used as a reserve to the first choice winger and captain Billy Barnes, and retired from football in 1914.
Debut: 16 Sep 1908 v Watford (A) 0-0 SL Div 1.

LAY Peter J
(CH) CD
b: Stratford, London, 4 Dec 1931
QPR: Jul 1956
Football League: 1-0. **FAC:** 0-0. **FLC:** 0-0.
Other: 0-0. **Total:** 1-0.

Peter arrived at Loftus Road, and stayed for two years. But the consistency and freedom from injury of the regular centre-half, Keith Rutter, ensured that Peter was never able to make his mark in the side.
Debut: 26 Dec 1956 v Crystal Palace (H) 4-2 Div 3 (S).

LAZARUS Mark
(OR) Wing 5′ 8″ 11st 3lbs
b: Stepney, London, 5 Dec 1938
QPR: (£3,000) Sep 1960
Football League: 37-19. **FAC:** 2-0. **FLC:** 3-1.
Other: 0-0. **Total:** 42-20.

Mark Lazarus

Mike Leach

QPR: (£15,000) Feb 1962
Football League: 81-28. **FAC:** 6-1. **FLC:** 1-0.
Other: 0-0. **Total:** 88-29.
QPR: (£10,000) Nov 1965
Football League: 88-29. **FAC:** 6-2. **FLC:** 11-4.
Other: 0-0. **Total:** 105-35.
Honours: League Cup winner's medal. Two 2nd Div runner's-up medals. 3rd Div championship medal.

Mark was one of a family of eight brothers plus five sisters, and he was a former boxer who was unbeaten in 10 fights. Two of his brothers, Harry and Lew Lazar, were also famous in the "ring". A powerfully built player, he had been on the books of Fulham as an amateur, before being taken in hand by Leyton Orient. Mark made his debut for the Os; in the London Challenge Cup match v Charlton Athletic, scoring two brilliant goals, and he signed professional forms in November 1957. He was noted as being very fast and aggressive, by Alec Stock, who watched him on several occasions before eventually signing him.

Mark became a big favourite of the crowd at Loftus Road. However, after just one season he became a big money signing for Wolves, but was back at Loftus Road four months later. In 1964 he agreed to a move to Brentford where he was equally popular during his near two year stay. Mark made a second return to QPR, and in two years added another 105 games to produce a grand total of 235 with 84 goals. In 12 years of League football, Mark notched up a total of 134 goals in 442 League appearances. He went on to run his own transport business in Romford, Essex.
Debut: 17 Sep 1960 v Colchester United (A) 1-0 Div 3.

LEABURN Carl Winston
(CF) Striker 6′ 3″ 13st 0lbs
b: Lewisham, London, 30 Mar 1969
QPR: 2002
Football League: 1-0. **FAC:** 0-0. **FLC:** 0-0.
Other: 0-0. **Total:** 1-0.

Carl created a new club record, when he had the shortest first team career for QPR, with just a three minute appearance!
Debut: 5 Jan 2002 v Reading (A) 0-1 Div 2.

LEACH James M
(LH) Def 5′ 10″ 11st 8lbs
b: Spennymore, County Durham, July 1890
d: 1951
QPR: Jul 1922
Football League: 1-0. **FAC:** 0-0. **FLC:** 0-0.
Other: 0-0. **Total:** 1-0.

Jim was an excellent player, who was brainy, witty, always looked confident on the ball, and always seemed to have plenty of time in which to manoeuvre. Unfortunately a very bad injury kept him out of the side for the whole of the 1919/20 season, which forced him to miss the Aston Villa Cup final v Huddersfield Town. Jim retired from football in 1923 after leading the reserves at Loftus Road.
Debut: 26 Aug 1922 v Watford (H) 1-2 Div 3 (S).

LEACH Michael J C
Mid 6′ 0″ 12st 0lbs
b: Hackney, London, 16 Jan 1947
QPR: Feb 1964
Football League: 313-61. **FAC:** 23-3. **FLC:** 19-6.
Other: 6-0. **Total:** 361-70.
Honours: 2 England youth caps. 2 2nd Div runner's-up medals.

Mike could always be relied on to give 100%

Emmanual Ledesma

effort in a match and was one of the many debutants to have scored in their opening match. Some of the crowd did not appreciate his running off the ball, as he never appeared to be moving fast but in this he was deceptive. It wasn't until his fifth season at Loftus Road that Mike became more or less a regular in the first team. Alec Stock brought Mike into the team for the last five matches of the 1967/68 season, and this inclusion proved to be a master stroke. For during this period Mike struck-up an instant relationship with Rodney Marsh and he scored three goals in five matches as Rangers clinched a place in the First Division. Mike's stay at QPR was to last 14 years in total, when over 300 League matches were played. Mike moved out to the USA in 1978, but soon returned and played for Cambridge United, until moving into the non-League world.
Debut: 26 Feb 1965 v Colchester United (H) 5-0 Div 3.

LEARY Stuart Edward

(CF) Striker 5' 9" 10st 9lbs
b: Cape Town, South Africa, 30 Apr 1933
d: August 1988
QPR: Dec 1962
Football League: 94-29. **FAC:** 7-3. **FLC:** 3-0.
Other: 0-0. **Total:** 104-32.

Stuart's movement off the ball was superb and his shooting was excellent, he was a very good opportunist and a shrewd distributor of the ball. His services were in demand all year round, for cricket was his other sport. Stuart accumulated 16,000 runs and took 140 wickets at an average of 33.67 for Kent. He retired from football in 1966 and died on Table Mountain, South Africa in 1988, his body being discovered on 23rd August; Stuart had been missing for five days.
Debut: 15 Dec 1962 v Brighton & Hove Albion (A) 2-2 Div 3.

LEATHER John

Goal 6' 0" 11st 10lbs
b: 1875
QPR: 1898
Southern League: 2-0. **FAC:** 0-0. **FLC:** 0-0.
Other: 0-0. **Total:** 2-0.

Jack was a reserve to the other goalkeepers at Arsenal as well as at QPR. He played in eight League and two FA Cup matches as well as 58 reserve matches for the Gunners.
Debut: 26 Mar 1904 v Wellingborough (H) 3-0 SL Div 1.

LEDESMA Emmanuel Jorge

Mid
b: Quilmes, Argentina, 24 May 1988
QPR: (Loan) Jun 2008

Sammy Lee

Football League: 17-1. **FAC:** 2-0. **FLC:** 4-3.
Other: 0-0. **Total:** 23-4.

Rangers beat off stiff competition from a number of Serie A clubs for Emmanuel's signature when they swooped to clinch the signing of the highly-rated Argentinean midfielder in June 2008. The youngster, who was born in Quilmes but has an Italian passport, agreed a season-long loan deal (from Genoa) with Rangers who had the option to buy the player for three million Euros at the end of his year-long stay. Despite becoming a favourite with the fans, Emmanuel returned to Italy in February 2009 on loan to Serie B side Salernitana.
Debut: 9 Aug 2008 v Barnsley (H) 2-1 Championship.

LEE Kieran Christopher

Mid 6' 1" 12st 0lbs
b: Stalybridge, 22 Jun 1988
QPR: (Loan) Jan 2008
Football League: 7-0. **FAC:** 1-0. **FLC:** 0-0.
Other: 0-0. **Total:** 8-0.
Debut: 5 Jan 2008 v Chelsea (A) 0-1 FA Cup third round.

LEE Samuel

Mid 5' 7" 10st 2lbs
b: Liverpool, 7 Feb 1959
QPR: (£200,000) Aug 1986
Football League: 30-0. **FAC:** 3-1. **FLC:** 2-0.
Other: 0-0. **Total:** 35-1.
Honours: 7 English youth caps. 6 U21 caps. 14 England caps. 2 European Cup winner's medals. 3 Div 1 championship medals. 4 Football League Cup winner's medals.

Sammy was the original "super-sub", at Liverpool, a fine all-round player and a complete midfield dynamo. He was an enthusiastic and strong runner, who was solid in the tackle and a fine distributor of the ball. All his honours were won while with Liverpool.
Debut: 30 Aug 1986 v Aston Villa (H) 1-0 Div 1.

LEGGE Albert Edward

(IR) Mid 5' 7" 10st 4lbs
b: Hednesford, Walsall, 19 Jan 1901
d: July 1988
QPR: Jun 1930
Football League: 9-1. **FAC:** 0-0. **FLC:** 0-0.
Other: 0-0. **Total:** 9-1.
Honours: 3rd Div (North) championship medal.

The son of a coalminer, Bert was a hard working and reliable inside-right who played the game until he was 38 years old. With retirement came the almost inevitable pub management, in Heathtown and Wolverhampton, followed by a job for the Goodyear Tyre Company until he reached pensionable age. At the time of his death he was resident in Wednesfield and died in New Cross Hospital.
Debut: 30 Aug 1930 v Thames Association (H) 3-0 Div 3 (S).

LEIGERTWOOD Mikele Benjamin

Mid 6' 2" 12st 3lbs
b: Enfield, 12 Nov 1982
QPR: (£900,000) Aug 2007
Football League: 82-7. **FAC:** 2-0. **FLC:** 2-0.
Other: 0-0. **Total:** 86-7.
Honours: 3 Antigua and Barbuda caps.

Rangers completed the signing of Mikele from Sheffield United on the final day of the 2007 summer transfer window. The no-nonsense midfielder soon became one of the first names on the team sheet and is fast approaching his 100th QPR appearance. Eligible for Antigua and Barbuda as well as England, Mikele made his international

debut on 5 November 2008 in a 3-2 defeat against Trinidad and Tobago but went on to score his first goal in their next match against Guyana.
Debut: 1 Sep 2007 v Southampton (H) 0-3 Championship.

LEIGH Thomas

(FB) Def 5′ 8″ 11st 3lbs
b: Hollins, Bury, 1888
QPR: 1910
Southern League: 4-0. **FAC:** 0-0. **FLC:** 0-0.
Other: 0-0. **Total:** 4-0.

Tommy is described in contemporary sources as, "a dandy who was both bold and vigorous, and very fast." He was also noted for his hard and low clearances. Tommy won many prizes for cycling, swimming, and at football where he could play on either flank, thereby being a reserve for both full-backs.
Debut: 19 Nov 1910 v Bristol Rovers (H) 1-2 SL Div 1.

LENNON Alexander Victor

(IL) Mid
b: Glasgow, Scotland, 23 Oct 1925
QPR: Jan 1947
Football League: 1-0. **FAC:** 0-0. **FLC:** 0-0.
Other: 0-0. **Total:** 1-0.

A surfeit of inside-forwards at Loftus Road led to the free transfer of this player to Mansfield Town. Alex played just three matches for them before they too released him.
Debut: 4 Dec 1948 v Coventry City (H) 0-3 Div 2.

LENNOX Stuart

(RH) Def
b: Scotland
QPR: 1900
Southern League: 11-0. **FAC:** 0-0. **FLC:** 0-0.
Other: 0-0. **Total:** 11-0.

Stuart was a typical Scottish player plying his trade south of the border. He was kept as a reserve at QPR and stood in as substitute for Keech when he was out of the side.

Debut: 29 Dec 1900 v Reading (H) 0-0 SL Div 1.

Mikele Leigertwood

LEWIS Dudley Reginald James

(CF) Striker 5′ 11″ 12st 0lbs
b: Kensington, London, 19 Nov 1909
d: Bath, 24 Apr 1987
QPR: 1929
Football League: 1-0. **FAC:** 0-0. **FLC:** 0-0.
Other: 0-0. **Total:** 1-0.

Dudley was still an amateur when he played for QPR, scoring a goal on his debut, and didn't sign pro forms until a few weeks later. During the 1931/32 season he appeared in 20 reserve team matches and scored five goals.
Debut: 2 May 1931 v Bournemouth and Boscombe Athletic (H) 3-0 Div 3 (S).

LEWIS James William

(IR) Mid 5′ 9″ 12st 0lbs
b: Hackney, London, 2 Dec 1905
d: March 1976
QPR: 1931
Football League: 11-4. **FAC:** 0-0. **FLC:** 0-0.
Other: 0-0. **Total:** 11-4.
Honours: 13 English Amateur caps. Member of a tour to South Africa winning 2 caps. Full England wartime cap as a substitute. 3 Athenian League championship medals.

Jim Lewis senior was the leading amateur of his day and QPR engaged him to play in their team in the 1931/32 season at the White City Stadium (just up the road from Loftus Road, where the reserve team played). Lewis had scored over 300 goals in his career and was a sound player in most aspects of the game, being able to seize a scoring opportunity at a moment's notice. But the hopes of the player and the club came to nothing when the team ended the season in 13th place in the division.
Debut: 29 Aug 1931 v Brentford (A) 0-1 Div 3 (S).

LILLIE John

(LB) Def 5′ 9″ 12st 0lbs
b: Newcastle
QPR: 1924
Football League: 3-0. **FAC:** 0-0. **FLC:** 0-0.
Other: 0-0. **Total:** 3-0.

John was a member of the reserve squad at Liverpool before he moved to QPR, staying for a season before he moved to East London.
Debut: 30 Aug 1924 v Newport County (A) 0-0 Div 3 (S).

LINIGHAN Andrew

CD 6′ 3″ 13st 10lbs
b: Hartlepool, 18 Dec 1962

QPR: (Loan) Mar 1999
Football League: 7-0. **FAC:** 0-0. **FLC:** 0-0.
Other: 0-0. **Total:** 7-0.
Honours: 4 England B caps. Div 1 championship medal. Football League Cup winner's medal. FA Cup winner's medal. European Cup Winners' Cup winner's medal.

Andrew was born into a footballing family, for his father played for Lincoln City and Darlington, while his brothers, Brian and David, played for Bury and Mansfield Town respectively.
Debut: 5 Apr 1999 v Ipswich Town (A) 1-3 Div 1.

LINTOTT Evelyn Henry

(HB) Def 5' 9" 12st 4lbs
b: Godalming, Surrey, 2 Nov 1883
d: July 1918
QPR: 1907
Southern League: 31-1. **FAC:** 2-0. **FLC:** 0-0.
Other: 2-0. **Total:** 35-1.
Honours: 7 full English caps. 5 England Amateur caps. Southern League championship medal. 1 Football League cap.

A schoolmaster by profession, he stayed an amateur throughout his career. Lintott was noted at the time as a player that followed in the footsteps of Needham and Forrest. A contemporary of the time wrote "He was a vigorous and clever player, tackling and passing with fine judgement." Evelyn was the club's first ever full international, when he played for England in February 1908. For a time he was the chairman of the Players' Union, however, he resigned from the post in 1911. Like so many others he volunteered to serve in the army in the 1914/18 conflict and served in the Light Infantry as a subaltern on the Somme in Flanders, where he lost his life.
Debut: 7 Sep 1907 v New Brompton (H) 2-2 SL Div 1.

LISBIE Kevin Anthony

Striker 5' 8" 10st 7lbs
b: Hackney, London, 17 Oct 1978
QPR: (Loan) Dec 2000
Football League: 2-0. **FAC:** 0-0. **FLC:** 0-0.
Other: 0-0. **Total:** 2-0.
Honours: English youth caps. 2 caps Jamaica.

Kevin, very fast and skilful on the ball and able to play as a central striker or on the wing, was on loan at Loftus Road for a short period.
Debut: 2 Dec 2000 v Sheffield Wednesday (A) 2-5 Div 1.

LOCK Herbert

Goal 5' 8" 12st 0lbs
b: Southampton, 22 Jan 1887
d: Southampton, 16 Mar 1957
QPR: Aug 1921
Football League: 6-0. **FAC:** 0-0. **FLC:** 0-0.
Other: 0-0. Total: 6-0.

By all accounts, Bert was a daring and acrobatic keeper who was noted for his uncanny anticipation when he was facing penalty kicks. In the days when the goalkeeper had to stand still on the goal-line, he would pace up and down rather like a caged lion and eventually position himself slightly off centre. The penalty taker would invariably shoot towards the larger gap and Bert, anticipating correctly, would make the save. On retirement he settled in his home town of Southampton and worked as a carpenter and joiner for the South Western Railways.
Debut: 12 Nov 1921 v Aberdare Athletic (H) 1-0 Div 3 (S).

LOCKE Leslie C

(IL) Mid
b: Perth, Scotland, 24 Jan 1934
QPR: May 1956
Football League: 76-24. **FAC:** 3-2. **FLC:** 0-0.
Other: 3-3. **Total:** 82-29.
Honours: Scottish Amateur international.

Steve Lomas

Les helped in no small part to ensure Rangers' Third Division survival. The top 11 clubs of each Division (North and South) were to form the new Third. QPR just managed it with 50 points, and by finishing in 10th place. During this period Les notched up another four goals to end the season with 13, the second highest scorer. His stay at Loftus Road only lasted four seasons, and in 1960 he drifted into non-League football.
Debut: 27 Aug 1956 v Plymouth Argyle (H) 3-0 Div 3 (S).

LOFTHOUSE James

(OL) Wing 5' 6" 11st 4lbs
b: St Helens, Lancashire, 24 Mar 1898
QPR: May 1926
Football League: 80-27. **FAC:** 1-0. **FLC:** 0-0.
Other: 0-0. **Total:** 81-27.

A short, stocky winger who was both tricky and very fast, Jimmy possessed an excellent shot. He was very experienced, having played during the 1914/18 conflict for Manchester United and was ever-present for QPR in the 1926/27 season. After retirement he worked and played for the GPO.
Debut: 28 Aug 1926 v Crystal Palace (A) 1-2 Div 3 (S).

LOGAN W

(FB) Def 5' 8" 11st 6lbs
b: Scotland, 1885
QPR: 1909
Southern League: 7-0. **FAC:** 0-0. **FLC:** 0-0.
Other: 0-0. **Total:** 7-0.

A reserve defender who stood in for any injuries or absentees at full-back during the 1909/10 season, he could play at either right- or left-back.
Debut: 1 Sep 1909 v Watford (H) 4-3 SL Div 1.

LOMAS Stephen

Mid 6' 0" 12st 8lbs
b: Hanover, Germany, 18 Jan 1974
QPR: Aug 2005
Football League: 55-2. **FAC:** 2-0. **FLC:** 0-0.
Other: 0-0. **Total:** 57-2.
Honours: 45 Northern Ireland caps.

Although he was 31 at the time he signed, Steve added vital experience to Rangers' squad when he swapped Upton Park for Loftus Road on a free transfer after eight years with West Ham United during which time he won 45 caps for Northern Ireland. Steve had established his reputation as a combative midfielder with Manchester City in the 1990s and stayed two years at QPR before moving to Gillingham. March 2009 saw him appointed player/manager of St Neots Town FC in the Eagle Bitter United Counties Premier League.
Debut: 10 Sep 2005 v Southampton (A) 1-1 Championship.

LONEY Basil (Reverend)

(RB) Def
QPR: 1914
Southern League: 1-0. **FAC:** 0-0. **FLC:** 0-0.
Other: 0-0. **Total:** 1-0.
Honours: FA Amateur Cup winner's medals.

The Reverend Basil played for QPR on one solitary occasion, when he was passing through London!
Debut: 24 Apr 1915 v Crystal Palace (H) 3-2 SL Div 1.

LONGBOTTOM Arthur

(IL) Striker 5' 8" 10st 12lbs
b: Leeds, Yorkshire, 30 Jan 1933
QPR: Mar 1954
Football League: 201-62. **FAC:** 11-4. **FLC:** 0-0.
Other: 3-1. **Total:** 215-67.

Arthur had a touch of mischief in his play, which endeared him to many supporters. He kept his hair close cropped and later changed his surname to Langley (some say in order not to be ridiculed when he moved to Millwall). He equalled the feats of Addinall and Smith by heading the goalscorers for three years running from 1956/57 to 1958/59. Yet strangely, apart from this "purple" patch, his scoring was infrequent, for in his other four seasons at QPR he could manage only 11 League goals in total. During his nine years at Loftus Road he made over 200 first team appearances. In 1963, Arthur was transferred to Millwall together with Jim Towers, but neither made any impact, and Arthur moved on to Oxford United less than a year later. Two further short periods followed before he dropped down to non-League football.
Debut: 12 Mar 1955 v Leyton Orient (A) 0-3 Div 3 (S).

LOPEZ Jordi

Mid 6' 0" 12st 2lbs
b: Granollers, Spain, 28 Feb 1981
QPR: (Loan) Feb 2009
Football League: 10-1. **FAC:** 0-0. **FLC:** 0-0.
Other: 0-0. **Total:** 10-1.
Debut: 28 Feb 2009 v Barnsley (A) 1-2 Championship.

LOWE Henry Pratt

(IL) Striker 5' 7" 11st 0lbs
b: Keetle, Fife, Scotland, 24 Feb 1907
d: Calne, Wilts, Oct 1988
QPR: Jun 1935
Football League: 161-40. **FAC:** 10-0. **FLC:** 0-0.
Other: 0-0. **Total:** 171-40.

QPR definitely got the better of the exchange deal when they brought Harry Lowe to Loftus Road and let Ted Goodier go to Watford. In one match for the Vicarage Road side, he scored a goal, but also failed with a penalty, on his wedding day, in a 4-1 victory over Swindon Town. Harry was a direct inside-forward who had a powerful long range shot in his right foot, and he made over 160 Football League appearances during his four years at Loftus Road. Shortly after moving to Guildford City, war broke out and so effectively cutting short his playing career. He became a successful Chelsea scout in 1943, then in 1945 took the manager's job at Guildford City. In 1947 he became the Bournemouth manager and the same position followed at Yeovil Town in 1951. In 1954 he was scouting for Watford, and finally became the Cheshunt manager in 1955.
Debut: 31 Aug 1935 v Millwall (H) 2-3 Div 3 (S).

LOWE Keith

Def 6' 2 ''13st 3lbs
b: Wolverhampton, 13 Sep 1985
QPR: (Loan) 2006
Football League: 1-0. **FAC:** 0-0. **FLC:** 0-0.
Other: 0-0. **Total:** 1-0.
Debut: 4 Feb 2006 v Leeds United (A) 0-2 Championship.

LOWE O

(LB) Def
QPR: 1907
Southern League: 2-0. **FAC:** 0-0. **FLC:** 0-0.
Other: 0-0. **Total:** 2-0.

Replaced regular left-back Fidler for the last two Southern League games of the 1907/08 season.
Debut: 25 Apr 1908 v Southampton (A) 2-5 SL Div 1.

LOWE W

(IL) Mid
QPR: 1919
Southern League: 1-0. **FAC:** 0-0. **FLC:** 0-0.
Other: 0-0. **Total:** 1-0.

This player stood in just once for the injured Jack Gregory when he was out of the team.
Debut: 8 Nov 1919 v Millwall (H) 1-2 SL Div 1.

LUMSDON Francis L

(OR) Wing
b: Sunderland
QPR: Apr 1935
Football League: 38-8. **FAC:** 1-0. **FLC:** 0-0.
Other: 0-0. **Total:** 39-8.

Frank was a very fast and tricky winger whose best match by far was that against Cardiff City at Loftus Road, when he scored a hat-trick in a 5-1 victory for QPR.
Debut: 29 Sep 1935 v Swindon Town (A) 2-2 Div 3 (S).

LYON Frank H

(FB) Def 5' 8" 11st 3lbs
b: Crewe, Cheshire, 23 Sep 1879
QPR: 1903
Southern League: 56-0. **FAC:** 4-0. **FLC:** 0-0.
Other: 0-0. **Total:** 60-0.
Honours: Played for Cheshire v Lancashire. 2 Cheshire Senior Cup medals plus a runner's-up medal. Southern Professionals v the Amateurs. In the Ilford side that toured Denmark. He was also with Chelsea when they toured Holland.

Frank established the reputation for his exceptional pace by being a competitive sprinter and held many trophies. Injury forced his early retirement from the game. He later opened a business in Crewe.
Debut: 24 Oct 1903 v Fulham (A) 2-2 SL Div 1.

Jordi Lopez

M

MACDONALD John
MADDIX Daniel Shawn
MAGUIRE Gavin Terence
MAHON Gavin Andrew
MAHONEY-JOHNSON Michael Anthony
MALCOLM Andrew
MALCOLM Robert
MALLETT Joseph
MANCIENNE Michael McHale
MANCINI Terence John
MANNING John Thomas
MARCH Richard
MARCROFT Edward Hollows
MARNEY Dean Edward
MARSDEN Benjamin
MARSH Rodney William
MASON William Sidney
MASSON Donald Sandison
MATTHEWS F W
MAYES Thomas
McADAMS William J
McALLISTER William
McCAIRNS Thomas
McCARGILL H
McCARTHY Alan James
McCARTHY Leonard Daniel
McCELLAND John Bonar
McCONNELL Alexander
McCREERY David
McCULLOCH Andrew
McDERMOTT Andrew
McDONALD Alan
McDONALD John
McEWAN David
McEWAN Robert
McEWAN William
McFLYNN Terence
McGEE Paul G
McGOVERN Brian
McGOVERN Michael John
McGOVERN Thomas
McGOWAN Frank
McKAY John
McKAY William
McKENZIE Thomas
McKIE Daniel
McKINLAY
McKINNEY E
McLARNEY P
McLEAN John C
McLEOD George J
McLEOD Kevin Andrew
McLEOD Robert
McLINTOCK Francis
McMAHON Hugh J
McNAB John S
McNAUGHT John William
McQUADE Terrance J
McQUEEN Hugh
MEAKER Michael John
MERRICK Jack
METCHICK David J
MICKLEWHITE Gary
MIDDLEMISS Herbert
MIDDLETON John
MIKLOSKO Ludek
MILANESE Mauro
MILLAR Harry
MILLBANK Joseph H
MILLER Adam
MILLER James
MILLER Liam
MILLINGTON Thomas
MILLS Donald G
MILWARD George
MITCHELL Archibald P
MOBLEY Victor J
MOFFATT Hugh
MOGER
MOLLOY Peter
MOORE James
MOORE Stefan
MORALEE William Ernest
MORGAN Ian Arthur
MORGAN Roger Ernest
MORRIS Samuel
MORROW Steven Joseph
MORTIMORE John Henry
MOUGHTON Colin E
MOUNTFORD George Frederick
MUIR Ian James
MUIR William M
MULHOLLAND Scott
MURDIN Steven H
MURPHY Daniel Thomas
MURPHY Neil
MURRAY Paul
MUSSLEWHITE John
MUSTARD John
MYERS Colin Ernest

MACDONALD John

(OR) Wing 5' 10"
b: England
QPR: 1908
Southern League: 18-0. **FAC:** 2-0. **FLC:** 0-0.
Other: 0-0. **Total:** 20-0.
Honours: 2 Scottish Junior caps.

Although John was born in England, he first played for the Scottish junior side Glasgow Ashfield. (NB: some contemporary publications spell his name as McDonald but this spelling is incorrect).
Debut: 1 Sep 1908 v West Ham United (A) 0-2 SL Div 1.

MADDIX Daniel Shawn

CD 5' 11" 12st 2lbs
b: Ashford, 11 Oct 1967
QPR: Jul 1987
Football/Premier League: 292-13: **FAC:** 23-2.
FLC: 28-3. **Other:** 5-0. **Total:** 348-18.
Honours: 2 caps for Jamaica

Danny is a tough defender who has the ability to mark a man out of a match. He became the most popular player at the club, both with the supporters and with his fellow players. Danny suffered a serious foot injury which kept him out of the side for a long spell, but made a comeback as a substitute on the opening day of the 1994/95 season at Old Trafford. Then, in 2000, a knee injury meant another long lay-off. He never made a successful return to the QPR squad, adding just one League appearance, to a previous impressive record. His 14 years at Loftus Road saw him play in nearly 350 first team matches for the Rangers, during which time he scored a modest 18 goals.

In the summer of 2001, he moved up north, and in a strange twist of fate it was to the club that he had made his debut against 14 years earlier. After adding 61 Football League appearances to his record he was released by the Blades in the summer of 2003 and joined Barnet.
Debut: 28 Nov 1987 v Sheffield Wednesday (A) 1-3 Div 1.

MAGUIRE Gavin Terence

CD 5' 10" 11st 8lbs
b: Hammersmith, London, 24 Nov 1967
QPR: Oct 1985
Football League: 40-0. **FAC:** 6-0. **FLC:** 3-0.
Other: 0-0. **Total:** 49-0.
Honours: 7 caps for Wales. 1 B cap.

A hard, uncompromising defender, who had undoubted skills and was adept at creating attacks by long and accurate passes out of defence. Gavin"s mother came from the Rhondda and his father came from Ireland, so he was eligible for any one of the three home countries. He chose Wales.
Debut: 27 Dec 1986 v Oxford United (A) 1-0 Div 1.

MAHON Gavin Andrew

Mid 6' 1" 13st 2lbs
b: Birmingham, 2 Jan 1977
QPR: Jan 2008
Football League: 51-3. **FAC:** 3-0. **FLC:** 3-0.
Other: 0-0. **Total:** 57-3.

Originally a trainee with Wolverhampton Wanderers, Gavin failed to secure a professional contract at Molineux but was signed by Hereford United in 1996. He spent two years there before lengthy spells with Brentford and Watford brought him to Loftus Road. A solid and reliable midfield general who captained Watford to the Premiership in 2006 after a play-off victory over Leeds United, Gavin signed initially on an emergency loan basis but the transfer was soon made permanent.
Debut: 1 Jan 2008 v Leicester City (H) 3-1 Championship.

MAHONEY-JOHNSON Michael Anthony

Striker 5' 10" 12st 0lbs
b: Paddington, London, 6 Nov 1976
QPR: Apr 1995

Gavin Mahon

Football League: 3-0. **FAC:** 0-0. **FLC:** 0-0.
Other: 0-0. **Total:** 3-0.

A striker who had pace and was given a couple of chances to prove himself but failed to do so, Mike was given a free transfer.
Debut: 2 Oct 1996 v Port Vale (H) 1-2 Div 1.

MALCOLM Andrew

(RH) Mid 5' 9" 11st 4lbs
b: East Ham, London, 4 May 1953
QPR: (£12,000) Oct 1962
Football League: 84-5. **FAC:** 8-1. **FLC:** 2-0.
Other: 0-0. **Total:** 94-6.
Honours: Schoolboy & Youth international. 1 Football League cap. 2nd Div championship medal.

Andy was a wholehearted player who would give his all on the field of play during a match. His serious expression during it, earned him the nickname of smiler. When his playing career was finished he worked for Lyons (on the ice cream side) until 1977. Andy then became a public house manager in Maldon, then later in Latchendon. In 1986 he emigrated to South Africa.
Debut: 22 Oct 1962 v Hull City (H) 4-1 Div 2.

MALCOLM Robert

Mid 5' 11" 11st 2lbs
b: Glasgow, Scotland, 12 Nov 1980
QPR: (Loan) Nov 2007
Football League: 11-0. **FAC:** 0-0. **FLC:** 0-0.
Other: 0-0. **Total:** 11-0.
Honours: 1 Scotland U21 cap and 1 B cap.
Debut: 24 Nov 2007 v Sheffield Wednesday (H) 0-0 Championship.

MALLETT Joseph

(IR) Mid 5' 7" 11st 0lbs
b: Gateshead, 8 Jan 1916
QPR: (Loan) 1937
Football League: 29-4. **FAC:** 2-0. **FLC:** 0-0.
Other: 1-0. **Total:** 32-4.
QPR: (£800) Feb 1939
Football League: 41-7. **FAC:** 5-2. **FLC:** 0-0.
Other: 1-0. **Total:** 47-9.

Joe was a very classy player, a true midfield general who could command the play with subtle touches and deft passes from a defensive position. He had two spells at QPR, both before the war, during which time he notched up a total of 79 first team appearances. After the hostilities he commanded a large transfer fee when he moved to Southampton, despite being aged 31 at the time. In fact he was still playing, for Nottingham Forest reserves, at the age of 43 in 1959. He became the Birmingham City coach in 1964 then the manager one year later. Joe went to Greece in 1970 to coach Panionios, but five years later he was in the USA coaching New York Cosmos, Washington Diplomats

Robert Malcolm

in 1979 and finally San Jose Earthquakes in 1982. He returned to England a year later to become chief scout at Southampton. On his retirement, Joe moved to St Leonards, Sussex.
Debut: 23 Oct 1937 v Crystal Palace (H) 1-0 Div 3 (S).

MANCIENNE Michael McHale

Def 6′ 0″ 11st 9lbs
b: Isleworth, 8 Jan 1988
QPR: (Loan) Oct 2006
Football League: 58-0. **FAC:** 2-0. **FLC:** 1-0.
Other: 0-0. **Total:** 61-0.

Michael has been described as "one of England's brightest young talents" and was spotted at the age of nine by Chelsea while playing for Kingstonian. The youngster debuted for the Chelsea Reserves while still at school and signed a professional contract in January 2006. Michael's Stamford Bridge career in his first three seasons consisted of being an unused substitute in the final match of the 2005/06 campaign but he gained vital experience on loan at Loftus Road.
Debut: 21 Oct 2006 v Sheffield Wednesday (A) 2-3 Championship.

MANCINI Terence John

(CH) CD 6′ 0″ 12st 0lbs
b: Camden Town, London, 4 Oct 1942
QPR: (£20,000) Oct 1971
Football League: 94-3. **FAC:** 12-2. **FLC:** 5-0.
Other: 0-0. **Total:** 111-5.
Honours: 5 caps for Eire. 2nd Div runner's-up medal. South African League championship medal. 3rd Div championship medal.

Terry had an Italian father and an Irish mother and came from a family more renowned for their prowess in the boxing ring than on the football pitch. He was a tall, unflappable, self confident player, solid in the air but somewhat erratic on the ground, he knew his limitations and played to his strengths. Terry was one of the most colourful and popular characters to turn out for the club in the early 1970s and had an infectious sense of humour which was liked by spectators and players alike. While with QPR he played for Eire. In retirement he became the Fulham coach and later the Luton Town assistant manager for a while. He was then involved in running a car hire business followed by a long period working for Barwood Leisure, a sports travel company, as their sports events director.
Debut: 16 Oct 1971 v Sheffield Wednesday (A) 0-0 Div 2.

Michael Mancienne

Terry Mancini

MANNING John Thomas

(OR) Wing 5′ 9″ 11st 12lbs
b: Boston, Lincs, 1886
QPR: Jul 1920
Football League: 22-5. **FAC:** 2-0. **FLC:** 0-0.
Other: 0-0. **Total:** 24-5.
Honours: Central League championship medal.

John was a hefty winger who could brush aside the opposition with a repertoire of tricks and tremendous acceleration, who also had a bullet like shot to boot. One contemporary writer noted in 1913, "impervious to hard knocks, he gets through by weight alone, where lighter men would be hustled off the ball".
Debut: 23 Oct 1920 v Swansea Town (A) 3-1 Div 3.

MARCH Richard

(RH) Def 5′ 7″ 10st 8lbs
b: Washington, County Durham, 9 Oct 1908
d: 1987
QPR: 1932
Football League: 220-3. **FAC:** 14-0. **FLC:** 0-0.
Other: 7-0. **Total:** 241-3.

Tenacity, fearlessness and willingness were the attributes of this man. Dicky was a fiery red haired stripling who was revered by the spectators for his style of play. He played for QPR until 1941/42,

M N O

Rodney Marsh

a total of 10 seasons. He clocked-up an extra 59 wartime appearances bringing his total to 300 overall; a true one club man. During the pre-war years he was a regular in the Football League team for nine seasons. After his retirement from playing he was made catering manager at the club.
Debut: 24 Dec 1932 v Torquay United (A) 1-3 Div 3 (S).

MARCROFT Edward Hollows

(OR) Wing 5' 6" 10st 2lbs
b: Rochdale, Lancashire, April 1910
QPR: May 1932
Football League: 29-8. **FAC:** 4-1. **FLC:** 0-0.
Other: 0-0. **Total:** 33-9.

When Ted signed for Great Harwood, he was said to have scored 66 goals in a run of 63 matches for his previous club. This prompted Middlesbrough to sign him but despite scoring on his debut, this match proved to be his only outing for the club. However, not only was Ted a fast and tricky winger but he was an excellent piano player too, for those after match sing-a-longs.
Debut: 27 Aug 1932 v Brentford (H) 2-3 Div 3 (S).

MARNEY Dean Edward

Mid
b: Barking, London, 31 Jan 1984
QPR: (Loan) Jan 2004
Football League: 2-0. **FAC:** 0-0. **FLC:** 0-0.
Other: 0-0. **Total:** 2-0.
Honours: 1 England U21 cap.
Debut: 17 Jan 2004 v Brighton & Hove Albion (H) 2-1 Div 2.

MARSDEN Benjamin

(RB) Def 5' 9" 12st 6lbs
b: Hanley, Stoke, 1898
QPR: 1920
Football League: 126-6. **FAC:** 6-0. **FLC:** 0-0.
Other: 0-0. **Total:** 132-6.

Ben became the backbone of the QPR defence in the early days of the Third Division. It was acknowledged that he had an exceptionally hard kick, so he became the penalty expert of the side, and in his 132 appearances for the first team he netted six goals. He only played two matches for Reading during the 1925/26 season after which they released him. Ben served out the rest of his football career in minor non-League football.
Debut: 27 Dec 1920 v Brentford (H) 1-0 Div 3.

MARSH Rodney William

Striker 6' 0" 12st 6lbs
b: Hatfield, Herts, 11 Oct 1944
QPR: (£15,000) Mar 1966
Football League: 181-89. **FAC:** 9-8. **FLC:** 16-17.
Other: 0-0. **Total:** 206-114.
Honours: Young England cap. 2 U23 caps. 9 England cap. 3rd Div championship medal. League Cup winner's medal. 2nd Div runner's-up medal. League Cup runner's-up medal.

At the risk of repetition, Alec Stock's most inspired buy on the transfer market was Rodney Marsh from Fulham. At the time Rodney was an out of form player who had sustained an horrendous injury in 1965 which left him partially deaf. In form he was a flamboyant individual with a bountiful amount of skill and flair. Rodney was the top player during the most successful period in the club's history, in the mid-1970s. The cry of "Rod-nee, Rod-nee" would reverberate from the terraces at Loftus Road during his reign at the club. Among his many achievements, he created a new seasonal club goalscoring record when he netted 44 in the 1966/67 season. After six seasons at Loftus Road he moved on to Manchester City for a huge fee, before making his first move to the USA. In 1978 he became the general manager of Tampa Bay Rowdies.
Debut: 19 Mar 1966 v Peterborough United (A) 1-1 Div 3.

MASON William Sidney

Goal 5' 10" 11st 8lbs
b: Wimbledon, 31 Oct 1908
d: Bognor Regis, Nov 1995
QPR: 1933
Football League: 154-0. **FAC:** 6-0. **FLC:** 0-0.
Other: 10-0. **Total:** 170-0.
Honours: Represented a Surrey Amateur XI. London Challenge Cup winner's medal. London Combination runner's-up medal.

A former amateur player at Wimbledon, Bill then spent five years at Fulham before his move to QPR. Bill was a strong, muscular goalkeeper who played for the club into the Second World War (after being given a benefit match in 1939), adding over 70 matches to his total for the club. Besides becoming a War Reserve policeman, he then worked in a munitions factory from 1943 to 1947 before rejoining the police. He was a PC in the Wimbledon Division for 20 years and then worked as a security

guard until his retirement in 1975.
Debut: 18 Jan 1934 v Coventry City (A) 1-0 Div 3 (S).

MASSON Donald Sandison

Mid 5' 8" 10st 12lbs
b: Banchory, Scotland, 28 Aug 1946
QPR: (£100,000) Dec 1974
Football League: 116-18. **FAC:** 8-1. **FLC:** 12-3.
Other: 8-2. **Total:** 144-24.
Honours: 19 Scottish caps. 4th Div championship medal. 1st Div runner's-up medal.

Don entered First Division football at the age of 28 in December 1974, and gave the impression that a decade had been wasted for the gifted Scottish player. Don had the apparent time to find his openings and distribute with precision and style. Don is a fine example of talent finding its own reward no matter at what level it is exposed. He was a fiercely competitive and highly creative player who became the general of the attack in the mid-1970s. After three years at Loftus Road, further moves were made before he switched to the USA. After he returned from the USA he became, for a time, the player/manager of Kettering, and later ran the Gallery Hotel in Nottingham.
Debut: 14 Dec 1974 v Sheffield United (H) 1-0 Div 1.

Don Masson

MATTHEWS F W

Goal
QPR: 1913
Southern League: 2-0. **FAC:** 0-0. **FLC:** 0-0.
Other: 0-0. **Total:** 2-0.

An amateur goalkeeper who deputised for Nicholls at the end of the 1913/14 season, Matthews successfully managed to keep a blank sheet on both occasions.
Debut: 23 Apr 1914 v Brighton & Hove Albion (H) 3-0 SL Div 1.

MAYES Thomas

(IR) Mid
QPR: 1902
Southern League: 4-0. **FAC:** 0-0. **FLC:** 0-0.
Other: 0-0. **Total:** 4-0.

Tom was the man who turned out in different forward positions when a player was absent or injured, in the early days of the club.
Debut: 6 Dec 1902 v Watford (A) 2-0 SL Div 1.

McADAMS William J

(CF) Striker 5' 11" 11st 9lbs
b: Belfast, Northern Ireland, 20 Jan 1934
QPR: (£5,000) Sep 1964
Football League: 33-11. **FAC:** 3-1. **FLC:** 2-0.
Other: 0-0. **Total:** 38-12.
Honours: 15 Northern Ireland caps. 4th Div championship medal. 4th Div promotion medal.

A product of the Grosvenor Secondary School, Belfast, Billy worked as an apprentice heating engineer and turned down a career with Burnley after trials. A thrustful and courageous player, he had a fine burst of speed. Billy retired from football in 1968.
Debut: 25 Sep 1964 v Hull City (H) 2-1 Div 3.

McALLISTER William

(LH) Mid 5' 8" 11st 4lbs
b: Glasgow, Scotland, 1900
QPR: Oct 1926
Football League: 26-1. **FAC:** 0-0. **FLC:** 0-0.
Other: 0-0. **Total:** 26-1.
Honours: Represented the Southern League v the Central League.

Billy was noted as a, "Brilliant ball player but very temperamental". A story goes that when the Scotsman signed for Brighton & Hove Albion from Ebbw Vale, the club played a friendly against his former Welsh team later that season as part of the deal. However, Billy threw a clod of earth into the crowd following a dispute with a number of fans on the terraces and had to be escorted into the dressing room at the end of the match. In the course of the same evening the fans caught up with him in a local restaurant and further ugly scenes developed. However, it was trouble caused in another match, when he was sent off, which resulted in a one month suspension.
Debut: 23 Oct 1926 v Millwall (A) 1-2 Div 3 (S).

McCAIRNS Thomas

(CF) Striker 5' 9" 11st 10lbs
b: Dinsdale, County Durham, 22 Dec 1873
d: Willesden, 1932
QPR: May 1903
Southern League: 1-0. **FAC:** 2-0. **FLC:** 0-0.
Other: 0-0. **Total:** 3-0.
Honours: Northern League championship medal. Football League v Irish League.

Tommy ended his career as a journeyman, with a whirlwind tour of nine clubs in seven years. At Grimsby Town he scored 104 goals in 154 competitive matches, including six goals in a 7-1 victory over Leicester Fosse in 1896. Although it was reported that he was slow during his time at QPR he nevertheless still possessed excellent ball control and had the knack of being in the right place at the right time. Alas he never got the chance to prove himself at the club, for he only played one match in place of Milward who was ill at the time.
Debut: 24 Oct 1903 v Fulham (A) 2-2 SL Div 1.

McCARGILL H

(LH) Mid
QPR: 1905
Southern League: 4-0. **FAC:** 0-0. **FLC:** 0-0.
Other: 0-0. **Total:** 4-0.

McCargill was the man that stood in for Downing at wing-half when he was injured.
Debut: 14 Apr 1906 v Fulham (A) 0-1 SL Div 1.

McCARTHY Alan James

CD 5' 11" 12st 10lbs
b: Wandsworth, London, 11 Jan 1972
QPR: Dec 1989
Football League: 11-0. **FAC:** 1-0. **FLC:** 0-0.
Other: 1-0. **Total:** 13-0.
Honours: Youth cap for England. B cap for Wales. 3 U21 caps for Wales.

A reliable defender who was comfortable on the ball and tackled strongly, Alan was one of the few players to have represented two countries in the same sport, both Wales and England. He suffered an injury just as he was about to join Northampton Town in 1998.
Debut: 24 Nov 1990 v Arsenal (H) 1-3 Div 1.

M
N
O

McCARTHY Leonard Daniel

(IR) Mid 5' 7" 11st 6lbs
b: Cacrau, Wales
QPR: Jun 1937
Football League: 22-9. **FAC:** 4-1. **FLC:** 0-0.
Other: 1-1. **Total:** 27-11.
Honours: London Challenge Cup winner's medal.

Although not making many appearances or being a prolific goalscorer for the first team, Len netted 27 goals in 30 matches when the reserve side finished in second place to Arsenal in the London Combination, and won the London Challenge Cup in 1939.

Debut: 30 Oct 1937 v Notts County (A) 2-2 Div 3 (S).

McCELLAND John Bonar

(OR) Wing 5' 8" 10st 10lbs
b: Bradford, Yorkshire, 5 Mar 1935
QPR: (£14,000) Sep 1961
Football League: 71-22. **FAC:** 7-1. **FLC:** 1-0.
Other: 0-0. **Total:** 79-23.

The son of much travelled Jimmy, of Middlesbrough fame and the younger brother of Charlie. John proved to be a consistent player who was fast, skilful and always supplied a good amount of goals during the season. He retired in 1969 having scored over 100 goals in less than 400 matches.

Debut: 23 Sep 1961 v Watford (A) 2-3 Div 3.

Alan McDonald

McCONNELL Alexander

(LB) Def 5' 8" 11st 10lbs
b: Glenbuck, Scotland, 1875
QPR: Jul 1899
Southern League: 51-0. **FAC:** 13-0 **FLC:** 0-0.
Other: 0-0. **Total:** 64-0.

Alex was a full-back of the highest quality and was noted by the sports writers of the day as "A powerful kicker and a splendid tackler".

He had a younger brother, John, who also played for Grimsby Town around the same period. When Alex's playing days were over he became the reserve team manager of Grimsby Town in 1908.

Debut: 9 Sep 1899 v Tottenham Hotspur (A) 0-1 SL Div 1.

McCREERY David

Mid 5' 6" 10st 7lbs
b: Belfast, Northern Ireland, 16 Sep 1957
QPR: (£200,000) Aug 1979
Football League: 57-4. **FAC:** 2-0. **FLC:** 8-1.
Other: 0-0. **Total:** 67-5.
Honours: Northern Ireland school, youth and U21 caps. 67 full caps. 2nd Div promotion medal. FA Cup winner's medal. FA Cup runner's-up medal.

A Tommy Docherty signing during his second stay at Loftus Road. The "Doc" described him as "The bargain of the century". David was a strong running enthusiastic player, who possessed an endless amount of energy; he was very fiery and full of action. He was appointed the Carlisle United player/manager in 1992, and two years later the same at Hartlepool United. He became a Barnet scout in 1995 and a Blyth Spartans consultant later that year.

Debut: 19 Sep 1979 v Bristol Rovers (H) 2-0 Div 2.

McCULLOCH Andrew

Striker 6' 2" 13st 11lbs
b: Northampton, 3 Jan 1950
QPR: Oct 1970
Football League: 42-10. **FAC:** 1-0. **FLC:** 4-1.
Other: 0-0. **Total:** 47-11.
Honours: Scottish U23 cap. 4th Div promotion medal. 3rd Div promotion medal.

Andy was the team-mate of Steve Perryman, when he played in the Spurs Metropolitan League side of the late 1960s. Andy obtained a degree in Civil Engineering at the time and was still an amateur footballer who didn't turn professional until he joined QPR. He was sold on to Cardiff City after two years and nearly 50 senior side outings. Andy was a brave and bighearted striker who was the son of a former Scottish centre-forward.

Debut: 17 Oct 1970 v Birmingham City (H) 5-2 Div 2.

McDERMOTT Andrew

Def 5' 9" 11st 3lbs
b: Sydney, Australia, 24 Mar 1977
QPR: Aug 1995
Football League: 6-2. **FAC:** 0-0. **FLC:** 0-0.
Other: 0-0. **Total:** 6-2.
Honours: Australian U23.

Andy had his contract cancelled by Notts County in the summer of 2001 to allow him to return to Australia whereupon he signed on for the NSL club Northern Spirit.

Debut: 14 Dec 1996 v Southend United (H) 4-0 Div 1.

McDONALD Alan

CD 6' 2" 12st 7lbs
b: Belfast, Northern Ireland, 12 Oct 1963
QPR: Aug 1981
QPR: May 1983
Football/Premier League: 402-13. **FAC:** 33-2.
FLC: 43-3. **Other:** 5-0. **Total:** 483-17.
Honours: Northern Ireland school & youth caps. 52 full caps. League Cup runner's-up medal.

The captain of his club and country on many occasions, Alan became a vastly experienced and imposing stopper, and the joker in the team. Although he was very likable, Alan was a tough defender who was good in the air and a real threat from free-kicks in the opposing penalty area. Signed as a schoolboy, it was several seasons before he got his first team chance, having spent a loan spell at Charlton Athletic in 1983.

He played nine matches and even in those early days, he showed his poise and composure, in the centre-half position that was quite incredible for a youngster of 19 years. It was reported in those early days that Charlton tried to buy him for £50,000. But Alan remained loyal to Rangers, and in the next 14 years amassed no less than 402 League games, hence making him one of the top all-time players for appearances. During his long career at QPR he made his many appearances for Northern Ireland and also played in the UEFA Cup. He was ever-present in the League in 1985/86, and on three occasions missed just three games each season. After 16 years at Loftus Road, Alan was given a free transfer, and he moved to Swindon Town in 1997. He had the unusual experience of playing in goal in one match when the Swindon keeper was dismissed; the game was at QPR!

Debut: 24 Sep 1983 v Wolverhampton Wanderers (A) 4-0 Div 1.

McDONALD John

(RB) Def 5′ 10″ 12st 7lbs
b: Ayr, Scotland, 1882
QPR: 1907
Southern League: 182-0. **FAC:** 13-0. **FLC:** 0-0.
Other: 3-0. **Total:** 198-0.
Honours: 2 Southern League championship medals.

John played reserve to the famous Bob Crompton, the England captain, while playing for Blackburn Rovers, staying a couple of seasons there before he moved to Leeds City. John was described as, "a quiet fellow who was unassuming, whose play was more solid than showy and was a useful man to have in any defence". He retired from playing in 1913.

Debut: 14 Sep 1907 v Tottenham Hotspur (A) 2-3 SL Div 1.

McEWAN David

Striker 6′ 0″ 11st 0lbs
b: Westminster, London, 2 Nov 1977
QPR: Jul 2001
Football League: 5-0. **FAC:** 0-0. **FLC:** 1-0.
Other: 0-0. **Total:** 6-0.

Dave arrived on a six month contract in the summer of 2001 and although supposedly playing well in the reserves, he failed to impress in the seniors and he was released in January 2002.

Debut: 25 Aug 2001 v Reading (H) 0-0 Div 2.

McEWAN Robert

(LB) Def 5′ 10″ 12st 8lbs
b: Scotland, 1881
QPR: 1908
Southern League: 1-0. **FAC:** 0-0. **FLC:** 0-0.
Other: 0-0 **Total:** 1-0.
Honours: FA Cup winner's medal

Bob was used as a reserve to Joe Fidler and was called upon just once on Boxing Day 1908.

Debut: 26 Dec 1908 v Southampton (A) 4-1 SL Div 1.

McEWAN William

(OR) Wing
b: Glasgow, Scotland, 29 Aug 1914
d: Gravesend, Dec 1991
QPR: Jun 1938
Football League: 96-17. **FAC:** 12-3. **FLC:** 0-0.
Other: 2-0. **Total:** 110-20.
Honours: 3rd Div (South) championship medal.

A terrier-like winger who could strike panic into an opposing defender, Billy was on tour in Burma at the end of the war with an Army XI and although he had lost a lot of his pace from 1939, he was nevertheless still able to reproduce his tricks. As with others, the war deprived Billy of part of his football career, and his peacetime appearances span each side of the conflict. He made 76 wartime appearances scoring 34 goals and at the age of 38 years, along with Johnny Pattison, he was transferred to Leyton Orient to make another 21 appearances before his move to Gravesend & Northfleet.

Debut: 4 Mar 1939 v Crystal Palace (A) 1-0 Div 3 (S).

McFLYNN Terence

Mid 5′ 11″ 12st 2lbs
b: Magherafelt, Northern Ireland, 27 Mar 1981
QPR: May 1998
Football League: 2-0. **FAC:** 0-0. **FLC:** 0-0.
Other: 0-0. **Total:** 2-0.
Honours: Northern Ireland school and youth caps. 7 U21 caps.

Terry was the captain of the Under-19 side that reached the final of the Premier League Youth Academy play-offs in 2001. Yet he was one of 15 players to be released by the club in the summer that year.

Debut: 28 Apr 2001 v Stockport County (H) 0-3 Div 1.

McGEE Paul G

Striker 5′ 9″ 11st 7lbs
b: Sligo, Eire, 19 Jun 1954

Billy McEwan

QPR: Nov 1977
Football League: 39-7. **FAC:** 2-0. **FLC:** 3-1.
Other: 0-0. **Total:** 44-8.
Honours: Youth international. 2 U21 caps. 15 caps at full level. Canadian League championship medal. 3rd Div championship winner's medal. 3 times the Irish school champions. FA Cup of Ireland winner's medal. Football League of Ireland League championship medal.

Paul was a somewhat bubbly and confident character renowned for his speed off the mark. A much travelled striker, who remained at Loftus Road for two years – one of his longest stays! He helped his school, Summerhill College, to win the All-Ireland schools title in successive seasons netting a hat-trick in one of the finals, and made his debut for Sligo Rovers as a 16 year old.
Debut: 19 Nov 1977 v Coventry City (A) 1-4 Div 1.

McGOVERN Brian
CD 6' 3" 12st 7lbs
b: Dublin, Eire, 28 Apr 1980
QPR: (Loan) Dec 1999
Football League: 5-0. **FAC:** 0-0. **FLC:** 0-0.
Other: 0-0. **Total:** 5-0.
Honours: 2 U21 caps for Eire. Youth caps for Eire.

Brian was loaned-out by Arsenal in December 1999 for three months to gain experience. Good in the air and a strong tackler, he uses the ball well, especially at set-pieces. Brian stayed for just a month, but left after suffering an injury.
Debut: 28 Dec 1999 v Crewe Alexandra (H) 1-0 Div 1.

McGOVERN Michael John
Mid 5' 11" 12st 0lbs
b: Hayes, Middlesex, 15 Feb 1951
QPR: Nov 1966
Football League: 12-0. **FAC:** 1-0. **FLC:** 0-0.
Other: 0-0. **Total:** 13-0.

Mick began his apprenticeship in July 1966 at the age of 16 years. He made just 13 appearances in four and a half years at Loftus Road, but went on to a long career outside the League.
Debut: 26 Dec 1967 v Plymouth Argyle (A) 1-0 Div 2.

McGOVERN Thomas
(RH) Mid 5' 9" 11st 0lbs
b: Glasgow, Scotland
QPR: 1920
Football League: 2-0. **FAC:** 0-0. **FLC:** 0-0.
Other: 0-0. **Total:** 2-0.

Tom played in the first two matches of the newly formed Division 3, both defeats, and three team changes were then made, of which McGovern was one. He never played for the senior squad again.
Debut: 28 Aug 1920 v Watford (H) 1-2 Div 3.

John McKay

McGOWAN Frank
(IL) Striker
QPR: 1903
Southern League: 7-3. **FAC:** 2-0. **FLC:** 0-0
Other: 0-0. **Total:** 9-3.

Frank scored on his debut for the club and indeed netted three goals in the first three matches. However, he only played when Blackwood was out of the side, and added just four more games to his total.
Debut: 19 Sep 1903 v Tottenham Hotspur (H) 2-0 SL Div 1.

McKAY John
(OL) Wing
b: Port Glasgow, Scotland, 27 Jun 1927
QPR: Mar 1949
Football League: 17-1. **FAC:** 0-0. **FLC:** 0-0.
Other: 0-0. **Total:** 17-1.

John was one of five tried in the outside-left position in 1950. Then Ernie Shepherd arrived the next year, and that effectively put an end to the left-wing problem. The club was relegated in 1952 and McKay was given a free transfer.
Debut: 19 Nov 1949 v Bury (H) 1-0 Div 2.

McKAY William
(OR) Wing
b: Rothsay, Scotland, 10 Mar 1927
QPR: Jul 1955
Football League: 6-0. **FAC:** 0-0. **FLC:** 0-0.
Other: 0-0. **Total:** 6-0.

Billy was a tiny winger who was tricky and shared the right-wing spot with three others. In 1956 he joined Fred Durrant at Dover.
Debut: 30 Aug 1955 v Brentford (A) 0-2 Div 3 (S).

McKENZIE Thomas
(CF) Striker
b: Inverness, Scotland
QPR: 1908
Southern League: 9-1. **FAC:** 0-0. **FLC:** 0-0.
Other: 0-0. **Total:** 9-1.

Tommy played centre-forward for the opening seven matches of the season, when the team scored just three goals. That season the club had to play all their matches in mid-week and it was not until W O Steer was recruited that things started to improve.
Debut: 1 Sep 1908 v West Ham United (A) 0-2 SL Div 1.

McKIE Daniel
(CF) Striker
QPR: 1910
Southern League: 68-28. **FAC:** 1-2. **FLC:** 0-0.
Other: 1-0. **Total:** 70-30.

A fine opportunist centre-forward who could find the net with rewarding regularity, Daniel possessed a very hard shot and was the team's penalty taker. He was the club's leading goalscorer during the second championship season. Unfortunately during the following campaign, after suffering a very bad injury during the close season tour of Germany, he faded from the scene.
Debut: 12 Sep 1910 v West Ham United (H) 0-2 SL Div 1.

McKINLAY
(HB) Mid
QPR: 1901
Southern League: 4-0. **FAC:** 0-0. **FLC:** 0-0.

Other: 0-0. **Total:** 4-0.

McKinlay was a reserve who filled in for the likes of Seeley, Bowman, Keech and McQueen.

Debut: 26 Oct 1901 v Luton Town (A) 0-1 SL Div 1.

McKINNEY E

(OR) Wing

QPR: 1914

Southern League: 2-0. **FAC:** 0-0. **FLC:** 0-0.

Other: 0-0. **Total:** 2-0.

This winger appeared twice in consecutive matches in place of Thompson who was injured at the time. The youngster obviously didn't impress and he was not given another chance.

Debut: 27 Feb 1915 v Gillingham (H) 3-0 SL Div 1.

McLARNEY P

(RH) Def

QPR: 1905

Southern League: 8-0. **FAC:** 0-0. **FLC:** 0-0.

Other: 0-0. **Total:** 8-0.

McLarney replaced Lyon who had been injured during the close season. However, as soon as Lyon recovered, McLarney faded from the scene.

Debut: 2 Sep 1905 v New Brompton (H) 4-0 SL Div 1.

McLEAN John C

(CH) CD 5' 6" 12st 7lbs

b: Port Glasgow, Scotland, 22 May 1872

QPR: May 1906

Southern League: 41-0. **FAC:** 1-0. **FLC:** 0-0.

Other: 2-0. **Total:** 44-0.

Honours: 2 County caps for Renfrewshire. Scottish Junior international cap. Southern League championship medal.

John arrived at the club at the end of his career with the reputation of being a hard grafter as well as fearless in the tackle. By today's standards he was short for a central defender but this was evidently not unusual for this era.

Debut: 1 Sep 1906 v Luton Town (A) 1-1 SL Div 1.

McLEOD George J

(OL) Wing

b: Inverness, Scotland, 30 Nov 1932

QPR: (£8,000 + Lazarus) Jan 1964

Football League: 41-4. **FAC:** 0-0. **FLC:** 1-0.

Other: 0-0. **Total:** 42-4.

A good buy for Brentford, George remained at Griffin Park for over five years, before being sold within a part-exchange deal to QPR. He was at Loftus Road for little over a year before retiring in 1965. George emigrated to South Africa and around the same time Mark Lazarus returned to Loftus Road.

Debut: 17 Sep 1963 v Bristol Rovers (A) 0-0 Div 3.

Kevin McLeod

McLEOD Kevin Andrew

Mid 5' 11" 11st 0lbs

b: Liverpool, 12 Sep 1980

QPR: (£250,000) 2003

Football League: 70-6. **FAC:** 2-0. **FLC:** 4-1.

Other: 0-0. **Total:** 76-7.

Initially signed on loan from Everton during the 2002/03 season, Kevin impressed with his commanding and consistent performances which saw him dominate on the left flank and he was instrumental in Rangers' push for the play-offs. Such was the impact that the Everton Youth Academy graduate had, Ian Holloway signed him permanently in August 2003 although his sojourn at Loftus Road was to last less than two years. He moved to Swansea City in February 2005 and has since played for Colchester United and Brighton & Hove Albion.

Debut: 22 Mar 2003 v Wigan Athletic (H) 0-1 Div 1.

McLEOD Robert

Goal 6' 0"

b: Scotland

QPR: 1914

Southern League: 38-0. **FAC:** 3-0. **FLC:** 0-0.

Other: 0-0. **Total:** 41-0.

Honours: Scottish Cup winner's medal.

Bob was noted as an outstanding goalkeeper. He saved two penalties in a match for Newport County on Xmas Day 1913 to enable them to take the points.

Debut: 1 Mar 1914 v Millwall (A) 1-3 SL Div 1.

McLINTOCK Francis

CD 5′ 10″ 11st 4lbs
b: Glasgow, Scotland, 28 Dec 1939
QPR: (£20,000) Jun 1973
Football League: 127-5. **FAC:** 14-0. **FLC:** 14-1.
Other: 8-0. **Total:** 163-6.
Honours: 9 Scottish caps. 1 U23 cap. 3 FA Cup runner's-up medals. 3 League Cup winner's medals. London FA Challenge Cup medal. Inter Cities Fairs Cup winner's medal. League championship medal plus FA Cup winner's medal (the Double). Footballer of the Year.

Frank was a natural leader of men, a very resolute and skilled player. He was transferred to Arsenal for a record fee for a wing-half, it was also the highest amount that Arsenal had until then paid for a player. Even after 18 years playing experience he still commanded a transfer fee when he moved to Loftus Road. He captained the QPR side to the runner's-up spot in the First Division (1976) and to the quarter-finals of the UEFA Cup one year later. After four years with Rangers, he retired from playing in 1977, having enjoyed a career which spanned 20 years, and in which he played well over 600 League matches.

Frank first became the Leicester City manager, then was appointed the QPR coach in 1982. The Brentford manager post followed in 1984 and finally the Millwall assistant/manager in 1988. He went on to run a chain of Cash Converter shops and kept busy as an after dinner speaker.
Debut: 22 Sep 1973 v Birmingham City (H) 2-2 Div 1.

Frank McLintock

McMAHON Hugh J

(OL) Wing 5′ 10″ 10st 8lbs
b: Grangetown, Yorkshire, 24 Sep 1909
d: 1986
QPR: May 1936
Football League: 41-3. **FAC:** 3-1. **FLC:** 0-0.
Other: 1-1. **Total:** 45-5.

Hugh sampled football in the First Division as well as life in the Third in both North and South Division! QPR were lucky that he came into form at the right time, for what was known as the Bank of England club, Sunderland, paid £3,000 for him to cash strapped Rangers. Hugh continued to play football until well after the Second World War.
Debut: 12 Sep 1936 v Notts County (A) 2-1 Div 3 (S).

McNAB John S

(RH) Mid 6′ 1″ 11st 7lbs
b: Cleland, Scotland, 17 Apr 1895
d: 2 Jan 1949
QPR: Jun 1928
Football League: 54-2. **FAC:** 5-0. **FLC:** 0-0.
Other: 0-0. **Total:** 59-2.
Honours: 1 Scottish cap. 2 League championship medals.

John was described as a tall, rawboned, long-legged defender who was tough in the tackle and strong in defence. With him went the reputation of being the most likely winner of most 50/50 situations. John was noted as the hard man of the 1920s, after being banned for a six week period in 1925, after having been sent off in a match. In his retirement he became a licensee in Bootle.
Debut: 25 Aug 1928 v Torquay United (A) 4-1 Div 1 (S).

McNAUGHT John William

(OR) Wing
QPR: 1908
Southern League: 57-5. **FAC:** 5-1. **FLC:** 0-0.
Other: 1-0. **Total:** 63-6.

John made his debut for the club, in the Charity Shield replay match at Stamford Bridge in place of Pentland who had moved up north to Middlesbrough. As an amateur he was signed from Hounslow, and made nearly 60 first team appearances for the Rangers over the following three years.
Debut: 29 Aug 1908 v Manchester United 0-4 Charity Shield.

McQUADE Terrance J

(OL) Wing
b: Hackney, London, 21 Feb 1941
QPR: Jul 1963
Football League: 20-2. **FAC:** 3-0. **FLC:** 1-0.
Other: 0-0. **Total:** 24-2.
Honours: 4th Div championship medal.

Alec Stock acquired this winger along with the Brady brothers in 1963, but Terry made little impression at Loftus Road, playing in only 20 League matches in the next 14 months before he moved back across London.
Debut: 17 Sep 1963 v Bristol Rovers (A) 0-0 Div 3.

McQUEEN Hugh

(OL) Wing 5′ 8″ 11st 7lbs
b: Harthill, Scotland, 1 Oct 1867
d: Norwich, 8 Apr 1944
QPR: May 1901
Southern League: 26-9. **FAC:** 3-0. **FLC:** 0-0.
Other: 0-0. **Total:** 29-9.
Honours: Roseberry Charity Cup winner's medal. Edinburgh Shield winner's medal. 2 FA Cup runner's-up medals. 2nd Div championship winner's medal.

Hugh's father was a pit manager and father to nine more boys. Hugh was the Victorian equivalent of a play-maker with his skill, courage and enthusiasm much to the fore. The speed and accuracy of his crosses gained him a fine reputation and he was voted the best player on the losing side (Derby County) in the 1898 FA Cup final by the *Football Chat* magazine. He was near the end of his career when he joined QPR, but moved on after a year, and continued for three more. On his retirement he acquired a newsagent's shop in Norwich which he kept until the Second World War.
Debut: 7 Sep 1901 v Watford (H) 0-1 SL Div 1.

MEAKER Michael John

Mid 5′ 11″ 11st 5lbs
b: Greenford, Middlesex, 18 Aug 1971
QPR: Feb 1990
Football/Premier League: 34-1. **FAC:** 3-1.
FLC: 2-1. **Other:** 2-0. **Total:** 41-3.
Honours: Welsh B international. 2 caps at U21 level.

Although Mike was born in England he claimed Welsh nationality on his mother's side. A tricky performer with exciting attacking skills on a good day, on others his potential remained unfulfilled.
Debut: 20 Nov 1990 v Southampton (A) 0-4 FL Cup round two.

MERRICK Jack

Goal
b: Great Barr, Scotland, 1900
QPR: 1919
Southern League: 38-0. **FAC:** 1-0. **FLC:** 0-0.
Other: 0-0. **Total:** 39-0.

Jack was the goalkeeper who played in the team for the last season of the club's Southern League days.
Debut: 30 Aug 1919 v Bristol Rovers (A) 2-0 SL Div 1.

Mike Meaker

METCHICK David J

(IF) Mid 5' 8" 11st 0lbs
b: Bakewell, Derbyshire, 14 Aug 1943
QPR: Aug 1968
Football League: 3-1. **FAC:** 0-0. **FLC:** 1-0.
Other: 0-0. **Total:** 4-1.
Honours: 7 England youth caps.

Dave was a highly promising midfield player who had flair in his younger days for scoring goals. Alas he was too small for a striking role and he was played out of position on the wing. He joined Arsenal for a small fee and served the reserve side well, being a great influence on the youngsters of the day.

Debut: 5 Oct 1968 v WBA (A) 1-3 Div 1.

MICKLEWHITE Gary

(OR) Wing 5' 7" 10st 4lbs
b: Southwark, London, 21 Mar 1961
QPR: Jul 1979
Football League: 106-11. **FAC:** 6-1. **FLC:** 13-5.
Other: 2-0. **Total:** 127-17.
Honours: FA Cup runner's-up medal. 2 2nd Div championship medals. 3rd Div promotion medal.

Gary was a hard working, energetic midfield player, who was full of class, having come from Manchester United on a free transfer. A fringe first team player, playing in about half the games, nearly six years later Derby County paid £90,000 for him and he made 112 consecutive appearances for them. Gary was used as a full-back at his next, and last, Football League club, Gillingham.

Debut: 3 Oct 1981 v Blackburn Rovers (H) 2-0 Div 2.

MIDDLEMISS Herbert

(OL) Wing 5' 10" 11st 5lbs
b: Newcastle, 19 Dec 1888
d: Brixham, Devon, 28 Jun 1941
QPR: Jun 1920
Football League: 16-1. **FAC:** 0-0. **FLC:** 0-0.
Other: 0-0. **Total:** 16-1.
Honours: 4 trial matches for England. South v North. Football League v Southern League. 2nd Div runner's-up medal.

Bert was a very fine winger, always keen to cut inside and take a shot at goal. He joined QPR in their first season in the Football League, but was, by then, near the end of his playing career.

Debut: 28 Aug 1920 v Watford (H) 1-2 Div 3.

MIDDLETON John

(IR) Mid 5' 10" 12st 6lbs
b: Sunderland, 19 Apr 1898
QPR: May 1925
Football League: 54-9. **FAC:** 0-0. **FLC:** 0-0.
Other: 0-0. **Total:** 54-9.

Although John was an inside-forward he was gradually converted into a half-back. In fact he eventually became a player able to play right across the half-back line, playing centre-half for Aldershot until 1937. On hanging up his boots he became the trainer/coach at the Hampshire club.

Debut: 29 Aug 1925 v Gillingham (A) 0-3 Div 3 (S).

Gary Micklewhite

Ludo Miklosko

MIKLOSKO Ludek

Goal 6′ 5″ 14st 0lbs
b: Ostrava, Czechoslovakia, 9 Dec 1961
QPR: (£50,000) Oct 1998
Football League: 57-0. **FAC:** 6-0. **FLC:** 2-0.
Other: 0-0. **Total:** 65-0.
Honours: 44 caps for Czechoslovakia. B I U23.

A tall and commanding goalkeeper who was released by QPR during the summer of 2001. After a lengthy stay at West Ham, Ludo moved across London to Loftus Road during the 1998/99 season. He began the 2000/01 season as understudy to Lee Harper before playing his first match of the season in November. Ludo retained his place until March 2001 before being dropped. After he was released, he took up the post of goalkeeping coach at West Ham United.

Debut: 3 Oct 1998 v Grimsby Town (H) 1-2 Div 1.

MILANESE Mauro

Def 6′ 1″ 12st 6lbs
b: Trieste, Italy, 17 Sep 1971
QPR: 2005
Football League: 40-0. **FAC:** 2-0. **FLC:** 2-0.
Other: 0-0. **Total:** 44-0.

Ian Holloway brought more continental talent to Loftus Road in the summer of 2005 with the signing of Italian left-back Mauro Milanese. The hugely experienced defender – who had previously been on the books of Inter Milan, Parma, Napoli and Torino – made the left-back berth his own in his first season with the club. Mauro made 26 League appearances as Rangers ensured their Championship survival but could not prevent the club being on the wrong end of 0-3 scorelines against Northampton Town and Blackburn Rovers in the Carling Cup and FA Cup respectively. It was not a match made in heaven, however, and Mauro returned to his native country in 2007.

Debut: 20 Aug 2005 v Coventry City (A) 0-3 Championship.

MILLAR Harry

(CF) Striker 5′ 9″ 12st 0lbs
b: Paisley, Renfrewshire, Scotland, 1874
QPR: 1901
Southern League: 24-7. **FAC:** 3-5. **FLC:** 0-0.
Other: 0-0. **Total:** 27-12.

Harry was recognised as one of the cleverest strikers in the Victorian era, although his playing career was apparently quite short. Unfortunately little has been traced in print of this player. Probably his most memorable matches for Bury were his four goals v Crewe Alexandra in 1894 and the same tally for Stockton in the FA Cup in 1897. He also scored a quartet of goals for QPR in an FA Cup match v West Norwood in 1901.

Debut: 7 Sep 1901 v Watford (H) 0-1 SL Div 1.

MILLBANK Joseph H

(CH) CD
b: Edmonton, London, 30 Sep 1919
QPR: Jul 1948
Football League: 1-0. **FAC:** 0-0. **FLC:** 0-0.
Other: 0-0. **Total:** 1-0.

Transferred to Crystal Palace at the beginning of the war, Joe was unlucky in that footballwise, he was born at the wrong time. Of the 87 appearances he made for Crystal Palace only 29 were in the League, the rest being wartime matches.

Debut: 11 Sep 1948 v Barnsley (H) 2-2 Div 2.

Mauro Milanese

Adam Miller

MILLER Adam

Mid 5' 11" 11st 6lbs
b: Hemel Hempstead, 19 Feb 1982
QPR: Nov 2004
Football League: 15-0. **FAC:** 0-0. **FLC:** 1-0.
Other: 0-0. **Total:** 16-0.
Debut: 4 Dec 2004 v Nottingham Forest (A) 1-2 Championship.

MILLER James

(CF) Striker
b: Glasgow, Scotland
QPR: 1913
Southern League: 63-28. **FAC:** 8-3. **FLC:** 0-0.
Other: 0-0. **Total:** 71-31.

Jimmy was a very tough centre-forward who lost the better part of his playing days while in the trenches at Flanders. When peace came and he returned home from France, he seemed a different person; in 1921 he moved to Hartlepool where he played for the United in the North Eastern League.
Debut: 1 Sep 1913 v Swindon Town (A) 0-3 SL Div 1.

MILLER Liam

Mid 5' 7" 10st 6lbs
b: Cork, Republic of Ireland, 13 Feb 1981
QPR: Jan 2009
Football League: 13-0. **FAC:** 0-0. **FLC:** 0-0.
Other: 0-0. **Total:** 13-0.
Honours: 19 Republic of Ireland caps.
Debut: 27 Jan 2009 v Blackpool (A) 3-0 Championship.

MILLINGTON Thomas

(RB) Def
b: Manchester, 1887
QPR: 1914
Southern League: 28-0. **FAC:** 3-0. **FLC:** 0-0.
Other: 0-0. **Total:** 31-0.

Tom turned out quite regularly for the club up to the First World War. He started out as an inside-forward at Bury but settled in nicely at full-back at QPR. There is no trace of him after the Great War.
Debut: 1 Sep 1914 v Millwall (A) 1-3 SL Div 1.

MILLS Donald G

(IL) Mid 5' 10" 10st 6lbs
b: Rotherham, 17 Aug 1928
d: Torquay, Feb 1994
QPR: Aug 1946
Football League: 45-6. **FAC:** 3-3. **FLC:** 0-0.

Liam Miller

Other: 0-0. **Total:** 48-9.
QPR: Jan 1950
Football League: 31-3. **FAC:** 0-0. **FLC:** 0-0.
Other: 0-0. **Total:** 31-3.
Honours: Represented the 3rd Div (South) 3 times. 3rd Div (South) championship medal. 4th Div promotion medal.

Spotted at the age of 16 years old playing football in a mining community in Bramley, near Rotherham, Don signed professional forms for QPR on his 17th birthday. Loaned to Torquay United because of his frailty, it was thought that a spell of sea air would help to fill out his frame. The "Don", as he became known was so popular at the Devonshire club that they tried to buy him, and eventually they did in 1952. Don stayed there for 20 years as a player, coach and scout. Later he became a traffic warden in Torquay.

Debut: 25 Sep 1946 v Bournemouth & Boscombe Athletic (H) 3-0 Div 3 (S).

MILWARD George

(CF) Striker
b: Chesterfield, 1879
d: Whittington, 16 Jan 1909
QPR: May 1903
Southern League: 46-14. **FAC:** 0-0. **FLC:** 0-0.
Other: 0-0. **Total:** 46-14.

George, or Paddy, as he was generally known, was a deadly finisher, well liked by spectators. Unfortunately he sustained a bad injury that caused the onset of a serious illness from which he never recovered. Paddy returned to Chesterfield to open a tobacconist shop until his premature death at the age of 29 years.

Debut: 5 Sep 1903 v Brentford (H) 1-0 SL Div 1.

MITCHELL Archibald P

(CH) CD 5′ 8″ 12st 0lbs
b: Smethwick, 15 Dec 1885
d: Apr 1949
QPR: 1907
Southern/Football League: 306-11. **FAC:** 24-1. **FLC:** 0-0. **Other:** 1-0. **Total:** 331-12.
Honours: 2 Southern League championship medals. 7 Southern League caps. Represented an FA XI & the League.

The captain who became a legend in the side, who was later to become manager, Archie was to play many matches for the club, for including wartime appearances he totalled 467, during which time he scored 22 goals.

Strong and wiry, he developed into one of the pivots in the Southern League, and being an excellent header of the ball and a good tackler, he was probably the most influential player in the early history of the Rangers. After retirement from playing, Archie became the manager of Brentford for a time and then coached on the Continent for two years. When he returned he managed Dartford in 1928. He finally embraced the job of manager at QPR in 1930.

Debut: 2 Sep 1907 v Tottenham Hotspur (H) 3-3 SL Div 1.

MOBLEY Victor J

(CH) CD 6′ 0″ 13st 8lbs
b: Oxford, 11 Oct 1943
QPR: (£55,000) Oct 1969
Football League: 25-0. **FAC:** 3-0. **FLC:** 3-0.
Other: 0-0. **Total:** 31-0.
Honours: Capped by Young England. 13 caps for the U23. 1 Football League cap.

Vic must have been one of the unluckiest players in the Football League during the middle to late 1960s. First of all a poisoned foot prevented him from winning an England cap in 1964, then badly damaged ankle ligaments caused him to miss the 1966 FA Cup final. He was a big, solid, fair haired man and was the club's most notable signing to that date. Shortly after joining QPR it was discovered that he suffered from osteoarthritis in his knees. A court case ensued, in which the Rangers sued for their money back, but it was to no avail. After hanging his boots up, in 1971, he became involved in the part-time management of Oxford City. In the end, however, Vic elected to emigrate to New Zealand where he became the coach to Papatoetoe.

Debut: 4 Oct 1969 v Middlesbrough (H) 4-0 Div 2.

MOFFATT Hugh

(OR) Wing 5′ 4″ 9st 2lbs
b: Camerton, Cumberland, 1900
QPR: 1929
Football League: 15-3. **FAC:** 0-0. **FLC:** 0-0.
Other: 0-0. **Total:** 15-3.

A tiny winger who was mainly used as a reserve to Coward, Hugh was fast and tricky and moved between quite a few clubs in the 1920s.

Debut: 31 Aug 1929 v Crystal Palace (A) 1-1 Div 3 (S).

MOGER

Goal
QPR: 1905
Southern League: 3-0. **FAC:** 0-0. **FLC:** 0-0.
Other: 0-0. **Total:** 3-0.

One thing certain about Moger is that he is not the same goalkeeper that played for Manchester United, despite what some references generally state. Although detailed research has not revealed anything further about this man.

Debut: 21 Apr 1906 v Northampton Town (A) 1-1 SL Div 1.

MOLLOY Peter

(LB) Mid 5′ 10″ 12st 0lbs
b: Haslington, Lancashire, 20 Apr 1904
d: St Albans, 16 Feb 1993
QPR: Jul 1935
Football League: 3-0. **FAC:** 0-0. **FLC:** 0-0.
Other: 0-0. **Total:** 3-0.
Honours: Northern Ireland League XI v Northern Ireland Regional League. 3rd Div (North) Cup winner's medal.

A shilling each-way bet on a horse called King of Clubs changed Peter's life completely, when it won, and he ran away from home to join the Kings Royal Rifles. Pete was released after three months and found a job as a fairground boxer before turning to professional football. Playing in the reserves wherever he went, he did manage three senior games for QPR before moving on. He performed alongside such greats as Len Shackleton during the war, and notched up over 60 wartime matches for Bradford City together with 26 for Accrington Stanley.

Peter completed an FA coaching course in 1947, and became the manager of the Turkish national side in 1949. He once refereed a championship decider in Turkey, and abandoned the match after a sending-off and a penalty decision prompted a pitch invasion. A full apology was received from the Turkish FA. Turning down an offer from Chile, Peter joined Watford as their trainer in 1951 and stayed until 1992.

Debut: 14 Sep 1935 v Aldershot (H) 5-0 Div 3 (S).

MOORE James

(IL) Mid 5′ 8″ 10st 8lbs
b: Bolden Colliery, Durham, 1 Sep 1891
d: Dec 1972
QPR: Nov 1924
Football League: 26-5. **FAC:** 0-0. **FLC:** 0-0.
Other: 0-0. **Total:** 26-5.
Honours: FA Cup winner's medal.

Neat with his footwork and particularly clever at heading the ball, Jimmy was effectively rediscovered by Southampton in 1916 while he was helping to construct aeroplanes, being a carpenter by trade, in a boatyard in Cowes on the Isle of Wight. He guested for the Saints in several wartime matches and was persuaded to sign on a permanent basis in May 1919. Jimmy had the unfortunate distinction of being the first ever Southampton player to be sent off in a League match. After several moves he came to QPR but only stayed for part of the 1924/25 season. After a spell at Crewe, in 1927 he moved to NAC Breda, in Holland, as a coach. When he retired from the game he ran a public house for a time in Barnsley, then he purchased a greengrocery business, and after the Second World War he became a director

Stefan Moore

of Barnsley FC.
Debut: 30 Aug 1924 v Newport County (A) 0-0 Div 3 (S).

MOORE Stefan

Striker 5' 10" 10st 12lbs
b: Birmingham, 28 Sep 1983
QPR: Jun 2005
Football League: 39-3. **FAC:** 1-0. **FLC:** 2-0.
Other: 0-0. **Total:** 42-3.

Stefan came through the Aston Villa academy alongside his brother Luke (Villa and WBA) but, despite arriving with a glowing reputation, the striker's first season at Loftus Road was something of a disappointment for staff and fans alike, with the pacey front-man scoring just twice in 25 League appearances. As a result, Stefan was transfer-listed by Gary Waddock in April 2006. A loan spell with Port Vale preceded a return to Rangers' first team under new manager John Gregory but it was decided that his future lay elsewhere and Stefan has since appeared for Walsall and Kidderminster Harriers.
Debut: 6 Aug 2005 v Hull City (A) 0-0 Championship.

MORALEE William Ernest

(LH) Mid 5' 9" 10st 10lbs
b: Crook County, Durham, 3 May 1906
d: 1967
QPR: June 1936
Football League: 22-0. **FAC:** 0-0. **FLC:** 0-0.
Other: 1-0. **Total:** 23-0.

Billy was noted as a stalwart who was both loyal as a player and as a person. He was used mainly as a reserve, substituted for Dicky March, and retired in 1938.
Debut: 23 Jan 1937 v Clapton Orient (A) 0-0 Div 3 (S).

MORGAN Ian Arthur

(OR) Wing 5' 8" 11st 0lbs
b: City of London, 14 Nov 1946
QPR: Sep 1964
Football League: 173-26. **FAC:** 6-1. **FLC:** 11-1.
Other: 0-0. **Total:** 190-28.
Honours: 3rd Div championship medal. 2nd Div championship medal. FA tour of America & the Far East.

The Morgan twins on either wing were a familiar sight at QPR. In his heyday Ian was a fast and skilful winger, who was very adaptable in switching from left to right during a match and would probably finish it in midfield. He was bought by his former skipper, Mike Keen, who became manager of Watford. However, Ian sustained an injury which eventually brought about the cancellation of his contract and he retired from

full-time football.
Debut: 25 Sep 1964 v Hull City (H) 2-1 Div 3.

MORGAN Roger Ernest

(OL) Wing 5' 8" 11st 0lbs
b: City of London, 14 Nov 1946
QPR: Sep 1964
Football League: 180-39. **FAC:** 13-1. **FLC:** 13-4.
Other: 0-0. **Total:** 206-44.
Honours: 5 England youth caps. 1 U23 cap. 3rd Div championship medal. League Cup winner's medal. 2nd Div championship medal.

The career of Roger followed a close parallel course to that of his identical twin Ian. The similarity did not end there, for they were not only alike in appearance but also in style, as both were fast, tricky wingers who could cross the ball accurately or cut in for a shot. Of the two, Roger was probably regarded as slightly better. However, the pair proved a real handful for opposing defences. In 1969, Roger signed for Spurs and made his debut for them at Loftus Road against his old club, and who included his brother in the opposition line-up. Sadly, Roger was forced into a premature retirement in the summer of 1973.

He worked for Harringay Council as a recreation officer for a time before returning to football as the West Ham Community Development Officer.
Debut: 3 Oct 1964 v Gillingham (A) 2-2 Div 3.

MORRIS Samuel

(CH) CD
b: Handsworth, Birmingham
QPR: 1907
Southern League: 42-2. **FAC:** 2-0. **FLC:** 0-0.
Other: 0-0. **Total:** 44-2.

Sam was a totally dedicated player who stayed with the club for four years. Morris stood in for McLean on at least two occasions in the championship season of 1908. However, the following season with Lintott moving to Bradford City and McLean suffering from injuries, Sam was called upon to play quite often. When Hartwell came onto the scene, Sam played mostly reserve team football.
Debut: 25 Apr 1907 v Southampton (A) 2-5 SL Div 1.

MORROW Steven Joseph

Def 6' 0" 11st 6lbs
b: Belfast, Northern Ireland, 2 Jul 1970
QPR: (£500,000) Mar 1997
Football League: 91-2. **FAC:** 3-0. **FLC:** 6-0.
Other: 0-0. **Total:** 100-2.
Honours: FA Youth Cup medal. European Cup winner's medal. League Cup winner's medal. Northern Ireland schoolboy caps. 3 youth caps. 3 U21 caps. B cap. 39 full caps. Football Combination

Steve Morrow

championship medal. European Cup Winners' Cup finalist's medal. European Super Cup finalist medal.

Steve turned out in the Irish League when he was 15 years of age, and won the first of his 39 caps before he had even made his debut for Arsenal. In the Gunners' League Cup victory he scored his first ever goal in senior football and then broke his arm in the celebratory horseplay after the final whistle. A half million pound signing for QPR late in the 1996/97 season, he spent four years at Loftus Road, making exactly 100 first team appearances, then moved on to Peterborough, before crossing the Atlantic to play for Dallas Burn in the USA. He is one of the few professionals to wear contact lenses.

Debut: 5 Apr 1997 v Bolton Wanderers (A) 1-2 Div 1.

MORTIMORE John Henry

(CH) CD 6′ 0″ 11st 9lbs
b: Farnborough, 23 Sep 1934
QPR: (£8,000) Sep 1965
Football League: 10-0. **FAC:** 0-0. **FLC:** 0-0.
Other: 0-0. **Total:** 10-0.
Honours: Youth caps for England. 17 Amateur caps. Football League Cup winner's medal. 2nd Div runner's-up medal.

John was a commanding pivot, especially in the air, becoming the star of the side. Unfortunately he left after a short spell to become the player/coach of Sunderland. In the 1970s he took over as the manager of Portsmouth and later the same position in Greece, before becoming the assistant manager of Southampton. In the 1980s John led Benfica as manager, followed by Betis, Seville and finally Belenenses of Portugal. In this role he won the Portuguese League once and the Portuguese Cup three times running.

Debut: 11 Sep 1965 v Reading (H) 0-2 Div 3.

MOUGHTON Colin E

(LH) Mid 6′ 0″ 10st 8lbs
b: Harrow, Middlesex, 30 Dec 1947
QPR: Dec 1965
Football League: 6-0. **FAC:** 0-0. **FLC:** 0-0.
Other: 0-0. **Total:** 6-0.

Colin showed promise as an apprentice but was allowed to leave for Colchester United after a two month trial. They in turn released him the following year.

Debut: 21 May 1966 v Bournemouth (H) 5-0 Div 3.

MOUNTFORD George Frederick

(OR) Wing 5′ 9″ 11st 0lbs
b: Kidderminster, 30 Jan 1921
d: Kidderminster, 14 Jun 1973
QPR: Oct 1952
Football League: 35-2. **FAC:** 3-0. **FLC:** 0-0.
Other: 0-0. **Total:** 38-2.

George made occasional appearances in the Stoke City side when Stanley Matthews was unavailable. After the Second World War, George kept Matthews out of the side which resulted in Stan being transferred to Blackpool in 1947. In the summer of 1950, George, along with Neil Franklin and Charlie Mitten of Manchester United, went to play their soccer in British Columbia which was then outside the domain of FIFA. Mountford became immensely popular in Bogota, where he became known as the bald arrow, and stayed for the season. On his arrival back in England he was suspended for six months without pay for playing outside of FIFA regulations. The FA fined him £250 and George was never the same again. Much resentment was felt among the spectators at Loftus Road with the swap of Des Farrow (who was much liked) with that of the renegade George Mountford. With his football career in tatters he became a GPO engineer and played minor football till the end of his playing days.

Debut: 25 Oct 1952 v Crystal Palace (A) 2-4 Div 3 (S).

MUIR Ian James

For 5′ 8″ 10st 13lbs
b: Coventry, 5 May 1963
QPR: Sep 1980
Football League: 2-2. **FAC:** 0-0. **FLC:** 0-0.
Other: 0-0. **Total:** 2-2.
Honours: England schoolboy & youth caps. 4th Div runner's-up medal. Leyland Daf Cup winner's medal. 3rd Div runner's-up medal. Leyland Daf Cup runner's-up medal.

Ian only played two games for Rangers, and in the first he scored his two goals for the club. His ability was badly misjudged at Loftus Road, and indeed by a string of managers throughout the country, until the summer of 1985, when Frank Worthington took him under his wing at Tranmere Rovers.

Debut: 25 Apr 1981 v Cambridge United (H) 5-0 Div 2.

MUIR William M

(OR) Wing
b: Ayr, Scotland, 27 Aug 1925
QPR: Feb 1949
Football League: 16-4. **FAC:** 0-0. **FLC:** 0-0.
Other: 0-0. **Total:** 16-4.

Muir was a Scottish born winger who had breakneck speed down the flank and could cross the ball with some accuracy.

Debut: 3 Feb 1951 v Birmingham City (H) 2-0 Div 2.

MULHOLLAND Scott

Mid 5′ 8″ 10st 5lbs
b: Bexleyheath, 7 Sep 1986
QPR: Jul 2004
Football League: 1-0. **FAC:** 0-0. **FLC:** 0-0.
Other: 0-0. **Total:** 1-0.
Debut: 19 Apr 2005 v Burnley (A) 0-2 Championship.

MURDIN Steven H

(CF) Striker
QPR: 1925
Football League: 1-0. **FAC:** 0-0. **FLC:** 0-0.
Other: 0-0. **Total:** 1-0.

Steve was just one of nine centre-forwards to be tried during the dismal 1925/26 season. QPR ended the campaign in Division 3 (South), bottom of the table with just 21 points, 14 points less than the next placed team Charlton Athletic.

Debut: 25 Feb 1926 v Aberdare Athletic (H) 1-3 Div 3 (S).

MURPHY Daniel Thomas

Def 5′ 6″ 10st 8lbs
b: Southwark, London, 4 Dec 1982
QPR: Dec 1999
Football League: 23-0. **FAC:** 1-0. **FLC:** 0-0.
Other: 0-0. **Total:** 24-0.
Honours: Eire Youth.

Danny is a left-sided defender who is quick to the tackle and passes the ball well. Only a fringe player in the first team squad, by the end of the 2002/03 season he had not established a regular slot and was signed by Swindon Town in July 2003.

Debut: 26 Dec 2001 v Chesterfield (A) 3-2 Div 2.

MURPHY Neil

(CF) Striker
b: Ireland
QPR: 1903
Southern League: 51-11. **FAC:** 2-1. **FLC:** 0-0.
Other: 0-0. **Total:** 53-12.
Honours: 3 Irish international caps.

Neil was the first QPR player to be capped by Ireland. Many tributes were written about him in the local papers of the time, an example being: "Fast and clever is Murphy the Ranger... As a forward to fans he's no stranger... Fast as a flash, then a loud thud... Bet your boots that it's 'Spud'... With his lightning-like drives that spell 'danger'."

Debut: 26 Sep 1903 v Luton Town (A) 0-1 SL Div 1.

MURRAY Paul

Mid 5′ 8″ 10st 5lbs
b: Carlisle, Cumberland, 31 May 1976
QPR: (£300,000) Mar 1996
Premier/Football League: 140-7. **FAC:** 9-0.
FLC: 8-1. **Other:** 0-0. **Total:** 157-8.

Paul Murray

Honours: England youth caps. 4 U21 caps. 1 B cap.

A highly talented left-footed player who looked to be comfortable at defending or attacking. At QPR he broke his leg once and his ankle twice, hence missing much of the 2000/01 season. During a five year career at Loftus Road, Paul notched up nearly 160 first team matches, before joining Southampton.

Newcastle United had also been interested, but he signed a one year contract with the Saints. However, just one substitute appearance was made for the south coast team, and a few months later he joined Oldham Athletic on a free Bosman transfer, where he met up again with manager Iain Dowie. The end of the 2002/03 season saw Paul up against his former team in the Second Division play-off semi-final.

Debut: 5 May 1996 v Nottingham Forest (A) 0-3 PL.

MUSSLEWHITE John

(CH) CD
QPR: 1896
Southern League: 2-0. **FAC:** 0-0. **FLC:** 0-0.
Other: 0-0. **Total:** 2-0.

John was the reserve team captain and centre-half for many years, even before the club were playing in the Southern League. He filled in for Hitch in 1900 and again in 1902.

Debut: 14 Apr 1900 v Bedminster (H) 2-1 SL Div 1.

MUSTARD John

(OR) Wing 5′ 8″ 11st 0lbs
b: Boldon, County Durham, 1905
QPR: Nov 1926
Football League: 37-4. **FAC:** 1-0. **FLC:** 0-0.
Other: 0-0. **Total:** 38-4.
Honours: Welsh Cup winner's medal. Welsh Cup runner's-up medal.

John was described as "handily versatile. A strong raiding winger, who carries a good shot and often uses it, as well as crossing the ball very accurately". Discovered by QPR, he was a noted sprinter and in his later career he also took a sweet penalty kick. On joining New Brighton he was immediately appointed captain, although he relinquished it shortly afterwards, stating that outside-right was not a suitable position to supervise players. He retired from the game in December 1938 at the age of 33.

Debut: 11 Dec 1926 v Plymouth Argyle (A) 0-2 Div 3 (S).

MYERS Colin Ernest

(IL) Striker 5′ 11″ 11st 12lb,
b: Wortley, Yorkshire, July 1894
QPR: 1924
Football League: 17-3. **FAC:** 5-7. **FLC:** 0-0.
Other: 0-0. **Total:** 22-10.

Noted as a brilliant player, Colin scored on his introduction to League football, for Bradford City, in 1919. But he was a journeyman who played for a different club virtually every season. His most successful match of all was for QPR in a cup-tie against Clapton at Loftus Road, when he scored all four goals in a 4-4 draw.

Debut: 25 Oct 1924 v Millwall (H) 0-0 Div 3 (S).

Dean Neal

N-O

NARDIELLO Daniel
NASH Robert G
NEAL Dean J
NEARY Harold Frank
NEEDHAM David William
NEIL Andrew
NEILL Warren Anthony
NELSON David
NELSON William E
NEWBIGGING Alexander
NEWLANDS George
NGONGE Felix Michel
NICHOLAS Charles Brian
NICHOLLS A
NIXON Thomas
NUTT Phillip J
NYGAARD Marc Stephen Griffith

O'BRIEN Michael Terrance
O'CONNER Mark Andrew
O'DONNELL Dennis
OGLEY William
OLI Dennis Chiedozie
OLISEH Egutu Chukwuma
OLSEN C
O'NEILL John Patrick
O'ROURKE John
ORR Douglas M
OSBORN Simon Edward
OVENS Gilbert
OVENSTONE David Guthrie
OXLEY Richard Lambert

NARDIELLO Daniel

Striker 5' 11" 11st 4lbs
b: Coventry, 22 Oct 1982
QPR: Jun 2007
Football League: 8-0. **FAC:** 0-0. **FLC:** 0-0.
Other: 0-0. **Total:** 8-0.
Honours: 3 Wales caps.
Debut: 11 Aug 2007 v Bristol City (A) 2-2 Championship.

NASH Robert G

(LB) Def
b: Hammersmith, London, 8 Feb 1946
QPR: Feb 1964
Football League: 17-0. **FAC:** 1-0. **FLC:** 0-0.
Other: 0-0. **Total:** 18-0.

Bob had just consolidated himself into the left-back position, left vacant by Peter Angell's retirement, when he received an horrendous injury during a match at Scunthorpe. This paved the way for the transfer of Jim Langley to the club. Bob was transferred to Exeter City after his recuperation, but to no avail for he left the game for good during the following season.

Debut: 25 Sep 1964 v Hull City (H) 2-1 Div 3.

NEAL Dean J

Striker 5' 10" 12st 0lbs
b: Edmonton, London, 5 Jan 1961
QPR: Jan 1979
Football League: 22-8. **FAC:** 0-0. **FLC:** 1-0.
Other: 0-0. **Total:** 23-8.
QPR: (Loan) Jun 1988
Football League: 0-0. **FAC:** 0-0. **FLC:** 0-0.
Other: 0-0. **Total:** 0-0.
Honours: Football League Trophy winner's medal.

There cannot be many players who have come back to their original club as a loan player. However, on his return, Dean did not play for the club even though he was a striker who had a deceptive turn plus a hard shot. He was Millwall's top goalscorer in 1983.

Debut: 18 Aug 1979 v Bristol Rovers (H) 2-0 Div 2.

NEARY Harold Frank

(CF) Striker 5' 9" 12st 4lbs
b: Aldershot, Hants, 6 Mar 1921
QPR: Jul 1945
Football League: 9-6. **FAC:** 0-0. **FLC:** 0-0.
Other: 0-0. **Total:** 9-6.
QPR: (£7,500) Oct 1949
Football League: 18-5. **FAC:** 1-0. **FLC:** 0-0.
Other: 0-0. **Total:** 19-5.

Frank played his early football in Northern Ireland during the 1940s and then turned out for Fulham in wartime matches. QPR signed him from Finchley at the beginning of the pre-war period. His incredible pace and tremendous shooting power was the feature of his game and Neary scored 23 goals in 21 matches during the 1945/46 season. At Leyton Orient he was their top marksman in 1948 and again in 1949. Frank was remembered for forcing the Bristol Rovers goalkeeper, Jack Weare, backwards into the net as he attempted to save his penalty kick. Also Archie McFeat of Torquay United was knocked unconscious when he got in the way of a Neary drive. He made a brief return to QPR, before moving to Millwall, where he notched up 59 goals in 142 appearances. Frank scored a career total of 118 goals in 245 League games.

Debut: 4 Sep 1946 v Bournemouth & Boscombe Athletic (A) 1-1 Div 3 (S).

NEEDHAM David William

CD 6' 1" 12st 7lbs
b: Leicester, 21 May 1949
QPR: Jun 1977
Football League: 18-3. **FAC:** 0-0. **FLC:** 2-0.
Other: 0-0. **Total:** 20-3.
Honours: 4th Div championship medal.
3rd Div runner's-up medal. League championship medal. 2 League Cup medals. League Cup runner's-up medal.

David was brought into the side to replace Frank McLintock but he lasted just six months. The team only won two games with him playing in defence and Needham never seemed to be able to fit in. He went on to become a successful businessman in Leicester.

Debut: 20 Aug 1977 v Aston Villa (H) 1-2 Div 1.

NEIL Andrew

(WH) Def 5' 8" 11st 0lbs
b: Crosshouse, Scotland, 18 Nov 1892
d: Kilmarnock, 14 Aug 1941
QPR: May 1927
Football League: 106-1. **FAC:** 6-0. **FLC:** 0-0.
Other: 0-0. **Total:** 112-1.
Honours: London Challenge Cup runner's-up medal. League championship runner's-up medal.

Andy was a slightly built character who was both skilful and dazzling with his wonderful ball control. In his first spell at the Goldstone Ground he was ever-present in the 1922/23 season which led to his transfer to Arsenal. He was to play in the Gunners' best ever season in the 1920s when they were First Division runner's-up in 1925/26. He became the general of the QPR side, who guided the team to third position in the Third Division (South) in 1930. This was to be his last season, in a short but notable QPR career, during which he played over 100 League matches.

Debut: 27 Aug 1927 v Newport County (H) 4-2 Div 3 (S).

NEILL Warren Anthony

(RB) Def 5' 10" 11st 5lbs
b: Acton, Middlesex, 21 Nov 1962
QPR: 1980
Football League: 181-3. **FAC:** 12-1. **FLC:** 19-1.
Other: 3-1. **Total:** 215-6.
Honours: England schoolboy caps. FA Cup runner's-up medal. 2nd Div championship medal. League Cup runner's-up medal.

Warren was a defender who liked to come forward with the attack whenever possible. His stay at Loftus Road lasted nearly eight years, during which time he made over 200 first team appearances. Although not established by then in the first team, he stood in for his subsequent Watford manager, Glen Roeder, who was suspended for the FA Cup final replay, after the first game was drawn. From that time on he became a fairly regular first team player, but suffering from sciatica, he announced his retirement from the game in 1995. However, he turned out for Watford on a non-contractual basis, and made several appearances for their reserve side.

Debut: 30 Aug 1980 v Chelsea (A) 1-1 Div 2.

NELSON David

(HB) Def 5' 8" 11st 3lbs
b: Douglas Water, Scotland, 3 Feb 1918
d: USA, Sep 1988
QPR: Feb 1950
Football League: 31-0. **FAC:** 1-0. **FLC:** 0-0.
Other: 0-0. **Total:** 32-0.
Honours: 3 London Combination championship medals. London Challenge Cup runner's-up medal. Bath Coronation Cup winner's medal.

The move to Loftus Road stunned the Brentford supporters for he had been the backbone of their defence as well as their captain. Dave was a versatile player who was equally at home in defence or attack. He played regularly throughout the war and had made over 150 appearances for Arsenal, and was part of the swap deal that brought Ronnie Rooke to Highbury just after the hostilities. In 1954 he became the Ashford Town manager and later moved to the USA.

Debut: 18 Feb 1950 v Sheffield United (H) 1-3 Div 2.

NELSON William E

(FB) Def
b: Silvertown, London, 20 Sep 1929
QPR: Jul 1955
Football League: 9-0. **FAC:** 0-0. **FLC:** 0-0.
Other: 0-0. **Total:** 9-0.

Billy was the brother of Andy Nelson the skipper of Ipswich Town. At QPR he was used mainly as cover for Ingham and Woods.

Debut: 24 Sep 1955 v Torquay United (H) 3-1 Div 3 (S).

Marc Nygaard

NEWBIGGING Alexander

(For & Goal) 5' 9" 11st 3lbs
b: Larkhall, Scotland, 27 Dec 1879
QPR: Jul 1901
Southern League: 5-0. **FAC:** 2-1. **FLC:** 0-0.
Other: 0-0. **Total:** 7-1.
Honours: Scottish Junior international.

Alex played for QPR as an outfield player who scored his one goal while playing at centre-forward. Later at Nottingham Forest he became a very good goalkeeper and was selected to play for his country at junior level in that position in 1906. Newbigging lived a long life for he was at the centenary celebrations of the Glasgow Rangers FC aged 99.
Debut: 20 Oct 1901 v Tottenham Hotspur (H) 2-1 SL Div 1.

NEWLANDS George

(RB) Def 5' 7" 12st 9lbs
b: Govenhill, Glasgow, 1882
QPR: Aug 1900
Southern League: 174-1. **FAC:** 12-0. **FLC:** 0-0.
Other: 0-0. **Total:** 186-1.
Honours: Represented the London League v the Buckinghamshire League.

George was a hard tackling, sturdy full-back who was always in a position to defend his ranks and he could play in any position (except goalkeeper). In January 1909 a newspaper article gave the best summation of George: "If he could feed his forward, as well as he tackles he would be a great defender. You can depend on finding him where the fight is keenest." Newlands was the club captain and was proud to be so. He later joined John Bowman at Norwich City and stayed there until 1910. When his career in football was over, George returned to Scotland and became a bricklayer in Dunfermline.
Debut: 29 Sep 1900 v Kettering (A) 1-2 SL Div 1.

NGONGE Felix Michel

Striker 6' 0" 12st 8lbs
b: Huy, Belgium, 10 Jan 1967
QPR: (£50,000) Dec 2000
Football League: 13-3. **FAC:** 2-0. **FLC:** 0-0.
Other: 0-0. **Total:** 15-3.
Honours: 6 caps for the Democratic Republic of Congo.

Unable to hold down a regular place in the team at Loftus Road, Michel was released at the end of the 2001 season.
Debut: 16 Dec 2000 v Nottingham Forest (H) 1-0 Div 1.

NICHOLAS Charles Brian

(RH) Def 5' 9" 11st 7lbs
b: Aberdare, Wales, 20 Apr 1933
QPR: May 1950
Football League: 112-2. **FAC:** 7-0. **FLC:** 0-0.
Other: 0-0. **Total:** 119-2.
Honours: English Schools international. Represented the 3rd Div (South) v the 3rd Div (North).

Brian made his debut for QPR at the age of 16, and stayed at Loftus Road for five years, appearing in the Football League on 112 occasions. He was a tenacious tackler and a sound defender who proved his worth to the side in the days when substitutes were not allowed. On two separate occasions, he took over in goal when Harry Brown was injured, and he kept a clean sheet in both games.

First Division Chelsea paid a large fee for him, but after less than three years he moved on to Coventry City. Despite his notable balding patch, at the age of 24 years, he gave the Midland side over four years excellent service, before moving into non-League football.
Debut: 31 Aug 1950 v Notts County (A) 3-3 Div 2.

NICHOLLS A

Goal
QPR: 1911
Southern League: 37-0. **FAC:** 5-0. **FLC:** 0-0.
Other: 0-0. **Total:** 42-0.

With the departure of Charlie Shaw to Celtic in the close season of 1913, Nicholls became the main custodian of the side and stayed until the end of the season.
Debut: 20 Jan 1912 v Watford (H) 1-1 SL Div 1.

NIXON Thomas

(RB) Def 6' 0" 11st 4lbs
b: Newcastle
QPR: 1927
Football League: 51-1. **FAC:** 0-0. **FLC:** 0-0.
Other: 0-0. **Total:** 51-1.

Tom was brought into the side as a centre-half (and made his debut in a record-breaking 8-0 victory), but was not discovered until the new manager, Archie Mitchell, came along in 1931 and thought he would make a very good full-back. Tommy was used in that position mainly as a reserve, but with the arrival of Mick O'Brien, the next manager in 1933, Nixon was released.
Debut: 9 Mar 1929 v Merthyr Town (H) 8-0 Div 3 (S).

NUTT Phillip J

Striker 5' 11" 11st 8lbs
QPR: Jul 1975
Football League: 4-1. **FAC:** 0-0. **FLC:** 0-0.
Other: 0-0. **Total:** 4-1.

Phil never played a full 90 minutes in a match, always coming on as a substitute. However, in one game he made an impact by scoring the equaliser in a 1-1 draw at home to Derby County, to keep the club at the top of the First Division.
Debut: 29 Nov 1975 v Stoke City (H) 3-2 Div 1.

NYGAARD Marc Stephen Griffith

Striker 6' 5" 14st 5lbs
b: Copenhagen, Denmark, 1 Sep 1976
QPR: Jul 2005
Football League: 69-13. **FAC:** 1-0. **FLC:** 2-1.
Other: 0-0. **Total:** 72-14.
Honours: 7 Denmark caps.

The first eight years of Marc's professional career was played out in Holland – with SC Heerenveen, MVV Maastricht and Roda JC before he was signed by Italian Serie A side Brescia Calcio. Unfortunately, the tall striker only made 10 League appearances for the Italians without finding the back of the net and was loaned to Catania and Vicenza before signing for Rangers. At Loftus Road, the Dane (who speaks several languages including English, Dutch, Italian and Vietnamese) found his scoring touch, netting nine goals in his first campaign but he was released in February 2008 and returned to Denmark with Randers FC.
Debut: 9 Aug 2005 v Ipswich Town (H) 2-1 Championship.

Dennis Oli

O'BRIEN Michael Terrance

(CH) CD 6' 2" 13st 7lbs
b: Kilcock, County Down, 10 Aug 1893
d: Uxbridge, 1940
QPR: May 1920
Football League: 66-3. **FAC:** 4-1. **FLC:** 0-0.
Other: 0-0. **Total:** 70-4.
Honours: 4 caps as captain of the Republic of Ireland. 10 caps for Northern Ireland. Football League v The Army.

Mick's first job was as a handyman to the groundsman at St Anthony's Cricket club near Dublin. He then became assistant groundsman to the Durham Cricket club, and didn't start playing football until he was 18 years old. He served in the army before the First World War, in the navy during it, (getting sunk in the Battle of Jutland), and ended up with the Royal Flying Corps! In 1920 he joined QPR and won his first cap. He sampled soccer in the USA in the mid-1920s and retired from playing in 1933, when he became manager of QPR, then the assistant manager of Brentford, in 1935. One year later he became the Ipswich Town manager taking them into the Football League. Tragically his wife and daughter both died before he was badly beaten up by an ex-boxer. He bred Alsatians, ran a shop in Derby and had a tobacconist's shop in Norwich. Few men packed more into their 47 years than Michael O'Brien.

Debut: 26 Aug 1920 v Watford (H) 1-2 Div 3 (S).

O'CONNER Mark Andrew

Mid 5' 7" 10st 2lbs
b: Rochford, Kent, 10 Mar 1963
QPR: Jun 1980
Football League: 3-0. **FAC:** 0-0. **FLC:** 0-0.
Other: 0-0. **Total:** 3-0.
Honours: U21 cap for Eire.

Unable to find a regular place in the side, this nippy fleet-footed player was transferred to Bristol Rovers. Mark was a capable and consistent midfield player or wing-back before he broke his leg in two places. He later became the youth team coach at Portsmouth.

Debut: 26 Dec 1981 v Chelsea (H) 0-2 Div 2.

O'DONNELL Dennis

For 5' 10" 10st 12lbs
b: Willington Quay, Northumberland, 1880
QPR: May 1906
Southern League: 25-7. **FAC:** 2-0. **FLC:** 0-0.
Other: 0-0. **Total:** 27-7.

Dennis was a resourceful player whose accurate shooting and passing made him a favourite of the crowd. It seemed that he was an excellent prospect in the early Edwardian era but after the time he spent with Lincoln City, he seemed to be burnt out. Dennis was the elder brother of Magnas, who also played for Lincoln City.

Debut: 1 Sep 1906 v Luton Town (A) 1-1 SL Div 1.

OGLEY William

(LH) Def 5' 9" 12st 0lbs
b: Rotherham, Yorkshire, 1896
QPR: Jul 1924
Football League: 36-2. **FAC:** 5-0. **FLC:** 0-0.
Other: 0-0. **Total:** 41-2.

Billy started playing football in the army during the First World War. On his demob he joined Swansea Town who were at the time in the Southern League. Billy spent a year with QPR before he returned to Yorkshire.

Debut: 30 Aug 1924 v Newport County (A) 0-0 Div 3 (S).

OLI Dennis Chiedozie

Striker 6' 0" 12st 4lbs
b: Newham, 28 Jan 1984
QPR: Oct 2001
Football League: 23-0. **FAC:** 3-0. **FLC:** 1-0.
Other: 3-0. **Total:** 30-0.

Dennis was a youngster who twice appeared as a substitute in 2001/02, but managed to command a more regular place during the following season. The next campaign saw him loaned out to gain more first team experience but his Loftus Road career was over and he moved to Swansea City in July 2004.

Debut: 26 Feb 2002 v Wigan Athletic (H) 1-1 Div 2.

OLISEH Egutu Chukwuma

Mid 6' 0" 11st 9lbs
b: Lagos, Nigeria, 18 Nov 1980
QPR: Jul 2006
Football League: 2-0. **FAC:** 0-0. **FLC:** 1-0.
Other: 0-0. **Total:** 3-0.
Debut: 22 Aug 2006 v Northampton Town (H) 3-2 Carling Cup first round.

OLSEN C

(CH) CD
QPR: 1919
Southern League: 1-0. **FAC:** 0-0. **FLC:** 0-0.
Other: 0-0. **Total:** 1-0.

A trialist who played in place of Archie Mitchell on a single occasion.

Debut: 9 Apr 1920 v Newport County (A) 0-3 SL Div 1.

O'NEILL John Patrick

CD 6' 0" 13st 0lbs
b: Derry, Northern Ireland, 11 Mar 1958
QPR: (£150,000) Jul 1987
Football League: 2-0. **FAC:** 0-0. **FLC:** 0-0.
Other: 0-0. **Total:** 2-0.
Honours: 39 caps for Northern Ireland. U21 cap. 2nd Div championship medal. 3rd Div promotion medal.

An experienced, polished and cool defender

who played second fiddle to Alan McDonald, John came from Leicester, but was transferred to Norwich City, at a much reduced fee, just a few months later. John was just 34 minutes into his debut match when he received an injury which was to end his career. In 1990 he spent a two year spell as the manager of League of Ireland side Finn Harps. Two years later he kept a wine and spirits shop in Derry while he was sitting on the board of Derry City. In October 1994, John won a high court action against John Fashanu and Wimbledon FC (arising from the tackle that put him out of the game), for £70,000.
Debut: 31 Oct 1987 v Norwich City (A) 1-1 Div 1.

John O'Rourke

O'ROURKE John

Striker 5′ 8″ 10st 10lbs
b: Northampton, 11 Feb 1945
QPR: (£70,000) Oct 1971
Football League: 34-12. **FAC:** 2-0. **FLC:** 1-0.
Other: 0-0. **Total:** 37-12.
Honours: Youth international. U23 cap. 2nd Div runners-up medal. 2nd Div championship medal.

John was an opportunist with a fierce shot but at Loftus Road the goals dried-up. In his early days he was unable to make an impression at either Arsenal or Chelsea until he dropped down to the Fourth Division to play for Luton Town. Success with them provided a springboard for better times. John later moved to live and work, running a newsagent, in a seaside resort.
Debut: 19 Oct 1971 v Luton Town (H) 1-0 Div 2.

ORR Douglas M

(OL) Wing
b: Glasgow, Scotland, 8 Nov 1937
QPR: Jun 1957
Football League: 5-0. **FAC:** 0-0. **FLC:** 0-0.
Other: 0-0. **Total:** 5-0.
Honours: Scottish Amateur international.

Dougie was given a one year trial before returning to Hendon.
Debut: 16 Sep 1957 v Swindon Town (H) 2-1 Div 3 (S).

OSBORN Simon Edward

Mid 5′ 10″ 11st 4lbs
b: Croydon, Surrey, 19 Jan 1972
QPR: (£1,100,000) Jul 1995
Premier League: 9-1. **FAC:** 0-0. **FLC:** 2-0.
Other: 0-0. **Total:** 11-1.

Simon was one of Ray Wilkins' first transactions on his becoming manager at Loftus Road. He was a steady and composed midfield player with fine passing ability and a good shot. Unfortunately he later suffered from knee trouble due to a flaky cartilage, but had been involved in two £1m transfers.
Debut: 19 Aug 1995 v Blackburn Rovers (A) 0-1 PL.

OVENS Gilbert

(RH) Def
b: Bristol
QPR: 1911
Southern League: 103-3. **FAC:** 9-1. **FLC:** 0-0.
Other: 0-0. **Total:** 112-4.

Although Bert didn't turn out for the Chelsea side, he nevertheless was a regular senior squad player at QPR for three years and he was in the team that won the Southern League title for the second time in 1912. He was an important member of the side and could play anywhere in defence.
Debut: 30 Sep 1911 v Exeter City (A) 1-1 SL Div 1.

OVENSTONE David Guthrie

(OL) Wing 5′ 8″ 10st 12lbs
b: Coal Wynd, Scotland, 17 Jun 1913
d: Cardiff, 19 Jan 1983
QPR: Jun 1935
Football League: 15-3. **FAC:** 1-0. **FLC:** 0-0.
Other: 0-0. **Total:** 16-3.

Dave was in such devastating form when Cardiff City visited Loftus Road that the Welsh club snapped him up during the close season. Showing many fine touches he nevertheless found himself in the reserves for a lot of his time at Cardiff so he was released in the spring of 1937. To accommodate his wife he moved back to South Wales at the end of his career and played in non-League football, finishing as the player/manager of Ebbw Vale and working on the railway at the same time. At the time of his death from a heart attack, he was living in a Salvation Army hostel in Cardiff.
Debut: 9 Nov 1935 v Bournemouth & Boscombe Athletic (H) 2-0 Div 3 (S).

OXLEY Richard Lambert

(OR) Wing 5′ 10″ 11st 10lbs
b: Barrow-on-Furness, 10 Apr 1893
d: Wallsend, 17 Apr 1953
QPR: Aug 1923
Football League: 18-0. **FAC:** 0-0. **FLC:** 0-0.
Other: 0-0. **Total:** 18-0.

Though Dick was born in Barrow he spent much of his early life on Tyneside working in a munitions factory during the First World War.

Well known as a sprinter, having won the Powderhall Handicap, Oxley was noted as a speedy winger with a sense of ball control and a happy knack of placing it on the right spot.His private life was dogged by tragedy having lost his wife in 1927 just five years after they were married. Their only son Jack died of consumption at 20 years of age, in 1943, while on an Officer Cadet course, and within 10 years Dick himself had died of jaundice.
Debut: 8 Sep 1923 v Swindon Town (A) 0-0 Div 3 (S).

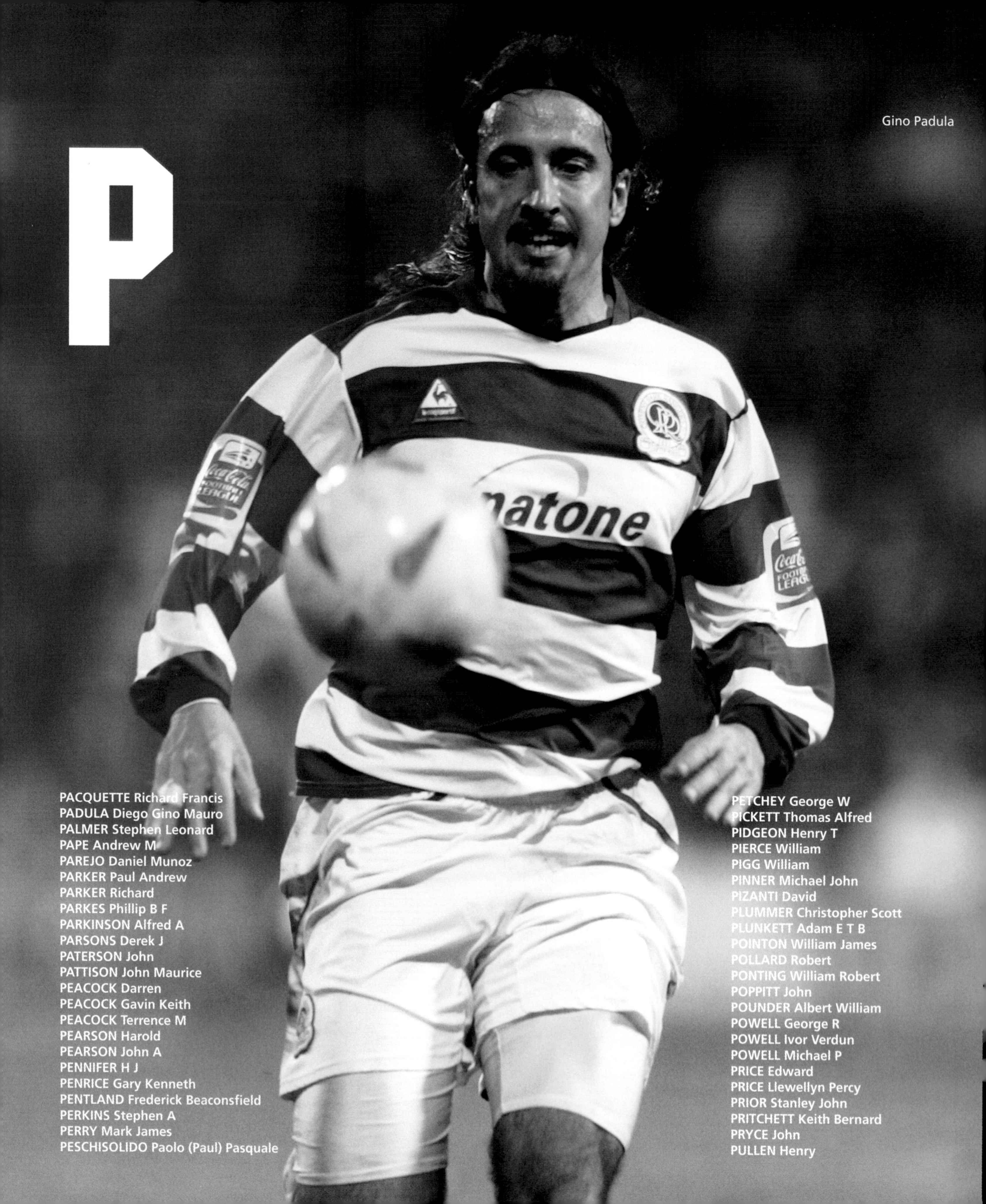

Gino Padula

P

PACQUETTE Richard Francis
PADULA Diego Gino Mauro
PALMER Stephen Leonard
PAPE Andrew M
PAREJO Daniel Munoz
PARKER Paul Andrew
PARKER Richard
PARKES Phillip B F
PARKINSON Alfred A
PARSONS Derek J
PATERSON John
PATTISON John Maurice
PEACOCK Darren
PEACOCK Gavin Keith
PEACOCK Terrence M
PEARSON Harold
PEARSON John A
PENNIFER H J
PENRICE Gary Kenneth
PENTLAND Frederick Beaconsfield
PERKINS Stephen A
PERRY Mark James
PESCHISOLIDO Paolo (Paul) Pasquale
PETCHEY George W
PICKETT Thomas Alfred
PIDGEON Henry T
PIERCE William
PIGG William
PINNER Michael John
PIZANTI David
PLUMMER Christopher Scott
PLUNKETT Adam E T B
POINTON William James
POLLARD Robert
PONTING William Robert
POPPITT John
POUNDER Albert William
POWELL George R
POWELL Ivor Verdun
POWELL Michael P
PRICE Edward
PRICE Llewellyn Percy
PRIOR Stanley John
PRITCHETT Keith Bernard
PRYCE John
PULLEN Henry

Richard Pacquette

PACQUETTE Richard Francis

Striker 6' 0" 12st 7lbs
b: Paddington, London, 28 Jan 1983
QPR: Feb 2000
Football League: 18-2. **FAC:** 1-0. **FLC:** 1-0.
Other: 1-0. **Total:** 21-2.
QPR: Jan 2003
Football League: 16-4. **FAC:** 0-0. **FLC:** 2-0.
Other: 0-0. **Total:** 18-4.

A strongly built striker who substituted for Andy Thompson during 2002, and made a reasonable number of appearances during the 2002/03 season, despite a short period out on loan, Richard has since become something of a journeyman footballer and has drifted into non-League football.

Debut: 21 Apr 2001 v Huddersfield Town (A) 1-2 Div 1.

PADULA Diego Gino Mauro

Def 5' 9" 12st 1lb
b: Buenos Aires, Argentina, 11 Jul 1976
QPR: 2002
Football League: 90-4. **FAC:** 3-0. **FLC:** 4-0.
Other: 6-1. **Total:** 103-5.

A quick and skilful left-back, who won several Man of the Match awards at Walsall with his determined tackling, ability in the air and readiness to move forward. Gino became a fan favourite and was part of the Rangers team that achieved promotion to the Championship in 2004 before joining Nottingham Forest in the summer of 2005.

Debut: 17 Aug 2002 v Barnsley (A) 0-1 Div 2.

PALMER Stephen Leonard

CD 6' 1" 12st 13lbs
b: Brighton, Suffolk, 31 Mar 1968
QPR: Jul 2001
Football League: 130-9. **FAC:** 4-0. **FLC:** 3-0.
Other: 2-0. **Total:** 139-9.
Honours: English schools cap.

Steve possessed height, strength and energy, and as a Cambridge Blue he captained his side in their second Varsity Match, in 1989. He went on to play Premier League football for Ipswich Town, and after a six year spell, he moved on for a similar period, to Watford. He then signed for QPR as a defender and also with a view to improving the Rangers stability in midfield. He immediately became the club captain and was the only ever-present player in the League side in 2001/02, which he repeated the following season. Steve signed for MK Dons in 2004, where he spent two seasons before retiring in late 2005 to take up a position as Tottenham Hotspur's Academy Performance Manager.

Debut: 11 Aug 2001 v Stoke City (H) 1-0 Div 2.

Steve Palmer

PAPE Andrew M

Goal 6' 0" 12st 0lbs
b: Hammersmith, London, 22 Mar 1962
QPR: 1980
Football League: 1-0. **FAC:** 0-0. **FLC:** 0-0.
Other: 0-0. **Total:** 1-0.
Honours: Middlesex schools & county honours. 15 semi-pro caps. Gola League championship medal. FA Trophy winner's medal. Middlesex Senior Cup winner's medal. Vauxhall championship medal.

Andy only played once for QPR, but his consistency between the sticks was valued very highly by the England semi-pro management, and non-League clubs, that he later moved on to.

Debut: 13 Apr 1980 v Charlton Athletic (A) 2-2 Div 2.

PAREJO Daniel Munoz

Mid 5' 11" 11st 11lbs
b: Madrid, Spain, 16 April 1989
QPR: (Loan) Aug 2008
Football League: 14-0. **FAC:** 0-0. **FLC:** 4-0.
Other: 0-0. **Total:** 18-0.
Debut: 9 Aug 2008 v Barnsley (H) 2-1 Championship.

PARKER Paul Andrew

Def 5' 7" 10st 13lbs
b: West Ham, London, 4 Apr 1964
QPR: (£500,000 joint fee) Jun 1987
Football League: 125-1. **FAC:** 16-0. **FLC:** 14-0.
Other: 5-0. **Total:** 160-1.
Honours: 3 England youth caps. 8 U21 caps. 3 B caps. 19 full caps. 2 Premier League championship medals. FA Cup winner's medal. League Cup runner's-up medal.

Paul was an adaptable defender who could play at wing-back or in the centre of defence. He was also excellent in the air for such a small man and could out-jump players much taller than himself. What he lacked in inches he compensated for with tremendous speed and astute reading of the game, he always seemed to have more time than anybody else. Parker moved from Fulham to QPR along with Dean Coney for a joint fee of £500,000. During his four years at Loftus Road he made 125 League

Paul Parker

appearances, but he really came to notice after his signing for Manchester United for £2 million. Later moves took him to various clubs before becoming the manager of Chelmsford City, and later the same at Welling United.
Debut: 15 Aug 1987 v West Ham United (A) 3-0 Div 1.

PARKER Richard

(CF) Striker 5' 8" 11st 3lbs
b: Stockton-on-Tees, 14 Sep 1894
d: Stockton-on-Tees, 1 Jan 1969
QPR: Jul 1922
Football League: 61-30. **FAC:** 5-4. **FLC:** 0-0.
Other: 0-0. **Total:** 66-34.

Dick was a fast, clever and crafty player who preferred the ball at his feet rather than in the air. The outcome of a pass, followed by a hard sizzling shot, would almost invariably culminate in a goal. Dick still holds the scoring record at Millwall with 40 goals in the 1926/27 season.
Debut: 26 Aug 1922 v Watford (H) 1-2 Div 3 (S).

PARKES Phillip B F

Goal 6' 3" 14st 9lbs
b: Sedgley, Staffordshire, 8 Aug 1950
QPR: (£15,000) Jun 1970
Football League: 344-0. **FAC:** 27-0. **FLC:** 27-0.
Other: 8-0. **Total:** 406-0.
Honours: 1 England cap. B cap. U21 cap. 6 U23 caps. 2nd Div runner's-up medal. 1st Div runner's-up medal. FA Cup winner's medal. League Cup runner's-up medal. 2nd Div championship medal.

Phil Parkes

Rated on a par with the other great QPR goalkeepers of the past, Phil was the second for Rangers to break the transfer record. Commanding in the air as well as the six yard box, he had lightning reflexes which made him very hard to beat. Phil would surely have won many more England caps if it hadn't been for Peter Shilton. With QPR in decline and regularly involved in relegation struggles, Phil jumped at the chance of joining West Ham United in February 1979. Parkesy set a club record of 22 clean sheets in the Hammers 1980/81 campaign.

His career spanned more than 800 League and Cup games and by a statistical quirk, he made exactly 344 League appearances each for QPR and West Ham United. He moved back to Loftus Road in 1991 to become the goalkeeper coach.
Debut: 22 Aug 1970 v Leicester City (H) 1-3 Div 2.

PARKINSON Alfred A

(LR) Mid
b: Camden Town, London, 30 Apr 1922
QPR: Sep 1943
Football League: 76-5. **FAC:** 3-2. **FLC:** 0-0.
Other: 0-0. **Total:** 79-7.

Alf was the reserve for such players as Joe Mallett, Ivor Powell and Don Mills, and effectively became a utility player. Alf retired from the game in 1951.
Debut: 1 Mar 1947 v Norwich City (A) 1-0 Div 3 (S).

PARSONS Derek J

(LH) Mid
b: Hammersmith, London, 24 Oct 1929
QPR: Feb 1950
Football League: 2-1. **FAC:** 1-0. **FLC:** 0-0.
Other: 0-0. **Total:** 3-1.

Derek joined the club as a 19 year old in 1952, and subsequently he was allowed to leave for Ashford Town after just one season.
Debut: 8 Nov 1952 v Torquay United (A) 1-1 Div 3 (S).

PATERSON John

(IL) Mid. 5' 9" 11st 0lbs
b: Fifeshire, Scotland, 1904
QPR: 1925
Football League: 36-6. **FAC:** 0-0. **FLC:** 0-0.
Other: 0-0. **Total:** 36-6.

John was one of the few players to stay with the club after the disastrous season of 1925/26. He emigrated to Canada in 1930 and played the game until he was 50. John visited England in 1977 when he was 72 years old.
Debut: 16 Jan 1926 v Merthyr Town (A) 0-1 Div 3 (S).

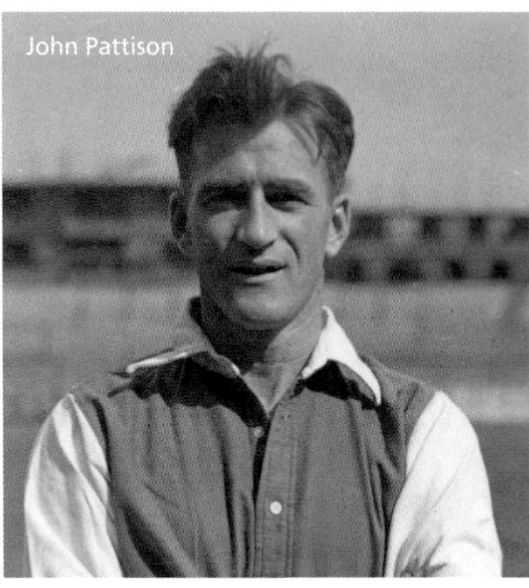
John Pattison

PATTISON John Maurice

(OL) Wing
b: Glasgow, Scotland, 19 Dec 1918
QPR: May 1937
Football League: 92-26. **FAC:** 9-5. **FLC:** 0-0.
Other: 2-0. **Total:** 103-31.
Honours: 3rd Div (South) championship medal.

John was an old fashioned type of winger, one that could turn on a sixpence, who was fast and tricky and enticed opponents to tackle him and had a sizzling shot to boot. But like so many of his age, the war robbed him of some of his best football playing years and consequently restricted his appearances. John played a further 44 matches for Leyton Orient until 1951 before teaming up with Fred Durrent at Dover. He later coached the Queensland club in Australia.
Debut: 12 Mar 1938 v Notts County (H) 2-1 Div 3 (S).

PEACOCK Darren

CD 6' 2" 12st 6lbs
b: Bristol, 3 Feb 1968
QPR: (£350,000) Dec 1990
Football League: 126-6. **FAC:** 3-0. **FLC:** 12-1.
Other: 2-0. **Total:** 143-7.
Honours: Welsh Cup winner's medal.

Darren's attempt to establish himself in the Newport County side came to an abrupt halt when a broken leg put him out of football for 18 months. He joined Hereford United when Newport County were wound up and gradually turned into a very good central defender. Late in 1990 he became a big money signing for QPR, where he spent the next four years. Eventually he became the country's most expensive defender (at that time), with Newcastle's record purchase of £2.7 million, in 1994.

Kevin Keegan, the Newcastle United manager, had persistently sought his signature. Another move and two loan signings followed, but an injury to

Darren Peacock

his neck in the League Cup tie at Fulham in the year 2000 led to his retirement from the game on medical grounds.
Debut: 23 Dec 1990 v Derby County (A) 1-1 Div 1.

PEACOCK Gavin Keith

Mid 5' 8" 11st 5lbs
b: Eltham, Kent, 18 Nov 1967
QPR: Nov 1984
Football League: 17-1. **FAC:** 1-0. **FLC:** 0-0.
Other: 0-0. **Total:** 18-1.
QPR: (£1,000,000) Nov 1996
Football League: 190-35. **FAC:** 9-3. **FLC:** 9-3.
Other: 0-0. **Total:** 208-41.
Honours: English school caps. 5 youth caps. 1st Div championship medal. Represented the Football League.

Gavin's ability to make threatening runs from midfield made him a potent attacking threat, always able to fire home quality strikes from midfield when he was in a scoring position. His twisting runs and quick turns were appreciated by his various clubs. He captained the England schools side and is the son of Keith Peacock the ex-Charlton player. His appearances for QPR were rare, and so he moved on to Gillingham.

Subsequent moves in the next nine years saw his value rapidly rise until he was bought for £1 million by Rangers, who had earlier released him for a relatively small fee. He gave nearly five years service in his second spell at Loftus Road, being a near ever-present during this period. After a loan spell at Charlton, he was not retained at the end of the 2001/02 season, and retired from playing.
Debut: 29 Nov 1986 v Sheffield Wednesday (H) 2-2 Div 1.

PEACOCK Terrence M

(CF) Striker 5' 9" 11st 3lbs
b: Hull, Humberside, 18 Apr 1935
QPR: Aug 1956
Football League: 16-4. **FAC:** 1-0. **FLC:** 0-0.
Other: 0-0. **Total:** 17-4.

Terry was a wholehearted genuine player who made an impressive start to his career at Loftus Road by scoring three goals in his first three matches. However, an injury that he received proved to be long term and he was forced to retire at the age of 23.
Debut: 15 Dec 1956 v Reading (H) 1-1 Div 3 (S).

PEARSON Harold

(OR) Wing 5' 7" 10st 6lbs
b: Birkenhead, Liverpool, 1910
QPR: 1938
Football League: 11-1. **FAC:** 3-0. **FLC:** 0-0.
Other: 1-0. **Total:** 15-1.

"Tich" was regarded as a future international at Prenton Park and made his debut at the age of 17. However, he turned out to be just another journeyman, and his career was cut short by the Second World War.
Debut: 8 Oct 1938 v Swindon Town (A) 2-2 Div 3 (S).

PEARSON John A

(IL) Mid
b: Isleworth, Middlesex, 23 Apr 1935
QPR: Jun 1958
Football League: 21-9. **FAC:** 0-0. **FLC:** 0-0.
Other: 0-0. **Total:** 21-9.

Manager Jack Taylor was a fan of John Pearson but with the arrival of Alec Stock as manager, he

Gavin Peacock

was released and in came Brian Bedford instead. John was given a free transfer to Kettering in 1960.
Debut: 1 Sep 1958 v Tranmere Rovers (A) 0-2 Div 3.

PENNIFER H J

(CF) Striker
QPR: 1913
Southern League: 3-0. **FAC:** 0-0. **FLC:** 0-0.
Other: 0-0. **Total:** 3-0.

Pennifer was one of the many youngsters who stood in for centre-forward Miller. He joined the army in 1914 and he was one of the many to lose his lives in the Battle of the Somme.
Debut: 13 Dec 1913 v Cardiff City (A) 0-3 SL Div 1.

PENRICE Gary Kenneth

Mid 5′ 7″ 10st 0lbs
b: Bristol, 23 Mar 1964
QPR: (£625,000) Oct 1991
Football/Premier League: 82-20. **FAC:** 4-1.
FLC: 7-2. **Other:** 1-0. **Total:** 94-23.

Gary was of small stature but was a very tricky player, and had plenty of guile and determination. His passing was a delight to watch and his ability to read a match was excellent. Both the Bristol clubs initially rejected Gary on account of his size, however, he rejoined Rovers in 1984. After a million pound move to Aston Villa, in which he appeared in just 15 League matches, he joined QPR. But in four years he only played in 82 League games before moving to Watford for a much reduced fee.
Debut: 2 Nov 1991 v Aston Villa (H) 0-1 Div 1.

Gary Penrice

PENTLAND Frederick Beaconsfield

(OR) Wing 5′ 9″ 11st 11lbs
b: Wolverhampton, 18 Sep 1883
d: Poole, Dorset, 16 Mar 1962
QPR: May 1907
Southern League: 37-14. **FAC:** 2-0. **FLC:** 0-0.
Other: 1-0. **Total:** 40-14.
Honours: 5 England caps. Represented the South v the North. Southern League championship medal.

Fred's unusual middle name stems from his father, a former Lord Mayor of Birmingham, who was an admirer of Benjamin Disraeli, the Earl of Beaconsfield. Fred was a fast and very talented winger who was tricky on the ball and could centre it with precision. QPR were lucky to acquire him at the start of their first Southern League championship. Pentland was coaching in Germany when the First World War broke out and he was interned for the duration. A telegram received in England via the Netherlands FA stated that he was allowed to "go about his business but he cannot leave Germany". After the war he coached in France and spent 15 years in Spain, coaching Athletico Bilbao until the outbreak of the Spanish civil war. When Fred returned to England he joined the coaching staff at Brentford and then became manager of Barrow from January 1938 until September the next year.
Debut: 2 Sep 1907 v Tottenham Hotspur 3-3 SL Div 1.

PERKINS Stephen A

Def 5′ 11″ 11st 0lbs
b: Stepney, London, 3 Oct 1954
QPR: Jun 1977
Football League: 2-0. **FAC:** 0-0. **FLC:** 0-0.
Other: 0-0. **Total:** 2-0.

Steve was transferred along with reserve player Haverson who was also a defender.
Debut: 1 Apr 1978 v Middlesbrough (H) 1-0 Div 1.

PERRY Mark James

Def 5′ 11″ 12st 10lbs
b: Ealing, Middlesex, 19 Oct 1978
QPR: Oct 1995
Football League: 66-1. **FAC:** 3-0. **FLC:** 5-0.
Other: 1-0. **Total:** 75-1.
Honours: England school and youth caps.

Mark is an excellent reader of the game, being comfortable on the ball and tackles and passes effectively. His normal position was on the right side of defence but he could play in a more forward midfield role when needed. Mark was given a free transfer in July 2002.
Debut: Sep 1996 v Barnsley (A) 3-2 Div 1.

PESCHISOLIDO Paolo (Paul) Pasquale

Striker 5′ 7″ 10st 12lbs
b: Scarborough, Canada, 25 May 1971

Paul Peschisolido

QPR: (Loan) Nov 2000
Football League: 5-1. **FAC:** 0-0. **FLC:** 0-0.
Other: 0-0. **Total:** 5-1.
Honours: 45 Canadian caps. 11 U23 caps. 2nd Div championship medal.

Paul produced some excellent performances full of commitment, anticipation and selfless running.
Debut: 4 Nov 2000 v Portsmouth (H) 1-1 Div 1.

PETCHEY George W

(RH) Mid
b: Stepney, London, 24 Jun 1931
QPR: Jul 1953
Football League: 255-22. **FAC:** 16-2. **FLC:** 0-0.
Other: 7-0. **Total:** 278-24.
Honours: 4th Div runner's-up medal. 3rd Div runner's-up medal.

George was one of the highest rated half-backs throughout the lower divisions, a tough tackler who would give no quarter nor ask for any. The fans at Loftus Road enjoyed his no nonsense attitude and were dismayed when he was transferred to Crystal Palace. Although he only spent seven years at Loftus Road, George chalked up nearly 300 first team appearances, and also netted 22 League goals. Later he became youth team manager and then assistant manager of the senior squad at Selhurst Park. In 1971 the Orient manager's job came along, followed in 1978 by the same at Millwall. In 1984 George became the assistant manager of Brighton & Hove Albion, later becoming the Youth Development Officer until 1986.
Debut: 19 Aug 1953 v Brighton & Hove Albion (H) 1-2 Div 3 (S).

PICKETT Thomas Alfred

Goal 5' 11" 12st 3lbs
b: Merthyr, Wales, 5 Feb 1909
QPR: 1929
Football League: 46-0. **FAC:** 6-0. **FLC:** 0-0.
Other: 0-0. **Total:** 52-0.

Not much is known about Pickett, except that he was the reserve to Joe Cunningham, and in 1932 he made way for Ernie Beecham. In fact Thomas' Football League career was short, and his 46 appearances for Rangers easily surpassed those that he made at the two Bristol clubs.
Debut: 16 Nov 1929 v Torquay United (H) 1-1 Div 3 (S).

PIDGEON Henry T

(OR) Wing 5' 7" 10st 7lbs
b: Tottenham, London
QPR: 1919
Southern League: 6-0. **FAC:** 0-0. **FLC:** 0-0.
Other: 0-0. **Total:** 6-0.

Henry played in the last six matches of the old Southern League.
Debut: 5 Apr 1920 v Merthyr Tydfil (H) 0-0 SL Div 1.

PIERCE William

(RB) Def 5' 9" 12st 7lbs
b: Howden-on-Tyne, Durham, 29 Oct 1907
d: 1976
QPR: 1922
Football League: 179-2. **FAC:** 14-1. **FLC:** 0-0.
Other: 0-0. **Total:** 193-3.

Bill was a hard tackling, never say die type of player who played for QPR throughout the 1920s. At 16 years of age he made his debut, and during his eight seasons, he saw the highs and lows at Loftus Road, including seeing the club applying for re-election, to that of finishing in third place.
Debut: 6 Oct 1923 v Swansea Town (A) 0-2 Div 3 (S).

PIGG William

(LH) Mid 5' 8" 11st 6lbs
b: High Spen, County Durham, 1897
QPR: Aug 1924
Football League: 21-0. **FAC:** 4-0. **FLC:** 0-0.
Other: 0-0. **Total:** 25-0.

Bill was an unrelenting tackler and was unlucky to be with the club at this period in their history. He arrived just after they had to apply for re-election and left two seasons later when they had to apply for the second time.
Debut: 7 Mar 1925 v Luton Town (H) 2-1 Div 3 (S).

PINNER Michael John

Goal
b: Boston, Lincolnshire, 16 Feb 1934
QPR: Jul 1959
Football League: 19-0. **FAC:** 2-0. **FLC:** 0-0.

Chris Plummer

Other: 1-0. **Total:** 22-0.
Honours: 4 Cambridge varsity blues. 52 England amateur caps. Represented Great Britain in the 1960 and 1964 Olympics. Represented the RAF.

Mike began as a 15 year old and was invited to join Aston Villa at 17. He did his National Service as a pilot officer and on his demob became a solicitor. He was regarded as one of the finest amateur goalkeepers of his day. At the age of 29 he signed his first professional contract, with Leyton Orient, and played over 80 matches for them. Besides playing for a variety of clubs he also toured with the famous Middlesex Wanderers.
Debut: 22 Aug 1959 v Swindon Town (H) 2-0 Div 3.

PIZANTI David

Def 5′ 10″ 11st 0lbs
b: Israel, 27 May 1962
QPR: 1987
Football League: 21-0. **FAC:** 4-1. **FLC:** 4-0. **Other:** 3-0. **Total:** 32-1.
Honours: 25 caps for Israel.

David took quite a while to acclimatise to the English game; however, when he did he was used mainly as a reserve or was substituted. He was released during the 1989 close season.
Debut: 17 Oct 1987 v Liverpool (A) 0-4 Div 1.

PLUMMER Christopher Scott

CD 6′ 2″ 12st 9lbs
b: Isleworth, London, 12 Oct 1976
QPR: Jul 1994
Premier/Football League: 62-2. **FAC:** 7-0. **FLC:** 2-0. **Other:** 0-0. **Total:** 71-2.
Honours: England youth caps. 5 U21 caps.

Chris is a tall central defender who looks very assured on the ball. He likes to get forward in set-pieces where he can cause problems for the opposing defenders. His first team appearances were fairly rare, and he missed the start of the 2001/02 season while he was recovering from a long term injury. Returning eventually to the side in November 2001, he then broke his ankle in only his second game back and was on the sideline for the remainder of the campaign. After a loan period at Bristol Rovers he returned to QPR but was not retained at the end of the 2002/03 season, and during the summer was signed by Barnet.
Debut: 5 May 1996 v Nottingham Forest (A) 0-3 PL.

PLUNKETT Adam E T B

(LB) Def 5′ 8″ 11st 0lbs
b: Blantyre, Scotland, 16 Mar 1903
d: 1992
QPR: Jul 1925
Football League: 15-0. **FAC:** 0-0. **FLC:** 0-0. **Other:** 0-0. **Total:** 15-0.

Adam was a nomad as far as football was concerned, for he never stayed at the same club too long. Released by QPR he later became the subject of crowd barracking during his time at Coventry.
Debut: 29 Aug 1925 v Gillingham (A) 0-3 Div 3 (S).

POINTON William James

(CF) Striker
b: Hanley, Staffordshire, 25 Nov 1920
QPR: (£10,000) Jan 1949
Football League: 26-6. **FAC:** 0-0. **FLC:** 0-0. **Other:** 0-0. **Total:** 26-6.

Perhaps Bill was a touch too delicate for a centre-forward, for he was not as brash as Durrant or Addinall. However, his move to Brentford brought about an exchange deal which brought Dave Nelson to Loftus Road, much to the chagrin of the Bees supporters.
Debut: 22 Jan 1949 v Barnsley (A) 0-4 Div 2.

POLLARD Robert

(RB) Def 5′ 11″ 11st 10lbs
b: Plattsbridge, Lancashire, 25 Aug 1899
QPR: 1929

Football League: 66-0. **FAC:** 7-0. **FLC:** 0-0.
Other: 0-0. **Total:** 73-0.

Bob was a stocky player, who had an aggressive streak in him and was seldom beaten in the air or on the ground. For nine years he had been regarded as one of the best full-backs in the Third Division. He eventually went on to coach in France.

Debut: 14 Sep 1929 v Northampton Town (A) 1-2 Div 3 (S).

PONTING William Robert

(LB) Def
b: Andover, Hampshire, 1872
d: Whetstone, Middlesex, 21 Mar 1952
QPR: 1900
Southern League: 1-0. **FAC:** 0-0. **FLC:** 0-0.
Other: 0-0. **Total:** 1-0.

Bill was a schoolmaster by profession and an amateur, but he left teaching to go into the insurance business in London. Later he was to become a very influential broker.

Debut: 22 Sep 1900 v Watford (H) 1-0 SL Div 1.

POPPITT John

(RB) Def
b: Bedlington, Durham, 20 Jan 1923
QPR: Sep 1950
Football League: 106-0. **FAC:** 5-0. **FLC:** 0-0.
Other: 0-0. **Total:** 111-0.

A very dour performer who was fast and direct when tackling for the ball, in earlier days John had been a junior athletics champion and at Derby County he was the substitute to the captain Bert Mozley. He helped QPR in 1953/54 to cope with their first season back in the Third Division by helping to ensure that valuable points were won in as many as 15 draws. After four years and 111 first team appearances, he dropped down to non-League football.

Debut: 23 Sep 1950 v Birmingham City (A) 1-1 Div 2.

George Powell

POUNDER Albert William

(OR) Wing 6′ 0″ 12st 7lbs
b: Charlton, London, 27 Jul 1931
QPR: (£500) Feb 1954
Football League: 53-6. **FAC:** 2-0. **FLC:** 0-0.
Other: 0-0. **Total:** 55-6.

Because Bert was a somewhat ungainly character on the right wing, his attitude and endeavours never really endeared him to the spectators. He ended his footballing days on the non-League scene becoming player/manager of Sheppey United in 1964.

Debut: 13 Feb 1954 v Exeter City (A) 0-0 Div 3 (S).

POWELL George R

(RB) Def
b: Fulham, London, 11 Oct 1924
d: 1989
QPR: Dec 1946
Football League: 145-0. **FAC:** 10-0. **FLC:** 0-0.
Other: 0-0. **Total:** 155-0.
Honours: 3rd Div (South) championship medal.

George was recommended by a supporter who had seen him play in Germany during the war for the BAOR side. On being demobbed he joined the club as an amateur. In the 1947/48 season's FA Cup run, the side beat Gillingham, Stoke City and Luton Town to reach the sixth round versus Derby County, then a power in the land. The teams drew 1-1 at Loftus Road, but at Derby the following week, Reg Allen fractured a bone in his hand a few minutes after the start and George Powell went in goal. George stayed at Loftus Road for seven years and played in 155 competitive matches, before moving to Kent to play for the Snowdon Colliery side.

Debut: 8 Nov 1947 v Reading (A) 2-3 Div 3 (S).

POWELL Ivor Verdun

(RH) Mid 5′ 7″ 11st 6lbs
b: Gilfach, Wales, 5 Jul 1916
QPR: Sep 1937
Football League: 110-2. **FAC:** 12-0. **FLC:** 0-0.
Other: 2-0. **Total:** 124-2.
Honours: 8 caps for Wales plus 4 wartime

PQR

Ivor Powell

appearances. 3rd Div (South) championship medal.

Ivor was the first post-war player to be capped by his country while at the club, a tenacious, short, stocky half-back possessing a biting tackle and a very long throw-in. During the Second World War he was a PT instructor with the RAF stationed at Blackpool and appeared for the seasiders. Ivor struck up a great friendship with Stan Matthews who was subsequently best man at his wedding. In his last wartime match for Wales, Powell broke his collar-bone and was substituted by the Englishman, Stan Mortenson. When Aston Villa secured Ivor's transfer it was the highest fee paid for a half-back at that time. Injury finally put paid to his playing career in 1954, however, he remained the manager of Bradford City until the following year. Ivor became a publican in Manningham but then returned to the game as a coach for Leeds United. In 1960 he became the manager of Carlisle United and two years later took them into the Third Division. Later he managed Bath City and then coached in Greece, subsequently returning to coach the university football team.

Debut: 28 Jan 1939 v Walsall (H) 3-0 Div 3 (S).

POWELL Michael P

(CH) CD 6' 2" 14st 4lbs
b: Slough, Berkshire, 18 Apr 1933
QPR: Jan 1951
Football League: 105-0. **FAC:** 3-0. **FLC:** 0-0.
Other: 0-0. **Total:** 108-0.

Mike was a tall, strong, hefty defender who filled the central defender's spot in the mid-1950s. He was brought into the side to replace Bill Spence, who was injured. Michael gradually made the position his own until the emergence of Keith Rutter, who became the preferred player. Although Powell was given a couple of games at centre-forward he was released in 1959.

Debut: 6 Sep 1952 v Norwich City (A) 0-2 Div 3 (S).

PRICE Edward

Goal
b: Walsall
QPR: 1920
Football League: 7-0. **FAC:** 0-0. **FLC:** 0-0.
Other: 0-0. **Total:** 7-0.

Ted appeared as the goalkeeper in the first two matches ever played by the club in the Football League. He then stood between the sticks in April 1921 during an injury crisis, but retired from the game during the close season that followed.

Debut: 28 Aug 1920 v Watford (H) 1-2 Div 3.

PRICE Llewellyn Percy

(OL) Wing 5' 9" 11st 7lbs
b: Caersws, Wales, 12 Aug 1898
d: Dec 1969
QPR: Jun 1928
Football League: 3-0. **FAC:** 0-0. **FLC:** 0-0.
Other: 0-0. **Total:** 3-0.
Honours: 1 cap for Wales. 2nd Div championship medal.

Originally Lew was an inside- or centre-forward until he was turned into a winger at Aston Villa. He came to QPR late into his career and played in the first three matches of the 1928/29 season.

Debut: 25 Aug 1928 v Torquay United (A) 4-3 Div 3 (S).

PRIOR Stanley John

(CF) Striker
b: Swindon, Wiltshire, 20 Dec 1910
d: Swindon, Wiltshire, 22 Jun 1972
QPR: (£150) Jun 1937
Football League: 6-3. **FAC:** 0-0. **FLC:** 0-0.
Other: 0-0. **Total:** 6-3.
Honours: 3rd Div (South) championship medal. 2nd Div runner's-up medal. 1st Div runner's-up medal.

When Stan hit Charlton Athletic's first ever goal in Division 1 it gave him the unique record of scoring the club's first goals in all three Divisions of the Football League. In minor matches he had already notched five v Islington Corinthians and eight v Woolwich Garrison. Having to play second fiddle to Tommy Cheetham, he was transferred to QPR for a nominal fee, but found his chances were limited there. After the Second World War he worked as a poultry farmer near Swindon, but at the time of his death he was a carpenter.

Debut: 15 Sep 1937 v Torquay United (A) 2-0 Div 3 (S).

PRITCHETT Keith Bernard

(LB) Def 5' 9" 11st 4lbs
b: Glasgow, Scotland, 8 Nov 1953
QPR: Jan 1975
Football League: 4-0. **FAC:** 0-0. **FLC:** 0-0.
Other: 0-0. **Total:** 4-0.
Honours: 2nd Div runner's-up medal. 4th Div championship medal. 3rd Div runner's-up medal.

Keith took over from Ian Gillard when the latter filled in for David Webb. Pritchett became the national coach of New Zealand in 1996 and also a successful soccer journalist.

Debut: 31 Mar 1975 v Newcastle United (A) 2-2 Div 1.

PRYCE John

(IR) Mid 5' 9" 11st 10lbs
b: Renton, Dunbartonshire, Scotland, 25 Jan 1874
QPR: May 1901
Southern League: 19-2. **FAC:** 3-0. **FLC:** 0-0.
Other: 0-0. **Total:** 22-2.
Honours: Scottish Cup runner's-up medal. 2 2nd Div promotion medals.

By the time John reached the club he had lost a lot of his drive and penetration, so he never fitted well in the side. He retired in 1905.

Debut: 7 Sep 1901 v Watford (H) 0-1 SL Div 1.

PULLEN Henry

(LB) Def 5' 10" 12st 7lbs
b: Wellingborough, 1888
QPR: 1910
Southern League: 168-1. **FAC:** 13-0. **FLC:** 0-0.
Other: 1-0. **Total:** 182-1.
Honours: Southern League championship medal. Played for the Southern League team.

Henry was a clever two-footed left-back who was a fine tackler. When he moved to Hartlepool in 1921 Henry had already played his last football match, for he was struck down with appendicitis and never did turn out for his new club.

Debut: 29 Apr 1911 v Plymouth Argyle (H) 1-0 SL Div 1.

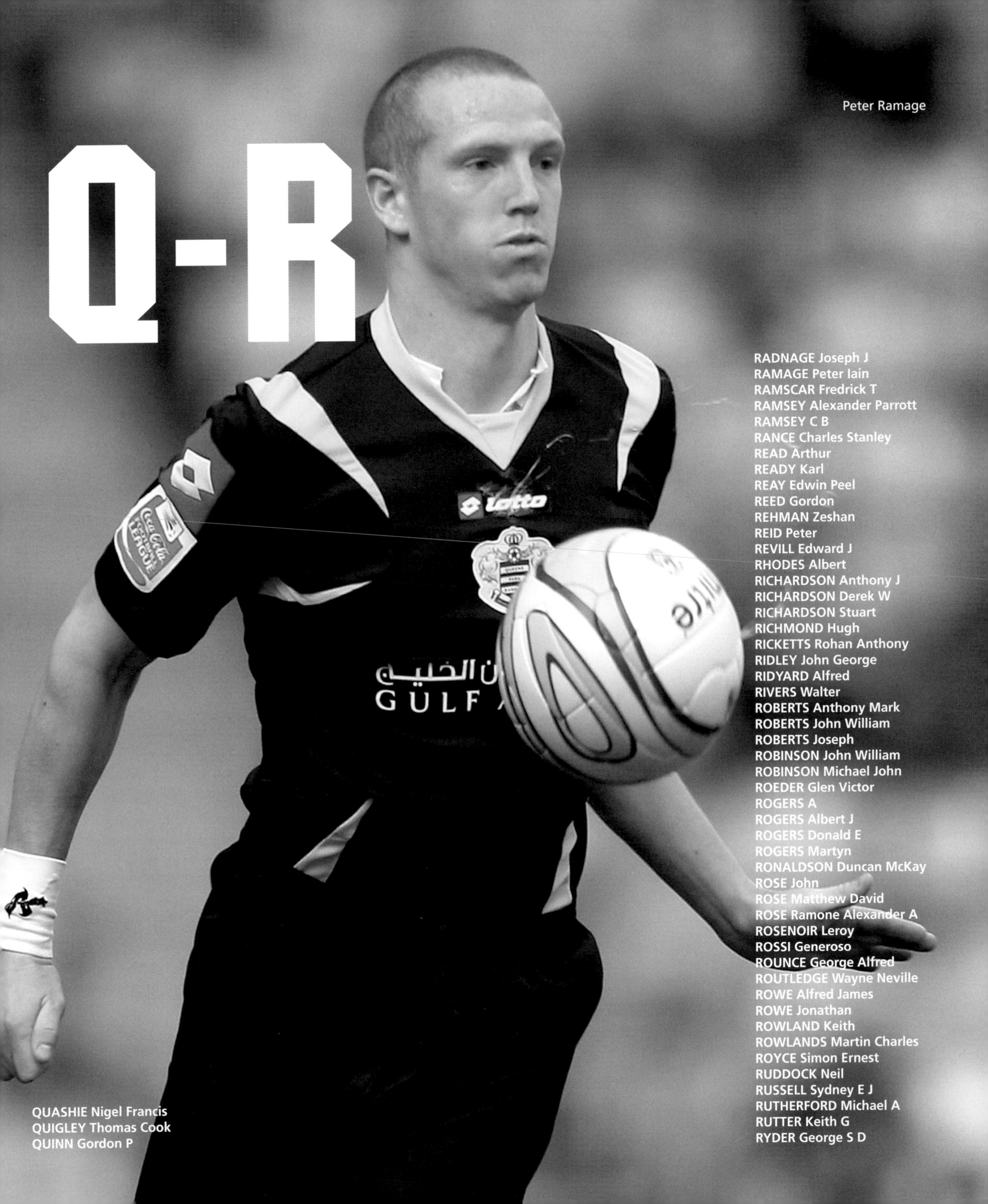

Peter Ramage

Q-R

RADNAGE Joseph J
RAMAGE Peter Iain
RAMSCAR Fredrick T
RAMSEY Alexander Parrott
RAMSEY C B
RANCE Charles Stanley
READ Arthur
READY Karl
REAY Edwin Peel
REED Gordon
REHMAN Zeshan
REID Peter
REVILL Edward J
RHODES Albert
RICHARDSON Anthony J
RICHARDSON Derek W
RICHARDSON Stuart
RICHMOND Hugh
RICKETTS Rohan Anthony
RIDLEY John George
RIDYARD Alfred
RIVERS Walter
ROBERTS Anthony Mark
ROBERTS John William
ROBERTS Joseph
ROBINSON John William
ROBINSON Michael John
ROEDER Glen Victor
ROGERS A
ROGERS Albert J
ROGERS Donald E
ROGERS Martyn
RONALDSON Duncan McKay
ROSE John
ROSE Matthew David
ROSE Ramone Alexander A
ROSENOIR Leroy
ROSSI Generoso
ROUNCE George Alfred
ROUTLEDGE Wayne Neville
ROWE Alfred James
ROWE Jonathan
ROWLAND Keith
ROWLANDS Martin Charles
ROYCE Simon Ernest
RUDDOCK Neil
RUSSELL Sydney E J
RUTHERFORD Michael A
RUTTER Keith G
RYDER George S D

QUASHIE Nigel Francis
QUIGLEY Thomas Cook
QUINN Gordon P

QUASHIE Nigel Francis

Mid 6′ 0″ 12st 4lbs
b: Peckham, London, 20 Jul 1978
QPR: Aug 1995
Premier/Football League: 57-3. **FAC:** 4-2.
FLC: 1-0. **Other:** 0-0. **Total:** 62-5.
Honours: 14 Scotland caps. England youth caps. 4 U21 caps. 1 B cap. 1st Div championship medal.

On his day, Nigel is a talented player with good passing ability and a powerful shot. After three years at Loftus Road, he cost Nottingham Forest an enormous fee, but only a quarter of this figure when he moved back south two years later. At Portsmouth, Nigel's vision, tackling and first touch made him one of the better players in the club's rise to the Premiership. It was during this period that he won the first of his Scottish caps.

Debut: 30 Dec 1995 v Manchester United (A) 1-2 PL.

QUIGLEY Thomas Cook

(CF) Striker
b: Mid-Calder, Lancashire, 26 Mar 1932
QPR: Jun 1956
Football League: 16-7. **FAC:** 0-0. **FLC:** 0-0.
Other: 1-0. **Total:** 17-7.

Nigel Quashie

Tom was one of four players to be tried in the centre-forward spot during the 1956/57 season, at the start of which he scored seven goals in nine matches. However, he had trouble settling in London, so he was released at the end of the season.

Debut: 18 Aug 1956 v Reading (A) 0-1 Div 3 (S).

QUINN Gordon P

(IF) Mid 5′ 11″ 11st 6lbs
b: Shepherds Bush, London, 11 May 1932
QPR: Aug 1952
Football League: 22-1. **FAC:** 1-0. **FLC:** 0-0.
Other: 0-0. **Total:** 23-1.

Gordon was a tall, slim player, who was excellent at controlling the ball and his passing was first class, but he somehow lacked that little bit of confidence. Plymouth Argyle signed him in an attempt to take the club back into the Second Division, but Gordon lasted just one season with the club, after failing to win a permanent place in the side.

Debut: 18 Oct 1952 v Newport County (H) 4-2 Div 3 (S).

RADNAGE Joseph J

(HB) Mid
QPR: 1909
Southern League: 3-0. **FAC:** 0-0. **FLC:** 0-0.
Other: 0-0. **Total:** 3-0.

Radnage is believed to have come from Reading and was a reserve player. He stood in for Hartwell and Wake.

Debut: 11 Sep 1909 v Clapton Orient (H) 2-1 SL Div 1.

RAMAGE Peter Iain

Def 6′ 1″ 12st 0lbs
b: Ashington, 22 Nov 1983
QPR: May 2008
Football League: 31-0. **FAC:** 1-0. **FLC:** 2-0.
Other: 0-0. **Total:** 34-0.

A lack of first team opportunities at St James' Park – just 51 League starts in almost five years as a professional – led to Peter signing for Rangers in 2008. The son of former semi-professional rugby union player and international RFU referee Iain Ramage clearly has sporting talent running through his veins and settled well at Loftus Road. A versatile and committed defender, Peter has the opportunity to represent either his country of birth or that of his father, Scotland.

Debut: 9 Aug 2008 v Barnsley (H) 2-1 Championship.

RAMSCAR Fredrick T

(IR) Mid 5′ 6″ 9st 6lbs
b: Salford, Lancashire, 24 Jan 1919
QPR: Oct 1947
Football League: 51-4. **FAC:** 6-1. **FLC:** 0-0.

Other: 0-0. **Total:** 57-5.
Honours: 3rd Div (South) championship medal.

Fred made his debut in the Football League for Manchester City, as an amateur, during the war period but signed for Stockport County in 1943, being offered terms with Manchester United on the same day.

A smooth and classy player with a good strong shot who became the general of the side that won the Third Division title in 1948. When his playing days were over he went back to Northampton to take charge of the Colts team and then finished up at Wellingborough in the late 1950s.

Debut: 25 Oct 1947 v Ipswich Town (A) 0-1 Div 3 (S).

RAMSEY Alexander Parrott

(OL) Wing 5′ 8″
b: Gateshead, 1899
QPR: Jun 1921
Football League: 6-0. **FAC:** 0-0. **FLC:** 0-0.
Other: 0-0. **Total:** 6-0.

Alex had been a gunner in the Machine Gun Corps in France and Egypt during the First World War, and cost the Newcastle club a £100 transfer fee from Swalwell in 1919. Stan Seymour was brought in from the Scottish club, Morton, to replace him the following year and Alex was transferred to QPR. Great things were expected of him but he disappointed many observers of the game, and only made six League appearances.

Debut: 27 Aug 1921 v Swindon Town (H) 0-0 Div 3 (S).

RAMSEY C B

(OR) Wing
QPR: 1919
Southern League: 12-1. **FAC:** 0-0. **FLC:** 0-0.
Other: 0-0. **Total:** 12-1.

Ramsey was just one of six outside-rights to be tried during this season, which was the last in the old Southern League. None of them were retained for the following campaign.

Debut: 6 Dec 1919 v Northampton Town (H) 5-1 SL Div 1.

RANCE Charles Stanley

(CH) CD 6′ 1″ 12st 4lbs
b: Bow, London 28 Feb 1889
d: Chichester, Sussex, 29 Dec 1966
QPR: Sep 1922
Football League: 13-0. **FAC:** 0-0. **FLC:** 0-0.
Other: 0-0. **Total:** 13-0.
Honours: Amateur Cup winner's medal. 2nd Div championship medal.

Charlie was an extraordinarily clever player, determined and intelligent, who always tried to be creative with his clearances out of defence.

Karl Ready

He played as an amateur for Clapton as a 15 year old and went on to represent London & Essex County and rapidly developed into one of the best amateur central defenders in the country. A goalscoring member of the Clapton FA Amateur Cup winning team, Charlie was selected as a reserve for the England amateur team on four occasions, but when he was picked for a match against Denmark, in 1910, it was postponed because of the death of King Edward VII. At QPR his appearances were limited so he moved back to non-League football, and was appointed manager of Guildford United in 1925. In 1930 he became coach to Wood Green.

Debut: 30 Sep 1922 v Brighton & Hove Albion (A) 0-2 Div 3 (S).

READ Arthur

(HB) Mid
b: Ealing, Middlesex, 1899
QPR: 1921
Football League: 21-0. **FAC:** 0-0. **FLC:** 0-0.
Other: 0-0. **Total:** 21-0.
Honours: 2 England Amateur international caps. FA Amateur Cup runner's-up medal.

Arthur was rather unobtrusive yet effective at all three wing-half positions. The ball was usually kept on the ground by him and passes were astutely placed. After leaving for Reading he received an injury which forced him to retire in 1923.

Debut: 27 Jan 1921 v Swindon Town (H) 0-0 Div 3 (S).

READY Karl

CD 6′ 1″ 13st 3lbs
b: Neath, Wales, 14 Oct 1972
QPR: Aug 1990
Premier/Football League: 226-10. **FAC:** 8-0. **FLC:** 12-1. **Other:** 0-0. **Total:** 246-11.
Honours: 5 Welsh caps. 2 B caps. 5 U21 caps. School caps.

Karl is comfortable both in the air and on the ground, a first class defender who can play anywhere across the back four. He came up through the club's youth system and signed as a pro in August 1990. He started as a right-back but after injury returned as a central defender, and was an excellent foil to Alan McDonald. He stayed at Loftus Road for 11 years, but it was around five seasons before he established himself as a first team regular.

However, he was unfortunate in never being able to gain the full support of some fans, often being accused of lack of pace. During his time at Loftus Road he was one of several players to wear the captain's armband. In the summer of 2001 Karl was one of 15 players to be released, and he was signed on by Motherwell. But in September 2002, he was temporarily released from his contract and journeyed back south to sign for ambitious Aldershot Town of the Ryman League. This was a coup for the Hampshire side, and Karl remained for much of the season, helping the Shots' promotion to the Conference.

Debut: 9 Oct 1991 v Hull City (H) 5-1 League Cup round two.

Edwin Reay

REAY Edwin Peel

(RB) Def
b: Tynemouth, North Shields, 5 Aug 1914
QPR: 1937
Football League: 34-0. **FAC:** 1-0. **FLC:** 0-0.
Other: 3-0. **Total:** 38-0.
Honours: 3rd Div (South) championship medal.

A loyal servant to the club despite his appearances being limited in a six year period, Ted was very unfortunate that his career coincided with the Second World War, around which period he did tour Italy with an Army 11 led by Stan Cullis.
Debut: 2 Apr 1938 v Watford (A) 1-3 Div 3 (S).

REED Gordon

(CF) Striker 5' 9" 11st 4lbs
b: Spennymore, Durham, May 1913
QPR: 1934
Football League: 9-4. **FAC:** 0-0. **FLC:** 0-0.
Other: 0-0. **Total:** 9-4.

Gordon was a dashing centre-forward who could find the net with certain regularity. However, his main claim to fame lay outside the football world, for he was an excellent saxophonist and became the lead of one of the most famous bands in London during the late 1930s.
Debut: 25 Aug 1934 v Swindon Town (A) 1-3 Div 3 (S).

REHMAN Zeshan

Def 6' 2" 12st 3lbs
b: Birmingham, 14 Oct 1983
QPR: Aug 2006
Football League: 46-0. **FAC:** 1-0. **FLC:** 2-0.
Other: 0-0. **Total:** 49-0.
Honours: 6 Pakistan caps.

Zesh signed a three year deal with Rangers in the summer of 2006 but has found it difficult establishing himself as a first team regular. As a result, the centre-half has found himself being loaned out to other clubs during his QPR career. Nevertheless, the Pakistani international has racked up almost half a century of appearances for the club. He has written himself into the history books, however, as the first British Asian to start a Premier League match and the first to have played in all four divisions of professional football in this country. He was also the first Pakistani international to play professional football in England.
Debut: 12 Aug 2006 v Southend United (H) 2-0 Championship.

REID Peter

Mid 5' 8" 10st 8lbs
b: Huyton, Lancashire, 20 Jun 1956
QPR: Feb 1989
Football League: 29-1. **FAC:** 0-0. **FLC:** 3-0.
Other: 0-0. **Total:** 32-1.
Honours: 2nd Div championship medal. FA Cup winner's medal. European Cup winner's medal. 2 1st Div championship medals. 13 England caps. 6 U21 caps. Voted Player of the Year in 1985.

Zesh Rehman

Peter Reid

A player of superb skill and vision who distributed the ball with precision and briskness, Peter rarely needed more than two touches of the ball; he would get it, move into space and demand it back, forever bringing colleagues into the game and opening up fresh avenues of attack. Peter's time at Loftus Road was towards the end of his football career, although he played for several clubs both before and after.
Debut: 11 Feb 1989 v Nottingham Forest (A) 0-0 Div 1.

REVILL Edward J

(IR) Striker
b: Bolsover, Nottinghamshire
QPR: Aug 1911
Southern League: 62-21. **FAC:** 4-1. **FLC:** 0-0.
Other: 1-1. **Total:** 67-23.
Honours: Southern League championship medal.

A prolific scorer for whichever team he played for, and on the continental tour of 1912, he scored six goals versus Saabrucken. Teddy was the eldest of three brothers, who all played for Chesterfield around this time. After his retirement from football he became a licensee at the Cross Keys Hotel in Bolsover.
Debut: 2 Sep 1911 v Plymouth Argyle (A) 1-0 SL Div 1.

RHODES Albert

(RB) Def
b: Dinnington, Yorkshire, 29 Apr 1936
QPR: Dec 1954
Football League: 5-0. **FAC:** 0-0. **FLC:** 0-0.
Other: 0-0. **Total:** 5-0.

Bert was the reserve, who stood in for Woods at right-back whenever he was injured or unavailable; which wasn't very often!
Debut: 14 Apr 1956 v Reading (A) 1-3 Div 3 (S).

RICHARDSON Anthony J

(RB) Def
b: Southwark, London, 7 Jan 1932
QPR: Apr 1951
Football League: 2-0. **FAC:** 0-0. **FLC:** 0-0.
Other: 0-0. **Total:** 2-0.

This was the season that relegation from the Second Division loomed large. George Powell stood in for left-back Tony Ingham, who was injured and Tony Richardson was the man to fill in at right-back.
Debut: 5 Jan 1952 v Bury (H) 3-2 Div 2.

RICHARDSON Derek W

Goal 6' 1" 14st 4lbs
b: Hackney, London, 13 Jul 1956
QPR: Apr 1976
Football League: 31-0. **FAC:** 0-0. **FLC:** 1-0.
Other: 0-0. **Total:** 32-0.
Honours: 2 England youth caps. 2 semi-pro caps.

Derek was Phil Parkes' understudy but after the horrendous season of 1978/79, he was released.
Debut: 8 Mar 1977 v Leeds United (H) 0-0 Div 1.

RICHARDSON Stuart

(LB) Mid 5' 9" 11st 0lbs
b: Leeds, 12 Jun 1938
QPR: Nov 1956
Football League: 1-0. **FAC:** 0-0. **FLC:** 0-0.
Other: 0-0. **Total:** 1-0.

Stuart received just one first team opportunity owing to the brilliant form of Peter Angell. He was therefore given a free transfer to Oldham Athletic, but unfortunately they had to apply for re-election that season, and manager Jack Rowley released him.
Debut: 3 Jul 1959 v Colchester United (A) 0-3 Div 3.

RICHMOND Hugh

(CH) CD 5' 11" 11st 10lbs
b: Kilmarnock, Scotland, 9 Mar 1893
QPR: May 1925
Football League: 10-0. **FAC:** 0-0. **FLC:** 0-0.
Other: 0-0. **Total:** 10-0.

Hugh served with Scottish clubs before the First World War and fought with the Seaforth Highlanders during it. He joined Leicester City and was initially regarded as a goalscoring inside-forward but was soon to demonstrate a natural ability at centre-half. He captained the Leicester City reserve team in the Central Alliance. At Coventry City, Hugh became known as "Rubberneck" and bagged a hat-trick of goals against Nelson in 1923. At QPR they were fighting for the second time in three years against re-election, when no less than 10 centre-halves were tried in the team, of which Hugh was one. The following season he was coaching at Blyth Spartans and in 1929, at Spennymore United.
Debut: 29 Aug 1925 v Gillingham (A) 0-3 Div 3 (S).

RICKETTS Rohan Anthony

Mid 5' 10" 11st 7lbs
b: Clapham, 22 Dec 1982
QPR: (Loan) Mar 2007
Football League: 2-0. **FAC:** 0-0. **FLC:** 0-0.
Other: 0-0. **Total:** 2-0.
Debut: 31 Mar 2007 v WBA (H) 1-2 Championship.

RIDLEY John George

(RB) Def 5' 6" 11st 11lbs
b: Bardon Mill, 19 Jan 1903
d: Prudhoe, 25 Dec 1977
QPR: 1934
Football League: 17-0. **FAC:** 1-0. **FLC:** 0-0.
Other: 3-0. **Total:** 21-0.
Honours: 2nd Div championship medal.

After the departure of Warney Cresswell in 1922 from South Shields to Arsenal, John Ridley made the left-back berth his own at the North-East club, once clocking up 110 consecutive appearances.
Debut: 8 Dec 1934 v Brighton & Hove Albion (H) 1-2 FAC.

RIDYARD Alfred

(CH) CD 6' 3" 13st 0lbs
b: Cudworth, 5 May 1908
d: West Bromwich, 1981
QPR: (£625) Mar 1938
Football League: 28-0. **FAC:** 4-0. **FLC:** 0-0.
Other: 1-0. **Total:** 33-0.
Honours: 3 Central League championship medals.

Tall, commanding and built like the side of a house, Alf was as tough as old boots and was regarded as a real stopper centre-half. He was milking a cow on his Handsworth farm when a representative from QPR signed him on the transfer deadline day in 1938. Most of Alf's matches for the club (over 200 of them), were played during the wartime period. Retiring in 1948 he became the assistant manager and later had a spell as chief coach, before becoming the club's head scout.
Debut: 9 Apr 1938 v Gillingham (H) 2-0 Div 3 (S).

RIVERS Walter

(RH) Mid 5' 11" 12st 7lbs
b: Throckley, Newcastle, 8 Jan 1909
QPR: May 1933
Football League: 3-0. **FAC:** 0-0. **FLC:** 0-0.
Other: 1-0. **Total:** 4-0.

A miner before he started playing football, Wally spent his whole career in the two Third Divisions making over 200 appearances. He was a tall, stalwart figure who was not easily shaken off the ball, opening up the game with his impressive distribution.
Debut: 26 Aug 1933 v Brighton & Hove Albion (H) 2-0 Div 3 (S).

ROBERTS Anthony Mark

Goal 6' 0" 12st 0lbs
b: Bangor, Wales, 4 Aug 1969
QPR: Jul 1987
Premier/Football League: 122-0. **FAC:** 11-0. **FLC:** 10-0. **Other:** 2-0. **Total:** 145-0.
Honours: Welsh youth caps. 2 U21 caps. 1 B cap. 1 Welsh cap. Welsh semi-pro caps.

Tony is a tall, commanding goalkeeper, who is something of a shot stopper, with a huge kick. He spent 11 years at QPR but was not often the first team keeper, hence only 122 League appearances during this long period. Unfortunately he suffered a hand injury which kept him out of the game for much of 1998. However, Tony made a comeback after a period with Millwall, St Albans City, and then with Dagenham & Redbridge in the Conference. He won his single (full) Welsh cap when he came on as substitute for Neville Southall during the World Cup qualifying game against Georgia in August 1996.
Debut: 18 Nov 1989 v Arsenal (A) 0-3 Div 1.

ROBERTS John William

(OL) Wing
b: Liverpool, September 1880
QPR: May 1905
Southern League: 22-1. **FAC:** 0-0. **FLC:** 0-0.
Other: 0-0. **Total:** 22-1.

"A wonderfully clever dribbler and if his shooting were only on par with his wizard-like manipulation of the ball, he would indeed be a great player." So wrote a newspaper during his first season at Brighton. John was transferred to QPR along with Andy Gardner in May 1905, but failed to impress.
Debut: 21 Oct 1905 v Norwich City (A) 0-4 SL Div 1.

ROBERTS Joseph

(OL) Wing 5' 7" 11st 0lbs
b: Tranmere, 2 Sep 1900
d: Watford, 9 Mar 1984
QPR: May 1927
Football League: 4-0. **FAC:** 0-0. **FLC:** 0-0.
Other: 0-0. **Total:** 4-0.

One of a large family, Joe was raised in Birkenhead and one of his first jobs was that of a plater and boilermaker on the docks. A widely travelled player, appearing with no less than 14 clubs in 10 years, he was a fast and clever winger who preferred to pass than shoot.

He was also a brilliant billiards player and an excellent golfer, right into his 80s. Joe took over his father-in-law's newsagent and tobacconist shop close to the Watford ground, and ran it for many years, while he continued as an avid Hornets supporter.
Debut: 5 Nov 1927 v Luton Town (A) 1-0 Div 3 (S).

ROBINSON John William

(IL) Mid 5' 8" 11st 9lbs
b: Grangetown
QPR: 1923
Football League: 5-1. **FAC:** 0-0. **FLC:** 0-0.
Other: 0-0. **Total:** 5-1.

John scored in his debut match for QPR, but the club ended the season at the bottom of the League.
Debut: 27 Oct 1923 v Northampton Town (H) 3-2 Div 3 (S).

Mike Robinson

ROBINSON Michael John

Striker 6' 0" 12st 7lbs
b: Leicester, 12 Jul 1958
QPR: (£100,000) Aug 1984
Football League: 48-5. **FAC:** 2-0. **FLC:** 8-1.
Other: 0-0. **Total:** 58-0.
Honours: 23 caps for Rep of Ireland. 1 B cap. FA Cup runner's-up medal. League championship medal. European Cup winner's medal. League Cup runner's-up medal.

Mike was an aggressive and hard working player, but injury forced him to retire from the game after two years with the Spanish club, Osasuna. However, he remained in the country and became a media star, as the co-host of the award winning TV football programme *El Dia Despues* (The Day After).
Debut: 29 Dec 1984 v Stoke City (A) 2-0 Div 1.

Glen Roeder

ROEDER Glen Victor

CD 6' 1" 12st 3lbs
b: Woodford, Essex, 13 Dec 1955
QPR: (£250,000) 1978
Football League: 157-17. **FAC:** 11-0. **FLC:** 13-1.
Other: 0-0. **Total:** 181-18.
Honours: 6 B caps for England. FA Cup runner's-up medal. 2nd Div championship medal. 2nd Div promotion medal.

The trademark of this player was to be unruffled and very cool. Glen was so elegant going forward that it seemed a pity to play him as a defender. He became the Watford manager in July 1993, and this lasted until February 1996. He became part of the England coaching staff before he joined West Ham in a similar capacity. With the departure of Harry Redknapp, he became the caretaker manager of West Ham United. Glen was appointed manager in June 2001.
Debut: 26 Jun 1978 v Nottingham Forest (H) 0-0 Div 1.

ROGERS A

(IR) Mid
QPR: 1907
Southern League: 32-10. **FAC:** 2-0. **FLC:** 0-0.
Other: 0-0. **Total:** 34-10.

Very little is known about this player, except that he became the second highest goalscorer during the season, when QPR were ordered by the Southern League to play all their matches in mid-week. After two years with Bristol Rovers, Rogers had drifted out of football altogether.
Debut: 2 Sep 1907 v Tottenham Hotspur (H) 3-3 SL Div 1.

ROGERS Albert J

(IL) Mid
b: Manchester
QPR: 1928
Football League: 12-4. **FAC:** 0-0. **FLC:** 0-0.
Other: 0-0. **Total:** 12-4.

Bert came onto the scene when Rounce was injured and out of the side; scoring twice on his debut. It is not known what happened to him after 1930.
Debut: 15 Dec 1928 v Coventry City (H) 3-1 Div 3 (S).

ROGERS Donald E

(OL) Wing 5′ 10″ 12st 10lbs
b: Paulton, Somerset, 25 Oct 1945
QPR: (Exchange deal) Sep 1974
Football League: 18-5. **FAC:** 1-0. **FLC:** 0-0.
Other: 0-0. **Total:** 19-5.
Honours: England youth caps. 2 U23 caps. Football League cap. FA Youth Cup runner's-up medal. 3rd Div runner's-up medal. League Cup winner's medal. Anglo-Italian Cup winner's medal. Anglo-Italian Inter-League winner's medal.

The spectators at Loftus Road were given the treat of watching one of the best wingers in the country at that time. Don combined an electrifying turn of speed with silky skills on the ball. An exchange for Ian Evans brought him to Shepherds Bush and an exchange again brought Peter Eastoe from Swindon Town. Don still lives in Swindon where he runs his own sports shop as he has for the last thirty-odd years.

Debut: 24 Sep 1974 v Everton (H) 2-2 Div 1.

Don Rogers

ROGERS Martyn

(RB) Def 5′ 9″ 11st 4lbs
b: Nottingham, 26 Jan 1960
QPR: Jul 1979
Football League: 2-0. **FAC:** 0-0. **FLC:** 0-0.
Other: 0-0. **Total:** 2-0.
Honours: 9 England schoolboy caps.

When Tommy Docherty became manager of QPR for the second time, he persuaded Martyn to join him. He played for the club twice before Terry Venables sacked him when he became manager in May 1981. Sadly Martyn's promise as a junior was never fulfilled, and he was to die tragically in a fume-filled hire car.

Debut: 26 Apr 1980 v Newcastle United (H) 2-1 Div 2.

RONALDSON Duncan McKay

(CF) Striker 5′ 8″ 12st 3lbs
b: Glasgow, 21 Apr 1879
d: Glasgow, 20 Sep 1947
QPR: Dec 1900
Southern League: 18-8. **FAC:** 0-0. **FLC:** 0-0.
Other: 0-0. **Total:** 18-8.
Honours: Scottish Junior international.

Duncan was a "have boots will travel", sort of player whose brainy manoeuvres on the pitch made him a wanted man throughout his career. Quick off the mark with an unselfish attitude, plus a sixth sense for openings in the opponents' defence. It was said that he had a good deep singing voice. Duncan was a tinsmith by trade.

Debut: 1 Dec 1900 v New Brompton (A) 1-2 SL Div 1.

ROSE John

(RB) Def
b: Sheffield, Yorkshire, 25 Oct 1921
QPR: Mar 1943
Football League: 17-0. **FAC:** 1-0. **FLC:** 0-0.
Other: 0-0. **Total:** 18-0.

Jack dominated the right-back position during the latter part of the 1946/47 season. He then suffered three cartilage operations within a year, which proved too much for this likeable player, so he decided to quit the game in 1948.

Debut: 31 Aug 1946 v Watford (H) 2-1 Div 3 (S).

ROSE Matthew David

CD 5′ 11″ 11st 1lb
b: Dartford, Kent, 24 Sep 1975
QPR: (£500,000) May 1997
Football League: 243-8. **FAC:** 5-0. **FLC:** 8-0.
Other: 5-0. **Total:** 261-8.
Honours: 2 England U21 caps. FA Youth Cup winner's medal.

Matt was the captain of Arsenal's Youth team when they won the 1994 FA Youth Cup, and three years later QPR paid a substantial fee for his signature. A relatively stylish and good tackler with passing skills, Matt began as a midfield player but moved to centre-back or sweeper.

He is an excellent defender but has often been hit by injuries, although he gradually earned himself a more or less regular slot in the first team. By the time he signed for Yeovil Town in February 2007, he had been with the club a decade and made a very creditable 243 Football League appearances.

Debut: 9 Aug 1997 v Ipswich Town (H) 0-0 Div 1.

ROSE Ramone Alexander A

Striker 5′ 10″ 11st 0lbs
b: Reading, Berkshire, 19 Jan 1990
QPR: May 2008
Football League: 3-0. **FAC:** 1-0. **FLC:** 0-0.
Other: 0-0. **Total:** 4-0.
Debut: 4 May 2008 v WBA (H) 0-2 Championship.

ROSENOIR Leroy

(CF) Striker 6′ 1″ 11st 10lbs
b: Balham, London, 24 Aug 1964
QPR: (£50,000) Aug 1985
Football League: 38-8. **FAC:** 4-0. **FLC:** 5-2.
Other: 0-0. **Total:** 47-10.
Honours: England Schoolboy international.

Leroy was a bustling type of player who sometimes seemed to lack a bit of refinement to his game. On other occasions he could be very effective and was especially good in the air and quick on the ground. In 1994 he went to Fleet Town as coach and two years later moved on to Gloucester City as the player/manager. Leroy went on to manage Torquay United and Brentford.

Debut: 3 Sep 1985 v Arsenal (H) 0-1 Div 1.

Matt Rose

Generoso Rossi

ROSSI Generoso

Goal 6' 3" 13st 5lbs
b: Naples, Italy, 13 Jan 1979
QPR: Jan 2005
Football League: 3-0. **FAC:** 0-0. **FLC:** 0-0.
Other: 0-0. **Total:** 3-0.
Debut: 23 Apr 2005 v Wigan Athletic (A) 0-0 Championship.

ROUNCE George Alfred

(IL) Striker 5' 8" 10st 7lbs
b: Grays, Essex, 1905
d: London, 2 Oct 1936
QPR: Jun 1928
Football League: 171-58. **FAC:** 17-12. **FLC:** 0-0.
Other: 0-0. **Total:** 188-70.
Honours: 2 appearances for the Middlesex Amateurs.

George was a direct player with a very hard shot who unfortunately was struck down with tuberculosis shortly before signing for Bristol Rovers. Aged just 31 he died in Victoria Park Hospital, Hackney.
Debut: 25 Feb 1928 v Merthyr Town (A) 4-0 Div 3 (S).

ROUTLEDGE Wayne Neville

Mid 5' 7" 10st 0lbs
b: Sidcup, 7 Jan 1985
QPR: (£600,000) Jan 2009
Football League: 19-1. **FAC:** 0-0. **FLC:** 0-0.
Other: 0-0. **Total:** 19-1.
Honours: 12 England U21 caps.
Debut: 10 Jan 2009 v Coventry City (H) 1-1 Championship.

ROWE Alfred James

(OL) Wing 5' 8" 10st 7lbs
b: Poplar, London
QPR: 1925
Football League: 4-1. **FAC:** 0-0. **FLC:** 0-0.
Other: 0-0. **Total:** 4-1.

Bob Jack, the manager of Plymouth Argyle, signed three players from Barking Town in 1921. Frank Richardson attained instant fame, Jack Leslie, after a slower start became an Argyle legend, but Alf Rowe spent four years at Home Park without becoming an automatic choice. At QPR, Alf played on the wing instead of at half-back and managed to score on his debut. However, within a year he was gone.
Debut: 5 Apr 1926 v Bournemouth & Boscombe Athletic (A) 1-4 Div 3 (S).

ROWE Jonathan

(LB) Def 5' 8" 10st 10lbs
b: Packmoor, Manchester, 1907
QPR: 1935
Football League: 52-0. **FAC:** 4-0. **FLC:** 0-0.
Other: 1-0. **Total:** 57-0.

Jonty was a very experienced player who could fill either full-back positions with ease. He retired during the ill-fated 1939/40 season when Port Vale's future went into abeyance because of the start of the war. Jonty appeared as a guest player for Crewe Alexandra once during the conflict.
Debut: 31 Aug 1935 v Millwall (H) 2-3 Div 3 (S).

ROWLAND Keith

Mid 5' 10" 10st 0lbs
b: Portadown, Northern Ireland, 1 Sep 1971
QPR: (Exchange deal) Jan 1998
Football League: 56-3. **FAC:** 2-0. **FLC:** 2-0.
Other: 0-0. **Total:** 60-3.

A left-sided player who can operate either as a wing-back or in a more traditional midfield role, Keith usually delivers one great cross during the course of the match. He came to QPR as part of the Trevor Sinclair deal with West Ham United. He stayed at Loftus Road for three years, during which time he made 60 senior appearances. He then moved on to Barnet and transferred to Hornchurch in July 2003.
Debut: 31 Jan 1998 v Stockport County (A) 0-2 Div 1.

Wayne Routledge

ROWLANDS Martin Charles

Mid 5′ 9″ 10st 10lbs
b: Hammersmith, London, 8 Feb 1979
QPR: Jul 2003
Football League: 188-33. **FAC:** 6-0. **FLC:** 8-4.
Other: 3-0. **Total:** 205-37.
Honours: 3 Republic of Ireland caps.

One of the bargains of the decade, Martin was signed on a free transfer from Brentford in July 2003 and has since gone on to make more than 200 appearances for Rangers. The midfielder notched 12 goals in his first season at Loftus Road and again hit double figures in the 2006/07 campaign and has twice been awarded the accolade of Supporters' Player of the Year. Such a rich vein of form earned him a recall to the Republic of Ireland squad under manager Giovanni Trapattoni.

Debut: 9 Aug 2003 v Blackpool (H) 5-0 Div 1.

Martin Rowlands

ROYCE Simon Ernest

Goal 6′ 2″ 13st 2lbs
b: Newham, Northumberland, 9 Sep 1971
QPR: (Loan) Aug 2002
Football League: 16-0. **FAC:** 0-0. **FLC:** 0-0.
Other: 0-0. **Total:** 16-0.
QPR: Jan 2005
Football League: 63-0. **FAC:** 3-0. **FLC:** 1-0.
Other: 0-0. **Total:** 67-0.

Loaned from Leicester City while Culkin and Day were injured, Simon was the third choice goalkeeper. QPR were so impressed with him when they played against him at Brighton & Hove on Boxing Day 2001 that this led to the loan deal. He stayed for much of the 2002/03 season, before eventually moving on to Charlton. Simon returned – initially on loan – in 2005 and enjoyed an extended run in the first team for the next two campaigns before moving to Gillingham.

Debut: 24 Aug 2002 v Peterborough United (H) 2-0 Div 2.

Simon Royce

RUDDOCK Neil

CD 6′ 2″ 12st 2lbs
b: Wandsworth, London, 9 May 1968
QPR: (Loan) Mar 1998
Football League: 7-0. **FAC:** 0-0. **FLC:** 0-0.
Other: 0-0. **Total:** 7-0.
Honours: 1 England cap. 1 B cap. 4 U21 caps. Youth caps. League Cup winner's medal.

Neil was a very effective defender, his seven match loan spell from Liverpool saving QPR from relegation in 1998. His imposing physical presence was supported by powerful tackling, strength in the air, and a great left foot.

Debut: 28 Mar 1998 v Huddersfield Town (A) 1-1 Div 1.

RUSSELL Sydney E J

(LB) Def 6′ 0″ 12st 7lbs
b: Feltham, Middlesex, 1 Oct 1911
QPR: 1933
Football League: 42-0. **FAC:** 1-0. **FLC:** 0-0.
Other: 2-0. **Total:** 45-0.

After three years Sid only made 45 first team appearances for the Rangers, and he moved on to Northampton Town. Tragically for Sid, he broke a leg at the end of the 1938/39 season while he was playing for the Cobblers at Southend on Easter Saturday. He was stretchered off and at Southend Infirmary he had to have the leg amputated after complications had set in. The brotherhood that exists in football showed itself with manager David Jack telling Northampton that he would let Southend help in any way possible, and Everton agreeing to play a charity match.

Debut: 4 Feb 1933 v Watford (A) 2-2 Div 3 (S).

RUTHERFORD Michael A

Mid 5′ 9″ 11st 10lbs
b: Sidcup, Kent, 6 Jun 1972
QPR: 1989
Football League: 2-0. **FAC:** 0-0. **FLC:** 1-0.
Other: 0-0. **Total:** 3-0.

A QPR trainee who was released at the end of the 1993/94 season, Mike became a valued member of the Welling United club that were at that time in the Vauxhall Conference.

Debut: 21 Oct 1989 v Charlton Athletic (H) 0-1 Div 1.

RUTTER Keith G

(CH) CD 6′ 0″ 11st 7lbs
b: Leeds, Yorkshire, 10 Sep 1934
QPR: Jul 1954
Football League: 339-1. **FAC:** 18-0. **FLC:** 5-0.
Other: 7-0. **Total:** 369-1.

Consistent, reliable and unflappable were the words used about this outstanding defender. Keith was arguably the best centre-half of the Third Division in the early 1960s, missing just seven matches in six seasons, which included three occasions when he was an ever-present. He ousted Taylor from the centre-half position and proved himself in that position. His stay at Loftus Road lasted nearly nine years, when he made an impressive 369 first team appearances in total, a very high average of around 40 per season. Yet he only ever scored one League goal, in his first season at Loftus Road. He moved to Colchester in 1963, and during the 1963/64 season scored another goal – this time for the opposition (an own goal versus Reading). Even at age 40, he was able to sign for another club, Romford, after 20 years as a full-time professional. 1964/65 was the last for Keith as a player.

Debut: 24 Aug 1954 v Southend United (A) 2-2 Div 3 (S).

RYDER George S D

(IL) Mid 5′ 8″ 11st 10lbs
QPR: 1904
Southern League: 69-20. **FAC:** 4-1. **FLC:** 0-0.
Other: 0-0. **Total:** 73-21.
Honours: Toured South Africa with the Corinthians.

George had the reputation of being a fast and tricky player at Oxford University where he was studying law. At QPR he ended the 1905/06 season as the top goalscorer.

Debut: 1 Oct 1904 v Northampton Town (H) 0-1 SL Div 1.

Neil Ruddock

David Seaman

S

SABIN Eric
SAHAR Ben
SALES Arthur Alfred
SALT Harold
SALVAGE Barry J
SAMUEL Daniel John
SANDERSON Keith
SANGSTER J
SANSOM Kenneth Graham
SANTOS Georges
SAPHIN Reginald Francis Edward
SAUL Frank Lander
SCULLY Anthony Derek Thomas
SEALY Anthony John
SEAMAN David Andrew
SEARY Raymond M
SEELEY George Alfred
SHANKS Donald
SHAW Charles
SHEPHERD Ernest
SHEPPARD William
SHERON Michael Nigel
SHIMMIN Dominic Libreville
SHITTU Daniel Olusola
SHUFFLEBOTTOM Thomas
SIBLEY Frank Phillip
SILKMAN Barry
SILVER Alan G
SIMEK Franklin
SIMONS Henry Thomas
SINCLAIR Scott Andrew
SINCLAIR Trevor Lloyd
SINGLETON Harold Bertram
SINTON Andrew
SKILTON Percy G
SKINNER Henry
SLACK Rodney Geoffrey
SLADE Steven Anthony
SMITH Albert W
SMITH Arthur R
SMITH Edward William Alfred
SMITH Frank A
SMITH George Casper
SMITH James Dean
SMITH John William
SMITH Norman
SMITH Norman
SMITH Stephen Charles
SMITH Stephen R
SMITH Thomas S
SMITH William Conway
SNELGROVE George W
SOMMER Juergen Peterson
SPACKMAN Nigel James
SPENCE William Joseph
SPENCER John
SPOTTISWOODE Joseph
SPRATLEY Alan S
SPRINGETT Peter J
SPRINGETT Ronald Deryk G
ST AIMIE Kieron Lloyd J Minto
STAINROD Simon Allan
STANDLEY Thomas L
STEER William Henry Owen
STEIN Mark Earl Sean
STEINER Robert Herman
STEJSKAL Jan
STEPHENSON Herbert L
STEPHENSON James
STEVENS Ronald Frederick
STEWART Damion
STEWART George
STEWART Ian Edwin
STEWART John
STOCK Alexander William
STRUGNELL H H
STURRIDGE Dean Constantine
SUGDEN Sidney H
SUTCH W H
SWAN John (formerly SWANN)
SWANN Herbert A
SWEETMAN Sidney C
SWINFEN Reginald
SYMES Ernest Herbert Charles

SABIN Eric
Forward 6' 0" 12st 0lbs
b: Sarcelles, France, 22 Jan 1975
QPR: Jun 2003
Football League: 10-1. **FAC:** 2-0. **FLC:** 1-0.
Other: 0-0. **Total:** 13-1.
Debut: 9 Aug 2003 v Blackpool (H) 5-0 Div 2.

SAHAR Ben
Striker 5' 10" 12st 5lbs
b: Holon, Israel, 10 Aug 1989
QPR: 2007
Football League: 9-0. **FAC:** 0-0. **FLC:** 0-0.
Other: 0-0. **Total:** 9-0.
Debut: 1 Sep 2007 v Southampton (H) 0-3 Championship.

SALES Arthur Alfred
(RH) Mid
b: Lewes, Sussex, 14 Mar 1900
d: Lewes, Sussex, 5 May 1977
QPR: 1930
Football League: 35-0. **FAC:** 0-0. **FLC:** 0-0.
Other: 0-0. **Total:** 35-0.

Arthur established a huge reputation for himself in the amateur football world, however, at Chelsea he was limited to just seven first team matches in five years. Upon leaving Stamford Bridge in May 1928 he played for several amateur clubs before joining QPR. Arthur was a fine athlete and once ran the 100 yards in 10.5 seconds.

Debut: 11 Oct 1930 v Swindon Town (A) 1-4 Div 3 (S).

Ben Sahar

SALT Harold
(RH) Mid 5' 9" 11st 7lbs
b: Sheffield, Yorkshire
QPR: May 1926
Football League: 5-0. **FAC:** 0-0. **FLC:** 0-0.
Other: 0-0. **Total:** 5-0.

This fair haired Yorkshireman was a centre-half as well as an inside-forward for Brighton & Hove, a left-winger for Port Vale and a wing-half at QPR. Bob Hewison was trying to build a side that wouldn't have to apply for re-election again, but Salt didn't fit the bill.

Debut: 2 Oct 1926 v Bournemouth (A) 2-6 Div 3 (S).

SALVAGE Barry J
Mid 5' 11" 11st 10lbs
b: Bristol, 21 Dec 1947
d: Eastbourne, 1986
QPR: (£9,000) Mar 1971
Football League: 21-1. **FAC:** 1-0. **FLC:** 1-0.
Other: 0-0. **Total:** 23-1.

Barry was a tall orthodox left-footed player who was most successful at Brentford and Millwall. At these clubs he found regular senior squad football. Tragically he died of a heart attack while he was on a charity run in Eastbourne, and still in his 30s.

Debut: 21 Aug 1971 v Middlesbrough (A) 2-3 Div 2.

SAMUEL Daniel John
(IL) Mid 5' 7" 10st 7lbs
b: Swansea, Wales, 1911
QPR: 1935
Football League: 9-3. **FAC:** 0-0. **FLC:** 0-0.
Other: 0-0. **Total:** 9-3.

Dan was just one of five players to be tried in this position during the season. But he quickly faded from the Football League, and it became evident that he was better suited playing the summer game of cricket.

Debut: 31 Aug 1935 v Millwall (H) 2-3 Div 3 (S).

SANDERSON Keith
Mid 5' 10" 11st 8lbs
b: Hull, Humberside, 9 Oct 1940
QPR: (£5,000) Jun 1965
Football League: 104-10. **FAC:** 9-2. **FLC:** 11-0.
Other: 0-0. **Total:** 124-12.
Honours: League Cup winner's medal. 3rd Div championship medal. 2nd Div runner's-up medal.

Malcolm Allison recruited Keith, a former Cambridge Football blue, as soon as he became manager of Bath City, and when he became the manager of Plymouth Argyle, the player followed him there, where he became a part-time pro. Keith had his critics at Plymouth, those arguing that as a part-timer he ought not to receive full wages, but he was championed by Allison who maintained that the player's value to the side was not appreciated

from the terraces. Alec Stock stepped in to buy Sanderson as soon as Allison left Plymouth, and he became an integral part of the QPR side and also the captain. Keith had a tireless attitude to the game and was a huge favourite with the spectators at Loftus Road. He lasted four seasons, whereupon he moved down into non-League Football.
Debut: 21 Aug 1965 v Brentford (A) 1-6 Div 1.

SANGSTER J

(OR) Wing
QPR: 1912
Southern League: 4-0. **FAC:** 0-0. **FLC:** 0-0.
Other: 0-0 **Total:** 4-0.

A reserve player who stood in for Bill Thompson on four occasions during the season and never once appeared on the losing side.
Debut: 21 Sep 1912 v Northampton Town (H) 3-2 SL Div 1.

SANSOM Kenneth Graham

(LB) Def 5' 6" 11st 8lbs
b: Camberwell, London, 26 Sep 1958
QPR: (£300,000) Jun 1989

Kenny Sansom

Reg Saphin

Football League: 64-0. **FAC:** 10-2. **FLC:** 7-0.
Other: 1-0. **Total:** 82-2.
Honours: South London, Surrey and England schoolboys. 5 youth caps. 8 U21 caps. 3 B level. 86 full England caps. FA Youth Cup medal. 2nd Div championship medal. League Cup winner's medal. League Cup runner's-up medal.

Kenny was regarded as the best left-back in the country at the time Arsenal paid a world record fee to secure his transfer. What made him a great player was his remarkable consistency, being very fast over short distances and the accuracy of his distribution of the ball. Spectators all agreed that his touchline sorties were a picture to behold. At 31 years old he still cost QPR a large transfer fee, and over 80 games and two years later he once again moved on. A succession of clubs still saw him playing in non-League Football at 41.
Debut: 19 Aug 1989 v Crystal Palace (H) 2-0 Div 1.

SANTOS Georges

Mid 6' 3" 14st 0lbs
b: Marseille, France, 15 Aug 1970
QPR: Jul 2004
Football League: 74-6. **FAC:** 1-0. **FLC:** 2-0.
Other: 0-0. **Total:** 77-6.

Signed from Ipswich Town in the summer of 2004 on a two-year contract, Georges' versatility was soon evident as he could capably slot into both defence and midfield. A journeyman footballer, Georges was one of five Sheffield United players sent off – against his former club – in the infamous Battle of Bramall Lane in March 2002 that saw the match against West Brom abandoned with the home side reduced to six players. The Frenchman turned out for Brighton & Hove Albion and Oxford United following his stint at Loftus Road but has since drifted into non-League football.
Debut: 7 Aug 2004 v Rotherham (H) 1-1 Championship.

SAPHIN Reginald Francis Edward

Goal
b: Kilburn, London, 8 Aug 1916
QPR: May 1946
Football League: 30-0. **FAC:** 2-0. **FLC:** 0-0.
Other: 0-0. **Total:** 32-0.
Debut: 4 Dec 1946 v Poole Town (A) 0-0 1st round Rep.

SAUL Frank Lander

(CF) Striker 5' 10" 11st 12lbs
b: Canvey Island, London, 23 Aug 1943
QPR: May 1970
Football League: 43-4. **FAC:** 3-0. **FLC:** 6-2.
Other: 0-0. **Total:** 52-6.
Honours: 7 England youth caps. Young England cap. FA Cup winner's medal.

Frank was something of a "Boy Wonder", playing

Tony Scully

for the Spurs reserves when only 15 years of age and then making his League debut at just 17. He was the stand-in for Bobby Smith, notching three goals in six matches in the famous Spurs double season. Frank was strong and eager and not lacking in skill, a fair haired youngster that always grafted hard, giving everything. After two years at Southampton he spent the next two or so at Loftus Road, when he notched up over 50 first team appearances. After his retirement from football he ran a building and decorating concern in Billericay in Essex and later a small fashion and knitwear business in London's East-End during the 1990s.
Debut: 15 Aug 1970 v Birmingham City (A) 1-2 Div 2.

SCULLY Anthony Derek Thomas

(OL) Wing 5' 7" 11st 12lbs
b: Dublin, Eire, 12 Jun 1976
QPR: (£155,000) Mar 1998
Football League: 40-2. **FAC:** 1-0. **FLC:** 5-0.
Other: 0-0. **Total:** 46-2.
Honours: Republic of Ireland school and youth caps. 1 B cap.

Although he was a skilful ball player, Tony was unable to command a regular first team place. He was loaned to Walsall but did not appear in any of the Saddlers line-ups.
Debut: 21 Sep 1998 v Stoke City (A) 1-2 Div 1.

SEALY Anthony John

(CF) Striker 5' 8" 11st 10lbs
b: Hackney, London, 7 May 1959
QPR: (£75,000) Mar 1981
Football League: 63-18. **FAC:** 1-0. **FLC:** 4-0.
Other: 0-0. **Total:** 68-18.
Honours: League Cup runner's-up medal. 2nd Div championship medal. 3rd Div championship medals.

Tony scored no less than 224 goals in schools and boys club football during the 1974/75 season. He signed for Southampton and made his reserve team debut at the age of 16 years. Sealy was a strong bustling player who was the leading scorer for QPR in their championship season of 1983. An astonishing record held by Tony is that of four championship medals, won by him with four different clubs in the space of 10 years.

As he played out the twilight years of his career in Hong Kong, he also trained as a physio. Tony went on to work as the sporting manager for Hong Kong FC.
Debut: 21 Mar 1981 v Derby County (H) 3-1 Div 2.

SEAMAN David Andrew

Goal 6' 2" 14st 10lbs
b: Rotherham, Yorkshire, 19 Sep 1963
QPR: (£225,000) Aug 1986
Football League: 141-0. **FAC:** 17-0. **FLC:** 13-0.
Other: 4-0. **Total:** 175-0.
Honours: 73 England caps. 10 U21 caps. 6 B caps. 1st Div championship winner's medal. 2 Premiership championship winner's medals. 3 FA Cup winner's medals. League Cup winner's medals. European Cup winner's medal. Charity Shield winner's medal.

Relaxed and composed both on and off the pitch, he was still the number one choice for England until 2002, despite his age. David is a strong, brave goalkeeper who is fast off his line, has a safe pair of hands and a strong kick. Seaman's distribution is excellent, varying between long and short to the wing-backs or long kicks to the strikers. Many attacking moves originate from his foresight and he is a great shot-stopper being exceptionally agile for a big man. In four seasons at Loftus Road, David was a first team fixture in the side and in 1989 he won the first of his 73 England caps when appearing against Scotland. It cost Peterborough United a modest fee to buy him from Leeds United. But a more realistic idea of his value was required for his signature at Birmingham City. George Graham, then manager of Arsenal, paid out a British record fee (£1.3 million) for a goalkeeper – nearly six times what he had cost QPR from Birmingham City – when he obtained Seaman's signature.
Debut: 23 Aug 1986 v Southampton (A) 1-5 Div 1.

Don Shanks

SEARY Raymond M

(LH) Def 5' 9" 10st 7lbs
b: Wallingford, Berkshire, 18 Sep 1952
QPR: Sep 1970
Football League: 1-0. **FAC:** 0-0. **FLC:** 0-0.
Other: 0-0. **Total:** 1-0.

Ray's only appearance for the club was as a substitute in September 1971. His contract was not renewed at Cambridge United in 1976, so he ended his days in non-League Football.

Debut: 4 Sep 1971 v Swindon Town (A) 0-0 Div 2.

SEELEY George Alfred

Wing 5' 6" 11st 7lbs
b: Ventnor, IOW, July 1877
d: Ventnor, 15 Oct 1921
QPR: 1901
Southern League: 19-2. **FAC:** 3-0. **FLC:** 0-0.
Other: 0-0. **Total:** 22-2.

A speedy, versatile and very tricky player who could centre the ball with remarkable precision, George was known as "the Lion Tamer", due to his once having entered a lion's cage in a circus in Southampton. Although he was marked down as a right-winger, he could also play on the left.

Debut: 7 Sep 1901 v Watford (H) 0-1 SL Div 1.

SHANKS Donald

(RB) Def 5' 11" 10st 8lbs
b: Hammersmith, London, 2 Oct 1952
QPR: (£35,000) Nov 1974
Football League: 180-10. **FAC:** 11-1. **FLC:** 14-0.
Other: 1-0. **Total:** 206-11.
Honours: 7 England youth caps.

Don was a regular defender who missed very few matches through injury. Arriving at Loftus Road in late 1974, it was three seasons or so before he established a regular place in the QPR line-up. Eventually, after seven seasons, he made over 200 appearances, and helped QPR to the runner's-up spot, behind Liverpool, in 1976. Following his time at Loftus Road, he first stopped off at Brighton for two years, before moving around the world, playing in the Far East, America and Malta, before returning to England. But he is also remembered for his reputation as a playboy on the London gambling scene and had a former Miss World, Mary Slavin, as his girlfriend.

Debut: 7 Dec 1974 v Burnley (A) 0-3 Div 1.

SHAW Charles

Goal 5' 6" 12st 0lbs
b: Twechar, Scotland, 21 Sep 1885
d: New York, USA, 27 Mar 1938
QPR: May 1907
Southern League: 232-0. **FAC:** 16-0. **FLC:** 0-0.
Other: 3-0. **Total:** 251-0.
Honours: Represented the Football League v Irish & Scottish Leagues. Scottish XI v English XI. Scottish League v Football League. 2 caps for the Southern League v Football League.
2 Southern League championship medals.
5 Scottish League championship medals.
2 Scottish Cup winner's medals.

Charlie was on a par with the rest of the goalkeeping greats that QPR have had in the history of the club. He was only 5' 6" tall with a small build but despite this he had a solid frame which kept him from being charged into the net, as was the norm in those far off days. A "wondrous little goalkeeper" was the cry from QPR & Celtic fans alike. After seven years with Rangers, he moved north to Scotland. At Celtic he was idolised and made a club total of 436 appearances and kept 240 clean sheets. He took over as skipper in September 1916 and "His voice could he heard shouting advice all over the pitch." Charlie died in New York, USA of pneumonia at the age of 52 years.

Debut: 2 Sep 1907 v Tottenham Hotspur (H) 3-3 SL Div 1.

SHEPHERD Ernest

(OL) Wing 5' 7" 11st 8lbs
b: Wombwell, Yorkshire, 14 Aug 1919
QPR: Aug 1950
Football League: 219-51. **FAC:** 12-2. **FLC:** 0-0.
Other: 1-0. **Total:** 232-53.

An old fashioned attacking winger, who was very fast and could beat the full-back with deft ball control and tricky play. There was certainly no doubting his speed off the mark for it had served him well during sporting events while in the RAF and it had also won him money in invitation races. The crowd at Loftus Road enjoyed his antics and he became their firm favourite. When Ernie retired from playing he became the Bradford Park Avenue trainer in 1957, the same at Southend United in 1959, then the assistant/manager in 1969, before becoming the physio/coach at Orient in 1973. Shepherd retired at the age of 61 years in 1979 after coaching for 2 years in the United Arab Emirates.

Debut: 13 Aug 1950 v Chesterfield (H) 1-1 Div 2.

Mike Sheron

SHEPPARD William

(IL) Mid 5' 11" 11st 4lbs
b: Ferryhill, Durham, 1906
d: Hemel Hempstead, 27 Dec 1950
QPR: Jun 1930
Football League: 13-4. **FAC:** 0-0. **FLC:** 0-0.
Other: 0-0. **Total:** 13-4.

Bill scored some 60 goals in two years at Ferryhill Athletic and did the same at Chilton Colliery as well as Crook Town. He was never in the Liverpool line-up but Sheppard scored 25 goals for Watford in his first season and 14 in the next, after that he seemed to fade out of the picture, except when scoring that famous penalty against Arsenal in 1933. Bill died of a heart attack on a Christmas visit to his local pub, King Henry Eighth, in Hemel Hempstead aged 44 years.
Debut: 25 Oct 1930 v Northampton Town (H) 0-2 Div 3 (S).

SHERON Michael Nigel

Striker 5' 10" 11st 13lbs
b: Liverpool, 11 Jan 1972
QPR: (£2,750,000) Jul 1997
Football League: 63-19. **FAC:** 2-0. **FLC:** 4-1.
Other: 0-0. **Total:** 69-20.
Honours: 16 England U21 caps.

A player with vision and skill to go with his sharpness around the box. A very skilful player linking up well with his colleagues and with the ability to beat opponents with ease. Mike Sheron was a £2.75 million move to QPR (a record for both Stoke and QPR), but he suffered a recurrence of a back injury and, after only 18 months, in January 1999, he moved to Barnsley.
Debut: 2 Sep 1997 v Reading (A) 2-1 Div 1.

SHIMMIN Dominic Libreville

Def 6' 0" 12st 7lbs
b: Bermondsey, 13 Oct 1987
QPR: Mar 2005
Football League: 3-0. **FAC:** 0-0. **FLC:** 1-0.
Other: 0-0. **Total:** 4-0.
Debut: 20 Aug 2005 v Coventry City (A) 0-3 Championship.

SHITTU Daniel Olusola

CD 6' 3" 13st 0lbs
b: Lagos, Nigeria, 2 Sep 1980
QPR: (£250,000) Oct 2001
Football League: 172-17. **FAC:** 3-0. **FLC:** 5-0.
Other: 5-0. **Total:** 185-17.
Honours: 16 caps for Nigeria.

Signed by QPR after two fans funded his £250,000 deal, Danny is a big solid central defender who won his first cap v Paraguay, while at Loftus Road, and had a memorable debut for QPR, being sent off. He soon became a popular player at Loftus Road and was a near ever-present in the first team during the 2002/03 and 2005/06 seasons before leaving for Watford in a £1.6 million deal in August 2006.
Debut: 23 Oct 2001 v Peterborough United (A) 1-4 Div 2.

Danny Shittu

SHUFFLEBOTTOM Thomas

(LH) Mid
b: 1881
QPR: May 1904
Southern League: 1-0. **FAC:** 0-0. **FLC:** 0-0.
Other: 0-0. **Total:** 1-0.

A young and enthusiastic player who was a reserve at most of his clubs, Tom travelled to Swindon along with John Bowman and played alongside him in his only match for the club.
Debut: 18 Mar 1905 v Swindon Town (A) 0-0 SL Div 1.

SIBLEY Frank Phillip

(LH) Mid 5' 10" 12st 4lbs
b: Uxbridge, Middlesex, 4 Dec 1947
QPR: 1963
Football League: 143-3. **FAC:** 10-1. **FLC:** 15-1.
Other: 0-0. **Total:** 168-5.
Honours: 4 England youth caps. Captain of the U18 squad. 3 U23 caps. 3rd Div championship winner's medal. League Cup winner's medal.

It was highly unfortunate that Frank received a severe knee injury which forced him to retire early in his career in 1974. He was immediately given the job of club coach and in 1977 followed on with the manager's job after Dave Sexton had left. When Steve Burtenshaw came onto the scene in 1978, Frank reverted to club coach again but then took the manager's job at Walsall, but only for a short time. He became the coach at Hounslow Town and in 1984 reverted to the job of caretaker/manager at QPR once again after Alan Mullery left the club. Jim Smith arrived in 1985 and Frank resumed the job as coach to the club becoming assistant/manager to Trevor Francis in 1988. In the 1990s he became the assistant/manager of Millwall. However, yet again he then returned to the job of coach at QPR.
Debut: 4 Sep 1963 v Aldershot (A) 1-3 FL Cup 1st Round.

SILKMAN Barry

Mid 5' 8" 10st 13lbs
b: Stepney, London, 29 Jul 1952
QPR: (£5,000) Oct 1980
Football League: 23-2. **FAC:** 2-0. **FLC:** 0-0.
Other: 0-0. **Total:** 25-2.
Honours: 3rd Div championship medal winner.

Barry was a flamboyant character who on his day was unstoppable. In November 2000, Silkman received plenty of plaudits after his 75th minute appearance for Harrow Borough (versus Wycombe Wanderers) made him the oldest player at 48 years, to play in the FA Cup since Sir Stanley Matthews turned out for Stoke City in the 1960s. He later became a football agent and also greyhound trainer in Kent.
Debut: 1 Nov 1980 v Grimsby Town (A) 0-0 Div 2.

Frank Sibley

SILVER Alan G
Goal
QPR: 1954
Football League: 0-0. **FAC:** 1-0. **FLC:** 0-0.
Other: 0-0. **Total:** 1-0.

Just two days before the second replay of a first round FA Cup match, Harry Brown the goalkeeper was injured in a League match at Bristol City. Silver was the only goalkeeper available to fill the gap. With a goalless first half on a mud churned pitch, all seemed well at the start of the second. Yet by 73 minutes QPR were down 0-4. Alan never played for the club again, in fact Brian Nicholas, the regular right-half was in goal for the next League match!
Debut: 29 Nov 1954 v Walthamstow Avenue (A) 0-4 FA Cup.

SIMEK Franklin
Def 6′ 0″ 11st 6lbs
b: St Louis, Missouri, USA, 13 Oct 1984
QPR: (Loan) Oct 2004

Scott Sinclair

Football League: 5-0. **FAC:** 0-0. **FLC:** 0-0.
Other: 0-0. **Total:** 5-0.
Honours: 5 caps for United States.
Debut: 19 Oct 2004 v PNE (A) 1-2 Championship.

SIMONS Henry Thomas
(IR) Mid 5′ 8″ 11st 4lbs
b: Hackney, London, October 1887
d: 1956
QPR: Aug 1914
Southern League: 19-7. **FAC:** 3-1. **FLC:** 0-0.
Other: 0-0. **Total:** 22-8.
Honours: Southern Counties Amateur championship medal.

Simons was very much respected in London amateur circles, showing uncanny anticipation in matches, often mastering the opposing defender. Tommy was one of several brothers who were prominent among amateur clubs around this time and was the son of a one-time groundsman at Clapton Orient.
Debut: 14 Nov 1914 v Exeter City (H) 0-2 SL Div 1.

SINCLAIR Scott Andrew
Striker 5′ 10″ 10st 0lbs
b: Bath, 25 Mar 1989
QPR: (Loan) Nov 2007
Football League: 9-1. **FAC:** 0-0. **FLC:** 0-0.
Other: 0-0. **Total:** 9-1.
Honours: Capped at U17, U18, U19 and U20 levels for England.
Debut: 6 Nov 2007 v Coventry City (H) 1-2 Championship.

SINCLAIR Trevor Lloyd
Mid 5′ 10″ 11st 2lbs
b: Dulwich, London, 2 Mar 1973
QPR: (£750,000) 1993
Premier/Football League: 167-16. **FAC:** 10-2.
FLC: 13-3. **Other:** 0-0. **Total:** 190-21.
Honours: England youth caps. 1 B cap. 14 U21 caps. 9 full caps.

Trevor's appetite for running at defenders was backed up by an indefatigable work rate which marked him out as a modern rarity. He was very much a skilful player who was difficult to dispossess when he was in full flight. Despite being a Londoner by birth, he was brought up in Manchester (where he became a City fan), and started in the Football League at Blackpool. After three seasons he became a big money QPR signing. After a further five years, and nearly 200 appearances, his value had trebled with his move across London. One of his best performances was for West Ham United against Derby County on Boxing Day 2002 when he scored with a spectacular 12 yard volley. By the end of the 2002/03 season, he had also played around 200 matches for the Hammers.

Trevor Sinclair

Debut: 18 Mar 1993 v Liverpool (H) 1-3 PL.

SINGLETON Harold Bertram
(OL) Wing 5′ 9″ 12st 3lbs
b: Prescot, Lancashire, 1877
d: Macclesfield, 5 Jul 1948
QPR: 1904
Southern League: 19-0. **FAC:** 0-0. **FLC:** 0-0.
Other: 0-0. **Total:** 19-0.

The left-wing spot was filled by Harry with capability during his time with the club, although he normally shared it with John Stewart.
Debut: 3 Sep 1904 v Plymouth Argyle (H) 2-1 SL Div 1.

SINTON Andrew
Mid 5′ 7″ 10st 7lbs
b: Newcastle, 19 Mar 1966
QPR: (£350,000) Mar 1989
Premier/Football League: 160-22 **FAC:** 13-2.
FLC: 14-0. **Other:** 3-1. **Total:** 190-25.
Honours: School caps. 3 B caps. 12 England caps. League Cup winner's medal.

A left-sided midfield player who added width to the attack and made things happen, Andy was an early ball specialist who could place an accurate

Andy Sinton

cross into the heart of the penalty area. A bargain buy from Cambridge United, still under 18 years old, he quickly became a great favourite at Griffin Park, and the fans were very disappointed when he moved the few miles to Loftus Road. Over four years, and 160 appearances later he moved north to Sheffield, then south again to Spurs. A radio reporter once boldly stated that, "It could be bad news for Andy Sinton – his knee is locked-up in the dressing room." Another player who tried to show off his silky skills at Cambridge United, at the same time as Sinton didn't meet with quite the same success. He kept falling over on an icy pitch and was promptly rejected. His name was Peter Beardsley!
Debut: 25 Mar 1989 v Sheffield Wednesday (A) 2-0 Div 1.

SKILTON Percy G

(CF) Striker 5' 10" 12st 2lbs
b: Harrow, Middlesex
QPR: 1903
Southern League: 62-22. **FAC:** 0-0. **FLC:** 0-0.
Other: 2-0. **Total:** 64-22.
Honours: Southern League championship medal.

A first class amateur, who played for the club over a number of years, Percy gave many fine performances but perhaps his best was in the 5-1 defeat of Swindon Town at Park Royal in 1909 in which he scored a hat-trick.
Debut: 30 Apr 1904 v Millwall (H) 2-1 SL Div 1.

SKINNER Henry

(LH) Mid 5' 9" 12st 0lbs
b: Middlesex, 1875
QPR: 1899
Southern League: 40-1. **FAC:** 6-0. **FLC:** 0-0.
Other: 0-0. **Total:** 46-1.
Honours: FA Amateur Cup winner's medal.

According to contemporary writers, Henry was a man with a pleasant disposition who could cope with the swiftest opponents. Quick on his feet he could hold his own with the fastest of wingers.
Debut: 16 Sep 1899 v New Brompton (H) 2-0 SL Div 1.

SLACK Rodney Geoffrey

Goal
b: Farcett, Cambridgeshire, 11 Apr 1940
QPR: Mar 1961
Football League: 1-0. **FAC:** 0-0. **FLC:** 0-0.
Other: 0-0. **Total:** 1-0.
Honours: Southern League runner's-up medal. Southern League championship winner's medal. Southern League Cup winner's medal.

Rodney was the understudy to Gordon Banks at Leicester City but he only made a single appearance for QPR. At Cambridge United, Rodney, made over 350 League & Cup appearances, and won the Player of the Year award on three separate occasions – 1963, 1965 and 1966.
Debut: 3 May 1962 v Halifax Town (A) 1-1 Div 3.

SLADE Steven Anthony

Striker 6' 0" 11st 2lbs
b: Hackney, London, 6 Oct 1975
QPR: (£350,000) Jul 1996
Football League: 68-6. **FAC:** 3-0. **FLC:** 7-1.
Other: 0-0. **Total:** 78-7.
Honours: 4 England U21 caps.

A right-sided attacker who also plays as a central striker, Steve is a hard runner who looks to create opportunities for others. Released in the summer of 2000 he joined Cambridge United on a weekly contract but was released in November 2000. Steve subsequently re-emerged at Luton Town in April 2001 where he had a trial with their reserves.
Debut: 28 Aug 1996 v Wolverhampton Wanderers (A) 1-1 Div 1.

SMITH Albert W

(LH) Mid
b: Stoke-on-Trent, 27 Aug 1918
d: 9 Jun 1992
QPR: May 1939
Football League: 62-2. **FAC:** 7-0. **FLC:** 0-0.
Other: 0-0. **Total:** 69-2.
Honours: 3rd Div (South) championship winner's medal.

Bert was a tough, uncompromising and aggressive player who challenged hard for the ball. During the war he was awarded the BEM at Dunkirk for bravery. Later in the war he served in the Middle East and then in Germany where he played for an army team, the winners of two Cups. Unfortunately a broken leg ended his career after a tackle by Fulham's Pat Beasley at Craven Cottage in October 1948. Later, Bert qualified as an FA coach and for 40 years was employed in that role at Harrow Borough FC. Later on he set up a fish and chip shop near Loftus Road with ex-team mate Arthur Jefferson.
Debut: 7 Sep 1946 v Walsall (A) 2-0 Div 3 (S).

SMITH Arthur R

(OR) Wing
b: Stourbridge, Birmingham, 1887
QPR: 1911
Southern League: 35-8. **FAC:** 1-0. **FLC:** 0-0.
Other: 1-0. **Total:** 37-8.
Honours: Southern League championship winner's medal.

A small and very fast winger who was a master of the early cross, Arthur was an amateur who was training at a London College to become a

Steve Slade

schoolteacher. Later he tutored at St Peters College, in Saltley, Birmingham. He became a very efficient and respected administrator in non-League football as secretary of Brierley Hill Alliance, before retiring in 1934.
Debut: 2 Sep 1911 v Plymouth Argyle (A) 1-0 SL Div 1.

SMITH Edward William Alfred

(IL) Mid 5′ 9″ 12st 2lbs
b: Marylebone, London, 23 Mar 1929
d: London, April 1993
QPR: Jul 1957
Football League: 17-1. **FAC:** 1-1. **FLC:** 0-0.
Other: 2-0. **Total:** 20-2.

Eddie was an aggressive player who was only a part-time professional, as he owned a chain of newsagent shops in London, which kept him out of full-time football.
Debut: 24 Aug 1957 v Brentford (H) 1-0 Div 3 (S).

SMITH Frank A

Goal
b: Colchester, Essex, 30 Apr 1936
QPR: May 1962
Football League: 66-0. **FAC:** 3-0. **FLC:** 2-0.
Other: 0-0. **Total:** 71-0.

Manager Alec Stock considered Peter Springett was too young to play regularly for the senior squad, so he signed Smith, the Spurs reserve goalkeeper, to share the position with him. Hence over his three years at Loftus Road he played 66 League games, almost exactly half the total number of matches possible.
Debut: 24 Sep 1962 v PNE (H) 1-2 FL Cup first round.

SMITH George Casper

(CH) CD 6′ 1″ 12st 2lbs
b: Bromley-by-Bow, London, 23 Apr 1915
d: Bodmin, Oct 1983
QPR: Jun 1947
Football League: 75-1. **FAC:** 8-0. **FLC:** 0-0.
Other: 0-0. **Total:** 83-1.
Honours: 3rd Div (South) championship medal.

George made his Football League debut in the final match before the Second World War for Charlton Athletic. Much of his playing career, he was aged 25, and his chance of honours, were negated by the conflict. He did win an England cap and a Cup winner's medal during this period, but these are not generally acknowledged, and in addition he appeared in many representative

Jimmy Smith

matches. George was a tall, unflappable centre-half who captained QPR to the championship in 1948. A year later he became the assistant/manager of Ipswich Town but resigned within three months. In 1950 Smith became the Chelmsford City manager, then the Redhill manager, and the boss of Eastbourne United followed. He then became the FA youth manager, the Sheffield United coach, then the Sutton United manager in 1957. In 1958 he became the manager of Crystal Palace and in 1960 the Sheffield United coach again. Finally he became the Portsmouth manager in 1960 culminating in the general manager's job at Portsmouth in 1970.
Debut: 23 Aug 1947 v Norwich City (H) 3-1 Div 3 (S).

SMITH James Dean

Mid 6' 0" 11st 0lbs
b: Newham, 7 Jan 1987
QPR: (Loan) Sep 2006
Football League: 29-6. **FAC:** 2-0. **FLC:** 0-0.
Other: 0-0. **Total:** 31-6.
Honours: Capped at U16, U17 and U19 levels for England.

Signed by Chelsea as a trainee in July 2005, Jimmy has only made one (substitute) appearance for his parent club and has spent the majority of his professional career on loan. However, he impressed when he arrived at Loftus Road and his initial month's loan was soon extended to the end of the 2006-07 campaign. The attacking midfielder notched six goals during his time with Rangers, including one on his home debut against Norwich City and a brace in the 4-2 victory over Crystal Palace in November 2006. Jimmy has since spent periods on loan with Norwich City, Sheffield Wednesday and Leyton Orient.
Debut: 30 Sep 2006 v Southampton (A) 1-2 Championship.

SMITH John William

(C.F) Striker 5' 8" 11st 0lbs
b: Derby, 1890
QPR: Apr 1919
Southern/Football League: 117-43. **FAC:** 5-2.
FLC: 0-0. **Other:** 0-0. **Total:** 122-45.
Honours: 3rd Div (South) championship medal.

Jack played for the club during the latter part of the war under the "guest" player system and signed for QPR directly peace had resumed. Neat and quick in all his actions he was a firm favourite of the crowd. An ever-present in their last season in the Southern League, Jack was in the side for the entire first season of the Football League. Dogged by injuries at his final club, Brighton & Hove Albion, he was released in May 1925 and left the first class game.
Debut: 30 Aug 1919 v Bristol Rovers (A) 2-0 SL Div 1.

SMITH Norman

(RB) Def 5' 8" 11st 1lb
b: Durham, 20 Sep 1897
d: Newcastle, 18 May 1978
QPR: May 1937
Football League: 68-2. **FAC:** 3-0. **FLC:** 0-0.
Other: 0-0. **Total:** 71-2.
Honours: 2 3rd Div (South) championship winner's medals.

Norman was a solid old fashioned full-back, who was made captain upon his arrival at the club. In July 1939 he became the Chelsea assistant/trainer and in May 1946 he was then made the head trainer for around seven years. After his retirement from football, Norman bought a newsagent in the Tottenham area of London.
Debut: 28 Aug 1937 v Brighton & Hove Albion (H) 2-1 Div 3 (S).

SMITH Norman

(LH) Mid 5' 8" 10st 9lbs
b: Newcastle-upon-Tyne, 15 Dec 1897
d: Newcastle-upon-Tyne, May 1978
QPR: Aug 1930
Football League: 26-0. **FAC:** 1-0. **FLC:** 0-0.
Other: 0-0 **Total:** 27-0.

Norman was made team captain as soon as he arrived at Loftus Road. When he left the club he took up coaching, and in 1933 joined the Swiss club Kreuzlingen. After two years he took a job at St Gallen, Switzerland until 1938 when he joined Newcastle United as trainer; he also trained England and the English representative sides. After the war, Norman was a vital part of the Newcastle United set up which clinched promotion and won three FA Cup finals. In 1961 at the age of 64 he became manager, until he stepped down in 1962.
Debut: 30 Aug 1930 v Thames Association (H) 3-0 Div 3 (S).

SMITH Stephen Charles

(OL) Wing
b: Hednesford, Staffordshire, 27 Mar 1896
d: Chichester, 1980
QPR: May 1928
Football League: 24-1. **FAC:** 1-0. **FLC:** 0-0.
Other: 0-0. **Total:** 25-1.

Steve was the son of an English international of the same name, who played for Aston Villa in the late 19th Century. Like his father, he was an outside-left who was a good passer of the ball and accurate with his crosses.
Debut: 6 Sep 1928 v Newport County (A) 0-0 Div 3 (S).

SMITH Stephen R

Goal
QPR: 1925
Football League: 2-0. **FAC:** 0-0. **FLC:** 0-0.
Other: 0-0. **Total:** 2-0.

An amateur goalkeeper who was on trial with the club and played in the last two matches of the 1925/26 season – the second re-election campaign for the club.
Debut: 24 Apr 1926 v Aberdare Athletic (A) 0-1 Div 3 (S).

SMITH Thomas S

(OR) Wing 5' 9" 11st 0lbs
b: Ashton-in-Makerfield, Lancashire, 1877
QPR: 1899
Southern League: 13-1. **FAC:** 8-3. **FLC:** 0-0.
Other: 0-0. **Total:** 21-4.

Tom arrived at Southampton from Preston North End, his new club thinking they had signed a star player. It was discovered that there were two Tom Smiths at the Lancashire club and that Spurs had signed the true star. Nevertheless QPR were only too happy to sign him for their initial season in the Southern League.
Debut: 9 Sep 1899 v Tottenham Hotspur (A) 0-1 SL Div 1.

SMITH William Conway

(IR) Striker 5' 7" 10st 12lbs
b: Huddersfield, Yorkshire, 13 Jul 1926
QPR: Mar 1951
Football League: 174-81. **FAC:** 6-3. **FLC:** 0-0.
Other: 1-0. **Total:** 181-84.

Always known by his second given name, Conway, he was the son of W H Smith, the old England and Huddersfield Town player who formed a celebrated partnership with Clem Stephenson. Conway was certainly a chip off the old block, although not reaching his father's standard, he nevertheless possessed a sizzling shot. Denied an earlier Football League playing career due to the war, he didn't make it at his home town team, and joined Rangers in 1951. He immediately became a near automatic first team choice, and in four out of the next six seasons that Smith was with QPR, he topped the scoring list and during this time made 181 appearances in total. In 1956, aged 30, he finished his League career with Halifax.
Debut: 17 Mar 1951 v Leeds United (A) 2-2 Div 2.

SNELGROVE George W

(IR) Mid 5' 8" 11st 0lbs
b: 1886
QPR: 1907
Southern League: 11-1. **FAC:** 0-0. **FLC:** 0-0.
Other: 0-0. **Total:** 11-1.

George was a reserve who appeared on three occasions during the 1908 championship year, taking the place of Cannon. During the following

Juergen Sommer

season, he was given an extended stay in the first team but to no avail.
Debut: 18 Apr 1908 v Northampton Town (H) 2-3 SL Div 1.

SOMMER Juergen Peterson

Goal 6' 4" 15st 12lbs
b: Manhattan, New York, USA, 27 Feb 1969
QPR: (£600,000) Aug 1995
Premier/Football League: 66-0. **FAC:** 3-0. **FLC:** 2-0. **Other:** 0-0. **Total:** 71-0.
Honours: 5 USA caps.

The son of a former SV Hamburg player who emigrated to America, Juergen showed signs of brilliance at QPR and he was virtually impregnable in the air. Although this huge goalkeeper was a good shot-stopper he came under some pressure when QPR were relegated, nonetheless holding on to his first team place, but – perhaps surprisingly – was passed over for the US Olympic squad in 1996.
Debut: 16 Sep 1995 v Leeds United (A) 3-1 PL.

SPACKMAN Nigel James

Mid 6' 1" 12st 4lbs
b: Romsey, Hampshire, 2 Dec 1960
QPR: (£500,000) Feb 1989
Football League: 29-1. **FAC:** 0-0. **FLC:** 2-1. **Other:** 2-0. **Total:** 33-2.
Honours: 2nd Div championship winner's medal. League Cup winner's medal. 3 Scottish Premier League championship medals. Scottish League Cup winner's medal. Scottish Cup winner's medal.

Nigel was a tall, hefty character with a tremendous shot. He had a good sense of humour which was loved by the fans and his colleagues alike. In 2001 he took over the manager's job at Barnsley but he was relieved of it shortly into the season.
Debut: 4 Feb 1989 v Millwall (H) 1-2 Div 1.

SPENCE William Joseph

(CH) CD
b: Hartlepool, 10 Jan 1926
QPR: Dec 1951
Football League: 56-0. **FAC:** 4-0. **FLC:** 0-0. **Other:** 0-0. **Total:** 60-0.

Bill was made team captain on his arrival at Loftus Road and the spectators saw a classy performance, although they were shocked to see such a small central defender. However, his ball control was pure class. Injury was the cause of his early retirement in July 1955.
Debut: 22 Dec 1951 v Coventry City (H) 1-4 Div 2.

SPENCER John

Striker 5' 6" 11st 7lbs
b: Glasgow, Scotland, 11 Sep 1970
QPR: (£2,500,000) Nov 1996
Football League: 48-22. **FAC:** 6-2. **FLC:** 2-0. **Other:** 0-0. **Total:** 56-24.
Honours: School & youth caps. 3 U21 caps. 14 full Scottish caps.

John was confined for long spells to the Glasgow Rangers reserve side but managed to score 18 goals in 49 appearances, before his initial big money move which took him to Chelsea. He became Rangers' second highest purchase when he moved to Loftus Road in 1996. A small, lively, bustling striker with a good finish, who had strength and a shrewd footballing brain which served him well, John was skilful and quick thinking, and turned defenders to make space for shooting. He also had

Nigel Spackman

John Spencer

the ability to retain the ball in tight situations.
Debut: 23 Nov 1997 v Reading (A) 1-2 Div 1.

SPOTTISWOODE Joseph

(OL) Wing 5' 9" 12st 0lbs
b: Carlisle, Cumberland, 1894
QPR: Jun 1925
Football League: 22-2. **FAC:** 0-0. **FLC:** 0-0.
Other: 0-0.**Total:** 22-2.
Honours: 3rd Div (South) championship winner's medal.

Joe was a winger of considerable ability but he had slowed down somewhat by the time he reached QPR. He settled into the side which finished the season bottom of the table for the second time in three years.
Debut: 25 Aug 1925 v Gillingham (A) 0-3 Div 3 (S).

SPRATLEY Alan S

Goal 5' 9" 11st 0lbs
b: Maidenhead, Berkshire, 5 Jun 1949
QPR: May 1967
Football League: 29-0. **FAC:** 2-0. **FLC:** 1-0.
Other: 0-0. **Total:** 32-0.

The arrival of Phil Parkes ended the period in which Alan was given to prove himself. Transferred to Swindon Town in 1973, his contract was terminated at the end of the following season, having played just seven matches for the Wiltshire club.
Debut: 4 Jan 1969 v Aston Villa (A) 1-2 FA Cup third round.

SPRINGETT Peter J

Goal 5' 10" 11st 6lbs
b: Fulham, London, 8 May 1946
d: Sheffield, 28 Aug 1997
QPR: May 1963
Football League: 137-0. **FAC:** 10-0. **FLC:** 13-0.
Other: 0-0. **Total:** 160-0.
Honours: 6 England youth caps. 6 U23 caps. 3rd Div championship winner's medal. League Cup winner's medal. 4th Div promotion medal.

Peter arrived aged just 17, and the highlight of his career at Loftus Road was being in the QPR side that came from behind to beat Jimmy Hagan's West Bromwich Albion in Wembley's first ever League Cup final. He went on to play 160 first team matches over four years. An exceptionally brilliant custodian who was quick to get down to a shot, confident in collecting the ball from a centre, and was never overshadowed by his brother's reputation. After retiring from the game he became a policeman, and died aged just 51 from a long term illness.
Debut: 18 May 1963 v Peterborough United (H) 0-0 Div 3.

SPRINGETT Ronald Deryk G

Goal 5' 10" 12st 6lbs
b: Fulham, London, 22 Jul 1935
QPR: Feb 1953
Football League: 88-0. **FAC:** 1-0. **FLC:** 3-0.
Other: 3-0. **Total:** 95-0.
QPR: (£16,000) Jun 1967
Football League: 45-0. **FAC:** 1-0. **FLC:** 3-0.
Other: 0-0. **Total:** 49-0.
Honours: 33 England caps. 9 Football League caps. 4 caps v Young England. 2nd Div championship winner's medal. 1st Div runner's-up medal. FA Cup runner's-up medal. 2nd Div runner's-up medal.

Ron kept goal with a mixture of brilliance, dependability and cat-like agility and with phenomenal anticipation. His first term at Loftus Road lasted five years, when he moved, like his older brother later, to Sheffield Wednesday. Nine years on, a unique deal in 1967 took his brother, Peter, to Sheffield Wednesday and Ron back to Loftus Road for a fee of £16,000. Ron had the distinction of being Sheffield Wednesday's most capped England player, having gained 33 between 1959 and 1966. In 1970 Ron owned a sports shop in Shepherds Bush.
Debut: 5 Nov 1955 v Norwich City (H) 2-3 Div 3 (S).

Ron Springett

ST AIMIE Kieron Lloyd J Minto

Mid 6' 1" 13st 0lbs
b: Brent, London, 4 May 1989
QPR: Jun 2007
Football League: 0-0, **FAC:** 0-0. **FLC:** 1-0.
Other: 0-0. **Total:** 1-0.
Debut: 14 Aug 2007 v Leyton Orient (H) 1-2 FLC first round.

STAINROD Simon Allan

Striker 6' 1" 11st 11lbs
b: Sheffield, Yorkshire, 1 Feb 1959
QPR: (£275,000) Nov 1980
Football League: 145-48. **FAC:** 12-5. **FLC:** 17-5.
Other: 3-3. **Total:** 177-61.
Honours: 3 England youth caps. 2nd Div championship winner's medal. FA Cup runner's-up medal.

Simon was a popular character at QPR enriching the game with a touch of class that didn't show at any of his other clubs, having a subtle style of play and scoring many memorable goals, Simon's only

Simon Stainrod

negative attribute was a fiery temper. He fitted in well at QPR, with his game developing under the coaching of Terry Venables.

His stay at Loftus Road lasted just over five years during which time he made 145 Football League appearances, whereupon his career continued in England, France and Scotland. At Dundee he became the player/manager and then manager, in 1992, followed by the same at Ayr United, which lasted just two months before he was sacked.
Debut: 22 Nov 1980 v PNE (A) 2-3 Div 2.

STANDLEY Thomas L

(CF) Striker
b: Poplar, London, 23 Dec 1932
QPR: May 1957
Football League: 15-2. **FAC:** 0-0. **FLC:** 0-0.
Other: 0-0. **Total:** 15-2.

Tom was the fifth of eight centre-forwards to be tried during the 1957/58 season. At Bournemouth he was turned into a very reliable half-back and stayed until he retired in 1965, notching up over 160 first team appearances.
Debut: 21 Dec 1957 v Brentford (A) 1-1 Div 3 (S).

STEER William Henry Owen

(CF) Striker 5′ 8″ 11st 6lbs
b: Kingston-upon-Thames, 1888
QPR: 1909
Southern League: 68-31. **FAC:** 8-6. **FLC:** 0-0.
Other: 0-0. **Total:** 76-37.
Honours: 6 Amateur caps for England. London League v Birmingham League. 2 caps for Southern League v Football League.

Bill was an amateur at QPR but turned professional at Chelsea. He played throughout the First World War and retired in 1918.
Debut: 1 Oct 1909 v Watford (H) 4-3 SL Div 1.

STEIN Mark Earl Sean

Striker 5′ 6″ 11st 10lbs
b: Cape Town, South Africa, 29 Jan 1966
QPR: (£300,000) Aug 1988
Football League: 33-4. **FAC:** 3-1. **FLC:** 4-2.
Other: 4-0. **Total:** 44-7.
Honours: England youth cap. League Cup winner's medal. Full Members' Cup runner's-up medal. Auto Trophy winner's medal. 2nd Div championship winner's medal.

One of three footballing brothers, he was a nimble opportunist and quick off the mark. Mark made several big transfer moves, and at 37 years of age was still playing in senior non-League football.
Debut: 27 Aug 1988 v Manchester United (A) 0-0 Div 1.

Rob Steiner

STEINER Robert Herman

Striker 6′ 2″ 13st 5lbs
b: Finsprong, Sweden, 20 Jun 1973
QPR: (Loan) Nov 1998
Football League: 8-1. **FAC:** 0-0. **FLC:** 0-0.
Other: 0-0. **Total:** 8-1.
QPR: (Loan) Mar 1999
Football League: 4-2. **FAC:** 0-0. **FLC:** 0-0.
Other: 0-0. **Total:** 4-2.
QPR: (£215,000) Jul 1999
Football League: 24-6. **FAC:** 2-0. **FLC:** 1-0.
Other: 0-0. **Total:** 27-6.
Honours: 4 Swedish international caps.

Steiner was at QPR on three separate occasions, twice as a loan player from Bradford City; and the last time a permanent £215,000 deal from the same club. But injuries blighted his career, and whilst with QPR Rob suffered a serious back injury which required surgery. Unfortunately he was unable to recover from it and had to prematurely retire.
Debut: 7 Nov 1998 v Bolton Wanderers (H) 2-0 Div 1.

STEJSKAL Jan

Goal 6′ 3″ 12st 0lbs
b: Czechoslovakia, 15 Jan 1962
QPR: (£625,000) Oct 1990

Jan Stejskal

Premier/Football League: 108-0. **FAC:** 3-0.
FLC: 11-0. **Other:** 1-0. **Total:** 123-0.
Honours: 4 Czech international caps. 1 U21 cap.

Jan was a very tall goalkeeper who was quickly confirmed as a favourite of the crowd at Loftus Road. Brought in to replace David Seaman, he generally shared the number one spot with Welsh international Tony Roberts, although Jan was a Czech international himself. During his four seasons at Loftus Road, he appeared in 108 League matches (missing only one in the 1991/92 season). In 1994 he returned to his former club, Sparta Prague, and later became the coach of rivals Slavia.
Debut: 20 Oct 1990 v Leeds United (A) 3-2 Div 1.

STEPHENSON Herbert L

(IR) Mid 5′ 11″ 11st 0lbs
b: London
QPR: 1930
Football League: 2-0. **FAC:** 0-0. **FLC:** 0-0.
Other: 0-0. **Total:** 2-0.

Both of the matches Herbert played in were against the same opposition, Southend United, and both matches ended in 2-0 defeats for the London club. Bert never turned out again for the Rangers, and detailed research has failed to reveal any further information.
Debut: 15 Nov 1930 v Southend United (A) 0-2 Div 3 (S).

Mark Stein

STEPHENSON James

(OR) Wing 5' 6" 11st 2lbs
b: New Delaval, Feb 1895
d: Newcastle-upon-Tyne, Feb 1960
QPR: 1927
Football League: 18-0. **FAC:** 0-0. **FLC:** 0-0.
Other: 0-0. **Total:** 18-0.

A class act on the right wing, Jimmy was one of a famous footballing family which included the great Clem, he was also the uncle of the cricketer/footballer, Bob Stephenson. Jimmy, who was the licensee of a public house in Watford, had to be persuaded to sign for QPR at the time.
Debut: 27 Aug 1927 v Newport County (H) 4-2 Div 3 (S).

STEVENS Ronald Frederick

(OL) Wing
b: Luton, Bedfordshire, 26 Nov 1914
QPR: 1938
Football League: 0-0. **FAC:** 0-0. **FLC:** 0-0.
Other: 1-0. **Total:** 1-0.

The only match that Ron played, in QPR colours, was a Third Division (South) Cup match which resulted in a draw. The replay was never played owing to the outbreak of war.
Debut: 4 May 1939 v Port Vale (H) 0-0 Div 3 (S) Cup.

STEWART Damion

Def 6' 3" 13st 8lbs
b: Jamaica, 8 Aug 1980
QPR: Jun 2006
Football League: 121-8. **FAC:** 5-0. **FLC:** 7-3.
Other: 0-0. **Total:** 133-11.
Honours: 36 full caps for Jamaica.

Having already impressed with two solid seasons at Loftus Road under his belt, Damion's 58th minute goal in the League Cup third round tie at Aston Villa in September 2008 ensured his continued popularity with Rangers fans as it proved the only goal of a game that ensured the Premiership outfit's dismissal from the competition. Indeed, Damion finished the season being voted both the Players' and Supporters' Player of the Year. The Jamaican-born defender joined QPR on a free transfer from Harbour View, having spent the 2005-06 campaign on loan with Bradford City.
Debut: 5 Aug 2006 v Burnley (A) 0-2 Championship.

STEWART George

(IR) Mid
b: Chirnside, Durham,16 Oct 1920
QPR: Mar 1948
Football League: 38-5. **FAC:** 2-0. **FLC:** 0-0.
Other: 0-0. **Total:** 40-5.

Damion Stewart

A quality player who was quick witted and clever on the ball, George was a real asset to the team in their final run-in to the championship of 1948. He was often kept out of the side by the brilliance of Freddy Ramscar.
Debut: 13 Mar 1948 v Ipswich Town (H) 2-0 Div 3 (S).

STEWART Ian Edwin

(OL) Wing 5' 6" 11st 9lbs
b: Belfast, N Ireland, 10 Sep 1961
QPR: May 1980
Football League: 67-2. **FAC:** 3-0. **FLC:** 14-2.
Other: 3-0. **Total:** 87-4.
Honours: N Ireland schools & youth caps. 31 full caps for N Ireland. 2nd Div championship winner's medal.

Early impressions at Loftus Road of Ian's talent were most favourable. He had a clever but direct style of play with complete control of the ball. However, he was labelled with the inconsistent tag, which stayed with him throughout his career.
Debut: 12 Dec 1981 v Barnsley (H) 1-0 Div 2.

STEWART John

(OL) Wing
QPR: 1901
Southern League: 23-3. **FAC:** 3-1. **FLC:** 0-0.
Other: 0-0. **Total:** 26-4.
QPR: 1904
Southern League: 13-2. **FAC:** 0-0. **FLC:** 0-0.
Other: 0-0. **Total:** 13-2.

Scoring on his debut for the club, this fast and tricky winger was the most popular of the players. John could play on either wing but he had to return home to Scotland for domestic reasons. After 1905 all trace of him disappears.
Debut: 5 Oct 1901 v Swindon Town (H) 4-0 SL Div 1.

STOCK Alexander William

(CF) Striker 5' 9" 10st 10lbs
b: Peasedown, Somerset, 30 Mar 1917
d: 2001
QPR: 1938
Football League: 16-3. **FAC:** 0-0. **FLC:** 0-0.
Other: 1-2. **Total:** 17-5.

As happened to so many players the war disrupted his career. Alec was drafted into the army in 1939 and became a Major in the Royal Armoured Corps and saw plenty of action, but played no serious football until 1947. On demobilisation he became the player/manager of Yeovil Town and masterminded that famous defeat of First Division Sunderland in the FA Cup of 1949. This catapulted him into the limelight and in August that year, Alec was appointed manager of Leyton Orient and he led them to the championship of the Third Division (South) in 1956. Stock turned down an offer from

Middlesbrough and joined Arsenal, staying there for just 53 days before returning to Orient. In August 1957 Roma of Italy offered him a job, and he returned to England in 1958. A year later he moved to QPR and so began one of the most exciting periods in the club's history. Alec later managed Luton Town, Fulham, became a QPR director, and then the caretaker/manager for a spell in 1978. He finally managed AFC Bournemouth in 1979 before becoming a director from 1981 to 1986.
Debut: 26 Feb 1938 v Reading (H) 3-0 Div 3 (S).

STRUGNELL H H

(IF) Mid
QPR: 1913
Southern League: 11-0. **FAC:** 0-0. **FLC:** 0-0.
Other: 0-0. **Total:** 11-0.

Nothing is known about Strugnell except that he was a reserve inside-forward who stood in for relevant players when they were injured.
Debut: 1 Sep 1913 v Swindon Town (A) 0-3 SL Div 1.

STURRIDGE Dean Constantine

Striker 5′ 8″ 12st 1lbs
b: Birmingham, 27 Jul 1973
QPR: Mar 2005
Football League: 11-0. **FAC:** 0-0. **FLC:** 0-0.
Other: 0-0. **Total:** 11-0.
Debut: 19 Mar 2005 v Rotherham (A) 1-0 Championship.

SUGDEN Sidney H

(IR) Mid 5′ 9″ 10st 2lbs
b: Battersea, London, 1880
QPR: Jan 1905
Southern League: 65-23. **FAC:** 2-0. **FLC:** 0-0.
Other: 0-0. **Total:** 67-23.

"A wonderfully dashing player with a splendid turn of speed and a deadly shot. However, he is not a good team man"; Sidney Sugden was so described by a contemporary reporter. Sid played just nine League matches during the first championship season of 1908 which was also his last.
Debut: 2 Sep 1905 v New Brompton (H) 4-0 SL Div 1.

SUTCH W H

(IL) Mid
QPR: 1919
Southern League: 1-2. **FAC:** 0-0. **FLC:** 0-0.
Other: 0-0. **Total:** 1-2.

A reserve who came into the side in place of the injured John Gregory, the captain, and scored two goals in a 7-1 victory against Bristol Rovers.
Debut: 3 Jan 1920 v Bristol Rovers (H) 7-1 SL Div 1.

SWAN John (formerly Swann)

(IL) Mid 5′ 10″ 11st 7lbs
b: Easington, Durham, 19 Jul 1892
d: Hendon, Jan 1990
QPR: (£300) Feb 1927
Football League: 28-5. **FAC:** 0-0. **FLC:** 0-0.
Other: 0-0. **Total:** 28-5.
Honours: FA Cup runner's-up medal. 2nd Div championship medal.

John possessed a very hard left footed shot and boasted that his right foot was just to stand on, his heading was not so bad either. However, there is a downturn to the story. Suspended by Leeds United for going absent without leave, John was transferred to Watford and was again suspended, this time *sine die*, along with another player, who was dismissed at the same time. Nothing was ever revealed as to the nature of his misdeed but in those days most indiscretions were alcohol related. In 1986 John was living in Hendon and it was believed at the time that there was no one still alive that had played in an earlier FA Cup final.
Debut: 12 Feb 1927 v Bristol City (A) 0-1 Div 3 (S).

Dean Sturridge

SWANN Herbert A

(IR) Mid 5′ 7″ 11st 8lbs
b: Lytham, Lancashire, 28 Mar 1882
QPR: 1909
Southern League: 4-1. **FAC:** 0-0. **FLC:** 0-0.
Other: 0-0. **Total:** 4-1.

Not much is known about this player, except that he once scored all five goals for Plymouth Argyle in a match v Millwall, in the Western League in 1906.
Debut: 9 Oct 1909 v Millwall (H) 1-2 SL Div 1.

SWEETMAN Sidney C

(RB) Def 6′ 0″ 12st 12lbs
b: London
QPR: 1925
Football League: 100-0. **FAC:** 2-0. **FLC:** 0-0.
Other: 0-0. **Total:** 102-0.
Honours: Willesden schools representative.

A QPR discovery who turned professional in 1925, Sid was a stylish full-back who could play on either flank, he was powerfully built and attracted much attention among the big clubs. Eventually Sid was transferred to Millwall and stayed there until the mid-1930s. He was also an expert billiards and table-tennis player.
Debut: 7 Feb 1925 v Merthyr Town (A) 3-2 Div 3 (S).

SWINFEN Reginald

(RB) Def
b: Battersea, London, 4 May 1915
d: October 1996
QPR: 1936
Football League: 26-5. **FAC:** 3-0. **FLC:** 0-0.
Other: 4-0. **Total:** 33-5.

A stocky, bustling player, who never really found his true position, Reg, unfortunately owing to the Second World War, had his most promising career interrupted.
Debut: 19 Sep 1936 v Clapton Orient (H) 2-1 Div 3 (S).

SYMES Ernest Herbert Charles

(LB) Def 5′ 9″ 11st 10lbs
b: Acton, London, 22 Aug 1892
d: 1977
QPR: 1924
Football League: 26-0. **FAC:** 4-0. **FLC:** 0-0.
Other: 0-0. **Total:** 30-0.

Ernie was one of the players dismissed after the club's second re-election year in three seasons.
Debut: 8 Nov 1924 v Gillingham (H) 1-1 Div 3 (S).

T

TAARABT Adel
TAGG Anthony
TAYLOR
TAYLOR Andrew
TAYLOR Brian
TAYLOR Gareth Keith
TAYLOR Geoffrey Arthur
TAYLOR James Guy
TEALE Richard G
TEMBY William
TENNANT William
THOMAS David
THOMAS Jerome William
THOMPSON A
THOMPSON Charles
THOMPSON Garry Linsey
THOMPSON J
THOMPSON Oliver
THOMPSON William T
THOMSON Andrew
THORNTON H V
THORPE Anthony
TILLSON Andrew
TIMOSKA Sampsa
TOMKYS Michael G
TOMMASI Damiano
TOSSWILL John Speare
TOWERS Edwin James
TOWNSEND Luke
TRAVERS James Edward
TRODD William H
TURNBULL Peter
TURNER William
TURPIE Robert P
TUTT Walter R

Dave Thomas

Adel Taarabt

TAARABT Adel
Striker 5' 11" 12st 0lbs
b: Fes, Morocco, 24 May 1989
QPR: (Loan) Mar 2009
Football League: 7-1. **FAC:** 0-0. **FLC:** 0-0.
Other: 0-0. **Total:** 7-1.
Honours: 3 full caps for Morocco.
Debut: 14 Mar 2009 v Southampton (A) 0-0 Championship.

TAGG Anthony
CD 6' 1" 11st 0lbs
b: Epsom, Surrey, 10 Apr 1957
QPR: Mar 1975
Football League: 4-0. **FAC:** 0-0. **FLC:** 0-0.
Other: 0-0. **Total:** 4-0.
Honours: 4th Div championship medal winner.

Tony Tagg played in the, arguably, best QPR side ever when they were beaten into second place on the last day of the season, by Liverpool, in the 1975/76 season. His debut match was the 5-1 defeat of Derby County at the Baseball Ground. Tony went on to play over 100 matches for Millwall.
Debut: 23 Aug 1975 v Derby County (A) 5-1 Div 1.

TAYLOR
(HB) Mid
QPR: 1905
Southern League: 2-0. **FAC:** 0-0. **FLC:** 0-0.
Other: 0-0. **Total:** 2-0.

Lost in the mists of time is any record of this man. He played right-half when Millwall defeated QPR 7-0. He then played centre-half, in place of McLean, in the 2-0 defeat by Spurs.
Debut: 26 Jan 1907 v Millwall (A) 0-7 SL Div 1.

TAYLOR Andrew
Def 5' 11" 11st 7lbs
b: Blackburn, 14 Mar 1986
QPR: (Loan) Jan 2006
Football League: 3-0. **FAC:** 0-0. **FLC:** 0-0.
Other: 0-0. **Total:** 3-0.
Debut: 14 Jan 2006 v Southampton (H) 1-0 Championship.

TAYLOR Brian
(FB) Def
b: Hammersmith, London, 2 Jul 1944
QPR: 1962
Football League: 50-0. **FAC:** 0-0. **FLC:** 2-0.
Other: 0-0. **Total:** 52-0.

Brian stepped into Roy Bentley's position once the latter had retired. He was a very good defender who stood in for all the first class players such as Keen, Angell and the Brady brothers. Even so he managed to accrue 50 League matches at QPR, before dropping down to the non-League scene, after three years.
Debut: 23 Mar 1963 v Watford (A) 5-2 Div 3.

TAYLOR Gareth Keith
Striker 6' 2" 13st 8lbs
b: Weston Super Mare, Somerset, 25 Feb 1973
QPR: (Loan) Mar 2000
Football League: 6-1. **FAC:** 0-0. **FLC:** 0-0.
Other: 0-0. **Total:** 6-1.
Honours: 9 Welsh caps. 7 U21 caps.

His style is limited but usually effective and he gets his fair share of yellow cards. Gareth is very much in the mould of the old fashioned centre-forward, his goals coming mainly from his head.
Debut: 18 Mar 2000 v Walsall (A) 3-2 Div 1.

TAYLOR Geoffrey Arthur
(OL) Wing 5' 8" 10st 0lbs
b: Henstead, Suffolk, 22 Jan 1923
QPR: Nov 1953
Football League: 2-0. **FAC:** 0-0. **FLC:** 0-0.
Other: 0-0. **Total:** 2-0.

In an astonishing career, Geoff appeared for six different Football League clubs, in an 11-year period, but made a total of only 10 outings, which must be record of sorts. He spoke both fluent French and German and also carved out a career in both countries, first as a player/coach, then as a coach with German clubs FC Idar Oberstein (from 1964), VFL Weierbach (1967), VSV Schwarzerden (1975) and SV Bundenbach (1984). Geoff finally retired at the age of 61 years.
Debut: 25 Dec 1953 v Colchester United (A) 0-5 Div 3 (S).

TAYLOR James Guy
(CH) CD
b: Cowley, Middlesex, 5 Nov 1917
QPR: Apr 1953
Football League: 41-0. **FAC:** 3-0. **FLC:** 0-0.
Other: 0-0. **Total:** 44-0.
Honours: 2nd Div championship winner's medal. Football League cap. 2 England caps (at 34).

Jim originally signed for Fulham as an inside-forward just before the Second World War, in which he served in the Navy, and this delayed his introduction to the first class game. He was 28 years old when he made his debut in August 1946, as a wing-half. Eventually he replaced the regular centre-half and became one of the best defenders in the country. Jim was well liked at Loftus Road and was made captain as soon as he arrived at the club. He was likened to Neil Franklin by reason of his strong, quick tackles and his good use of the ball, although he was regarded as rather weak in the air. Jim later became manager of Yiewsley, in 1958 and then the same at Uxbridge, in 1959.
Debut: 19 Aug 1953 v Brighton & Hove Albion (H) 1-2 Div 3 (S)

TEALE Richard G
Goal 6' 1" 13st 7lbs
b: Millam, Sussex, 27 Feb 1952
QPR: Jul 1973
Football League: 1-0. **FAC:** 0-0. **FLC:** 1-0.
Other: 0-0. **Total:** 2-0.
Honours: Amateur Cup final winner's medal.

Dick was a consistent and commanding goalkeeper who covered for Phil Parkes. He came to the notice of QPR in the Amateur Cup final of 1973. He went on to run a building firm and to play veteran football although outfield rather than in goal.
Debut: 7 Sep 1974 v Birmingham City (H) 0-1 Div 1.

TEMBY William
(IR) Mid
b: Dover, Kent, 16 Sep 1934
QPR: Feb 1955
Football League: 7-3. **FAC:** 0-0. **FLC:** 0-0.
Other: 0-0. **Total:** 7-3.

Bill's first two matches for the club were played at right-half. However, the following season he played at inside-right and scored three goals in his last three matches. He was then enticed into Kent League Football.
Debut: 5 Nov 1955 v Norwich City (H) 2-3 Div 3 (S).

TENNANT William

(CH) CD 5′ 10″ 12st 7lbs
b: Coatbridge, Scotland, 1874
QPR: 1899
Southern League: 12-5. **FAC:** 3-0. **FLC:** 0-0.
Other: 0-0. **Total:** 15-5.
Honours: A Scottish junior cap.

Bill was a clever player who came to the club with a great reputation. Although his position was centre-half he played at centre-forward on four occasions and scored five goals.

Debut: 9 Sep 1899 v Tottenham Hotspur (A) 0-1 SL Div 1.

Dave Thomas

THOMAS David

(OR) Wing 5′ 8″ 10st 10lbs
b: Kirkby-in-Ashfield, Nottinghamshire, 5 Oct 1950
QPR: (£165,000) Oct 1972
Football League: 182-28. **FAC:** 14-2. **FLC:** 17-3.
Other: 7-1. **Total:** 220-34.
Honours: Schoolboy international. 5 England youth caps. 11 U23 caps. 8 full caps. 2nd Div runner's-up medal. 1st Div runner's-up medal.

The capture of David Thomas was probably Gordon Jago's best signing for QPR. He was part of the team that ended the season as runners-up in the First Division.

Dave was a two-footed winger who could centre the ball with immaculate precision from any angle. Fast and direct he could destroy his opponent with a sleight of foot or a swerve of his body. He left QPR in 1977, and played for several clubs during the ensuing five years. On retiring as a player, he took up coaching, first at Bognor Regis Town then at Brentford, and later became a landscape gardener, living in Prinsted, Sussex.

Debut: 21 Oct 1972 v Sunderland (H) 3-2 Div 2.

THOMAS Jerome William

Wing 5′ 10″ 11st 10lbs
b: Wembley, 23 Mar 1983
QPR: (Loan) Mar 2002
Football League: 4-1. **FAC:** 0-0. **FLC:** 0-0.
Other: 0-0. **Total:** 4-1.
QPR: (Loan) Aug 2002
Football League: 6-2. **FAC:** 0-0. **FLC:** 0-0.
Other: 0-0. **Total:** 6-2.

Despite twice coming on loan to QPR, Jerome only played a handful of games on each occasion, although he was recognised as an exciting prospect.

Debut: 30 Mar 2002 v Tranmere Rovers (A) 3-2 Div 2.

THOMPSON A

(OR) Wing
QPR: 1905
Southern League: 23-7. **FAC:** 1-0. **FLC:** 0-0.
Other: 0-0. **Total:** 24-7.

Thompson was a reserve who scored a hat-trick when he replaced Neil Murphy. But when Pentland moved to QPR Thompson was released.

Debut: 28 Oct 1905 v Plymouth Argyle (H) 2-0 SL Div 1.

THOMPSON Charles

(RB) Def
b: Bighton Banks, Hampshire
QPR: 1921
Football League: 1-0. **FAC:** 0-0. **FLC:** 0-0.
Other: 0-0. **Total:** 1-0.

Charlie made his one and only appearance for QPR in a match v Brentford, replacing Ben Marsden in defence.

Debut: 29 Oct 1921 v Brentford (H) 1-1 Div 3 (S).

THOMPSON Garry Linsey

Striker 6′ 2″ 13st 3lbs
b: Birmingham, 7 Oct 1959
QPR: (£125,000) Aug 1991
Premier/Football League: 19-1. **FAC:** 0-0.
FLC: 5-3. **Other:** 1-0. **Total:** 25-4.
Honours: 6 England caps at U21 level. League Cup runner's-up medal.

Garry was a tall, well built target man who was extremely strong in the air. He was released from Northampton Town in the summer of 1998.

Debut: 21 Aug 1991 v Norwich City (H) 0-2 Div 1.

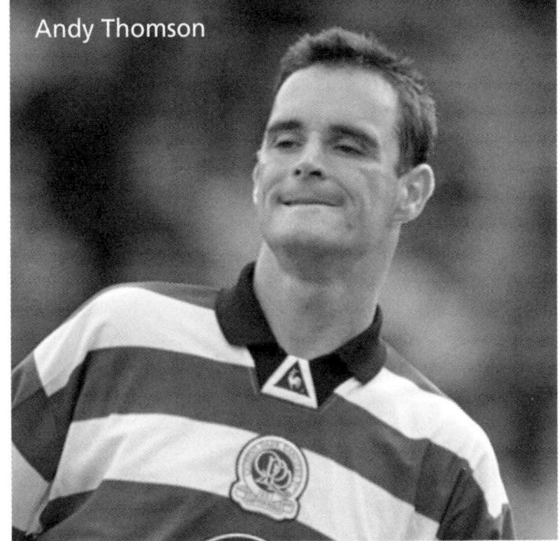
Andy Thomson

THOMPSON J

(RH) Mid
b: Willesden
QPR: 1924
Football League: 22-0. **FAC:** 4-0. **FLC:** 0-0.
Other: 0-0. **Total:** 26-0.

An ex-right-winger then a right-half and called upon to play in many positions, including centre-half and inside-right. This was the second time in three years that the club had finished bottom of the table, and Thompson was released at the end of the season.

Debut: 27 Dec 1924 v Newport County (H) 4-3 Div 3 (S).

THOMPSON Oliver

(LH) Mid 5′ 8″ 11st 2lbs
b: Gateshead, 11 May 1900
d: Chesterfield, 24 Jul 1975
QPR: May 1928
Football League: 18-0. **FAC:** 0-0. **FLC:** 0-0.
Other: 0-0. **Total:** 18-0.

Oliver was a constructive member of the team whose expertise at the time was invaluable. At Chesterfield, along with Shirley Abbott, he became the mainstay of the club. He coached the team and during the war took over as the first team trainer. He held the post until 1966 whereupon he took a slightly less active role as the club's masseur.

Debut: 1 Sep 1928 v Gillingham (H) 1-0 Div 3 (S).

THOMPSON William T

(OR) Wing 5′ 7″ 11st 0lbs
b: Morpeth, Aug 1886
d: Byker, 28 Dec 1933
QPR: 1912
Southern League: 119-6. **FAC:** 11-0. **FLC:** 0-0.
Other: 0-0. **Total:** 130-6.
Honours: Southern League v Football League.

Billy was known as 'Rubber' because of his elastic-type stature and spring-heeled displays down the right wing. He was brilliant at times but he could be very frustrating and temperamental too by all accounts. A very speedy and clever winger.

Debut: 5 Sep 1912 v Plymouth Argyle (H) 2-1 SL Div 1.

THOMSON Andrew

Striker 5′ 10″ 10st 13lbs
b: Motherwell, Scotland, 1 Apr 1971
QPR: Mar 2001
Football League: 90-29. **FAC:** 4-2. **FLC:** 2-2.
Other: 1-0. **Total:** 97-33.

Andy became the top goalscorer in the 2001/02 season although it was clear that he suffered from a back injury and was not fully fit when playing. He played in around half the matches in the 2002/03 season but lost his goalscoring form, netting just

two in League matches, and signed for Partick Thistle in July 2003.
Debut: 24 Mar 2001 v Burnley (A) 1-2 Div 1.

THORNTON H V

(IL) Mid
QPR: 1911
Southern League: 35-10. **FAC:** 1-0. **FLC:** 0-0.
Other: 1-0. **Total:** 37-10.
Honours: Southern League championship winner's medal.

Thornton joined the "Footballers Battalion" and became one of the casualties of the First World War, being killed in France.
Debut: 9 Oct 1911 v Reading (H) 3-0 SL Div 1.

THORPE Anthony

Striker 5' 9" 12st 0lbs
b: Leicester, 10 Apr 1974
QPR: (£50,000) Aug 2003
Football League: 41-10. **FAC:** 2-0. **FLC:** 0-0.
Other: 3-1. **Total:** 46-11.

Once the subject of a £1 million move (from Fulham to Bristol City in June 1998), Rangers signed Tony from financially-stricken Luton Town for a nominal fee in August 2003. The striker stayed two years at Loftus Road but was unable to repeat his previous goal ratio of one in just over two games and managed 11 in his 46 appearances for QPR. Spells with Rotherham, Swindon Town and Colchester United preceded a step down in non-League football in 2007.
Debut: 23 Aug 2003 v Bournemouth (H) 1-0 League 1.

TILLSON Andrew

CD 6' 2" 12st 10lbs
b: Huntingdon, Cambridgeshire, 30 Jun 1966
QPR: (£400,000) Dec 1990
Football League: 29-2. **FAC:** 0-0. **FLC:** 2-0.
Other: 1-0. **Total:** 32-2.

A good, dependable central defender whose heading and passing abilities from defence contributed enormously to a sound back four. A big money signing, he was at Rangers for less than two years, but remained at his next club for nearly eight.
Debut: 23 Dec 1990 v Derby County (A) 1-1 Div 1.

Tony Thorpe

TIMOSKA Sampsa

Def 6' 1" 11st 11lbs
b: Kokemaki, Finland, 12 Feb 1979
QPR: Jan 2007
Football League: 21-0. **FAC:** 0-0. **FLC:** 0-0.
Other: 0-0. **Total:** 21-0.

A free transfer signing from Finnish club MyPa-47 in January 2007, Sampsa quickly slotted into the Rangers defence and demonstrated his ability to play anywhere in the back four. The defender made just 21 appearances for the Loftus Road side before he was released from his 18-month contract by mutual consent and returned to MyPa-47 in early 2008.
Debut: 13 Jan 2007 v Hull City (A) 2-1 Championship.

TOMKYS Michael G

(OR) Wing 5' 8" 11st 0lbs
b: Kensington, London, 14 Dec 1932
QPR: Nov 1951
Football League: 91-19. **FAC:** 8-2. **FLC:** 0-0.
Other: 2-0. **Total:** 101-21.
Honours: English Youth international.

Mike was a genuine player who would give his all during a match, sometimes interchanging with the other winger or centre-forward. He made his debut at the age of 19 and was last heard of as the manager of Harrow Borough in 1978.
Debut: 17 Nov 1951 v Cardiff City (A) 1-3 Div 2.

TOMMASI Damiano

Mid 5' 11" 11st 9lbs
b: Negrar, Italy, 17 May 1974
QPR: Sep 2008
Football League: 7-0. **FAC:** 0-0. **FLC:** 0-0.
Other: 0-0. **Total:** 7-0.
Honours: 25 full caps for Italy.
Debut: 28 Oct 2008 v Birmingham City (H) 1-0 Championship.

TOSSWILL John Speare

(IR) Mid 5' 11" 12st 0lbs
b: Eastbourne, 1890
d: Brighton, 28 Sep 1915
QPR: May 1911
Southern League: 3-1. **FAC:** 0-0. **FLC:** 0-0.
Other: 0-0. **Total:** 3-1.

John joined the Royal Engineers at the outbreak of the First World War and was serving as a dispatch rider on the Western Front when he was wounded. He was brought home to Brighton but tragically died on the operating table.
Debut: 5 Apr 1912 v Southampton (H) 1-1 SL Div 1.

TOWERS Edwin James

(CF) Striker 5' 10" 12st 2lbs
b: Shepherds Bush, London, 5 Apr 1933

Damiano Tommasi

QPR: (Francis & Towers £8,000) May 1961
Football League: 28-15. **FAC:** 3-0. **FLC:** 2-1.
Other: 0-0. **Total:** 33-16.

Jim was a powerfully built, direct hustler for goals, who spelt danger to all opposing defenders. He was the other half of the duo that was known as the "Terrible Twins", the other half being George Francis. The "Terrible Twins" were the leading goalscorers for Brentford for seven seasons between 1955 and 1962. It is the only partnership traced in League Football to have scored 20 goals each in three consecutive seasons.

Debut: 19 Aug 1961 v Brentford (H) 3-0 Div 3.

TOWNSEND Luke

Striker 6' 0" 11st 10lbs
b: Guildford, 28 Sep 1986
QPR: Jul 2004
Football League: 2-0. **FAC:** 0-0. **FLC:** 0-0.
Other: 0-0. **Total:** 2-0.
Debut: 19 Apr 2005 v Burnley (A) 0-2 Championship.

TRAVERS James Edward

(CF) Striker 5' 8" 11st 6lbs
b: Birmingham, 4 Nov 1888
d: Birmingham 31 Aug 1946
QPR: May 1909
Southern League: 34-7. **FAC:** 7-1. **FLC:** 0-0.
Other: 0-0. **Total:** 41-8.
Honours: FA Cup winner's medal.

George, as he preferred to be called, was the son of Hyram Travers, the old-time music hall comedian known as the "Pearly King". His birth is still shrouded in mystery as a couple of other club histories have him born in different places, indeed the *Athletic News* states that he was born in Bow, London. It is known that he enlisted in the army in 1915 and it is said that he caught malaria while serving in the Far East, while others say he served in Salonika where he played for the British Army. He made six appearances for Spurs in wartime matches and retired from playing in 1931 aged 42.

Debut: 1 Sep 1909 v Watford (H) 4-3 SL Div 1.

TRODD William H

(RH) Mid
QPR: 1934
Football League: 6-0. **FAC:** 0-0. **FLC:** 0-0.
Other: 1-0. **Total:** 7-0.

Trodd took over from Dickie March when he was injured. This was at the time when one manager left the club and another arrived, and this proved to be his first and last season.

Debut: 13 Apr 1935 v Exeter City (H) 1-1 Div 3 (S).

TURNBULL Peter

(IL) Mid 5' 7" 11st 5lbs
b: Lanquhar, Scotland, 1875
QPR: Aug 1899
Southern League: 19-6. **FAC:** 6-7. **FLC:** 0-0.
Other: 0-0. **Total:** 25-13.

Blessed with natural athleticism, Peter knew how to control the ball at speed, a hard man to dispossess, yet he had to be in the mood, for not only did he show his brilliance at times but his inconsistency in other games. At Brentford he finished the season as top goalscorer in the Southern League with 15 goals.

Debut: 9 Sep 1899 v Tottenham Hotspur (A) 0-1 SL Div 1.

TURNER William

(LH) Mid 5' 10" 12st 0lbs
b: Southmoor, Durham, 22 Dec 1894
d: 1970
QPR: Jul 1927
Football League: 38-0. **FAC:** 1-0. **FLC:** 0-0.
Other: 0-0. **Total:** 39-0.
Honours: 3rd Div (S) championship winner's medal. FA XI v The Army.

Bill was a full-back who was quickly turned into a half-back at Southampton after an injury crisis. His last season as a professional was spent at Loftus Road. He was said to have been a very reliable player.

Debut: 27 Aug 1927 v Newport County (H) 4-2 Div 3 (S).

TURPIE Robert P

Mid 5' 7" 10st 8lbs
b: Hampstead, London, 13 Nov 1949
QPR: Nov 1967
Football League: 2-0. **FAC:** 0-0. **FLC:** 0-0.
Other: 0-0. **Total:** 2-0.

Bob was the substitute for Watson, who played at full-back for the club, and never really had a chance in a midfield position.

Debut: 13 Sep 1969 v Portsmouth (A) 3-1 Div 2.

TUTT Walter R

(OL) Wing
QPR: 1930
Football League: 7-3. **FAC:** 0-0. **FLC:** 0-0.
Other: 0-0. **Total:** 7-3.

Walter was one of the many left-wingers tried during this period. Eventually he became the substitute for Cribb.

Debut: 14 Jan 1931 v Bristol Rovers (A) 0-3 Div 3 (S).

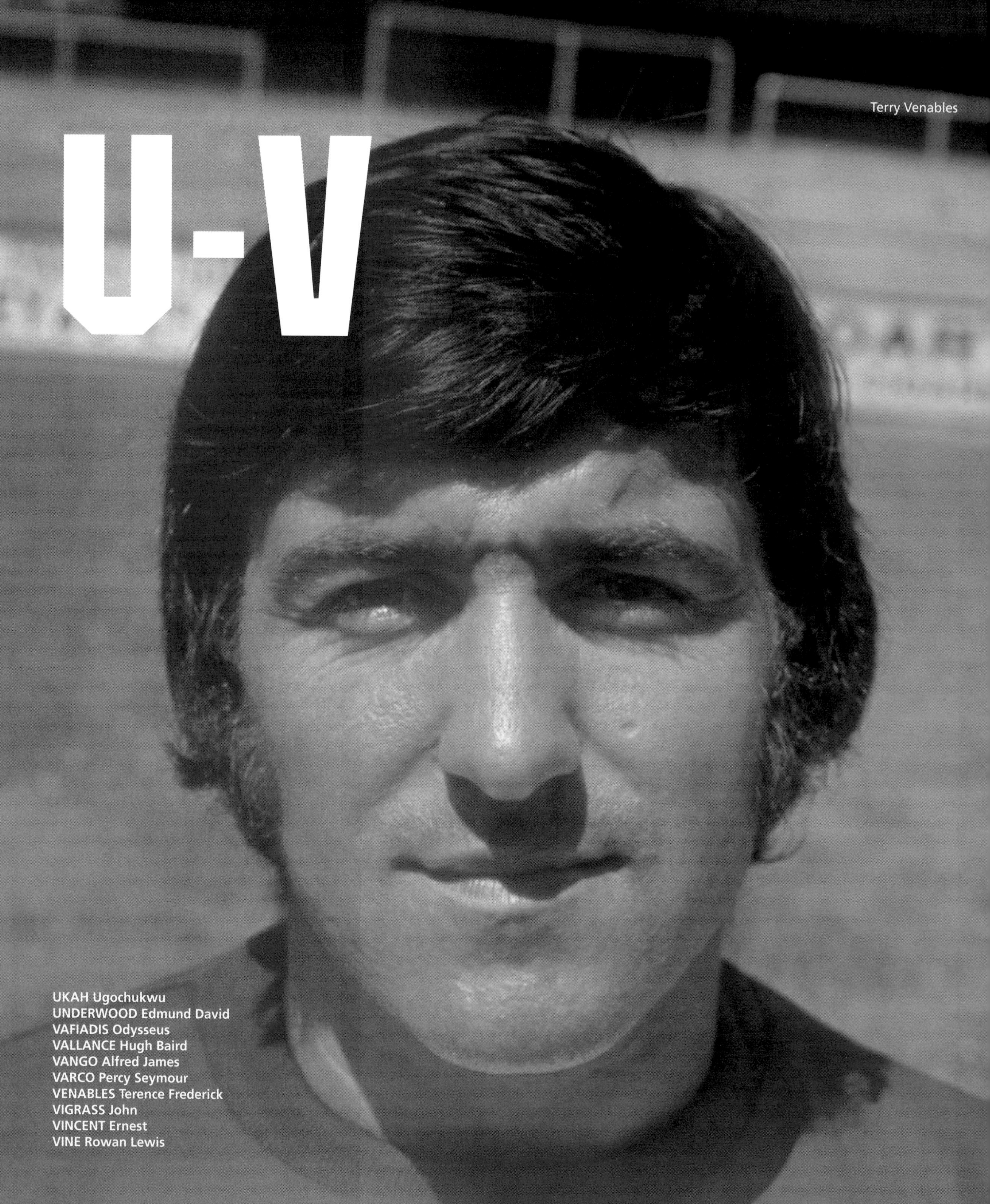

Terry Venables

U-V

UKAH Ugochukwu
UNDERWOOD Edmund David
VAFIADIS Odysseus
VALLANCE Hugh Baird
VANGO Alfred James
VARCO Percy Seymour
VENABLES Terence Frederick
VIGRASS John
VINCENT Ernest
VINE Rowan Lewis

UKAH Ugochukwu

Def 6' 1" 12st 11lbs
b: Parma, Italy, 18 Jan 1984
QPR: Aug 2005
Football League: 1-0. **FAC:** 0-0. **FLC:** 1-0.
Other: 0-0. **Total:** 2-0.
Debut: 20 Aug 2005 v Coventry City (A) 0-3 Championship.

UNDERWOOD Edmund David

Goal 6' 1" 13st 5lbs
b: St Pancras, London, 15 Mar 1928
d: South Africa, 1989
QPR: Dec 1949
Football League: 2-0. **FAC:** 0-0. **FLC:** 0-0.
Other: 0-0. **Total:** 2-0.

Dave was a genial and bubbly character who was the third choice goalkeeper at Loftus Road, after Harry Brown and Stan Gullan. He was given a free transfer to Watford, but within 18 months, Liverpool bought him to replace their regular keeper, Sidlow. However, when they dropped into the Second Division in 1954, Dave returned to Watford.

Debut: 19 Jan 1952 v Luton Town (H) 1-0 Div 2.

VAFIADIS Odysseus

Wing
b: London, 8 Sep 1945
QPR: Nov 1962
Football League: 15-4. **FAC:** 0-0. **FLC:** 0-0.
Other: 0-0. **Total:** 15-4.

After two years at Loftus Road, Odysseus first moved to Millwall before joining Jim Langley at Hillingdon Borough in 1965. He was with them when they sensationally beat Luton Town in the FA Cup in 1969.

Debut: 28 Sep 1963 v Millwall (H) 2-0 Div 3.

VALLANCE Hugh Baird

(CF) Striker 5' 11" 11st 12lbs
b: Wolverhampton, 14 Jun 1905
d: Birmingham, 1973
QPR: May 1928
Football League: 1-0. **FAC:** 0-0. **FLC:** 0-0.
Other: 0-0. **Total:** 1-0.

Hugh was a master at positioning himself, he also had a deceptive body swerve, but could not get into the side at QPR because of the form of record breaking George Goddard. So during the close season he was transferred to Brighton & Hove Albion, where he turned into a goalscoring phenomenon. He created a new club record, netting 30 in the League during the 1929/30 season.

Debut: 16 Feb 1929 v Watford (A) 1-4 Div 3 (S).

VANGO Alfred James

(CH) CD 5' 9" 11st 10lbs
b: Bethnal Green, London, 23 Dec 1900
d: Erith, 24 Nov 1977
QPR: 1930
Football League: 12-0. **FAC:** 0-0. **FLC:** 0-0.
Other: 0-0. **Total:** 12-0.
Honours: FA Amateur Cup winner's medal.

Alf was an amateur who was a very clever attacking centre-half but turned out for the club mostly at wing-half. He was a motor mechanic by trade.

Debut: 13 Jan 1931 v Bristol Rovers (A) 0-1 Div 3 (S).

VARCO Percy Seymour

(CF) Striker 5' 9" 13st 0lbs
b: Fowey, Cornwall, 17 Apr 1904
d: Fowey, 29 Jan 1982
QPR: Jun 1926
Football League: 16-4. **FAC:** 0-0. **FLC:** 0-0.
Other: 0-0. **Total:** 16-4.

Percy was a powerfully built player who was speedy and very hard to knock off the ball. Unfortunately at QPR he was out of the side for a long period owing to a fractured patella (knee-cap). When he recovered he was given a free transfer to Norwich City where he became very popular. On retirement from first class football he became a very successful fish merchant and later the Mayor of Fowey twice. He also became the official AFA coach in Cornwall in 1938.

Debut: 28 Aug 1926 v Crystal Palace (A) 1-2 Div 3 (S).

VENABLES Terence Frederick

(RH) Mid 5' 8" 11st 8lbs
b: Dagenham, Essex, 6 Jan 1943
QPR: (£70,000) Jun 1969
Football League: 177-19. **FAC:** 14-1. **FLC:** 15-2.
Other: 0-0. **Total:** 206-22.
Honours: England school caps, 1 amateur cap. 7 youth caps. Football League v Irish League. Young England v England. 4 caps at U23 level. 2 full England caps. FA Youth Cup winner's medals. 2nd Div runner's-up medal. League Cup winner's medal.

Terry was the first player to be capped by his country at all levels. On the field he was an accurate long range passer of the ball who had great vision for the game. Much of his career was spent at Chelsea and Spurs and he was at Loftus Road for a little over five years, where he managed more than 200 first team appearances, an average of 40 per season. After retiring from playing, Terry became the Crystal Palace manager in 1976, the same at QPR in 1980, and then Barcelona in 1984. The Spurs managership followed in 1988, the same for England in 1992, Australia in 1995, and Portsmouth in 1997, after which he became a TV football pundit. In 2002 he was appointed the manager of Leeds United, but was dismissed during the season.

Debut: 9 Aug 1969 v Hull City (H) 3-0 Div 2.

VIGRASS John

(CH) CD
b: Leek, Derbyshire
QPR: 1921
Football League: 66-1. **FAC:** 5-0. **FLC:** 0-0.
Other: 0-0. **Total:** 71-1.

John was a wing-half who was converted into a centre-half but when the club ended the season bottom of the Third Division (South) in 1924, he, along with many others, was sacked.

Debut: 22 Apr 1922 v Merthyr Town (H) 0-0 Div 3 (S).

VINCENT Ernest

(RH) Mid 5' 9" 11st 9lbs
b: Washington, Durham, 28 Oct 1907
d: Doncaster, 2 Jun 1978
QPR: Jun 1935
Football League: 28-0. **FAC:** 2-0. **FLC:** 0-0.
Other: 1-0. **Total:** 31-0.
Honours: Durham County schoolboy caps. Rest of the League v Wearside champions.

Ernie proved to be a strong and vigorous tackler who could play as a central defender in an emergency. He suffered a fractured ankle at Manchester United and on his recovery moved to QPR where he made 28 League appearances in two seasons. After his career in football Ernie worked at Haworth Colliery and later became the security officer there, retiring in 1972. He died six years later of cancer of the stomach. Ernie's brother played in the Football League for Durham City.

Debut: 31 Aug 1935 v Millwall (H) 2-3 Div 3 (S).

VINE Rowan Lewis

Striker 6' 1" 11st 12lbs
b: Basingstoke, 21 Sep 1982
QPR: (£1,000,000) Oct 2007
Football League: 38-8. **FAC:** 0-0. **FLC:** 0-0.
Other: 0-0. **Total:** 38-8.

Having begun his footballing career with Portsmouth as a trainee in 2000, Rowan found his first team chances limited and eventually signed for Luton Town at the end of the 2004/05 season. A big-money move to Birmingham City followed before he arrived – initially on loan – at Loftus Road. Three goals in 15 appearances preceded a fractured leg sustained during a freak training ground accident that kept him out for the majority of the 2008/09 campaign but he returned to full fitness in April 2009.

Debut: 3 Oct 2007 v Colchester United (A) 2-4 Championship.

Ray Wilkins

W-Z

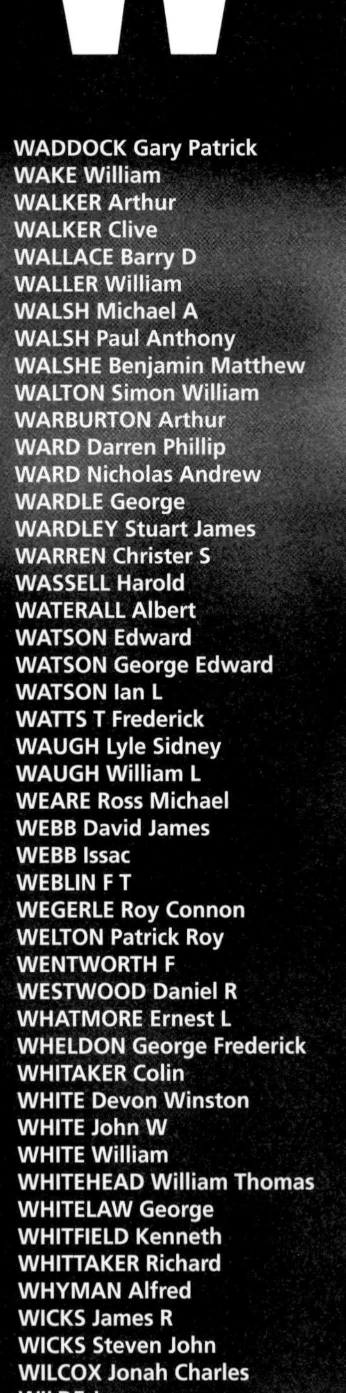

WADDOCK Gary Patrick
WAKE William
WALKER Arthur
WALKER Clive
WALLACE Barry D
WALLER William
WALSH Michael A
WALSH Paul Anthony
WALSHE Benjamin Matthew
WALTON Simon William
WARBURTON Arthur
WARD Darren Phillip
WARD Nicholas Andrew
WARDLE George
WARDLEY Stuart James
WARREN Christer S
WASSELL Harold
WATERALL Albert
WATSON Edward
WATSON George Edward
WATSON Ian L
WATTS T Frederick
WAUGH Lyle Sidney
WAUGH William L
WEARE Ross Michael
WEBB David James
WEBB Issac
WEBLIN F T
WEGERLE Roy Connon
WELTON Patrick Roy
WENTWORTH F
WESTWOOD Daniel R
WHATMORE Ernest L
WHELDON George Frederick
WHITAKER Colin
WHITE Devon Winston
WHITE John W
WHITE William
WHITEHEAD William Thomas
WHITELAW George
WHITFIELD Kenneth
WHITTAKER Richard
WHYMAN Alfred
WICKS James R
WICKS Steven John
WILCOX Jonah Charles
WILDE J
WILES George Harold
WILES Henry S
WILKINS Dean Mark
WILKINS Raymond Colin
WILKS Alan
WILLIAMS Brian
WILLIAMS Thomas Andrew
WILLIAMS William Thomas
WILLOCK Calum Daniel
WILSON Andrew Nesbit
WILSON Clive Euclid Aklana
WILSON Thomas
WILSON Thomas Carter
WINGROVE Joseph S
WITTER Anthony Junior
WOOD Arthur Basil
WOODHOUSE George F
WOODS Christopher Charles Eric
WOODS Patrick J
WOODWARD Horace John
WOODWARD Joseph Henry
WRIGHT Ernest
WRIGHT Paul H
WYATT A G
WYPER Henry Thomas Harley
YATES John
YATES Stephen
YENSON William
YOUNG Herbert
YOUNG John
YOUNG William A
YOUSSOUF Sammy
ZELIC Nedijeljko

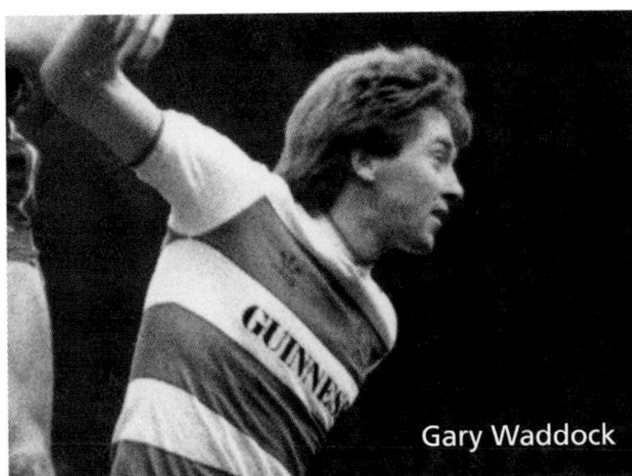
Gary Waddock

WADDOCK Gary Patrick

Mid 5′ 10″ 11st 12lbs
b: Kingsbury, London, 17 Mar 1962
QPR: Jul 1979
Football League: 203-8. **FAC:** 14-0. **FLC:** 22-2.
Other: 1-0. **Total:** 240-10.
QPR: Dec 1991
Football League: 0-0. **FAC:** 0-0. **FLC:** 0-0.
Other: 0-0. Total: 0-0.
Honours: Eire youth caps. 2 caps at B level. 1 cap at U21 level. 1 cap at U23 level. 21 full caps. 2nd Div championship medal. FA Cup runner's-up medal.

Gary was very much a defensive type of midfield player with a ferocious tackle, distributing the ball very quickly and accurately. He became one of the most popular QPR players at the time, qualifying to play for the Republic of Ireland through parentage, his father having been born in County Wexford. Locally born Gary's first club was QPR, where he stayed for over eight years, before he moved to Belgium. Very occasionally a professional footballer returns from a serious injury after a long period out of the game and is able to make a complete recovery. At one time it was widely believed that Gary's career was over after such an injury, yet his recovery was so complete that he won his 19th cap for Eire in 1990. Gary was released from Luton Town in 1998.
Debut: 15 Sep 1979 v Swansea City (A) 2-1 Div 2.

WAKE William

(LH) Mid 5′ 9″ 12st 0lbs
b: Bamburgh, Newcastle, 1887
QPR: 1909
Southern League: 175-1. **FAC:** 16-0 **FLC:** 0-0.
Other: 1-0. **Total:** 192-1.
Honours: 2 caps for London League v Birmingham League. Southern League v Scottish League. Southern League championship winner's medal.

Bill played for QPR for 10 years in total, turning out for them throughout the First World War, until retiring from the game in 1919. Hence four crucial years in his career were curtailed by the hostilities. By the end of the conflict he was aged around 32 and so just missed out (by a year or so) on appearing for the Rangers in their early Football League days.
Debut: 1 Sep 1909 v Watford (H) 4-3 SL Div 1.

WALKER Arthur

(CF) Striker 5′ 9″ 11st 0lbs
b: Ripley, Derbyshire, August 1888
QPR: 1907
Southern League: 28-15. **FAC:** 2-1. **FLC:** 0-0.
Other: 0-0. **Total:** 30-16.
Honours: Southern League championship medal.

Arthur was one of the top strikers of his day playing outside the Football League. He became the club's second top goalscorer in the 1907/08 championship season having been transferred from Nottingham Forest. He left for Notts County the following season but he was not as successful at his new club.
Debut: 14 Sep 1907 v Tottenham Hotspur (A) 2-3 SL Div 1.

WALKER Clive

(OL) Wing 5′ 8″ 11st 4lbs
b: Oxford, 26 May 1957
QPR: Dec 1985
Football League: 20-1. **FAC:** 4-0. **FLC:** 3-1.
Other: 0-0. **Total:** 27-2.
Honours: Oxford and England representative. 3 FA Trophy medals. Conference Player of the Year 1995. FA Representative XI v Isthmian League.

Clive was quick and had an unpredictable flair for scoring spectacular goals. In just under two years he made only 27 appearances for Rangers before moving on. Released by Brighton in May 1993, he had trials with Swansea City and Slough Town before joining Woking. For a short period Clive was the full-time player/assistant manager to Eddie May at Brentford in the 1997/98 season. He remained active in the GM Vauxhall Conference, not retiring from playing until May 1999, just a few days short of his 42nd birthday.
Debut: 17 Dec 1985 v Aston Villa (H) 0-1 Div 1.

Clive Walker

WALLACE Barry D

Def 5″ 9″ 11st 4lbs
b: Plaistow, Essex, 17 Apr 1959
QPR: Aug 1976
Football League: 25-0. **FAC:** 2-0. **FLC:** 1-0.
Other: 0-0. **Total:** 28-0.

After an unremarkable 25 League appearances in four years at Loftus Road, Barry visited, and then stayed on in the USA as a player during the 1980s.
Debut: 26 Oct 1977 v Aston Villa (A) 0-1 FL Cup first round.

WALLER William

(IL) Mid
b: Bolton, Lancashire
QPR: Feb 1924
Football League: 2-0. **FAC:** 0-0. **FLC:** 0-0.
Other: 0-0. **Total:** 2-0.

No fewer than six different players filled the position of inside-left in this re-election season, and Billy was sacked at the end of it.
Debut: 1 Mar 1924 v Bournemouth & Boscombe Athletic (H) 0-1 Div 3 (S).

Micky Walsh

WALSH Michael A

Striker 5′ 9″ 11st 5lbs
b: Chorley, Lancashire, 13 Aug 1954
QPR: (Exchange P Eastoe) Mar 1979
Football League: 18-3. **FAC:** 1-0. **FLC:** 1-0.
Other: 0-0. **Total:** 20-3.
Honours: 21 caps for the Republic of Ireland.

At his best, Micky was brave, quick and could control the ball at speed. However, he failed to show the fans at Loftus Road the sort of talent that they knew he had. On his return to England in 1989 he joined the backroom staff at non-League Slough Town where he remained until 1991. In February 1995 he was appointed joint manager of Chertsey Town. Micky was the proud father of quads in 1985.
Debut: 31 Mar 1979 v Derby County (H) 2-2 Div 1.

WALSH Paul Anthony

Striker 5' 7" 10st 8lbs
b: Plumstead, London, 1 Oct 1962
QPR: (Loan) Sep 1991
Football League: 2-0. **FAC:** 0-0. **FLC:** 0-0.
Other: 0-0. **Total:** 2-0.
Honours: 5 England caps. 9 youth caps. 4 caps at U21 level. London FA XI v England. European runner's-up medal. Championship winner's medal. Football League Cup runner's-up medal. FA Cup winner's medal.

Paul was loaned to QPR with a view to a permanent transfer. After an incident with Ray Clemence on the Spurs training ground, it did not materialise. Voted Young Player of the Year in 1984, he was tricky with the ball and was highly popular with an excellent work rate and 100% committal throughout his career. Finally in December 1997 he had to give up playing after an injury he sustained in February 1990.
Debut: 17 Sep 1991 v Luton Town (A) 1-0 Div 1.

WALSHE Benjamin Matthew

Wing 6' 1" 12st 12lbs
b: Hammersmith, London, 24 May 1983
QPR: Jul 2000
Football League: 2-0. **FAC:** 0-0. **FLC:** 0-0.
Other: 0-0. **Total:** 2.0

Ben made his League debut in the closing weeks of the 2000/01 season. He was a fast and direct winger who was a member of the U19 team that reached the final of the FA Premier Academy.
Debut: 28 Apr 2001 v Stockport County (H) 0-3 Div 1.

Nick Ward

Simon Walton

WALTON Simon William

Mid 6' 1" 13st 5lbs
b: Leeds, 13 Sep 1987
QPR: (£200,000) Jul 2007
Football League: 5-0. **FAC:** 0-0. **FLC:** 0-0.
Other: 0-0. **Total:** 5-0.
Debut: 11 Dec 2007 v Burnley (A) 0-2 Championship.

WARBURTON Arthur

(IR) Mid 5' 8" 10st 7lbs
b: Whitefield, Bury, Lancashire, 30 Oct 1903
QPR: Jun 1938
Football League: 17-0. **FAC:** 4-0. **FLC:** 0-0.
Other: 0-0. **Total:** 21-0.

Arthur was a hard working midfield player who showed boundless energy and put in some useful performances for the club in the last full season before the Second World War. He joined the RAF and became a PT instructor. As a guest during the hostilities he played for Rochdale, Bradford, Middlesbrough, Lincoln City and Bury.
Debut: 10 Sep 1938 v Brighton & Hove Albion (A) 1-3 Div 1 (S).

WARD Darren Phillip

CD 6' 0" 12st 6lbs
b: Harrow, Middlesex, 13 Sep 1978
QPR: (Loan) Dec 1999
Football League: 14-0. **FAC:** 1-0. **FLC:** 0-0.
Other: 0-0. **Total:** 15-0.

Darren was loaned from Watford for three months after an operation to remove a metal plate from his leg, and the move proved to be the making of him. Regaining his appetite for the game he soon became popular with the fans. But his loan period at an end, he returned to Watford in March 2000.
Debut: 18 Dec 1999 v Charlton Athletic (H) 0-0 Div 1.

WARD Nicholas Andrew

Mid 6' 0" 12st 2lbs
b: Perth, Australia, 24 Mar 1985
QPR: Jul 2006
Football League: 20-1. **FAC:** 1-0. **FLC:** 2-0.
Other: 0-0. **Total:** 23-1.
Honours: Capped at U20 and U23 level by Australia.

A rising star in his native Australia, Nick had trials with Leicester City and Brentford but chose to sign for Rangers in the summer of 2006. Despite scoring in his third outing, at home against Southend United, the attacking midfielder did not show enough promise to warrant a lengthy Loftus Road career and he found himself loaned to Brighton & Hove Albion in January 2007. He returned

Stuart Wardley

Down Under and signed for Melbourne Victory in December 2007.
Debut: 5 Aug 2006 v Burnley (A) 0-2 Championship.

WARDLE George

(OR) Wing 5′ 8″ 11st 7lbs
b: Kimbleworth, Durham, 24 Oct 1919
QPR: Jan 1949
Football League: 53-4. **FAC:** 1-0. **FLC:** 0-0.
Other: 0-0. **Total:** 54-4.

George was a very skilful player whose career was marred by the Second World War. He probably reached his summit during the conflict as a guest player; turning out in two Wembley Cup finals for Chelsea and in one scored a goal. Returning to Exeter City at the end of the war, George showed that he was in a class of his own. Often he would beat three or four players with the ball but his colleagues would not react quickly enough to take advantage. Accommodation was a problem in post-war Britain and unable to find a house in Exeter, he was transferred to Cardiff City. Two years later, aged nearly 30, he appeared for QPR for over two seasons during which time he appeared in over 50 matches.
Debut: 29 Jan 1949 v Southampton (H) 1-3 Div 2.

WARDLEY Stuart James

Mid 5′ 11″ 12st 7lbs
b: Cambridge, 10 Sep 1975
QPR: (£15,000) Jul 1999
Football League: 87-4. **FAC:** 5-3. **FLC:** 2-0.
Other: 1-0. **Total:** 95-7.

Gerry Francis, who plucked Les Ferdinand and Andrew Impey from non-League football, appeared to have found another gem of a player, for Stuart was voted the Player of the Year for the 1999/2000 season. He is mainly a right-sided midfield player but is extremely versatile and even took over in goal for QPR when Chris Day was injured. But after less than three years at Loftus Road, and nearly 100 appearances, he joined Rushden & Diamonds, after a loan period, in April 2002, and scored on his home debut.
Debut: 7 Aug 1999 v Huddersfield Town (H) 3-1 Div 1.

WARREN Christer S

Mid 5′ 10″ 11st 10lbs
b: Weymouth, Dorset, 10 Oct 1974
QPR: Jun 2000
Football League: 36-0. **FAC:** 1-0. **FLC:** 1-0.
Other: 0-0. **Total:** 38-0.

Chris came into the side when Paul Bruce was injured, but was unable to hold on to his place. He was one of four players to be tried in the left-back position by QPR in 2001/02 but after only a handful

Christer Warren

of appearances, and just two as substitute early in the 2002/03 season, he moved on to Bristol Rovers.
Debut: 28 Aug 2000 v WBA (A) 1-2 Div 1.

WASSELL Harold

(LB) Def
b: Stourbridge, Shropshire, 21 Sep 1879
QPR: 1905
Southern League: 3-0. **FAC:** 0-0. **FLC:** 0-0.
Other: 0-0. **Total:** 3-0.

A reserve defender who was never on the losing (first team) side at QPR, Harry was the cover for Newlands, and his final match was the 7-0 home defeat of Bristol Rovers.
Debut: 18 Nov 1905 v Watford (A) 4-3 SL Div 1.

WATERALL Albert

(CH) CD 5′ 7″ 11st 11lbs
b: Nottingham, 1 Mar 1889
d: 1963
QPR: 1926
Football League: 2-0. **FAC:** 0-0. **FLC:** 0-0.
Other: 0-0. **Total:** 2-0.
Honours: 3rd Div (North) championship winner's medal.

While Albert was clearly not lacking in skill, his greatest asset was his unquenchable thirst for the game. Following a disagreement with Notts County he went to Stockport County and developed into a versatile player who was equally adept as a wing-half as well as a centre-half. Both he and his football playing brother, Tommy, were called-up in February 1918, and Albert continued to play for Stockport until he was 37 years old. He made just two appearances for Rangers before his last move, to Clapton Orient. He retired in 1927 and returned to Nottingham where he became a pub landlord.
Debut: 18 Sep 1926 v Charlton Athletic (A) 0-2 Div 3 (S).

WATSON Edward

(RB) Def
b: Shotton, Durham, 1899
QPR: May 1922
Football League: 8-0. **FAC:** 0-0. **FLC:** 0-0.
Other: 0-0. **Total:** 8-0.

A reserve defender who usually covered the right-back position when injuries occurred.
Debut: 11 Sep 1922 v Brentford (A) 3-1 Div 3 (S).

WATSON George Edward

(OL) Wing 5′ 7″ 9st 2lbs
b: Shotton Colliery, Durham, 1914
QPR: 1934
Football League: 8-1. **FAC:** 0-0. **FLC:** 0-0.
Other: 0-0. **Total:** 8-1.

George had won several medals and trophies at junior level for the winter game but was more renowned for his ability at cricket in the summer.
Debut: 15 Sep 1934 v Brighton & Hove Albion (H) 2-1 Div 3 (S).

WATSON Ian L

(RB) Def 5′ 11″ 11st 11lbs
b: Hammersmith, London, 7 Jan 1944
QPR: (£10,000) Jul 1965
Football League: 202-1. **FAC:** 16-0. **FLC:** 14-0.
Other: 0-0. **Total:** 232-1.
Honours: 3rd Div championship winner's medal. 2 2nd Div runner's-up medals.

Ian signed professional forms for Chelsea after being at the club for two years. He never achieved a permanent place in the senior squad and was snapped-up for a song by manager Alec Stock, when he was languishing in the

Chelsea reserve team. Ian was a well built, burly defender, who gave great service to the club for nine years and played in the top three divisions of the Football League. However, he had a baptism of fire, being on the losing end of a 6-1 drubbing by local rivals Brentford. He was an ever-present in the First Division during the 1968/69 season, and missed just a few games on three other occasions. Just one solitary goal was scored, in the League, in 1969/70. Discounting his time at Chelsea, Ian was a true one club man, for he retired in 1974, aged 30.
Debut: 21 Aug 1965 v Brentford (A) 1-6 Div 3.

WATTS T Frederick

(LH) Def
b: London
QPR: 1919
Southern/Football League: 5-0. **FAC:** 0-0. **FLC:** 0-0. **Other:** 0-0. **Total:** 5-0.

An amateur full-back who occasionally turned out for the club when required to do so.
Debut: 3 Apr 1920 v Norwich City (H) 1-0.

WAUGH Lyle Sidney

(CH) CD
b: Newcastle-upon-Tyne, 1899
QPR: 1923
Football League: 5-0. **FAC:** 0-0. **FLC:** 0-0.

Ian Watson

WYZ

Dave Webb

Other: 0-0. **Total:** 5-0.

Lyle was an amateur reserve centre-half, who was not retained at the end of the season. He was one of many that suffered in the clear-out at the club at that time.

Debut: 12 Sep 1923 v Newport County (H) 0-3 Div 3 (S).

WAUGH William L

(OR) Wing
b: Edinburgh, Scotland, 27 Nov 1921
QPR: Jul 1950
Football League: 77-6. **FAC:** 2-0. **FLC:** 0-0.
Other: 0-0. **Total:** 79-6.

Billy's early football career was disrupted by the start of the Second World War and his permanent introduction to English League Football was not made until 1944, unusually during hostilities, at Luton Town. After six years he moved to QPR. He was an extremely fast and tricky winger who drifted past the opposition with ease. But his time at Loftus Road was limited to just three seasons. Billy retired from the game in M ay 1954.

Debut: 19 Aug 1950 v Chesterfield (H) 1-1 Div 2.

WEARE Ross Michael

Striker 6' 2" 13st 6lbs
b: Perivale, Middlesex, 19 Mar 1977
QPR: (£10,000) Mar 1999
Football League: 4-0. **FAC:** 1-0. **FLC:** 0-0.
Other: 0-0. **Total:** 5-0.

Gerry Francis discovered Ross playing for East Ham United and promptly captured him for QPR. Unfortunately he later sustained an injury which forced him to retire from the game.

Debut: 20 Nov 1999 v Walsall (H) 2-1 Div 1.

WEBB David James

Def 5' 11" 12st 11lbs
b: Stratford, London, 9 Apr 1946
QPR: (£100,000) Jul 1974
Football League: 116-10. **FAC:** 8-0. **FLC:** 14-2.
Other: 8-2. **Total:** 146-14.
Honours: FA Cup winner's medal. European Cup winner's medal. Charity Shield medal. League Cup runner's-up appearance.

A strong, robust and very versatile performer, who could play in almost any position on the field, Dave had a swashbuckling attitude to the game and was a favourite with players and spectators alike. When he joined QPR he partnered Frank McLintock at the back, as the club came within a whisker of clinching the championship of the old Division 1. The pair were reunited at Leicester City as manager McLintock attempted to shore up a hard-pressed defence. Disappointment was part of David's lot at both Leicester City and Derby County, but he was back on the promotion trail at AFC Bournemouth during his first stint at management in 1980. David also managed Torquay United in 1984, Southend United in 1986 and 1988, Milford in 1988, Chelsea in 1993 and Brentford from 1993 to 1997.

Debut: 17 Aug 1974 v Sheffield United (A) 1-1 Div 1.

Roy Wegerle

WEBB Issac

Goal 6' 1" 12st 0lbs
b: Worcester, 10 Oct 1874
d: Birmingham, March 1950
QPR: 1907
Southern League: 10-0. **FAC:** 0-0. **FLC:** 0-0.
Other: 0-0. **Total:** 10-0.
Honours: 2nd Div championship winner's medal.

Issie was a thoroughly reliable custodian, who had quick reflexes and was spectacular and agile. His early career was with various home town clubs, before 1904 when Sunderland paid £250 to West Brom for his services. Just 10 games for Rangers followed before a return to the Hawthorns. He retired in May 1910 to join the Army as a catering orderly. However, in August 1918, he made a comeback at the age of 43, when he turned out for West Brom.

Debut: 11 Mar 1907 v Brentford (H) 1-1 SL Div 1.

WEBLIN F T

(RB) Def
QPR: 1912
Southern League: 11-0. **FAC:** 0-0. **FLC:** 0-0.
Other: 0-0. **Total:** 11-0.

Weblin stood in for McDonald when he was injured.

Debut: 14 Dec 1912 v Merthyr Town (A) 0-0 SL Div 1.

WEGERLE Roy Connon

Striker 5' 8" 10st 2lbs
b: Johannesburg, South Africa, 19 Mar 1964
QPR: (£1,000,000) Dec 1989
Football League: 75-29. **FAC:** 11-1. **FLC:** 5-1.
Other: 1-0. **Total:** 92-31.
Honours: 2 full caps for USA plus U21 caps. League Cup runner's-up medal.

On his day a very exciting player who could be relied upon to pull something out of a dull match to brighten up the proceedings. Roy learnt his trade under the guidance of Rodney Marsh at Tampa Bay Rowdies. A wonderfully talented striker whose brilliant individualism was later sought after by a number of clubs in the 1990s. Roy was discovered in South Africa by the former Ipswich Town goalkeeper, Roy Bailey. He began to show his true potential while at Luton Town, which was sufficient to persuade QPR to pay a million pounds for him. It was here that he began to live up to his fee. His ability to twist and turn defenders inside out and score the most spectacular goals made him a great favourite with the crowd. His stay at Loftus Road lasted just over two years before he moved on for an even bigger transfer fee.

Debut: 16 Dec 1989 v Sheffield Wednesday (A) 0-2 Div 1.

WELTON Patrick Roy

Goal 6' 0"
b: Eltham, Kent, 3 May 1928
QPR: Mar 1958
Football League: 3-0. **FAC:** 0-0. **FLC:** 0-0.
Other: 0-0. **Total:** 3-0.
Honours: 3rd Div (South) championship medal.

30 year old Pat was transferred to QPR after turning out for Orient on nearly 300 occasions. He later went on to manage St Albans City and then Walthamstow Avenue before becoming the England youth team coach, and in 1969 Pat took the same role at Spurs, until 1976. He coached abroad for a time before becoming a PE teacher at a public school.

Debut: 31 May 1959 v Norwich City (A) 1-5 Div 3.

WENTWORTH F

(RH) Mid
QPR: 1909
Southern League: 7-0. **FAC:** 0-0. **FLC:** 0-0.
Other: 0-0. **Total:** 7-0.

A young solid player who only played for QPR during a single season, Wentworth was Archie Mitchell's stand-in.

Debut: 11 Sep 1909 v Clapton Orient (H) 2-1 SL Div 1.

WESTWOOD Daniel R

Striker 5′ 10″ 11st 5lbs
b: Dagenham, Essex, 25 Jul 1953
QPR: Jul 1974
Football League: 1-1. **FAC:** 0-0. **FLC:** 0-0.
Other: 0-0. **Total:** 1-1.

Danny came on as a substitute in the Boxing Day match v Leicester City and scored in the 4-2 victory, in his only appearance for the club.

Debut: 26 Dec 1974 v Leicester City (H) 4-2 Div 1.

WHATMORE Ernest L

(LH) Mid 5′ 9″ 11st 6lbs
b: Kidderminster, 25 Apr 1900
d: Kidderminster, 30 Jul 1991
QPR: Jun 1925
Football League: 78-3. **FAC:** 4-0. **FLC:** 0-0.
Other: 0-0. **Total:** 82-3.
Honours: Shropshire Senior Cup winner's medal. Birmingham & District League winner's medal.

His style of play led him to take more knocks during the course of a match than one can expect all season. Ernie was distinctive on the field of play with his bald head and there was no more an honest player on the pitch than this man. Ernie died a fortnight after breaking his hip in a fall at a Kidderminster nursing home.

Debut: 25 Aug 1925 v Torquay United (A) 4-3 Div 3 (S).

Devon White

WHELDON George Frederick

(IL) Mid 5′ 8″ 11st 5lbs
b: Langley Green, 1 Nov 1869
d: Worcester, 14 Jan 1924
QPR: 1901
Southern League: 14-6. **FAC:** 0-0. **FLC:** 0-0.
Other: 0-0. **Total:** 14-6.
Honours: 2nd Div championship winner's medal. 3 League championship winner's medals. FA Cup winner's medal (the famous double). 4 English caps. 4+ Football League caps.

Freddie was the youngest in a family of 10 and was a brilliant footballer, with an exceptional talent, and a great goalscorer, who simply loved the game. His intricate footwork often bemused the best defenders in the country. Fred also developed the art of the daisy-cutter shot; on bumpy pitches at this time, such a shot was a goalkeeper's nightmare and a high proportion of his goals were scored in this way! Fred was also a fine cricketer and played for Worcestershire from 1899 until 1906, and Carmarthenshire in 1910. In later life he became the landlord of the Farriers Arms in Worcester for a number of years. His brother, Sam, played for WBA.

Debut: 16 Nov 1901 v Reading (A) 1-7 SL Div 1.

WHITAKER Colin

(OL) Wing 5′ 10″ 11st 6lbs
b: Leeds, Yorkshire, 14 Jun 1932
QPR: Feb 1961
Football League: 8-0. **FAC:** 0-0. **FLC:** 0-0.
Other: 0-0. **Total:** 8-0.
Honours: League Cup runner's-up medal.

A speedy, skilful and confident winger who achieved some outstanding scoring feats, Colin recorded a century of goals from the wing in his League career, including eight hat-tricks, although ironically none for QPR in his brief career with the club. He was an all-round sportsman playing minor counties cricket for Shropshire and a single handicap golfer. He purchased a 40 acre farm and transformed it into a golf course. An RAF posting in Germany meant that he missed an England U23 cap while he was on Bradford Park Avenue's books.

Debut: 18 Feb 1961 v Hull City (H) 2-1 Div 3.

WHITE Devon Winston

Striker 6′ 3″ 14st 0lbs
b: Nottingham, 2 Mar 1964
QPR: (£100,000) Jan 1993
Premier League: 27-9. **FAC:** 0-0. **FLC:** 2-0.
Other: 0-0. **Total:** 29-9.
Honours: Anglo-Italian Cup championship winner's medal. 3rd Div championship winner's medal.

Devon was a big, cumbersome, awkward to mark striker, who was twice taken out of non-League Football to play in the professional ranks. After numerous transfers he was released in the summer of 1998 at the age of 34.

Debut: 27 Jan 1993 v Chelsea (H) 1-1 PL.

WHITE John W

(RB) Def 5′ 10″ 12st 6lbs
b: Manchester, 1880
QPR: May 1901
Southern League: 133-1. **FAC:** 7-0. **FLC:** 0-0.
Other: 0-0. **Total:** 140-1.
Honours: Southern League championship winner's medal.

Although christened Jabez, he always used the first name John. He was a ferocious tackler with a powerful kick. A football writer of the day wrote, "He had a cool and resourceful temperament about him." Brought out of non-League Football, John spent seven years at QPR during which time he averaged exactly 20 first team matches per season.

Debut: 28 Jan 1902 v Portsmouth (A) 0-1 SL Div 1.

WHITE William

(IF) Mid 5′ 9″ 12st 7lbs
b: Scotland, 1877
QPR: 1899
Southern League: 20-7. **FAC:** 5-1. **FLC:** 0-0.
Other: 0-0. **Total:** 25-8.

Bill hailed from the Scottish club Hearts and was good enough to walk straight into the Arsenal side and score on the opening day of the 1897/98 season. On his debut for Liverpool, Bill did the same again, scoring in the second minute of a Merseyside derby at Goodison Park.

Debut: 11 Nov 1899 v Chatham (A) 1-5 SL Div 1.

WHITEHEAD William Thomas

(CF) Striker
b: Saffron Walden, Cambridgeshire, 11 Sep 1897
QPR: 1925
Football League: 25-5. **FAC:** 4-0. **FLC:** 0-0.
Other: 0-0. **Total:** 29-5.

Bill was at Swansea Town when they won the Third Division (South) championship, but didn't play enough matches to qualify for a medal. Conversely at QPR, Bill was part of Bob Hewison's squad that had to apply for re-election for the second time in two years.

Debut: 17 Oct 1925 v Watford (H) 2-0 Div 3 (S).

WHITELAW George

(CF) Striker 6′ 0″ 12st 6lbs
b: Paisley, Glasgow, 1 Jan 1937
QPR: Mar 1959
Football League: 26-10. **FAC:** 0-0. **FLC:** 0-0.

Steve Wicks

Other: 1-0. **Total:** 27-10.
Honours: Scottish amateur international cap.

George was just one of six centre-forwards to be tried this season. He did, however, score on his debut for the club.
Debut: 15 Mar 1959 v Bradford City (H) 3-0 Div 3.

WHITFIELD Kenneth
(IF) Mid 5′ 10″ 12st 0lbs
b: Durham City, 24 Mar 1930
QPR: Jul 1959
Football League: 19-3. **FAC:** 4-0. **FLC:** 0-0.
Other: 0-0. **Total:** 23-3.

Full of promise in his early football days, Ken was in an exciting QPR side that ended the season in third place in Division 3. One year later, in 1961, he became the manager of Bideford Town for a time, then the coach of Luton Town and finally the assistant/manager of Cardiff City from 1974 until 1978.
Debut: 26 Sep 1959 v Tranmere Rovers (A) 3-0 Div 3.

WHITTAKER Richard
(RB) Def 5′ 9″ 11st 0lbs
b: Dublin, Eire, 10 Oct 1934
QPR: Jul 1963
Football League: 17-0. **FAC:** 0-0. **FLC:** 1-0.
Other: 0-0. **Total:** 18-0.
Honours: Irish schoolboy caps. 1 U23 cap. 1 full cap. 4th Div championship winner's medal.

This compact full-back became player/coach under Alec Stock, filling the gap left by Roy Bentley. Finally, in 1967, Dick became player/coach at Stamford.
Debut: 24 Aug 1963 v Oldham Athletic (A) 1-2 Div 3.

WHYMAN Alfred
(IL) Mid 5′ 10″ 12st 0lbs
b: Edmonton, London, 31 Oct 1884
d: South America, 1955
QPR: May 1909
Southern League: 153-22. **FAC:** 15-2. **FLC:** 0-0.
Other: 1-0. **Total:** 169-24.
Honours: Southern League championship medal.

Alf was a talented player who could fill any position except for goalkeeper. He gave QPR great service during the period leading up to the First World War. On retirement, Alf emigrated to South America in 1920.
Debut: 1 Sep 1909 v Watford (H) 4-3 SL Div 1.

WICKS James R
Goal 5′ 6″ 11st 0lbs
b: Reading, 1899
QPR: 1924
Football League: 5-0. **FAC:** 0-0. **FLC:** 0-0.
Other: 0-0. **Total:** 5-0.
Honours: Spartan League championship medal. Berks & Bucks Senior Cup winner's medal.

When Jim was at QPR, the club suffered a goalkeeper crisis and for a short period he was the only custodian available owing to injuries.
Debut: 8 Nov 1924 v Gillingham (A) 1-1 Div 3 (S).

WICKS Steven John
(CH) CD 6′ 2″ 13st 2lbs
b: Reading, Berkshire, 3 Oct 1956
QPR: (£300,000) Sep 1979
Football League: 73-0. **FAC:** 3-0. **FLC:** 6-0.
Other: 0-0. **Total:** 82-0.
QPR: (£250,000) Mar 1982
Football League: 116-6. **FAC:** 2-0. **FLC:** 17-0.
Other: 4-0. **Total:** 139-6.
Honours: 7 England youth caps. 1 U23 cap. 2nd Div championship winner's medal. Football League Cup runner's-up medal.

Steve graduated to the professional ranks from Chelsea juniors and was a first team regular at the age of 19 years old. A tall, solid and powerfully built player, who was dominant both in the air and on the ground, Steve was at the club twice for a total of six years. He eventually retired in 1988 after an injury which won him £202,000 in compensation, although a very brief comeback in non-League football was made the following year. Steve became the assistant manager at Portsmouth in 1989, the manager of Crawley Town in 1992, Scarborough in 1994, and had spells scouting for Lincoln City and Newcastle United. He finished his football career by coaching in the USA.
Debut: 25 Sep 1979 v Mansfield Town (A) 3-0 FL Cup.

WILCOX Jonah Charles
(CF) Striker 5′ 11″ 12st 0lbs
b: Coleford, Somerset, 19 Jan 1894
d: Shipham, 5 Aug 1956
QPR: May 1926
Football League: 9-2. **FAC:** 0-0. **FLC:** 0-0.
Other: 0-0. **Total:** 9-2.

Jonah was a natural goalscorer, although he didn't turn it on at Loftus Road. Scoring on his debut for Coleford, he later totalled 13 goals in eight matches for Bristol City during the First World War. At New Brighton he netted 35 goals in 42 League matches, which set a new club scoring record. At Bristol Rovers, Jonah became the top marksman in the 1925/26 season and the same for Gillingham in 1927/28 with 25 goals. In retirement he became the landlord of The Vine Hotel in Kidderminster until 1938, then the Golden Bowl in Bristol, followed by The New Inn at Blagdon for 14 years until 1955.
Debut: 28 Aug 1926 v Crystal Palace (A) 1-2 Div 3 (S).

WILDE J
(CH) CD
QPR: 1913

Southern League: 13-0. **FAC:** 0-0. **FLC:** 0-0. **Other:** 0-0. **Total:** 13-0.

The reserve centre-half who turned out in place of Archie Mitchell before the First World War. It is known that during the hostilities, he joined the "Footballers Battalion".

Debut: 23 Apr 1914 v Reading (A) 1-0 SL Div 1.

WILES George Harold

(FB) Def 5' 9" 11st 4lbs
b: East Ham, London, 1905
QPR: May 1929
Football League: 18-0. **FAC:** 0-0. **FLC:** 0-0. **Other:** 0-0. **Total:** 18-0.

A splendid all-round footballer, who during his career hardly ever committed a bad foul, George joined QPR as an amateur and embraced professionalism in 1930. He was physically a strong man who could battle it out with the toughest of characters, usually coming off best.

Debut: 5 Sep 1929 v Walsall (H) 2-2 Div 3 (S).

WILES Henry S

(CF) Striker 5' 8" 11st 0lbs
b: East Ham, London
QPR: 1929
Football League: 42-25. **FAC:** 1-0. **FLC:** 0-0. **Other:** 0-0. **Total:** 43-25.
Honours: Represented the United Services team in Egypt while in the RAF.

In the 1931/32 season at Loftus Road, Harry scored 11 goals in 11 matches. When he was transferred to Walsall the following campaign he notched 64 goals playing in the Midland Midweek League, the Birmingham Combination and various minor Cup competitions, plus in a handful of Third Division matches. He eventually left Fellows Park in 1935.

Debut: 31 Aug 1929 v Crystal Palace (A) 1-1 Div 3 (S).

WILKINS Dean Mark

Mid 5' 10" 12st 4lbs
b: Hillingdon, Middlesex, 12 Jul 1962
QPR: May 1980
Football League: 6-0. **FAC:** 0-0. **FLC:** 1-0. **Other:** 0-0. **Total:** 7-0.
Honours: Capped for Middlesex.

The younger brother of Ray, Dean was a stylish player who was dangerous at dead ball situations and was also an excellent passer of the ball. He retired in 1999 through injury.

Debut: 1 Nov 1980, Grimsby Town (A) 0-0 Div 2.

WILKINS Raymond Colin

Mid 5' 8" 11st 2lbs
b: Hillingdon, Middlesex, 14 Sep 1956
QPR: Nov 1989
Football/Premier League: 154-7. **FAC:** 13-2. **FLC:** 13-0. **Other:** 2-1. **Total:** 182-10.
QPR: Nov 1994
Football/Premier League: 21-0. **FAC:** 1-0. **FLC:** 3-0. **Other:** 0-0. **Total:** 25-0.
Honours: England schoolboy caps. 6 youth caps. 1 U21 cap. 2 U23 caps. 84 full caps. FA Cup winner's medal. Scottish Premier Division winner's medal.

Ray became Chelsea's youngest ever captain in April 1975 at the age of 18. Throughout his career he plied his services all around Europe. An elegant midfield general, he was at QPR twice, on the second occasion as the player/manager, during those last frantic seasons when he tried to keep the club in the Premier League. A regular in the England team, he made 84 appearances, and in total played in 200 matches for the Rangers. Ray resigned as QPR manager in 1996 and moved on to the same position at Fulham for a short time. From his TV appearances he was known for the overuse of the word "super" which led to a nickname of "Super Ray"! He finally finished his football career as the Chelsea coach.

Debut: 16 Dec 1989 v Sheffield Wednesday (A) 0-2 Div 1.

Ray Wilkins

WILKS Alan

Striker 5' 11" 11st 0lbs
b: Slough, Berkshire, 5 Oct 1946
QPR: May 1965
Football League: 50-14. **FAC:** 1-0. **FLC:** 3-5. **Other:** 0-0. **Total:** 54-19.
Honours: 3rd Div championship winner's medal. 2nd Div runner's-up medal. 4th Div runner's-up medal. England schoolboy caps.

A quiet and unassuming person off the pitch and on it he was cultured, gifted and sometimes a dazzling performer. Alan was a member of the squad that made the meteoric rise from the Third Division to the First in the late 1960s. In a League Cup match v Oxford United in 1967 he scored all five goals.

Debut: 27 Dec 1966 v Brighton & Hove Albion (A) 2-2 Div 3.

WILLIAMS Brian

(FB) Def 5' 8" 12st 12lbs
b: Salford, Lancashire, 5 Nov 1955
QPR: (£70,000) Jul 1977
Football League: 19-0. **FAC:** 2-0. **FLC:** 2-0. **Other:** 0-0. **Total:** 23-0.

A very dependable full-back but who was used mainly as a substitute at Loftus Road for just one season.

Debut: 20 Aug 1977 v Aston Villa (H) 1-2 Div 1.

WILLIAMS Thomas Andrew

Def 6' 0" 11st 8lbs
b: Carshalton, 8 Jul 1980
QPR: (Loan) Aug 2002
Football League: 29-1. **FAC:** 2-0. **FLC:** 1-0. **Other:** 1-0. **Total:** 33-1.
QPR: (Loan) Aug 2003
Football League: 5-0. **FAC:** 0-0. **FLC:** 0-0. **Other:** 0-0. **Total:** 5-0.

Tommy quickly became a crowd pleaser at QPR during the 2002/03 season with his charges from full-back and skilful play on the ball. He is a very confident player who always seems to have time to spare.

Debut: 10 Aug 2002 v Chesterfield (H) 3-1 Div 2.

WILLIAMS William Thomas

CD 6' 1" 13st 0lbs
b: Esher, Surrey, 23 Aug 1942
QPR: Jun 1961
Football League: 45-0. **FAC:** 2-0. **FLC:** 1-0. **Other:** 0-0. **Total:** 48-0.
Honours: England schoolboy caps. 8 England youth caps.

Bill was a powerful central defender, who was always dangerous from corners and free-kicks in the opponent's penalty area. He was converted into a central defender at WBA where he remained for three years. A long career in football followed, playing with several clubs, and then as coach to Sacramento Gold (USA) in 1979 and Atlanta Chiefs (1980). In 1981 he became the manager of Maidstone United, then the same in Durban (South Africa) in 1984. He returned to manage Maidstone 18 months later, followed by Gillingham and Dover Athletic. In May 2001 he became the director of football at Kingstonian.

Debut: 16 Sep 1961 v AFC Bournemouth (H) 1-1 Div 3.

Clive Wilson

WILLOCK Calum Daniel

Striker 5′ 11″ 12st 7lbs
b: London, 29 Oct 1981
QPR: (Loan) Nov 2002
Football League: 3-0. **FAC:** 0-0. **FLC:** 0-0.
Other: 0-0. **Total:** 3-0.

An excellent young striker who came on loan from Fulham, Calum prefers the ball played to his feet where his speed off the mark enables him to get behind the opposing defences.

Debut: 9 Nov 2002 v Northampton Town (H) 0-1 Div 2.

WILSON Andrew Nesbit

(IF) Mid 5′ 7′″ 12st 5lbs
b: Newmains, Scotland, 14 Feb 1896
d: Oct 1973
QPR: Oct 1931
Football League: 20-3. **FAC:** 3-0. **FLC:** 0-0.
Other: 0-0. **Total:** 23-3.
Honours: 12 Scottish full caps.

In 1915 Andy enlisted in the 6th Highland Light Infantry and was posted to France, losing his lance-corporal's stripes following a disagreement with another soldier. In 1918 a shell fragment shattered his left hand. Whilst in Stobhill Hospital, he was allowed out with the rest of the walking wounded to watch the Victory International between Scotland and England. Two of the Scottish players were delayed owing to a train breakdown, McMullan arriving in time, but not McNair, and Andy was drafted into a hurriedly re-arranged team, at centre-forward, and scored two goals!

He went on to make the position his own. He scored 23 of Scotland's 36 goals during the tour of Canada in 1922. Chelsea paid a record fee for him and he stayed for eight years. Andy later became manager of Clacton Town, then the Walsall manager until 1937 and finally the same at Gravesend & Northfleet. Still in London, he became a fine golfer, billiards player, and played bowls for England. He was a familiar figure at Stamford Bridge almost until he died.

Debut: 10 Oct 1931 v Norwich City (A) 1-2 Div 3 (S).

WILSON Clive Euclid Aklana

(LB) Def 5′ 7″ 10st 0lbs
b: Manchester, 13 Nov 1961
QPR: (£450,000) Jul 1990
Premier/Football League: 172-12. **FAC:** 8-1.
FLC: 16-1. **Other:** 3-1. **Total:** 199-15.
Honours: 2nd Div championship winner's medal.

This highly talented defender possessed speed and excellent passing ability as well as good ball control, and he was extremely popular with the fans. Clive was just as capable in midfield and was

widely thought of as the best uncapped defender in the country at the time. Yet, somehow his talents were never fully appreciated or put to the best use at Loftus Road, although for four of his five seasons he was a near ever-present in League matches. He made just one short of 200 first team appearances for Rangers, before moving on to Spurs for a four year spell.
Debut: 25 Aug 1990 v Nottingham Forest (A) 1-1 Div 1.

WILSON Thomas

(IF) Mid 5′ 8″ 11st 2lbs
b: London, Dec 1879
d: circa 1935
QPR: 1909
Southern League: 6-1. **FAC:** 0-0. **FLC:** 0-0.
Other: 0-0. **Total:** 6-1.

Little is known about this man, except that he was an amateur and he made his debut for the club on Christmas Day 1909, scoring the only goal of the match. His other five matches ended in draws.
Debut: 25 Dec 1909 v Norwich City (H) 1-0 SL Div 1.

WILSON Thomas Carter

(OL) Wing 5′ 6″ 11st 6lbs
b: Preston, Lancs, 20 Oct 1877
d: Blackpool, 30 Aug 1940
QPR: 1902
Southern League: 59-3. **FAC:** 3-0. **FLC:** 0-0.
Other: 0-0. **Total:** 62-3.
Honours: South v North international trial match.

Although he was on the small side, Tommy was sturdily built and was strong in possession. His forte was an ability to cross accurately from the wing and he was made captain as soon as he arrived at the club. A very popular player, he was described by one London correspondent as "One of the best outside-lefts in the Southern League." He married the daughter of an Oldham publican, and whilst with Bolton Wanderers was a publican himself. He became manager of Chorley of the Lancashire Combination in 1912 and finally was elected chairman of the board of directors at Rochdale in October 1919, running the club until 1923. Wilson also became proprietor of the Wellington Hotel in the town centre.
Debut: 3 Sep 1902 v Wellingborough Town (H) 2-0 SL Div 1.

WINGROVE Joseph S

(RB) Def
b: Southall, Middlesex
QPR: 1912
Southern League: 73-0. **FAC:** 3-0. **FLC:** 0-0.
Other: 0-0. **Total:** 76-0.

Joseph survived the conflict of the First World War after serving in the "Footballers Battalion" throughout but retired in 1921.
Debut: 23 Apr 1913 v Plymouth Argyle (A) 0-2 SL Div 1.

WITTER Anthony Junior

CD 6′ 1″ 13st 0lbs
b: London, 12 Aug 1965
QPR: (£125,000) Aug 1991
Premier League: 1-0. **FAC:** 0-0. **FLC:** 0-0.
Other: 0-0. **Total:** 1-0.

A tall, fast and mobile central defender who could use both feet and had a very fast turn of speed, keeping cool and calm under pressure, Tony was an expensive buy, for he was earlier rejected as a youngster, then made only one appearance in the first team. Three years later most of the transfer fee was recouped when he moved to Millwall. Tony was released in the summer of 1998 and became a cover player on a semi-permanent basis, but a knee injury in 1999 saw him dropping down to semi-pro level.
Debut: 14 Aug 1993 v Aston Villa (A) 1-4 PL.

Chris Woods

WOOD Arthur Basil

(IF) Mid 5′ 10″ 11st 1lbs
b: Southampton, Hampshire, 8 May 1890
QPR: 1923
Football League: 20-0. **FAC:** 0-0. **FLC:** 0-0.
Other: 0-0. **Total:** 20-0.

Arthur was a robust forward, who scored on his debut for Newport County against QPR which probably influenced the club to sign him the following season. However, he had the misfortune to play for four seasons out of five for the club that came bottom of the League: Gillingham – Southern League and the Third Division (South) – Newport County and finally QPR. Arthur finally retired from playing at the age of 37 due to a knee injury.
Debut: 15 Dec 1923 v Merthyr Town (H) 3-0 Div 3 (S).

WOODHOUSE George F

(RH) Mid
QPR: 1920
Southern League: 1-0. **FAC:** 0-0. **FLC:** 0-0.
Other: 0-0. **Total:** 1-0.

George Woodhouse "junior" played just one game for the club, his father George "senior", was an original member of the boys club, Christchurch Rangers, in 1882. Although moving to Berkshire, George senior, often journeyed to London to play, and was one of the pioneers responsible for the formation of QPR in 1886. Both father and son share what must be a unique distinction of having at various times been both player and director of the same club.
Debut: 3 Apr 1920 v Newport County (A) 0-3 SL Div 1.

WOODS Christopher Charles Eric

Goal 6′ 2″ 13st 5lbs
b: Swineshead, Lincolnshire, 14 Nov 1959
QPR: (£250,000) Jul 1979
Football League: 63-0. **FAC:** 1-0. **FLC:** 8-0.
Other: 0-0. **Total:** 72-0.
Honours: 9 England youth caps. 6 U21 caps. 43 full caps. 2nd Div championship winner's medal. 2 Football League winner's medals. 4 Scottish Premier Division championship winner's medals. 3 Scottish League Cup winner's medals.

Chris seemed an ideal replacement for Phil Parkes, possessing lightning reflexes and he could execute all the crafts of goalkeeping. Yet he lost his place to John Burridge. Chris later admitted that he lived too far from the QPR training ground and after 18 months he was transferred to Norwich City.
Debut: 18 Aug 1979 v Bristol Rovers (H) 2-0 Div 2.

WOODS Patrick J

(RB) Def 5′ 7″ 11st 6lbs
b: Islington, London, 29 Apr 1933
QPR: Jun 1950
Football League: 304-15. **FAC:** 20-0. **FLC:** 2-0.
Other: 7-1. **Total:** 333-16.

Pat was described by many critics as a fearless tackler and was noted for his well-timed clearances. A fine full-back and a cheerful character who left the club in 1961 to emigrate to Australia. During his 11 year long spell at Loftus Road, he made well over 300 appearances, and was an ever-present in the 1959/60 season Division 3 side. In the three previous seasons he

missed just five League matches. Pat returned to England some two years later to play for Colchester United for the 1963/64 season, where he appeared in most of the "U's" Third Division matches, at both left- and right-back. But he was soon to return to Australia.
Debut: 12 Sep 1953 v Walsall (H) 2-0 Div 3 (S).

WOODWARD Horace John

(CH) CD 5' 10" 11st 11lbs
b: Islington, London, 16 Jan 1924
QPR: (£10,500) Jun 1949
Football League: 57-0. **FAC:** 1-0. **FLC:** 0-0.
Other: 0-0. **Total:** 58-0.

After signing for Spurs straight from school, Horace was originally signed as a centre-forward and played as such as a 17 year old in the London War League. However, in 1942, he was sent to Finchley and turned out regularly for them. While serving in the Navy he was converted into a centre-half and made his debut in that position in September 1946. He was immediately made captain on his arrival at QPR in 1949. Leaving after two years, Horace finished his playing career at Stourbridge then became the Kingsbury Town manager in 1966 until 1971. He later worked as a bus driver for the British Oxygen Company.
Debut: 20 Aug 1949 v Leeds United (A) 1-1 Div 2.

WOODWARD Joseph Henry

Goal 6' 1" 12st 0lbs
b: Catford, Feb 1904
d: Lewisham, 1974
QPR: Feb 1928
Football League: 10-0. **FAC:** 1-0. **FLC:** 0-0.
Other: 0-0. **Total:** 11-0.

Joe was signed as cover for Joel Cunningham and indeed was generally the reserve goalkeeper at his other League clubs.
Debut: 17 Nov 1928 v Brighton & Hove Albion (H) 3-2 Div 3 (S).

WRIGHT Ernest

(IL) Mid 5' 9" 11st 7lbs
b: Middleton, Lancashire, 1912
QPR: Oct 1934
Football League: 1-0. **FAC:** 0-0. **FLC:** 0-0.
Other: 0-0. **Total:** 1-0.

Ernie joined the club as an amateur but after two months he became a professional. He was a schemer who could draw an opponent to create an open space before giving an accurate pass. The *Notts Post Football Annual* for 1937/38 described him as a "dextrous dribbler and a splendid shot."
Debut: 26 Jan 1935 v Brighton & Hove Albion (A) 1-5 Div 3 (S).

WRIGHT Paul H

Striker 5' 8" 10st 8lbs
b: East Kilbride, Scotland, 17 Aug 1967
QPR: (£275,000) Jul 1989
Football League: 15-5. **FAC:** 2-0. **FLC:** 2-1.
Other: 0-0. **Total:** 19-6.
Honours: Scottish youth caps. 3 U21 caps.

Paul, a phenomenal Scottish striker and scorer of over 100 goals in 350 Scottish matches, could not settle into the English game, so was soon transferred back to Scotland.
Debut: 19 Aug 1989 v Crystal Palace (H) 2-0 Div 1.

WYATT A G

(OR) Wing
QPR: 1909
Southern League: 10-0. **FAC:** 0-0 **FLC:** 0-0.
Other: 0-0. **Total:** 10-0.

A reserve player who stepped into the side when McNaught was injured, and only played in the latter part of the 1909/10 season.
Debut: 12 Mar 1910 v Exeter City (A) 0-0 Div 3 (S).

WYPER Henry Thomas Harley

(OR) Wing 5' 7" 10st 3lbs
b: Calton, Glasgow, 8 Oct 1900
d: Coatbridge, Scotland
QPR: Jun 1931
Football League: 11-0. **FAC:** 0-0. **FLC:** 0-0.
Other: 0-0. **Total:** 11-0.
Honours: 3rd Div (South) championship winner's medal.

Harry was a lightweight winger with sleek black hair and twinkling feet, who played for 10 clubs before QPR and moved on to five clubs after. On his retirement from the game, he took over the Peel Park Hotel (opposite the ground) in Accrington. He served in the RAF during the war, took over a guest house in Bournemouth then emigrated to Australia in 1949.
Debut: 28 Aug 1931 v Brentford (A) 1-1 Div 3 (S).

YATES John

(LH) Mid
b: Manchester 27 Nov 1903
QPR: 1929
Football League: 10-0. **FAC:** 0-0. **FLC:** 0-0.
Other: 0-0. **Total:** 10-0.

He was a player who hounded about the pitch like an "india-rubberman." John was a mobile left-half who deputised for Andy Neil during the 1929/30 season.
Debut: 9 Sep 1929 v Walsall (A) 0-4 Div 3 (S).

YATES Stephen

CD 5' 11" 11st 0lbs
b: Bristol, 29 Jan 1970
QPR: (£650,000) Aug 1993
Premier/Football League: 134-2. **FAC:** 7-0.
FLC: 8-0. **Other:** 0-0. **Total:** 149-2.
Honours: 3rd Div championship winner's medal.

Steve's career with Bristol Rovers was almost ended before it began. The club was in severe financial trouble in 1988 and without the generous offer of the supporters' club, who agreed to pay his wages in the first year of his career, he would have been released. Calm and solid, Steve had a no nonsense approach to the game and showed good aerial skills. He was voted The Young Player of the Year in 1989 at the age of 17. Steve was a big

Steve Yates

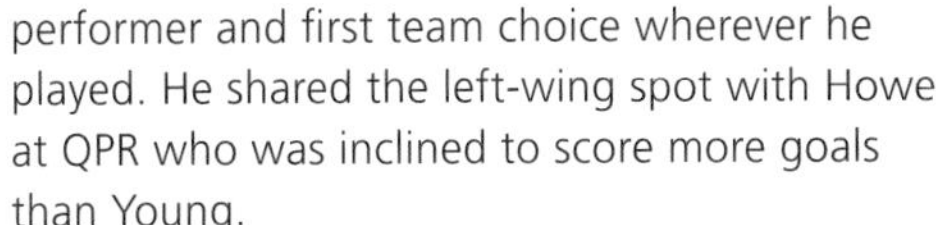

money buy by Rangers in 1993, and at Loftus Road he was noted as a fair opponent and a tough tackler.
Debut: 18 Aug 1993 v Liverpool (H) 1-3 PL.

YENSON William

(RH) Mid 5′ 9″ 12st 0lbs
b: Kingston Bagpuize, Oxfordshire, 1880
QPR: 1905
Southern League: 90-4. **FAC:** 4-0. **FLC:** 0-0.
Other: 0-0. **Total:** 94-4.
Honours: FA Cup runner's-up medal. Southern League championship winner's medal.

A tall, well built player who captained the side to the championship of the Southern League. Bill could use his strength in the tackle and was fond of throwing his weight about.
Debut: 2 Sep 1905 v New Brompton (H) 4-0 SL Div 1.

YOUNG Herbert

(OL) Wing 5′ 8″ 11st 7lbs
b: Liverpool, 4 Sep 1899
QPR: Jul 1929
Football League: 14-1. **FAC:** 1-0. **FLC:** 0-0.
Other: 0-0. **Total:** 15-1.

Bert was a fast and forceful winger, a consistent performer and first team choice wherever he played. He shared the left-wing spot with Howe at QPR who was inclined to score more goals than Young.
Debut: 31 Aug 1929 v Crystal Palace (A) 1-1 Div 3 (S).

YOUNG John

(LB) Def 5′ 10″ 12st 8lbs
b: Whitburn, Tyne & Wear, 1895
d: 1952
QPR: May 1926
Football League: 89-12. **FAC:** 2-0. **FLC:** 0-0.
Other: 0-0. **Total:** 91-12.
Honours: FA Cup runner's-up medal. 2nd Div runner's-up medal.

John was a left-winger who was converted into a full-back with considerable success. Upon his arrival at QPR he was given the captaincy and also became something of a penalty king. However, John was plagued by ill health and after a short spell with Accrington Stanley he decided to retire from the game, which enabled him to take over a farm near Sunderland.
Debut: 28 Aug 1926 v Crystal Palace (A) 1-2 Div 3 (S).

YOUNG William A

(IR) Mid 5′ 9″ 11st 6lbs
b: Ferrybridge, Durham, 1898
QPR: 1924
Football League: 8-2. **FAC:** 0-0. **FLC:** 0-0.
Other: 0-0. **Total:** 8-2.

Bill was an amateur who was released after the team ended the season bottom of the League for the second time in three years.
Debut: 21 Mar 1925 v Bournemouth (H) 0-2 Div 3 (S).

YOUSSOUF Sammy

Striker 6′ 0″ 13st 1lbs
b: Copenhagen, Denmark, 7 Sep 1976
QPR: Jan 2006
Football League: 6-0. **FAC:** 0-0. **FLC:** 0-0.
Other: 0-0. **Total:** 0-0.
Debut: 4 Feb 2006 v Leeds United (A) 0-2 Championship.

ZELIC Nedijeljko

Def 6′ 2″ 13st 8lbs
b: Sydney, Australia, 4 Jul 1971
QPR: (£1,250,000) Aug 1995
Premier League: 4-0. **FAC:** 0-0. **FLC:** 0-0.
Other: 0-0. **Total:** 4-0.
Honours: 33 Australian caps.

A big, strong midfield defender, who was captain of his country, and did an excellent job as a sweeper, Ned had to undergo an operation on his knee which was followed by a virus.
Debut: 23 Aug 1995 v Wimbledon (H) 0-1 PL.

THE MANAGERS 1907-2009

COWAN James
HOWIE James
LIDDELL Ned
HEWISON Robert
MITCHELL Archie
O'BRIEN Michael
BIRRELL William
VIZARD Edward
MANGNALL David
TAYLOR Jack
STOCK Alec
DODGIN William Jnr
DOCHERTY Tommy
ALLEN Leslie
JAGO Gordon
SEXTON Dave
SIBLEY Frank
BURTENSHAW Steve
VENABLES Terry
MULLERY Alan
SMITH James
FRANCIS Trevor
HOWE Don
FRANCIS Gerry
WILKINS Ray
HOUSTON Stewart
HARFORD Ray
HOLLOWAY Ian
WADDOCK Gary
GREGORY John
DE CANIO Luigi
DOWIE Iain
SOUSA Paulo
MAGILTON James

Terry Venables

COWAN James

1907-1913
b: Scotland, 17 Oct 1868
d: Scotland, 12 Dec 1918
Highest Achievement with QPR: Southern League championships, 1908 and 1912.

After James had retired from playing in June 1902, he coached the youngsters at Aston Villa for a while before taking the decision to move to QPR in 1907. The club had just moved to a new ground at Park Royal and had appointed their first ever manager. Jimmy Cowan gathered together eight new men and fitted them into a team. They were transformed into a title-winning combination, even drawing with Manchester United in the new FA Charity competition. QPR and Cowan repeated the feat four years later, and in the summer of 1912 the club undertook their first continental tour by visiting France and Germany, where all their matches were won. As the world was getting ready for hostilities, Jimmy offered his resignation on the grounds of ill health in 1913 to which the directors agreed. He went home to Scotland and died peacefully in his sleep.

HOWIE James

1913-1920
b: Ayrshire, Scotland, 19 Mar 1878
d: London, Jan 1963
Highest Achievement with QPR: 6th in the Southern League, 1920.

After playing for Kilmarnock, Kettering Town, Bristol Rovers, Newcastle United and Huddersfield Town, James was offered the job of manager of QPR in November 1913. Although the club was active throughout the First World War, the army commandeered the Park Royal ground in February 1915. So the club had to play out the rest of the war on their old Kensal Rise ground in Harvest Road. At the end of the war Rangers moved to the old Shepherd's Bush ground at Ellerslie Road in 1919, now known as Loftus Road. It was there that they played their last season of Southern League football. Howie left QPR in the spring of 1920 to manage Middlesbrough. Later he returned to London, where he ran a tobacconist's business. Howie died in January 1963.

LIDDELL Ned

1920-1924
b: Whitburn, Sunderland, April 1877
d: 22 Nov 1968
Highest Achievements with QPR: 3rd Division 3 (South), 1921; QPR 2 Arsenal 0, FA Cup 1921.

Ned was a centre-half who stood over 6' 0" tall and played his football for Sunderland, Southampton, Gainsborough Trinity, Clapton Orient, Southend United and Arsenal. Having retired from playing at the end of the First World War, Ned became manager of Southend United in their last season in the Southern League. He then became manager of QPR and discovered the likes of O'Brien and Chandler. Liddell was sacked in the close season of 1924 after the club had to seek re-election. Subsequently he was employed by Fulham as a scout and later he became manager. Ned guided Luton Town to promotion in 1937 and he was still actively involved in the game at the time of his death.

HEWISON Robert

1925-1931
b: Newcastle-upon-Tyne, 25 Mar 1889
d: Bristol, 1964
Highest Achievement with QPR: 3rd in Division 3 (South), 1929/30.

Before Bob Hewison took over the managerial seat at QPR the temporary manager, who was also acting secretary, Will Wood, ran the club. Hewison had been a wing-half in the Newcastle United team until after the First World War. In May 1920, Northampton Town paid £250 for Bob and made him their player/manager; he was there for five years. QPR secured him in 1925 and he managed the first side to play in the new blue and white hoops. Notably Hewison signed George Goddard, the club's all-time record goalscorer. Bob left QPR in the summer of 1931 and in March 1932 joined Bristol City where he spent 18 years, although from October 1938 until May 1939, he was suspended after a joint FA/League enquiry found several members of the club guilty of being involved in illegal payments. Hewison went on to manage Guildford City and Bath City.

MITCHELL Archie

1931-1933
b: Smethwick, Staffordshire, 15 Dec 1885
d: April 1949
Highest Achievement with QPR: 13th in Division 3 (South), 1932.

The original man to take over from Bob Hewison was John Bowman, an ex-player, ex-manager of Norwich City and Croydon Common and was at that time a QPR director. The club's move to the White City Stadium was imminent and Bowman was appointed manager in the summer of 1931. He was forced to stand down through illness before the new season had begun. However, the man who eventually took over from Bowman was Archie Mitchell, the ex-captain of QPR, who had managed Brentford from 1921 to 1925, then coached abroad and finally managed non-League Dartford before joining QPR again to coach the reserve team. The move up Wood Lane to the White City Stadium proved disastrous and although the new manager brought new blood into the side, attendances dropped dramatically and the club was forced to move back to Loftus Road. Within 18 months of taking over the managership of the club, Mitchell had gone, never to manage in the League again.

O'BRIEN Michael

1933-1935
b: Kilcock, Ireland, 10 Aug 1893
d: Uxbridge, Oct 1940.
Highest Achievement with QPR: 4th in Division 3 (South), 1934

Upon retiring from playing, O'Brien was immediately given the job of managing QPR in May 1933. He cleared out half the team and brought in six new players, but after the team ended the season in fourth position it suddenly collapsed to 13th the following year of 1935. O'Brien left the club in April, and later worked as the assistant/manager at Brentford, before taking up the job as manager of Ipswich Town, who were at that time in the Southern League and brought them into the Football League.

BIRRELL William

1935-1939
b: Celardyke, Fife, Scotland, 13 Mar 1897
d: November 1968
Highest Achievement with QPR: 3rd in Division 3 (South), 1937/38.

Middlesbrough captain Billy Birrell led them to the Second Division championship in 1927. Upon his retirement from playing he managed Raith Rovers, before spending five years at Bournemouth & Boscombe Athletic, where he struggled to keep the club afloat. In May 1935 he joined QPR and became the club's most successful manager since James Howie, missing out on promotion in 1938 by just three points. In May 1939 he took on the manager's job at Chelsea and steered the club to two wartime Cup finals plus two FA Cup semi-finals, before retiring in May 1952.

VIZARD Edward

1939-1944
b: Cogan, Wales, 7 Jun 1889
d: Wolverhampton, 25 Dec 1973
Highest Achievement with QPR: Won wartime "B" South League, 1940.

As a youth, Ted played football for Cogan Old Boys and rugby for Penarth, before joining Bolton Wanderers where he enjoyed a meteoric rise to fame. He soon made his debut for the senior squad and won his first international cap. Ted became the mainstay of the international side and was the caretaker/manager of Bolton Wanderers for a spell in 1919. In the first Wembley final year, he won an FA Cup medal in 1923 and another three years later. He played his last match in March 1931 at the age of 41 years. In 1933 he became the first full-time manager of Swindon Town, before, in the summer of 1939, taking over at QPR; but, alas, he only had wartime football to compete in. Nevertheless, the club was relatively successful throughout the war, and in April 1944 he was offered the manager's job at Wolves, for which over 100 applicants had applied. He was sacked in 1948 and finally took the job as manager of Cradley Heath in 1949.

MANGNALL David

1944-1952
b: Wigan, Lancashire, 21 Sep 1905
d: Penzance, 10 Apr 1962.
Highest Achievements with QPR: Champions Division 3 (South), 1948, 13th in Division 2, 1949

In his playing days, Dave was a bustling centre-forward who had a deceptive body swerve and was a prolific scorer. He once scored 10 goals in a reserve match for Leeds United but could not find a regular first team place, but was more successful after his move to Huddersfield Town. Dave Mangnall joined QPR in May 1939 and played for the club throughout the Second World War scoring many goals. He was reluctant to take the job of manager towards the end of the war, but in the end he accepted the offer and went on to build a fine side. The gradual break-up of the team, including Allen to Manchester United and Powell to Aston Villa, saw Mangnall leave the club after their relegation.

TAYLOR Jack

1952-1959
b: Barnsley, 15 Feb 1914
d: Barnsley, 22 Feb 1978
Highest Achievement with QPR: 10th in Division 3 (South), 1957 and 1958.

As a player Jack joined Wolves in 1931 staying with the club until 1938 when he joined Norwich City. After the war he played for Hull City and became the Weymouth player/manager in 1950 before becoming the QPR manager in 1952. At Loftus Road he was a solid if unspectacular manager who often picked up useful players from around the Leeds area. Taylor left QPR in May 1959 to take over the managership at Leeds United, who were relegated in 1960, but he resigned in March 1961, never to manage again.

STOCK Alexander

1959-1968
b: Somerset, 30 Mar 1917
d: Somerset, 16 Apr 2001
Highest Achievements with QPR: League Cup winners, 1967, Division 3 champions, 1967; 2nd in Division 2 (promoted to Division 1), 1968.

Alec, a miner's son, signed for Charlton Athletic, then joined QPR on loan in 1938, before signing permanently a year later. During the war he became a captain, and later major (after being wounded in the 1944 D Day landings). In the summer of 1946, Alec became the player/manager of Yeovil Town, and led them on their famous FA Cup run of 1949. That same year he joined Leyton Orient, won them the championship of the Third Division (South) in 1956, and had short spells at Arsenal and AS Roma. The managership of QPR followed, in August 1959, and one of the most exciting periods in the club's history unfolded during the next few years. By finishing eighth in the old Third South, he secured a place in the new Third Division in 1960, with a third final placing a year later. Four moderate seasons followed, before another third place in 1966, and at last the championship a year later plus the capture of the League Cup. Amazingly, Alec secured the runner's-up place in the Second Division the following season, just one point behind champions Ipswich Town, and so up to the First Division for the first time in the club's history. But after this nine year stint in charge, and before even selecting a First Division team, Stock resigned, and second in command, Bill Dodgin Jnr, took over as caretaker/manager. Stock later became the manager at Luton Town and Fulham, and a QPR director in 1977.

DODGIN William Jnr

Jun 1968-Nov 1968
b: Wardley, Durham, 4 Nov 1931
d: Jun 2000
Highest Achievement with QPR: (No complete season).

Coach Jimmy Andrews took over the managership for a very short period, before former Arsenal and Fulham player Bill Dodgin Jnr became caretaker/manager until the arrival of Tommy Docherty in November 1968. Bill went on to manage Fulham, Northampton Town in 1973 (and again in 1980), Brentford in 1976, and Woking.

Tommy Docherty

DOCHERTY Thomas

Nov 1968 and 1979-1980
b: Glasgow, Scotland, 24 Aug 1928
Highest Achievement with QPR: 5th in Division 2, 1979/80.

In November 1968, Scot and former Preston and Arsenal player Tommy Docherty was lured to Loftus Road. He wanted a move back to London and wished for First Division football again. But he soon realised he had made a mistake and sensationally quit the club after 28 days. Tommy had resented the influence of chairman Jim Gregory who wanted control over the signing of players and Docherty was refused permission to sign Brian Tiler from his former club Rotherham United. The ex-Chelsea manager was not out of work for long for he was snapped up by Aston Villa the following month. On his appointment as manager for the second time, in 1979, the much travelled and by now controversial Docherty stayed longer and the club ended the season fifth in the Second Division. However, by November of the following season and with the club in the relegation zone Tommy was sacked.

Les Allen

ALLEN Leslie

1968-1971
b: Dagenham, Essex, 4 Sep 1937
Highest Achievement with QPR: 9th in Division 2, 1970.

Les was one of the legendary Spurs players of the early 1960s who was part of the famous "Double team". He was transferred to QPR in a £21,000 deal from the north London club. Allen was made player/manager after the tempestuous 28 day reign of Tommy Docherty. He sold Roger Morgan to Spurs for £110,000 and then bought Terry Venables for

£50,000, both transfer fees breaking QPR records. Les remained at QPR until January 1971 after suffering immediate relegation back to the Second Division and two moderate seasons at that level.

JAGO Gordon

1971-1974
b: Poplar, London, 22 Oct 1932
Highest Achievements with QPR: Runners-up in Division 3, 1973; 8th in Division 1, 1974.

Former Charlton player Gordon Jago was Les Allen's assistant and it was natural that he took over the hot seat. He sold Rodney Marsh to Manchester City for £90,000, and took QPR into the First Division in 1973 followed by a very creditable eighth in the table a year later. In October 1974 Jago took over the managership of the Millwall club until 1978 when he emigrated to the USA, and became a successful soccer coach there.

Dave Sexton

SEXTON David

1974-1977
b: Islington, London, 6 Apr 1930
Highest Achievement with QPR: Runners-up to the League champions, 1976.

Former West Ham, Leyton Orient and Brighton player of the 1950s Dave Sexton became the manager of QPR 13 days after being sacked by Chelsea. In 1976 the club had its best ever season when they came second to Liverpool with only one point separating them. The club entered Europe and reached the quarter-finals of the UEFA Cup in 1977. The League Cup semi-finals were reached in the same year, but come summer and Dave was tempted away, with a lucrative offer, to Manchester United.

SIBLEY Frank

1977-1978 and 1984-1985
b: London, 4 Dec 1947
Highest Achievement with QPR: 19th in the 1st Division.

Former QPR player Frank Sibley, who had to retire prematurely due to injury, was promoted from head coach to manager after the departure of Sexton to Manchester United. Following the most successful period in the history of QPR, a season of woe was about to unfold. The club were lucky to cling on to their First Division status, but Sibley was at least responsible for the signing of Leighton James and Dave Needham. In July 1978 Sibley resigned and was replaced initially by Alec Stock, who was by then a director of the club, and eventually by Steve Burtenshaw. Frank, who on and off has spend a lifetime at QPR, made a brief return to the hot seat for a few months in 1984/85.

BURTENSHAW Steve

1978-1979
b: Portslade, Brighton, Sussex, 23 Nov 1935
Highest Achievement with QPR: 20th in Division 1 in 1978/79.

The former Brighton and Arsenal player Steve Burtenshaw was next in line. Steve's only season in charge at Loftus Road ended in disaster with QPR being relegated. Chairman Jim Gregory sacked him after only 10 months of his three year contract. Burtenshaw had been in charge at Hillsborough when they suffered the same fate. At Everton he lasted just a month as caretaker/manager in 1977.

VENABLES Terence

1980-1984
b: Bethnal Green, London, 6 Jan 1943.
Highest Achievements with QPR: FA Cup runner's-up after a replay, 1982; Division 2 championship, 1983; 5th in Division 1, 1984

After the second departure of Tommy Docherty, came the arrival of Terry Venables. The story of his career is well documented among the players. He is well known for his abilities as a coach and for man management. The championship of the Second Division was won in 1983 with 10 points to spare over their nearest rivals. A huge offer to manage Barcelona was received from Spain and so Venables left the club with his assistant Allan Harris.

MULLERY Alan

1984
b: Notting Hill, London, 23 Nov 1941
Highest Achievement with QPR: (No complete season).

Chairman Jim Gregory wished Terry Venables the best of luck and promptly appointed Alan Mullery in his place in June 1984. Alan had managed Brighton & Hove Albion, Charlton Athletic, Crystal Palace and now QPR. Jago stood-in for a short while but Mullery was sacked by Gregory in December 1984. Sibley once again took over for the rest of the season.

SMITH James

1985-1988
b: Sheffield, 17 Oct 1940.
Highest Achievements with QPR: League Cup runners-up, 1986; 5th in the 1st Division, 1988

Within a year Smith had taken QPR to the League Cup final at Wembley. He brought many fine players to Loftus Road including David Seaman, Paul Parker and Dean Coney. The other teams to be managed by Smith had been Boston United, Colchester United, Blackburn Rovers, Birmingham City and Oxford United and after leaving QPR he went on to manage Newcastle United, Portsmouth and Derby County.

FRANCIS Trevor

1988-1989
b: Plymouth, Devon, 19 Apr 1954.
Highest Achievement with QPR: 9th in the 1st Division, 1989

A schoolboy wonder, he was the first 16 year old to score four goals in a League match. Later he became the first English player to be transferred for £1,000,000. Francis had an unhappy spell as player/manager and the club struggled in the First Division during his spell in charge. Trevor tried to be a disciplinarian which didn't really suit his temperament and the players didn't respond. There was also some adverse publicity after the firing of a player who had decided to attend the birth of his first born rather than appear in the first team squad. It was an error of judgment on Trevor's part and he was sacked shortly afterwards.

Trevor Francis

HOWE Donald

1989-1991
b: Wolverhampton, 12 Oct 1935
Highest Achievement at QPR: 11th in the 1st Division, 1990.

At the time of his appointment Don was the coach at QPR. As well as a former player, he had been the manager of Arsenal and the England assistant/manager. Don had worked in Turkey and in Saudi Arabia and despite his qualifications and respect in the game, and a reasonable record at Loftus Road, he did not enjoy the job, and after only 18 months, he left and moved across London to Wimbledon.

Don Howe

FRANCIS Gerald

1991-1994 and 1998-2001
b: Chiswick, Middlesex, 6 Dec 1951
Highest Achievement with QPR: 5th in the Premier League, 1993.

Gerry Francis (who hardly needs an introduction) was appointed, and under him QPR ended their first season in the Premier League in fifth position, becoming the top London club in 1992/93. But his future at Loftus Road was in some doubt after talk of the possibility of selling his stars, Les Ferdinand and Andy Sinton to balance the books. Francis was reluctant to sell despite pressure from the boardroom. He was also in charge in 2001 when they dropped into Division 2 and went into administration.

Gerry Francis

WILKINS Raymond

1994-1996
b: Hillingdon, Middlesex, 14 Sep 1956
Highest Achievement with QPR: 8th in the Premier League, 1995.

Much travelled and then current player (since 1989), former England captain Ray Wilkins took over the combined player/manager job when Gerry Francis left for Spurs in 1994. At the end of his first season he lifted the team from near the bottom to a very respectable eighth. But relegation genuinely hit him hard, and it became too much for this elegant midfield general and so he left the club.

HOUSTON Stewart

1996-1997
b: Dunoon, Scotland, 20 Aug 1949
Highest Achievement with QPR: 9th in the 1st Division, 1997.

Ex-Manchester United defender Stewart Houston sat in the managerial seat at QPR during this period when caretaker boss Frank Sibley moved aside in September 1996. His one complete season was moderately successful, but in December 1997 he stepped down to make way for Ray Harford.

Stewart Houston

HARFORD Raymond

1997-1998
b: Halifax, Yorkshire, 1 June 1945
d: 9 Aug 2003
Highest Achievement with QPR: 21st in the 1st Division, 1998.

Ray was the most successful manager ever to lead Luton Town, yet he still ended up getting the sack, with the chairman stating that he didn't smile enough. Retiring as a player in 1976, he became the youth team coach at Fulham and eventually became their manager. He managed Wimbledon and was also part of the Blackburn Rovers set up when they won the Premiership. His time as manager at QPR was both limited and disastrous despite his high pedigree elsewhere. Ray died in August 2003.

Ian Holloway

HOLLOWAY Ian

2001-2006
b: Kingswood, 12 Mar 1963
Highest Achievements with QPR: Runners-up in the 2nd Division, 2004; 11th in the Championship 2005.

When the club went into administration in 2001, Gerry Francis was sacked from the manager's job and Ian Holloway was brought in. Once a player with QPR, he had played alongside a number of former Bristol Rovers team-mates, Dennis Bailey, Gary Penrice, Devon White and Steve Yates. He is the son of the well-respected local amateur, Bill Holloway. Ian is a great credit to his profession on and off the field and remains one of the club's most popular characters, and there can be no finer example for any young footballer to emulate. Ian exceeded all expectations, and performed marvels at the club when he guided the club to the divisional play-off final at Cardiff in 2003. The lottery of the play-offs were not needed the following campaign as Ian led the club to promotion behind champions Plymouth Argyle, the club he joined in June 2006. This position lasted until November 2007 when Ian joined Leicester City but relegation brought an end to his time in charge at the Walkers Stadium and Ian's next position was as manager of Blackpool in May 2009.

WADDOCK Gary

Feb 2006-Sep 2006

b: Kingsbury, 17 Mar 1962

Highest Achievement with QPR: (No complete season).

A QPR stalwart with more than 200 appearances between 1979 and 1987, Gary took charge after Ian Holloway's departure to pastures new. Having played for numerous clubs such as Charleroi (Belgium), Millwall, Bristol Rovers and Luton Town – including being a seasoned member of the Republic of Ireland squad – during a distinguished career, Gary's wealth of experience was vital with Rangers battling to preserve their Championship status. A poor start to the 2006/07 season, however, saw Gary replaced although he did stay on as assistant/manager until appointed manager of Aldershot Town in May 2007.

GREGORY John

2006-2007

b: Scunthorpe, 11 May 1954

Highest Achievement with QPR: 18th in the Championship, 2007.

John Gregory was an extremely experienced manager by the time he arrived at Loftus Road in September 2006. Another former QPR player, John had also enjoyed lengthy spells with Northampton Town, Aston Villa, Brighton & Hove Albion and Derby County before hanging up his boots in 1990. His managerial career began at Portsmouth but also included stints in charge of Plymouth Argyle, Wycombe Wanderers, Aston Villa and Derby County before sitting in the Rangers hotseat. Taking over from his predecessor, the club was at the bottom of the Championship but survival was secured. As with Gary Waddock, however, a poor run of results at the start of the 2007/08 campaign saw his contract terminated on 1 October.

John Gregory

DE CANIO Luigi

2007-2008

b: Matera, Italy, 26 Sep 1957

Highest Achievement with QPR: 14th in the Championship, 2008.

A relative unknown when he took the manager's job at QPR, having spent his playing and managerial career in Italy with teams such as Matera and Pisticci, Luigi De Canio arrived at Loftus Road and transformed the team's fortunes. A decent run of results led to a comfortable 14th placed finish in the Championship but the popular Italian's contract was terminated by mutual consent in May 2008. It has been alleged that Luigi returned to his home country in an effort to save his marriage.

Luigi De Canio

DOWIE Iain

May 2008-Oct 2008

b: Hatfield, 9 Jan 1965

Highest Achievement with QPR: (No complete season).

A former Northern Ireland international striker who scored 12 times in 59 appearances for his country, Iain's playing career ranged from non-League (with Cheshunt) to the Premiership (with Southampton). His managerial career kicked off with a caretaker stint at QPR after Ray Harford's departure in 1998 before moving on to Oldham Athletic, Crystal Palace, Charlton Athletic and Coventry City. Appointed manager at Loftus Road in May 2008, Iain's tenure lasted just 15 games despite the fact that QPR were then ninth in the Championship. He signed up in April 2009 to help Alan Shearer at Newcastle United but the pair were unable to prevent the Magpies' relegation from the Premiership.

SOUSA Paulo

2008-2009

b: Viseu, Portugal, 30 August 1970

Highest Achievement with QPR: (No complete season).

One of Portugal's treasures, Paulo was regarded as one of his country's best footballers and he plied his trade with the likes of Benfica, Juventus, Borussia Dortmund and Inter Milan before injury forced a premature halt to his playing days in 2002. He had, by this time, won 51 caps for Portugal and appeared at Euro '96 and Euro 2000. His appointment as QPR manager in November 2008 was his first managerial position but he did not see out the end of the 2008/09 season after being sacked following a fall-out with his employers. Paulo was offered the Swansea City manager's job in June 2009.

MAGILTON James

2009 to date

b: Belfast, Northern Ireland, 6 May 1969

Highest Achievement with QPR: (No complete season).

Rangers' latest manager, Jim Magilton, is a household name following a playing career that took in clubs such as Oxford United, Southampton and Ipswich Town as well as more than 50 caps for Northern Ireland. Indeed, it was at Portman Road that Jim began his managerial career when he took over from the departed Joe Royle in June 2006. He led the Tractor Boys to mid-table security during his time in charge of the Championship outfit but a failure to make the play-offs led to his dismissal in April 2009. Jim would not be unemployed for long however, as less than two months later he was installed in the Loftus Road hotseat.

Jim Magilton

The Complete Roll Call: 1907-2009

Name:	From:	To:
James Cowan	August 1907	May 1913
James Howie	August 1913	April 1920
Ned Liddell	April 1920	May 1924
Robert Hewison	August 1925	May 1931
Archie Mitchell	November 1931	May 1933
Mick O'Brien	May 1933	April 1935
Billy Birrell	April 1935	May 1939
Ted Vizard	May 1939	April 1944
Dave Mangnall	April 1944	May 1952
Jack Taylor	June 1952	May 1959
Alec Stock	August 1959	June 1968
Bill Dodgin Jnr	June 1968	November 1968
Tommy Docherty	November 1968	November 1968
Les Allen	December 1968	January 1971
Gordon Jago	January 1971	October 1974
Dave Sexton	October 1974	July 1977
Frank Sibley	July 1977	July 1978
Steve Burtenshaw	July 1978	May 1979
Tommy Docherty	May 1979	October 1980
Terry Venables	October 1980	May 1984
Alan Mullery	June 1984	December 1984
Frank Sibley (Caretaker)	December 1984	June 1985
Jim Smith	June 1985	December 1988
Trevor Francis	December 1988	November 1989
Don Howe	November 1989	May 1991
Gerry Francis	May 1991	November 1994
Ray Wilkins	November 1994	September 1996
Stewart Houston	September 1996	November 1997
John Hollins (Caretaker)	November 1997	December 1997
Ray Harford	December 1997	September 1998
Iain Dowie (Caretaker)	September 1998	October 1998
Gerry Francis	October 1998	February 2001
Ian Holloway	February 2001	February 2006
Gary Waddock	February 2006	September 2006
John Gregory	September 2006	October 2007
Mick Harford (Caretaker)	October 2007	October 2007
Luigi De Canio	October 2007	May 2008
Iain Dowie	May 2008	October 2008
Gareth Ainsworth (Caretaker)	October 2008	November 2008
Paulo Sousa	November 2008	April 2009
Gareth Ainsworth (Caretaker)	April 2009	June 2009
Jim Magilton	June 2009	To date

ACKNOWLEDGEMENTS

This book has been compiled using previously published statistics. Should fans reading this book be able to substantiate statistics that we have not been able to reference, please write to the author care of the publisher's address and we will make every effort to correct for future editions. Every effort has been made to check and clarify entries. We apologise if we have missed or been unable to substantiate some data.

With thanks to Francis Atkinson of QPR for his help with this project and for providing a large number of images included in this book. The publisher would like to thank Rebecca Ellis and Ellie Charleston for their hard work on this project.

The pictures in this book were provided courtesy of the following:

GETTY IMAGES
101 Bayham Street, London NW1 0AG

QPR
Loftus Road, South Africa Road, Shepherds Bush, London W12 7PA

Creative Director: Kevin Gardner

Design and Artwork: Jane Stephens

Picture research: Ellie Charleston

Published by Green Umbrella Publishing

Publishers Jules Gammond and Vanessa Gardner

Written by Ian Welch